Future Organizational Design

Wiley Series in Information Systems

Future Organizational Design

The Scope for the IT-based Enterprise

LARS GROTH

JOHN WILEY & SONS, LTD

Chichester · New York · Weinheim · Brisbane · Singapore · Toronto

Other Wiley Editorial Offices

John Wiley & Sons, Inc., 605 Third Avenue,
New York, NY 10158-0012, USA

WILEY-VCH Verlag GmbH, Pappelallee 3,
D-69469 Weinheim, Germany

Jacaranda Wiley Ltd, 33 Park Road, Milton,
Queensland 4064, Australia

John Wiley & Sons (Canada) Ltd, 22 Worcester Road,
Rexdale, Ontario M9W 1L1, Canada

John Wiley & Sons (Asia) Pte Ltd, 2 Clementi Loop #02-01,
Jin Xing Distripark, Singapore 129809

British Library Cataloguing in Publication Data

A catalogue record for this book is available from the British Library

ISBN 0-471-98893-6

Typeset in 10/12 pt Times by C.K.M. Typesetting, Salisbury, Wiltshire
Printed and bound in Great Britain by Biddles Ltd, Guildford and King's Lynn.
This book is printed on acid-free paper responsibly manufactured from sustainable forestry,
in which at least two trees are planted for each one used for paper production.

"Man is not the sum of what he has already, but rather the sum of what he does not yet have, of what he could have."

Jean-Paul Sartre, *Temporalité*, in *Situations* (1947–49)

Contents

Foreword

I have always been irked by the writings on the effect of information technology on organization. They reminded me of that joke about the consultant who sits on the edge of the bed each night and tells his wife how good it's going to be. Some years ago, I attended a conference on the subject at the Harvard Business School. Eventually I reached my limit: You guys have had thirty years to investigate the issue. What exactly have you done since that Levitt and Whistler article back in the 1950s? Then Lars Groth came along. I never would have looked at his material: it was on this same damnable subject, and a couple of hundred pages longer than what you see here. But he enticed me by sending a brief excerpt, which seemed unusual. So I called him. He sent me more and we arranged to meet at a stopover I had in Oslo airport. I read the material as the plane landed and was fascinated.

There he informed me that this labour of love was written over the previous eight years as a doctoral thesis to be submitted to the Sociology Department at the University of Oslo. He did this doctorate in classic European fashion: you meet your supervisor at the outset, disappear for years, and then show up and dump this huge document on his desk. Trouble was the man passed away, and Lars was having trouble getting anyone else to read it.

The rules in Norway are that another university can get involved, if it so chooses. Lars had made a contact at the Norwegian School of Economics and Business Administration in Bergen, and I reinforced this with a call to Torge Reve who was there at the time. Eventually they invited Lars to defend it there. Only one problem: they asked me to be the outside examiner. How could I refuse?

The deeper I got into this, and I must repeat that there was more material here originally, the more fascinated I became. This was not your usual thesis, not in its history, not in its style, not in its substance, not in its approach. But it was damn good—the first thing I can remember reading that really brings some insight to the slippery question of the impact of information technology on organization. Lars defended this unusual document on a memorable day in Bergen.

In my comments there, I explained why this thesis should be unacceptable: the subject is too broad, the topic is too vacuous, no systematic empirical work was done, the document is too long. All of which is to say that there is no formula for writing a thesis, any more than for applying IT. Don't trust the professors when it comes to these things. In fact, this is an extraordinary piece of work on all fronts: depth, creativity, language, structure, historical perspective. It is a testimonial to scholarship without socialization: few of the highly indoctrinated doctoral students do this well. I disagree with the author in places, but adore the way his labour of love glows from beginning to end. This is what scholarship should be about. So Lars received his doctorate, a tribute to the School in Bergen.

I urged Lars to get it published. It was already as much a book as a thesis, save being too long and belabored in places. So, being dragged kicking and screaming by the likes of me and the publisher, Lars whittled it down to the document you see before you.

I hate those endorsement blurbs on the back of books, and usually refuse to do them or allow them to be done on my books. (Greatest thing since sliced bread, etc.) I don't like to do Forewords either: for one thing, you should really read the book, for another, you should often be saying no, even to nice people and good friends. But when Lars asked me (remember, I had already read it all), how could I refuse?

Henry Mintzberg
1998

Preface

"Sometimes a scream is better than a thesis."
Emerson, *Journals*, 1836

This book began its life as a research project and doctoral dissertation. Normally, then, it should not have ended up in your hands, as doctoral dissertations belong to that peculiar class of texts whose meaning lies in the writing, not in the reading. As I started out, however, the thought of spending years of my life writing for an examining committee and the library shelves became too much to bear, and I decided to write a book rather than a thesis. I also wanted to write a text that was accessible and interesting for both organization people and computer people. This combination turned into a greater challenge than anticipated, and kept me busy for more years than I like to think of. Eventually, however, I had the good fortune of being accepted both at the Norwegian School of Economics and Business Administration in Bergen, Norway (for the degree of dr. oecon) and at John Wiley & Sons (for publication), and I can now finally say that it was a worthwhile effort! I hope you will enjoy reading it, and I welcome feedback. You will find me at *www.lars.groth.com*.

Changes have been made for the book edition though. Some of the chapters have been rather heavily edited, long quotations and detailed explanations needed for purely academic purposes have been shortened or omitted, the number of associative detours originally made as a personal therapy during the long years of writing have been pared down. However, I have not eradicated them completely. It is those small sparks springing from the associative cortex that makes the process of writing endurable, and I could not bring myself to carry out a complete purge—since doing so, I might even deprive the reader of some associations, insights, and new ideas. So please bear with me if you think I am straying somewhat from the subject: I will soon return.

Writing a cross-disciplinary book, I have also run into the problems associated with addressing quite different professional and scientific communities: In addition to the danger of breaching professional community tenets, explanations included to serve one group may tax another's patience.

Clearly, there is no panacea that can resolve this dilemma, and I have had to make a number of choices. The central decision has been to stick to my background as an organization sociologist and make the organization perspective the dominating one. It has nevertheless been impossible to avoid a certain dose of computerese, and I have tried to explain as I go along. If you are a complete stranger to computers, and find the explanations insufficient, you are welcome to visit my website and download a summary of the history of computing originally included in the dissertation as an appendix. There are also a number of books on the subject available. *Bit by Bit* by Stan Augarten is unfortunately out of print now, but you might try *A History of Modern Computing: 1945–1995* by Paul E. Ceruzzi or *A History of the Information Machine* by Martin Campbell-Kelly (details in the list of references in the back of the book).

Similarly, for those who feel they need some background on organization, a brief overview of the many-faceted field of organization theory (the second appendix to the dissertation) can also be found on my website. For a more elaborate exposition, I recommend the book *Organizations: Rational, Natural and Open Systems* by Richard W. Scott (details in the list of references).

Throughout the book, I have tried to use examples to illustrate the properties of computers and information technology in general. Many of them are actual systems that are or have been in operation; but because my main objective is to say something about the kind of arrangements that should be possible, not just what has been done already, I cannot stop there. To illustrate and explain what I see as the potential of information technology, and its fundamental strengths and weaknesses, I have also used imagined examples or thought models of systems that are possible but not yet realized.

This immediately raises an important question about which level of technology those models should assume. To allow only existing products as bases for reasoning would be unduly restrictive when the pace of development is as fast as it demonstrably is in the IT industry (this text alone has resided on four generations of computer systems and has been edited with the help of three different word processing programs in a total of seven versions). Any conclusion would then be overtaken by new developments before the document left the printer. On the other side, speculations based on potential technological capabilities fifty years from now would not be very interesting either, since a) we do not have the foggiest idea of what that technology will look like and what its capabilities will be and b) it would be of no use for those who would like to do something about their organizations today or in the coming decade, since the capabilities assumed might not be available within the span of their entire careers.

I have tried to hit the middle of the road in this matter, by only assuming capabilities that computer-based systems already possess or are likely to attain in the near future. The trends in the development of the most fundamental parts of computer systems, such as microprocessors, memory, and mass storage have shown great stability in the pace of development for several decades; the present level of chip complexity was in fact predicted fairly accurately by Gordon Moore in 1964 (Noyce 1977). He overshot the target by less than a factor of 10, which is not bad at all when you bear in mind that the number of components per chip today (1999) is *several million times higher* than it was in 1964.

We therefore have every reason to believe that the established trends will continue for a substantial number of years. Moreover, we also know that most mainstream products today were at the laboratory or prototype stage ten years ago, and it is not unreasonable to assume that most of the mainstream products that will be available in the next decade can already be seen in today's laboratories. There are, of course, always surprises, but as an industry matures the number of surprises and completely new product classes tends to diminish. During the ten years that have elapsed since I started to write this text, I have followed the development fairly closely, and no dramatic and unexpected new systems capabilities have surfaced. I therefore believe that we are on pretty safe ground if we assume that the basic capabilities we can expect from computers in the next couple of decades have already been demonstrated, and that the improvements in their capacity can be predicted with sufficient accuracy. Windows may be ousted as the dominating operating system and Microsoft may go bust (market share for actual products is impossible to forecast), but the fundamental capabilities of computers will prevail.

Series Preface

The information systems community has grown considerably since 1984, when we began publishing the Wiley Series in Information Systems. We are pleased to be a part of the growth of the field, and believe that this series of books is playing an important role in the intellectual development of the discipline. The primary objective of the series is to publish scholarly works which reflect the best of research in the information systems community.

THE PRESENT VOLUME

As the information systems field continues to mature, there is an increased need to carry the results of its growing body of research into practice. The series desires to publish research results that speak to important needs in the development and management of information systems, and our editorial mission recognizes explicitly the need for research to inform the practice and management of information systems. Lars Groth's book *Future Organizational Design: The Scope for the IT-Based Enterprise* serves such a purpose wonderfully. The author has provided an intriguing interpretation of how information technology could both inform and transform organizations. To this end, Groth sees organizations as 'constructible' in their own right and he traces how organizations have been constrained because of human limitations. To overcome these limitations, mankind has developed a variety of tools and techniques, typically in the form of alternative organizational structures. In his analysis, Groth draws heavily on work of Henry Mintzberg who has extensively explored the various forms of organizational structuring. Extending Mintzberg's view of organizations, Groth proposes the possibility of new forms of organizations because of the advancements in information technology. He postulates the existence of new organizational opportunities that heretofore were unimaginable. New structural configurations, made possible because of IT, will offer great promise to industry and government. This book provides some of the most innovative thinking to hit the field in a long time. It will be of interest to anyone who has even remotely considered what IT could do for organizations.

Rudy Hirschheim

Wiley Series in Information Systems

Editors

RICHARD BOLAND   Department of Management Information and Decision
   Systems, Weatherhead School of Management, Case Western Reserve
   University, 10900 Euclid Avenue, Cleveland, Ohio 44106-7235, USA
RUDY HIRSCHHEIM   Department of Decision and Information Systems,
   College of Business Administration, University of Houston, Houston,
   Texas 77202-6283, USA

Advisory Board

NIELS BJØRN-ANDERSEN   Copenhagen Business School, Denmark
D. ROSS JEFFERY   University of New South Wales, Australia
HEINZ K. KLEIN   State University of New York, USA
ROB KLING   Indiana University, USA
TIM J. LINCOLN   IBM UK Limited, UK
BENN R. KONSYNSKI   Emory University, Atlanta, USA
FRANK F. LAND   London School of Economics, UK
ENID MUMFORD   Manchester Business School, UK
MIKE NEWMAN   University of Manchester, UK
DANIEL ROBEY   Georgia State University, USA
E. BURTON SWANSON   University of California, USA
ROBERT TRICKER   Warwick Business School, UK
ROBERT W. ZMUD   University of Oklahoma, USA

Acknowledgments

"Gratitude is the poor man's payment."
English proverb

The impetus behind this project was my desire to be able to say something sensible about the interrelationship of information technology and organization. However, without the funding generously supplied by a number of organizations, I would not have been able to probe the question in real depth. I am therefore very grateful to the Research Council of Norway for their early and bold support, which enabled me to attract support also from the the County of Akershus, Elkem Aluminium, the Ministry of Government Administration, the Norwegian National Bank, Norsk Data (later taken over by Siemens), and Norsk Hydro. Norsk Data and the County of Akershus supported the participation of Akershus Central Hospital. In each of these organizations, there are many people who have helped with this project, and I feel grateful to them all. Without their support, this effort could never have succeeded. I would also like to thank my employer during the first half of the project, Avenir, for gracious understanding when the project started to slip behind schedule. Finally, I would like to express my gratitude to my partners in Pharos, who generously provided me with the necessary overdraft facilities when my income dwindled during the intensive last year and a half of writing.

When I started to explore the possibilities for this project, I received crucial support from four persons. First of all I must thank Marie Haavardtun, then managing director of Avenir, who strongly encouraged me to go on and was very helpful in providing contacts with possible sponsors. Tron Espeli, who was secretary of the governing committee for the Research Council's program "Man, Computer, and Work Environment," went out of his way to help me structure the project to meet the Research Council's requirements. Professor Sverre Lysgaard at the Department of Sociology at the University of Oslo volunteered without hesitation to review my work—as he did more than a decade earlier when I wrote my master's thesis. Finally, my colleague Peter Hidas both urged me on and volunteered to act as my mentor toward the Research Council.

Sadly, both Sverre Lysgaard and Marie Haavardtun died before the dissertation was finished, and before I could present them with the final results of their generous support. Their premature deaths were a blow to all of us who knew them and regarded them as friends.

Also, Professor Erling S. Andersen (the Norwegian School of Management, Oslo), Professor Per Morten Schiefloe (The Norwegian University of Science and Technology, Trondheim), Pål Sørgaard (then Associate Professor at the University of Oslo, now at the Directorate of Public Management) and Professor Ivar Lie (University of Oslo), Professor Kjell Grønhaug, and Professor Leif B. Methlie (both of the Norwegian School of Economics and Business Administration, Bergen), Åge Borg Andersen, and Otto Stabenfeldt (both old colleagues from Avenir), Eivind Jahren (Ministry of Trade and Industry), Jan Heim (then at the Norwegian Computing Center), and Kamar Singh (GE Aircraft Engines) gave of their valuable time to read and comment. Professor Tjerk Huppes (University of Groningen) found time to receive me and offer advice, and Assistant Professor Jan Brage Gundersen (University of Oslo) helped me with some of my philosophical excursions. My colleagues in Avenir and in Pharos have also been both helpful and supportive, prodding me on with their interest. I would especially like to thank Dag Solberg for his interest and suggestions. Dag is certainly one of the most experienced practitioners in the field of modeling in Norway, and he is also theoretically better versed in the subject than many academic specialists. His comments have been very useful.

However, during the writing process, two people have rendered more help and support than others, and without any formal obligation to do so.

First of all, I would like to thank Lee Gremillion for all his support and encouragement over the last eight years. Lee and I first met when I called on him in Boston early in 1990 following an article in *Datamation* on rapid prototyping, where a project that Lee managed was highlighted. Together with two colleagues, I contacted him to hear more about his experiences, and Lee, in his characteristically forthcoming and friendly way, freely shared his hard-won knowledge with the strangers from a small country far away. Later that year, he came over to Norway as the main speaker at a conference that Avenir organized in Oslo on the same subject. When he heard about my doctoral work, he expressed interest and offered to read my drafts and comment on them. Since then he has been my main reviewer, and whenever I sent something over, his comments returned with a promptness worthy of a rather more profitable client. With his doctorate from Harvard University, his background from academic appointments at Harvard, Indiana University, and Boston University School of Business, and his experience as a partner in PricewaterhouseCoopers in the U.S., his advice and criticism have been invaluable to me. He has also been an inexhaustible source of encouragement, which has helped greatly in pulling me through the deep troughs that invariably occur in such projects.

The second person I would like to single out is Associate Professor Gunnar Christensen at the Norwegian School of Economics and Business Administration in Bergen. We met during work on the Norwegian government's 1992–95 plan for developing the use of information technology in Norwegian industry, and afterward on one of the projects under that plan. I immediately seized upon the chance of recruiting Gunnar as an informal reviewer, and, by and by, he quietly accepted the role as sounding board. Patiently, he responded to my questions, offered suggestions, and listened to my occasional tales of frustration. During the final year, he also read and commented on the complete text, and thus effectively assumed the role Professor Sverre Lysgaard had before his death. As one of the few researchers in Norway who is equally well versed in organization theory and computer-based systems, Gunnar has been of great help. Of special importance was his assistance during and after my decision to stand for the doctorate in Bergen rather than at my alma mater in Oslo. His help with the formalities as well as with access to the other people there who had to look at my work was vital for the final success of my efforts.

During this last phase, when the final draft was out there begging for the final comments, I also had the good fortune of attracting the attention of Henry Mintzberg, whose organization models constitute the platform for reasoning about computer-based organization in this book. His instant enthusiasm rekindled my dwindling fires of inspiration and provided the fresh energy sorely needed to finally complete the project. When he accepted a request from the Bergen school to serve on my examining committee, it was another morale booster, and his kind support during my hunt for a publisher was invaluable. Thank you for bothering to look under the small stones along the road, Henry. You are living proof that success need not lead to aloofness.

Lastly, I want to thank my family for enduring the hardships with me. I have read many such statements of gratitude toward a family through the years, and until a few years ago I viewed them as perhaps little more than a social reflex. Now I know better. To have one of the parents strained by dissertation work year after year, often working both evenings and weekends, is an experience most families could well do without. I am very grateful that you put up with me, supporting me even through the nth delay and then again through the editing of the book manuscript. I hope I shall never test your love and tolerance in this way again.

I
A Platform for the Investigation

In this part, my purpose is to build the foundation for the main analytic thrust of the book. In Chapter 1, *Recourse to Reason*, I delineate the project's point of departure and the approach chosen for the analysis: to use the basic human preconditions for organizing as a starting point, and investigate how they are enhanced by technology—first by pre-computer technology and then by information technology itself. The chapter summarizes the main findings, outlines the other chapters and provides a short note on some central terms.

In Chapter 2, *Organization and Tools—the Human Advantages*, I set out to establish the (in my view) crucial link between organization and technology and explain the concept *space of constructible organizations*. The chapter ends with a delineation of the scope of the analysis.

In Chapter 3, *The Basic Preconditions for Organizing*, I discuss the subject of organization, especially how organizations are defined and what their basic elements of structuring are. The structural configurations of Henry Mintzberg are adopted as the main framework for the analysis. The discussion concludes that coordination is the linchpin of all organization, and a taxonomy of coordinating mechanisms (based on Mintzberg's definitions) is proposed. The chapter ends with the definition of what I see as the basic human preconditions for organizing, which will serve as the foundation for my main analysis.

1
Recourse to Reason

"A man's behavior is the index of the man, and his
discourse is the index of his understanding."
Ali Ibn-Abi-Talib, *Sentences*, 7th century.

SUSTAINED SUCCESS GROWS FROM KNOWING WHY

This is not a quick-fix book. It will not teach you simple prescriptions
for turning stagnating enterprises into dynamic winners with the help of
the latest in information technology. Neither will it inundate you with
computerese—although it *will* introduce a number of novel concepts
and hopefully coin a few new words. It is guaranteed *not* to admonish
you to turn your company into a knowledge-based learning organization,
virtualized into multidisciplinary, networked teams, assembled on the
go for each new challenge, meeting and working over the Internet and
delivering their products in digital form directly to the prosumer. Indeed,
you will not even find a separate chapter on the Internet.

This book is written on the presumptions that knowledge is better than
slogans and comprehension is better than prescription—that the real
key to a sustained, profitable exploitation of information technology is
a thorough knowledge of the technology, of organizations, of people,
and—above all—a well-founded understanding of how they interact
and can be combined.

A Quest for Practical Directions

In course of the 1980s, the interest in the relationship between information
technology and organization was picking up. One of the most intriguing
statements a speaker could make at the time was that a widespread adoption of advanced computer systems would make it possible to build new

organization structures, more efficient and flexible than the ones we were used to. This was always a sure hit, especially with the more well-groomed professional audiences in the chip-chip-hurrah community. From time to time, however, uninitiated participants would have the temerity to ask "*how*" or "*what kind of structures*," instantly creating that special kind of embarrassed silence experienced in close-knit congregations when newcomers ask "stupid" questions about central dogmas.

That also happened to this speaker a few times, and time and again I had to fall back on the well-worn examples of American Hospital Supply Corporation and American Airlines (and, fortunately, a couple of credible local cases). However, they did not quite seem to fit the bill. The companies in question had undoubtedly changed some aspect of the way they did business, and with notable success, but the systems' organizational impacts were questionable, apart from eliminating a number of positions associated with the old routines.

Often I ended up saying that the ways and means here were not quite clear yet, as we were all in the forefront of a development that was just taking off, and that, consequently, the new structures and ways of working had yet to emerge. It was hardly a satisfying answer for the audience, and definitely not a satisfying experience for me. I was in dire need of a qualified answer, and my quest for this answer escalated into the research effort behind this book.

My viewpoint was and is a practical one. I have been working as a consultant since 1980, and my clients always expect practical advice that will produce concrete improvements in their organizations. That is what they pay to get, and that is what I strive to provide. The basic goal for my research has therefore been to offer my clients better advice and perhaps also help others who needed to understand how their organizations could really come to grips with this new and exciting technology. The basic questions I wanted to answer were no more and no less than those I had encountered during my talks:

- What will the organizations look like that really take advantage of the full power of information technology?
- How should they be structured?
- How will they function?
- What will be their benefits and drawbacks?
- Are the opportunities the same across the board, or do they vary among organizations of different kinds?

If I could answer these questions, I felt I would also be in a much better position to help my clients both to take advantage of contemporary systems and to stake out the road ahead—since I would then be able to tell if their particular organizations could benefit from intensive use of information technology, what they would need to do in order to exploit it, and (just as important) how they could *not* exploit it.

Most of the literature in this field is prescriptive and refers to concrete examples. Prescriptions may be helpful for organizations very similar to those described, and good examples can be inspiring, but organizations always differ more than one should believe from a cursory look. Blind attempts to replicate other organizations' achievements may easily turn into disaster, since successful adaptation always requires more than mimicry. Without real understanding of the strengths and limitations of information technology, and how and why it enables certain organizational designs and not others, it is very difficult to determine where the greatest potentials are—and equally hard to stake out the most advantageous path into the future. This book is an attempt to establish such an understanding.

Venturing Beyond Prescriptions

It may seem brash to imply that this is a new approach—but the literature on the organizational effects of information technology largely ignore the substantial, established body of knowledge about organizations. It is as if the advent of the computer has at one and the same time obliterated history and changed human nature beyond recognition. However, IT is just a technology (albeit powerful), it is not some kind of magic; it is not impenetrable to reason. It does not throw everything into a turmoil or invalidate all previous knowledge about technology, organizations and how humans use technology. Our natural abilities and dispositions have hardly changed at all in historic times; our basic social habits and the way we prefer to pattern interpersonal relationships are also remarkably stable. We therefore have every reason to believe that major parts of existing organizational and psychological theory are valid also in the age of information technology.

As a machine, the computer is also something we can comprehend. We can analyze its actual and possible contributions in depth, just as we have done with previous organization technology—for the computer is certainly not the first tool we have created to improve on our natural capabilities for organizing. Tracing the history of human civilization, we will notice the impacts of innovations like networks of posting stations, roads, sailing ships, railroads, cars, airplanes, telegraph, telephone and radio—not to mention the art of writing, the most momentous innovation of them all. Throughout history, we have time and again used these tools creatively to expand the *space of constructible organizations*—the sum of all the variations in organization allowed by our biology, our tools and our mores. We have literally millennia of experience with organizations, with organizational tools and their interrelations, and for at least a century we have been studying these matters scientifically in the modern sense of the word. To discard such established knowledge can never be wise, even if it may sometimes be fashionable.

In this book, the main link to established organization theory will be the organizational configurations Henry Mintzberg first presented in his book *The Structuring of Organizations* in 1979. They are particularly well suited to the purpose, since they in an excellent way sum up the work of numerous others, provide very useful concepts for the analyses, and are sufficiently well-known to serve as a frame of reference for a large part of today's managers.

My main arguments and findings are summarized in Tables 1-1 to 1-3 on pages 6–8. The basic notion is that our use of technology—any technology—has its roots in our desire to overcome limitations in our natural, physiologically defined capabilities, and that this also applies to the construction of organizations. To gain an understanding of how we might exploit information technology in organizations, I therefore first had to define our most important limitations with respect to organization-

Table 1-1: *Overview: The basic human abilities and constraints and the resulting organizational configurations.*

Basic Human Abilities	Basic Human Constraints
Versatile and creative in work.	*Serial: Only one task at a time.*
Memory with great capacity and flexibility.	*Short term (working) memory extremely limited, long term memory fickle and unsuited for precise administrative information.*
Flexible information processing capacity, good mechanisms for integration and simplification.	*Limits in working memory severely restricts human ability to tackle complexity.*
Versatile communication abilities, great capacity for visual processing.	*Verbal communication slow and serial.*
Communication range well adapted to simple, local communication.	*Severe limitations in range; communication over distance depends on messengers.*
Emotions always important—we are less rational than we like to believe. Emotions are the source of both cohesion ...	*... and conflict.*

Archaic Configurations: Emergent Organizations		
Simple Structure	Feudal Form	Adhocracy

Table 1-2: *Overview: The basic contributions of pre-computer tools, the remaining constraints and the resulting organizational configurations.*

Contributions of Pre-Computer Tools	Remaining Constraints
Writing provides unlimited information storage without loss of content and implicit coordination of work.	*Laborious search and retrieval, implicit coordination limited by need for physical file access.*
By augmenting the working memory, writing greatly improves the human ability for complex processing. It also allows monitoring of complex events, extensive distribution of tasks and automation.	*Processing still bound to the human mind and thus limited by the capacity of the living humans.*
Physical transport revolutionized, information exchange doubly so (telegraph, telephone, radio).	*Fast, large volume point-to-point communication expensive, basic human communication capacity unchanged.*
Some improvements in the speed with which we can absorb and disseminate information, significant improvements in information accessibility.	*Basic human input/output limitations still an iron constraint.*
Some improvements in the management of emotions.	*Emotions still just as important for both cohesion and conflict.*

Main new organizational opportunities with Pre-Computer Tools
– Revolutionary increases in productivity and quality through automation.
– Revolutionary development of mechanical energy.
– Ability to tackle much more complex undertakings.
– Explicit design of organizations.
– Ability to organize and support really large organizations.

Modern Configurations: Explicitly Designed Organizations		
Machine Bureaucracy	Professional Bureaucracy	Divisionalized Form

building and how they constrain us in establishing and maintaining organizations (Table 1-1). I then explored the range of organizations built on these basic capabilities alone (the archaic configurations at the bottom of the table).

To isolate the possible contributions of information technology, I first looked into the most important of the pre-computer technologies and how they helped us overcome some of our basic limitations (Table 1-2). The most important new opportunities these tools provided are also listed in the table. The art of writing towers over all other inventions, as it liberated us from the crushing constraint of having to remember every single piece of information we needed to retain.

Table 1-3: Overview: The basic contributions of information technology, the remaining constraints and the resulting organizational configurations.

Contributions of Information Technology	Remaining Constraints
Revolutionary improvements in information storage and implicit coordination.	*Use of information still limited by human reading capacity.*
Information processing outside the mind, vastly extended scope for automation.	*Human internal processing capacity is still unchanged.*
Vastly increased bandwidth for electronic communication, dramatically lower prices.	*Basic human communication capacity unchanged.*
Much improved comprehension of complex information.	*Basic human input/output limitations still an iron constraint.*
No improvements in the management of emotions.	*Increasingly abstract work with systems that can also be relentless and pacing may induce strain.*

Main new organizational opportunities with Information Technology
– Extensive elimination of work and increased flexibility through hyperautomation and implicit coordination, possibilities for much larger and more responsive organizations. – Support for extremely large, organized entities that are not organizations in the classic sense. – Close coupling of separate organizations in extended value chains, wholly or partly automated. – Extensive centralization of power through informating. – Increased decentralization through improved information availability, de-specialization and increased depth of control. – Elimination of routine jobs through increases in personal productivity. – Improved group cooperation over distance, improved cohesion in teams and groups who cannot otherwise meet.

Computer-based Configurations: Model-driven Organizations				
Joystick Organization	Flexible Bureaucracy	Interactive Adhocracy	Meta-Organization	Organized Cloud

Some of the potential created by this expanding inventory of tools was exploited fairly early; some remained dormant. In fact, it was not until the advent of the Industrial Revolution that the potential was explored to any depth, and it was not until the twentieth century that the three modern organizational configurations were developed to a point where we finally came up against the limits of pre-computer tools. In contrast with the archaic organizations, which more or less emerged from tradition and

custom and remained remarkably stable over time, these modern configurations were to a substantial degree consciously designed, and thus
open to continuous improvement. The requirements were analyzed, the
positions described and the work of each employee detailed, often to a
substantial degree. The main organizational achievement of this age was
the archetypal Modern Organization—the *Machine Bureaucracy*—which
proved to be the configuration required to harness the new production
and transport technologies and to create the wealth of modern society.

Against this background, then, the contributions of computer-based
systems could be isolated. To ensure that all important aspects of the
technology were covered, I both analyzed the properties of the technology
as it stands today and looked into the main trends of development for the
next ten years as a basis for analyzing information technology's potential
for organizational innovation. The technology's four most significant contributions according to this analysis are outlined in Table 1-3, together
with the realization that our emotions are still with us, and may be in
serious conflict with some of the properties of computer-based systems
and the way we use them. In the table you will also find the main new
organizational opportunities afforded by these contributions, together
with the five proposed computer-based configurations.

Organization—A Human Endeavor

The Dawn

In prehistoric times, before we had developed significant tools, the level of
organization was modest in scale and scope. Archeology and anthropology indicate that there were two basic organizational configurations,
the Adhocracy and the Simple Structure, building on the two primeval
coordinating mechanisms: mutual adjustment and direct supervision.
These are typical for the hunting band and the patriarchal family,
respectively.

These two configurations are very different when it comes to scal-
ability—the ability to support larger structures. Adhocracies do not
scale well; the volume of communication needed to support mutual adjustment increases geometrically with the number of people involved. The
closest we can get is a representative system of some kind, as pioneered
in the Greek city states. The Simple Structure, however, can easily be
scaled up by encapsulation and delegation, preferably with geography
and lineage as structuring elements: the chief simply delegates power to
subordinate lords to rule separate parts of the kingdom. They, in turn,
may delegate power to rule even smaller parts, until one reaches the bottom
unit, which is always small enough to be managed by one person.

The beauty of such a system from a cognitive point of view lies in the extreme economy it offers in information processing, communication, and memorizing. Based on land rights and family lineage, it contains its own structuring information; that information is moreover constantly enacted in everyday life, and thereby reinforced in everyone's memory. By delegating total authority to his vassals over their fiefdoms and the people who live there, the king effectively encapsulates the information required to run the fiefdoms and shields himself from it. He now has to worry only about the loyalty of his vassals (often no small worry, unfortunately), the size of their tributes, and their contributions to his army. The number of people with whom he must deal is drastically reduced.

The feudal type of organization can in fact be viewed as a forerunner of the Divisionalized Form, which set separate objectives for the divisions, duplicated operating functions across them, eliminated the need for interdivisional coordination, and thereby strongly limited the need for information flows across division boundaries. A divisionalized organization thus provides a wide span of control for top management, which was also exactly the goal of the feudal system—developing out of the need to build large organizational structures with minimal requirements for memorizing, information processing, and communication.

The basic organizational forms of preliterate societies, then, relied either on the rule of one or on a form of rule by consensus or council. For larger structures, where one ruler or one council could not manage the complexity, the iron-clad constraints on human memory, communication, and information processing capabilities forced a reliance on two principles: the *delegation of authority* and the *encapsulation of information*.

Modern Times

The art of writing was the first breakthrough technology for organizational purposes. By making it possible to externalize memory, it lifted many of the constraints placed upon us by our limited recall. The ability to write down intermediate results and collect written information also made it possible to process much more complex problems individually and to time-slice (work on many problems more or less in parallel) much more easily. But the real revolution was found in the way writing let us distribute large tasks among a vast number of persons, synchronize and coordinate their activities, and communicate intermediate results between them. This allowed a literate society to routinely tackle tasks so massive that they would completely overwhelm any illiterate society.

Of great importance was also the coordinative effects of the active file of written records—once you can base your work on the information in a file, which is constantly updated by the results of what you did, your work is automatically coordinated with the work of all the others who use that particular file in the same way. Such a file will provide an *implicit coordination* of all those who work with it; and because of their common base of information, they will be able to act with considerable consistency without ever talking to each other. The fact that this information will not disappear with the user also means that both private and public administration can survive even sudden and unexpected changes in personnel. This was the first technology-dependent coordinating mechanism, and it marked a watershed in organization history.

Once the memory barrier was lifted, communication quickly became the bottleneck for organization building. Even though we know of regular courier services as early as 2000 BC, communication technology capable of serving as an infrastructure for mainstream organization building had to wait for the industrial revolution—for the steamship, the railroad, regular postal services, the telegraph, and finally the telephone. Mass distribution and mass media also became important tools for erecting and sustaining large organizations. Finally, mechanical automation has helped us overcome our limited ability to carry out physical operations in parallel, since automation can be viewed as "canned" action—as the enactment of previous design.

It took a long time to discover and exploit the new organizational possibilities opened up by the evolving technology. Long after the invention of writing, the state remained the chief domain for organization, and the feudal structure the main organization type. Administrative technologies provided by literacy were used only to support already existing organization practices, and literacy itself was limited to a select few. The best explanation we can give for this is that there were no pressing needs for new organizational forms. However, when industrial development started in earnest, the needs arose.

The first steps toward industrial production and modern organizational forms consisted of a more intensive exploitation of traditional approaches within the Simple Structure model. However, traditional organizational practices could not be scaled up to accommodate the fine-grained specialization that was now developing. The new specialization and mechanization required much more emphasis on coordination and control than the craft shop approach and its derivatives. The key is that it entailed splitting all the problems of design and production—an integral part of the craftsman's work—away from the worker. Those tasks now had to be carried out by specialists in design and planning, and the workers were required only to carry out their ordained tasks. Specialization in production therefore called for a much more sophisticated approach to planning and administration, and therefore to information processing, communication, and, consequently, to organization. The division of tasks, hierarchical supervision, detailed rules, precision, clarity and reliability that was required could not be fully realized within the framework of a traditional Simple Structure. The configuration that Mintzberg (1979) calls the Machine Bureaucracy was born.

Its development depended not only on technology but on the emergence of a new concept for coordination. March and Simon (1958) have pointed to a new and vastly more efficient method than the direct orders of traditional organizations, namely, *coordination by plan*—which is roughly equivalent to Mintzberg's *standardization of work process*. By pre-programming coordination, an explicit routine is formulated, and the need for communication-intensive *coordination by feedback*, on which both direct supervision and mutual adjustment depend, is dramatically reduced. The principle of pre-programmed work is, of course, carried to its logical conclusion in automation. The penalty is the cost of its conception and also of change—the efforts needed to analyze the requirements and construct and modify the programs are considerable, not to mention the construction of new machines.

In the modern organization, then, work is no longer organized in accordance with custom and tradition, but according to a *conscious* design based on an *explicit* analysis of the desired outcome and the available means. In my view, this represents a decisive break with the past and marks the transition to a new paradigm for the organization of human work. While traditional organizations more or less *emerged* from the social context, like a natural order of things, the new paradigm built on conscious analysis and explicit design, and focused on the coordination of interdependent, specialized tasks. The creators of the new organizations would almost gleefully break with tradition, if that was instrumental to improvements in effectiveness and efficiency.

By explicating analyses and design and committing them to paper, the new organizers also created (unknowingly) the first explicit conceptual models of organizations. By lifting the models out of the subconscious world of tacit knowledge, and literally spelling them out, they also opened them up for conscious inspection and improvement. This is the foundation for the modern organization.

The Contributions of Information Technology

As compared to earlier technology, information technology's single most significant contribution is the way it allows us—for the first time in history—*to process information outside the human mind*. This is a contribution fully on par with the memory revolution brought about by the art of writing, even if the kind of processing power provided by the computer is much more narrow than the capabilities of the human mind. However, the computer's outstanding (and rapidly improving) capabilities in quantitative data processing and logical operations definitely provide revolutionary new possibilities within the fields of computation (from finite element analysis to weather forecasting), of automation, and of monitoring extremely large amounts of information and exceedingly complex chains of events. Rather than marking the end of straightforward automation, as a number of people argue, the computer in my view inaugurates the age of *hyperautomation*—both in material production and in the provision of immaterial products and services.

The second most important contribution is the way computer-based systems improve our information storage capabilities. Even if writing has allowed us to store almost unlimited amounts of information (the Earth is large, and there is always a clean sheet of paper available), the accessibility of that information has been very limited. The larger the files, the more labyrinthine they become, and the establishment and maintenance of anything but the simplest keys are extremely time-consuming. Moreover, to access a paper-based file, you have to walk up to it or have somebody do it for you.

The database, on the other hand, allows us to store very large volumes of information in a form that allows very efficient search and retrieval, and access can be had from anywhere as long as there is an electronic link available. The most revolutionary aspect of this is not the free-form information base, however—it is the structured database, where information is stored in predetermined fields. In a structured database, information can be accessed not only as individual tidbits, but selections and aggregations can be made to produce reports, statistical methods can be applied, and very sophisticated analyses can be performed. The most awesome aspect of the structured database, however, is its coordinative power. Its precursor, the paper-based file, was also a powerful instrument for coordination, but the number of persons who can work with the same paper-based file is quite limited, access to information requires physical access to it, and the flexibility of the file is also poor—it has generally only one key (usually name, address or date), and it is close to impossible to scan it for other information items.

The structured database, on the other hand, has a vast (and rapidly increasing) capacity, it can have multiple keys (all fields can be keys if your system is powerful enough), and it can be accessed from almost anywhere in the world. The largest database systems today are probably the airline reservation systems, where the largest ones are approaching 200 000 terminals with real-time access. All those users—mostly travel agents and airline personnel (and even customers)—are completely coordinated by the database without ever having to talk to each other. While you are on the telephone in the late afternoon with your travel agent in Cincinnati, mulling over if you should book that last available seat on the first flight from London to Milan on Christmas Day, it may be snatched by an early riser in Oslo, Norway—and you will know it and suffer the consequences in the same instant (give or take a few seconds, depending on the current response time of the system and the alertness of your agent).

The sheer volume of the coordination that takes place every day through these databases is—even in theory—impossible to carry out without computers, and this great coordinative power of the structured database is the engine behind the lion's share of business applications. It is also the secret behind most of the famous examples of Business Process Reengineering. Together with budding hyperautomation, it is driving the increases in efficiency and the downsizing, reorganization and delayering going on in large corporations today. It also promises even greater revolutions ahead.

Only after these two primary qualities of computer-based systems comes communication—today perhaps computing's most touted feature. The most important aspects of this (when we are talking about organization) are *not* personal communication and networking, but rather remote access to (structured) databases and direct machine-to-machine communication. This is not to say that personal communication and networking are unimportant, but they have limited potential compared to other uses of computer-based systems. The reason is that there are a number of iron constraints that apply to human communication, no matter how advanced the channel is: we cannot speak, listen, write, read or comprehend information in verbal form faster than our forbears, and the limiting nozzles sit in our own heads. No matter how wide the hoses you lead up to those nozzles, their basic throughput will remain more or less constant. Any communication across the network will therefore reduce the time available for other communication activities, and even if computer-based systems make verbal communication both faster, more convenient, and somewhat quicker to effect, the total increase in communication capacity will be quite modest—especially when compared to the quantum leaps we can achieve in other areas of computer use.

The conclusions to this analysis run counter to a number of the claims that have been made over the last few years about the impact of information technology—that networking is the main impact of information technology, that hierarchy is being supplanted by networked teams, that classic automation is outdated and that the large firms of today are doomed in the competition with the agile, virtual organizations of tomorrow.

I claim instead that many of those assertions are based on superficial analyses and a lack of understanding both of the basics of organization, of human cognition and of the distinctive properties of information technology. In this book, I propose a different framework for understanding the interrelations of information technology and organization, a framework I believe is more complete, and therefore provides a better basis for a deep understanding of what the unique contributions of information technology are and how we can best exploit them without abusing ourselves in the process.

Model-driven Organizations

Configuring Mintzberg for Computers

Each of the contributions of information technology briefly outlined above does of course open up possibilities for organizational innovations. However, the greatest opportunities will come from combining them through the use of ever more comprehensive and integrated systems that are woven into the very fabric of work, providing a new basis for automation, task elimination and system-mediated coordination in organizations. By transforming the way we produce, the way we work and the way organizations are coordinated, computer-based systems expand the space of constructible organizations, opening up new territory for organizational innovations.

Organizations that use information technology extensively will be very complex entities. On the surface, they will not necessarily look more complex than organizations used to do—they may even look simpler, with their lean complexion and seemingly effortless production and service fulfillment. However, the introduction of computer-based systems creates a new level of sophistication, of complexity, and of abstraction—actions are increasingly tied to symbols, and the formalization of computer programs permeates much of the dialogues and strongly influences the work situation of those who use them.

While most modern organizations were designed with the help of a fairly simple explicit model reflected in organization charts and verbal descriptions of positions, tasks and workflows, the new computer-based organizations will require a more sophisticated approach. We will in fact need to use some of the tools that are mandatory when designing and developing large computer programs, to ensure that organization and systems are fully integrated and harmonized. A main tool here is the *conceptual model*, which contains a quite formal and precise description of the main objects and events in an organization—whether they are to be incorporated in a computer program or handled by organization members. This modeling process is considerably more refined and precise than the modeling efforts inherent in a traditional organizational design, and computer-based systems and the future organizations relying on them are therefore much more clear-cut representations of conceptual models than previous organization structures.

A computer-based system will in fact incorporate its own model, while at the same time representing that model's expression—or at least a part of it, as there will usually be human actors involved in the dialogue as well. Even that dialogue will be strongly constrained by the system's inherent model, which can only allow actions (accept input) that are defined within it. In addition to being descriptive, therefore, the model inherent in a computer-based system is also *active*, in the sense that it becomes a directive part in the ongoing patterns of actions constituting the organization.

When systems multiply, their fields of operation will increasingly meet or overlap, resulting in a need to integrate their operations. In turn, this will necessitate a more comprehensive conceptual model of the organization's problem domain. If this web of systems becomes sufficiently comprehensive, we will reach a situation where the major part of the operative actions (the interactions that are directly relevant to the organization's purposes) constituting the organization will be directed toward and through the computer-based systems, and not directly toward other humans. Somewhere around that point we will cross a threshold: the main constituting part of the organization will be the integrated computer-based systems, their programmed patterns of action, and, implicitly, *the conceptual model they are based on.* The coordination of the organization members will be mediated mainly by the systems, and thereby (logically) by the model, not by direct human communication. Such an organization will not only be model-based; it will be *model-driven.* The model, integrating several of the computer-dependent coordinating mechanisms, will constitute a supermechanism for coordinating the organization.

My analysis suggests the possibility of five such model-driven configurations, three of them modifications of configurations originally proposed by Mintzberg (1979), and two new ones. They are listed at the bottom of Table 1-3. They will be based on models of different basic designs, utilizing different combinations of computer-based systems.

The Joystick Organization

The Joystick Organization is the entrepreneur's dream: an organization where computers provide top management with detailed, real-time information about all vital activities (like sales), and where the employees' activities are highly circumscribed by the systems they work with—systems that can be continually modified through parameterization directed by the top management team or even the president him/herself. Developments in this direction can already be seen, especially in large retailing operations. It will rely on a *regulating model*, where the controlling and automating aspects of information technology is exploited to the maximum.

The Flexible Bureaucracy

The Flexible Bureaucracy represents the natural evolutionary path for the Machine Bureaucracy. The key to the transformation of this classic modern organization is the IT-based transition from inflexible to flexible standardization combined with much more efficient internal coordination. Hyperautomation, programmed routines and (often) implicit coordination will combine to make these organizations dramatically more agile than before. The lean (but often very large) Flexible Bureaucracy in my view seems a much more likely successor to this century's dominant organizational form than the small, more craft-oriented flexible specialization firms proposed by Piore and Sabel (1984) and others. That also applies to the largest of them, which are now in a period of contraction due to process reengineering and increasing automation. After a period of consolidation, these behemoths of the corporate world may well start to grow again. After all, information technology is a technology for automation and coordination—it should allow us to construct larger organizations, not only smaller ones.

The Flexible Bureaucracy will also rely on a regulating model, but it will be less comprehensive (relative to the total task structure of the organization) than the model powering the Joystick Organization. The larger the proportion of professionals in the organization, the more likely it is that there will also be strong elements of an *assisting model* present, focused on enhancing the professional qualities of the work.

The Interactive Adhocracy

The Interactive Adhocracy is perhaps the most intriguing of the first three configurations. Adhocracy is an organization where coordination mainly takes place through mutual adjustment. It is typically team-oriented and creative, producing unique solutions to unique problems. Adhocracies are extremely communication intensive, and spend a large percentage of their energy and resources on coordination. Therefore, they cannot compete with more efficient organizations in turning out standardized products or services.

The most promising way of transforming these organizations is not to use groupware or similar solutions to make communication among organization members smoother and more efficient; we will still come up against the iron constraints of the basic human communication capacities outlined in the previous section. Rather, the solution is to use the technology to eliminate the need for most of the communication in the first place. If the organization's main tasks can be modeled with sufficient precision and incorporated into a computer system (or an integrated suite of such systems), the members of an Interactive Adhocracy may be coordinated simply through their work with the system—in the same way that all travel agents who use the Amadeus or SABRE reservation systems are perfectly coordinated in their seat reservations without ever having to talk together. An early example may be the organization that produced the structural design of Boeing's new 777 jetliner. If we can thus eliminate most of the communication overhead in the Adhocracy while retaining its creative strengths, the result could be a formidable competitor in the territory between mass production and the one-of-a-kind designer shop.

The Interactive Adhocracy will have to rely on a *mediating model*, which constitutes both a tool for work and a medium for communication.

The Meta-Organization

The Meta-Organization is the first of the two new configurations suggested by my analysis. It is an entity consisting of two or more closely coupled organizations, coordinated by a common system or suite of systems. Early examples are the clusters constituted by a number of modern car manufacturers and their main subcontractors, located around the perimeter of the central factory. Working to the drumbeat of the main factory's production control system, all these separate organizations are synchronized to the point that they effectively function as one integrated organization, with the subcontractors delivering parts directly to the pertinent positions on the main assembly line only minutes before they are required.

There are two kinds of Meta-Organizations—the Supplier Cluster, organizing subcontractors around a main producer, and the Equal Partnership, where no single member has a dominating position. The Meta-Organization relies on a regulating model.

The Organized Cloud

Finally there is the Organized Cloud—a phenomenon that is not an organization in the classical sense, but that is nevertheless highly organized. We have already mentioned two examples—the airline reservation systems Amadeus and SABRE. Trading systems for stocks or currency are others. While the Meta-Organization typically comprises a small number of organizations that are tightly coordinated for most of their activities, the members of an Organized Cloud are only coordinated in a very narrow and specific area. Clouds are also typically much larger, indeed, they can become exceedingly large. The high performance, on-line database systems that form the core of Organized Clouds have up to now been very expensive, and the formation of Clouds have been limited to high-yield, time-critical activities. However, as costs continue to fall while performance improves, the Cloud will be viable for a much wider range of purposes. Clouds rely on highly specific mediating models that are restricted to a very narrow set of tasks.

From Analysis to Action

It is possible to work for improvement in an organization on several levels, from the discharge of a single task to the structuring of the total organization. However, single tasks are normally not very interesting targets, and to obtain a satisfactory level of insight and understanding in a larger part of the organization, it is usually necessary to analyze the organization's total field of operation quite carefully in order to secure both a tenable technological solution and a good implementation of it. It is also very important that the initial analysis aims at getting behind existing work arrangements to capture the gist of the work at hand—or, rather, its objectives, since the work itself (the present tasks) may be superfluous within a new framework.

This is not a trivial requirement, and the best methodology to follow the initial analysis is to devise a number of coaxing exercises to promote creativity. To avoid being trapped by existing procedures, it is necessary to employ a top-down approach in the initial analysis, starting with the primary objectives at the highest organizational level relevant to the project: what is, quite simply, the nature of the products and services we aim to provide? The goal should be to describe the desired implementation of these objectives at the level of products, services, customers or clients, and to chart the way they are related. I would propose an object-oriented approach for this, which will force us to focus precisely on the central objects and help us avoid function analysis—which all too easily becomes bogged down in a detailed escription of existing tasks and routines.

The analysis should then proceed along one or more of three dimensions, depending on what is appropriate for the project in question: product-related possibilities, process-related possibilities, and structure-related possibilities.

Product innovation based on information technology is nothing new—indeed, information technology has already become one of the main enablers both for improvements in products and services and the development of totally new kinds of products and services. Very often, such advances hinge on one particular aspect of the technology. For instance, the development of services so diverse as today's extremely flexible and efficient airline reservation, automatic teller machines and electronic toll fee stations has been totally dependent on the existence of powerful databases with remote access. A fuller understanding of the strong and weak points of the technology will make it easier to pinpoint the most promising possibilities.

Process orientation has become the collective mantra of the business community over the last few years. Practically all medium to large organizations will have a number of processes that are central to their operations, some of which will produce and deliver products and services to outside customers/clients, and some of which will serve vital, administrative needs. The key to these processes is coordination—coordination of the efforts of all those who are part of the process, as well as coordination with customers, suppliers and other groups and individuals both inside and outside the organization. The comprehensive analysis of computer-dependent coordinating mechanisms presented here should point to the most tenable approaches.

Compared to the situation a couple of decades ago, where systems were still viewed mainly as specific tools for rather narrow functions in the organization, today's focus on processes is a really significant step forward. It is also a step up onto a higher level of complexity, perhaps the highest level we presently can handle with some confidence. However, as we gradually integrate our processes, they will themselves become candidates for closer integration and coordination. We then reach a level where the whole organization—and often a part of its environment as well—must be described in the same model and served by a set of integrated systems. This involves rising to yet a higher level of complexity—today barely within reach, and only for organizations with a well defined and fairly narrow problem domain. To tackle integration at the organization level will require thorough understanding of the relationship between work, technology and organization, and we will need advanced methods for analysis, description and modeling. At this level, organization structure becomes one of the paramount issues.

Organization structure is of course a subject of considerable interest already at the process level, as key processes can involve large numbers of people and many organization units. To achieve the best possible results, it is always important to choose structures that match our objectives, the nature of the required processes, and the systems central to those processes. Sometimes, one will have a choice between process designs calling for different structures, and it is important to know the strengths and weaknesses of those structures if the desired results are to be achieved. However, structure first becomes a paramount concern when we approach not only a single process, but try to go one step further and integrate processes, support functions, systems and system use across the total organization. An understanding of the potential of conceptual modeling will then become mandatory, paving the way for the use of such models as a basis for really comprehensive computer-based systems—thus allowing organizations to achieve new levels of integration and coordination. The analysis in this book of the potentials for different types of organizations should also make us more aware of the potentials of our own organization and the ways in which it could (and could not!) be transformed.

A KEY TO THIS BOOK

As indicated in the Preface, I have tried to write a narrative that is easy to follow and pleasant to read. However, even with the best intentions on my side, readers may at places be confronted with leaps of thought that remain invisible to one who has been steeped in this material for years. I will therefore say a few words about how each part and each chapter fits into the scheme.

Part I: A Platform for the Investigation

In Part I, my purpose is to build the foundation for the analysis itself. In *Recourse to Reason*, I have just delineated my approach and summed up the main conclusions.

In *Organization and Tools—the Human Advantages*, I set out to establish the crucial link between organization and technology, and explain the concept *space of constructible organizations*, ending with a delineation of the scope of my analysis.

In *The Basic Preconditions for Organizing*, I discuss the subject of organization, especially how organizations are defined and what their basic elements of structuring are. The goal is to identify a suitable framework from the body of organization theory on which I could base my own analysis. Mintzberg's structural configurations are adopted as the main framework, and the discussion concludes that coordination is the linchpin of organization. A taxonomy of coordinating mechanisms, based on Mintzberg, is proposed. The chapter ends with a definition of the basic, human preconditions for organizing, which are to serve as the foundation for the analysis of technology use.

Part II: Individual Capacity and Organization before the Computer

In Part II, my purpose is to analyze the contributions of pre-computer technology. *Confined by Physiology* begins by looking at the six basic human preconditions in more detail. I also discuss important, traditional methods for alleviating or circumventing some of these constraints.

In *The Dawn of Organization*, I explore the problems of organization-building in societies without significant tools for organizational purposes, and try to determine the extent of the space of constructible organizations in such societies. The analysis focuses on the methods and techniques used to build and maintain pre-literate organizations. The analysis corroborates the conclusion that coordination is the essence of organization, and ends with what I see as the basic principles of preliterate organization.

In *The Power of Technology*, I discuss the nature of tools and the way the most important pre-computer technologies have alleviated our original constraints, gradually allowing for extensions of the space of constructible organizations. The single, most important innovation was undoubtedly the art of writing, and the great impact writing has had on our mental capacities is explored. Next, I discuss the communications revolution of the nineteenth century, and the chapter ends with some thoughts on complexity and the nature of automation.

In *The Modern Organization*, I try to assess the relationship between the development of pre-computer tools and the emergence of the modern organization. I conclude that the new forms of organization, especially the Machine Bureaucracy, were based on a new and vastly more efficient concept of coordination: the transition from direct to indirect supervision through standardization of work processes in the form of explicit routines and automation. I also propose that the emergence of the modern organization involved another breakthrough: the emergence of the explicit conceptual model and the concomitant explicit design of organizations. The chapter ends with a short discussion of the effect of culture on organizational forms.

Part III: IT and the Preconditions for Organizing

Now the platform for analyzing the impact of information technology is finally in place, and I start out in *Information Technology Characteristics* by assessing the state of the art of the technology and the likely achievements in basic performance improvements during the next decade. In *The IT-Based Preconditions*, I proceed to analyze how information technology can improve the capabilities of the individual over and beyond the contributions of earlier technology. This provides the foundation for the subsequent analysis of possible new organization forms and practices.

While working on this part, I felt it was necessary to balance the fairly technocentric analysis in Chapter 9, and underline that human nature is not exclusively defined by logic and reason. In Chapter 10, ***Emotional Barriers and Defenses***, I therefore discuss how our emotional side may put a spoke in the best technological wheel.

Part IV: Extending the Space of Constructible Organizations

In ***The Individual and the Group*** I then start on a prelude to the kernel by analyzing the possibilities information technology provides on the individual and group level. This is necessary both because they represent the primordial elements of organization as well as the fundamental building blocks of larger organizations, and because there are a number of application types (among them some of the most hyped-up ones) that apply first and foremost to this level.

Then, I move on to the core of the matter: the larger organizational context and the tools and potentials that apply to the organization as a whole. First I look at ***Routines and Automation***. Automation will in my view continue to represent an extremely important contribution to the development of modern societies, allowing enormous increases in productivity—something which will also have a number of interesting side effects. Computer-based automation also includes automatic routines at various levels, which is a very important prerequisite for two later themes. One of them, ***Coordination by Default***, is about how databases can contribute to the age-old problem of coordinating work, both improving on existing arrangements as well as providing new ones. The second I have called ***Comprehension and Control***; it is about how information technology can improve our understanding and control of both our work and our organizations by making information more accessible and even procure information that was previously unavailable. This has clear implications for organization structure and the way organizations can be run.

At the end of each of these three chapters, I discuss the possible extensions information technology may offer to the space of constructible organizations.

Part V: The New Organizations

I then close in on the final target in Part V. First, in ***Toward the Model-driven Organization***, I discuss what it really means to build organizations with information technology: that computer programs become ever more prominent parts of the organizational fabric, and therefore also become part of the very patterns of actions that constitute organizations. Next, I return to the conceptual model: After computers and computer programming were introduced, the model and modeling activities have become very explicit, and are becoming extremely important within the *computerate paradigm*. In my view, active models will make up the central element in most organizations in the future.

In **The New Configurations**, I first discuss if and how the extensions to the space of constructible organizations combine to modify Mintzberg's configurations, and find three significant new variants: the *Joystick Organization*, an entrepreneur's dream evolving from the Simple Structure, the *Flexible Bureaucracy*, a formidable fighter growing forth from the Machine Bureaucracy, and the *Interactive Adhocracy*—an Adhocracy where system-mediated communication allows true mutual adjustment to work in much larger settings than before. I then end by proposing two altogether new configurations: the *Meta-Organization*, a closely coupled group of separate organizations, and the *Organized Cloud*, which challenges our notions of what an organization really is. Finally, in **Concluding Considerations**, I discuss the practical need for theory, provide some ideas on how to use the book and discuss the relations between flexibility, cost, and productivity and why computers increase the ante in the race for improvements—and why superior IS and organization professionals and really gifted *Organization Design Managers* may be the ultimate competitive instrument.

2

Organization and Tools—the Human Advantages

"Man is a tool-using animal ... Without tools he is nothing, with tools he is all."
Thomas Carlyle, *Sartor Resartus*, 1833–34.

A CRUCIAL LINK

The basic notion behind this book is that technology has been a very important factor in the emergence, development, and design of organizations throughout history, and that changes in organization-relevant technology will spur changes in the structure and functioning of organizations as well. Why do I believe this?

Apart from the commonsense assumption that telephones and computers must matter, and convincing empirical evidence that railroads and the telegraph did so in the past (Chandler 1977, Beniger 1986), there are also theoretically well-founded reasons for believing so, and I would like to elaborate a little on this theme before proceeding to identify which of our abilities and limitations are most relevant for our organizing efforts.

To Be Human Is to Be Organized...

Everything we know about ourselves tells us that organizing is a fundamental part of human life—for as long as we know, humans have organized themselves in order to accomplish tasks that are not within the reach of single individuals. All that archeology and anthropology have discovered supports this; humans are and have always been social animals, and the isolated individual is an anomaly. Organization may well be rudimentary, as in the small bands of hunter/gatherers believed to constitute the primordial form of human society, but they nevertheless have a social structure and a basal role diversification, and a number of the hunter/gatherers we know of from historic (and present) times in fact have quite sophisticated social structures. Some of the oldest texts known, such as the Epic of Gilgamesh (believed to have been written down as early as in the beginning of the second millennium BC), contain descriptions of elaborate social organization. In the opening verse in the Epic of Gilgamesh alone, there are mentions of the king, of nobles, of warriors, and the concept "shepherd of the people/city" (Sandars 1964).

The Bible even contains concrete directions—and reasons—for organizing, as in Exodus 18:13–23, where Moses' father-in-law saw that the task Moses had taken upon himself—to pass judgement on all matters, large and small, for all of his people—was too big for one man. To resolve the situation, he devised a method in the form of an organizational structure to share the work among many, leaving Moses only with the most important cases.

Implicit in these examples lies another, decisive factor: Not only are humans born as organizers, they accumulate their experience and increase their collective skill from generation to generation. For even if every innovation must spring forth from an individual mind, it is (if successful) rapidly absorbed into the collective consciousness of the inventor's society, and may even spread beyond to other societies if there is sufficient contact between them.

Even if the pinnacles of individual creativity throughout history are impressive, then, it is as a collective phenomenon, as a meta-mind stretching through time and space, spanning thousands of generations, that the human intellect really shines. And the basis for this is our ability to organize—our ability to congregate in groups, tribes, and societies where knowledge and skills can accumulate and be transferred to new generations, who, in their turn, can develop them further. Although individual contributions are recognizable, they are indeed impossible to separate from the collective consciousness of humanity. As Boulding says, discussing the levels of theoretical discourse for systems theory (1956, p. 8), "... it is not easy to separate clearly the level of the individual human organism from the next level, that of social organizations".

To become masters of the Earth, we had to organize, and so we have done—in modern civilizations, the inventory of organizations is large and extremely diverse; they are a part of everyday life for nearly every human, and only the hermit escapes daily contact with them.

...and to Use Tools

Humans are not the only organizers in the animal kingdom, however, although undoubtedly they are the most accomplished. An even more distinguishing characteristic is our ability to make tools, particularly the way in which we use the process of collective accumulation of knowledge and experience to develop ever better tools, tools with increasing power and complexity.

Our array of tools and methods have grown large and diverse, and we apply them—or at least try to apply them—wherever we come up against challenges that go beyond our bare physical and mental powers. It is hardly possible to imagine that the realm of organizing should be exempted from this; the only possible reason would be that our abilities for organizing had no bounds, and that we never experienced any gap between them and our ambitions.

While this may hold true for our Lord, we—as mere humans—must rather content ourselves with the fact that the unaided human is an animal with definite physical and mental limitations, restricting the amount of work or the amount of information any single individual can cope with. As March and Simon say (1958, p. 11):

> This, then, is the general picture of the human organism that we will use to analyze organizational behavior. It is a picture of a choosing, decision-making, problem-solving organism that can do only one or a few things at a time, and that can attend to only a small part of the information recorded in its memory and presented by the environment.

Not only do we have limitations that can only be (partly) overcome by organization, but those very limitations even restrict the nature and size of the organizations we are able to build.

To organize on the scale necessary for the conquest of the Earth, we had to go beyond the social organization in the family, group and village, which built directly on our innate abilities. We had to develop tools and methods for building larger and more effective organizations, as we have done for so many other ends. The digital computer is no more than the newest of these tools, although it may prove to be the most powerful of them all so far.

THE POINT OF LEVERAGE

Earlier, I underlined how our success as a species derives from the powerful interplay between individual creativity on the one side and collective actions and accumulation of knowledge on the other. This field of force is evident in the theories of organization as well, but there has been a tendency to simplify the picture, by downplaying either the role of the individual, the role of the environment, or both. I feel distinctly uncomfortable with this—perhaps because my career as a consultant has awarded me with practical experience with a fairly large number of organizations. In every one of them, I think, I have seen the crucial role of both the individuals that make them up and the environment they work in.

Organizations Are Constructed

Theories are by their very nature always simplifications of reality, not least when the subject is human behavior in and around organizations—and the reason is not only differences in contingencies such as history, cultural settings, ages, and power structures. It is easy to lose sight of the simple fact that organizations are not physical entities acting and behaving on their own, but *derived* entities—wholes that are constituted through the actions of the individual human beings that make them up. Those humans have their own peculiar characteristics, dreams, objectives, and preferences, and the character of the organization, its successes and failures, is the result of an interplay both between those individuals and between them and other individuals outside the organization itself.

My experience therefore supports most of the basic views of Silverman, Weick, Berger and Luckmann, the social constructivists, and some (ontological) postmodernists such as Clegg. Organizations are constituted through the daily actions of their members and of the people they deal with in the environment, directly or indirectly. Organizations do not act; it is the people constituting them who act. Even single individuals can be of decisive importance in shaping the fate of very large organizations. The spectacular rise of ITT, for instance, is probably attributable to Harold Geneen (and, arguably, so is its fall), and the growth of IBM up to around 1950 was no doubt to a large degree a result of the vision, ruthlessness, and willpower of Thomas Watson, Sr. Further, IBM's phenomenal success as a computer company in the following four decades was not the result of an inevitable development, but primarily a consequence of the stubborn effort displayed by Tom Watson (son of Thomas). Keenly interested in the new machines, he defied his father's skepticism and, together with a small team of corporate mavericks, managed to develop and produce first the 701, IBM's first digital computer, and then the remarkably successful 650—all against strong, persistent opposition from IBM's planning department, who could not see any need for machines more powerful than the company's existing punched card equipment (Augarten 1984).

There is also no doubt that Henry Ford was the driving force behind the ascendancy of Ford Motors, or that (in Norway) there would have been no Norsk Hydro (or even Elkem) without Sam Eyde's vision, tenacity, and unsurpassed energy.

Even in the absence of such singular entrepreneurs, two organizations that are formally very similar—for instance, two municipal administrations of the same size and in the same part of a country—can be very different in how they work, how efficient they are, what their main problems are, and how receptive they are to change. Many of the dissimilarities can simply be traced back to the differences between the actual persons working in the two organizations, especially the differences between their most significant members (which usually include not only managers and local trade union representatives, but also strong personalities with informal influence over others). Even persons who no longer work in the organization may cast long shadows, clearly visible in the daily proceedings—both as symbols of unity (or discord) and through their legacies in the form of policies and procedures.

When organization members act, however, they will of course be influenced—often heavily—by the interpretations of meaning that their roles in the organization imbue them with. They act within a set of frames[1] (Goffman 1974) that to a large degree incarnate the collective interpretations of both other organization members and important persons and collectives outside the organization. Persons with important roles in an organization are therefore often perceived as acting for the organization, and the organization as "acting" through those persons. Clegg's concept of *modes of rationality* also fits neatly into this framework. Acting within their local frames, agents will use the means available and allowable to construct their organizations in a way that meets their purposes. Since frames will be different in different parts of the world, and even within different local regions in the same society, modes of rationality will also differ, and no single organizational solution will achieve total domination—although solutions that are successful in certain settings may inspire actors elsewhere to adopt certain aspects of them that are compatible with

---

[1] A *frame* is a scheme of interpretation that makes it possible for us to interpret, organize, and make sense of particular events and actions. Frames are therefore also expressions of the generally accepted norms in the social domains where they are valid. The same event may have very different interpretations in different frames. For instance, crying in a funeral is generally positively regarded and readily understood, while laughing would meet with strong resentment. In a meeting with old friends, however, laughter would be the normal thing, and crying would be met with puzzlement and concerned questions about the reasons. In a ceremony such as the opening of a new session in parliament, both laughter and crying would be regarded as improper. We all recognize a very large number of frames. Some are more or less universal, many are common to most people within a particular society, and many are local.

the local conditions. Wholesale transplantations may also be tried, but are sure to run into trouble.

Over time, there will of course be recurring patterns of action in organizations, certain actions will acquire a commonly understood meaning, and expectations about the durability of certain patterns of action will grow. It is these recurring patterns of action that constitute and define the organization in daily life; it is when we confront these patterns through interaction with organization members that we sense and experience the organization itself.

The patterns themselves and the expectations they generate are normally quite resilient; organizations can retain a remarkable degree of stability even with a high turnover of people, and can endure great stress without breaking. They can also continue to cling to life through year after year of unsuccessful operation (Meyer and Zucker 1989). Even when an organization is economically and legally dissolved, as after a bankruptcy, it happens—not infrequently—that a number of the people who constituted that organization will reconstitute themselves as a new organization with roughly the same purpose and many of the habits of the old one. The ingrained resistance to any change of routines and ways of working in almost any organization is another manifestation of the strength of recurring patterns of action.

But They Are also Systems

However, organizations also clearly exhibit systemic properties. A defining characteristic of a system is that it is more than the sum of its parts (Bertalanffy 1973). That is, if we study the individual cells that make up a fox, we cannot deduce the full nature or the behavior of the fox. By dissecting the fox, we destroy it and lose sight of its systemic properties. The same is true for social systems: if we only study isolated individuals, we cannot understand cooperation. By focusing solely on isolated, single acts carried out by the members of an organization, we cannot comprehend its structure and dynamics—and, just as important, neither can we understand the isolated acts, since their meaning is largely derived from their organizational (systemic) context—from the frames within which their are conceived. Actions in organizations are also very often responses to actions by other organization members. People thus receive feedback on their own actions and may modify them according to their interpretations of this feedback. Their interaction (interlocked behavior, in Weick's [1979] terms)—and hence the organization itself—therefore acquires a systemic character.

Even people who are not intended targets of a particular action may choose to interpret it as something that concerns them, and act accordingly, with ramifications not only for the original actor but for others in the organization as well. The universe of actions that constitute an organization is therefore dynamic, with patterns of actions and reactions reverberating through it, over time creating those recurring patterns of action that define the organization. We then have a system that exhibits both stability and dynamism. It shows stability in the sense that it is a recognizable social entity with roughly defined roles and a relatively predictable behavior. It is dynamic in the sense that its constituting members will change and that they over time will come up with new actions and establish new patterns of action.

Since organization members also have relations with people in the organization's environment (indeed its business transactions are built upon such contact) organizations are also open systems. Changes in the outside relations, in the problems and opportunities they represent, will provide major impetuses for internal changes. Organizations where the members, especially the leading members, are not able to interpret important changes in the environment in an adequate way, or do not respond to them, will soon be in trouble, which testifies to the fact that the stability of open systems is a precarious stability: it requires continuous effort to maintain it. This is, by the way, in accord with Ashby's law of requisite variety (Ashby 1956), which says that to survive, a system must contain within itself greater variety than the variety it is confronted with by its environment[2].

If organizations are systems, then, it follows that they have characteristics that arise from their systemic nature, and not from the actions of any single individual. This is a salient point—and a point of controversy for at least some action theorists, as Silverman (1970) notes. For if organizations are constituted only through the actions of their individual members, there seems to be no room for characteristics that are not traceable to one or a number of individuals.

I think this paradox is resolved when we take a closer look at the nature of systems—both systems in general and the peculiar class of systems that we call organizations. Systems are composed of parts, and real systems[3]—such as foxes and organizations—can be physically divided into their

---

[2] Humans are so successful as biological systems because they are extremely flexible with respect to food, organization, and tool use. Insects and bacteria flourish because of their prodigious breeding capacity, which allows a very rapid proliferation of successful genetic combinations or mutants. Humans, insects and bacteria thus all possess a large capacity for rapid variation. Most large animals do not: an example is the koala, whose numbers dwindle in step with the diminishment of the Australian eucalyptus forests.

[3] There are also conceptual systems, such as logic and mathematics (Bertalanffy 1973).

constituent parts. However, the systems are not defined only as the sum of their parts, but also (and indeed primarily) through the *interrelations* of these parts.

This means that the systems characteristics of organizations emanate first and foremost from the *interactions* of their members. Of course, they have to be manifested through concrete actions by concrete people, but since the conception of every significant action in the organization is influenced (to some degree) by the complex interactions and the established expectations within the organization or toward people in its environment (often both), the systems characteristics emerge *as a quality of the individual actions themselves.*

And Contingencies Matter

If organizations are systems, then, their systems characteristics become important. What are the recurring patterns of action like? Are they different from organization to organization, or are there similarities? Maybe some internal and environmental conditions are important?

This is leading toward the questions posed by contingency theory, and I see no reason to back away from them, since I think there are regularities in the systems characteristics of organizations, even if no two organizations are completely alike—just as most people have two arms and two legs despite their individual differences, and most small children giggle when tickled, no matter what culture or nationality they belong to. Galbraith (1977) addressed this question (Is there a general theory relevant to a specific organization?) in the introduction to his book *Organization Design* (pp. 7–9). His conclusion, based on interpretations of empirical studies, was that 50% to 75% of the variance in organizations could be accounted for by general theoretical propositions, leaving the rest to specific factors peculiar to the individual organizations. This means that no organization can be understood apart from its history, its particular setting, and the particular individuals who dominate it, but neither is any organization isolated from more general relationships.

One can probably differ in opinion on how much of the variance can be explained by general propositions—that proportion will vary, among other things, according to the cultural homogeneity of the sample—but there is, in my view, ample evidence that there is indeed a mix. Therefore, we have no choice but to approach the analysis of organizations on several levels: that of the individual actor, that of the single system, and that of the system in its environment. Important insights can be gained on either level; they are all significant for organization design and organization change, and all are relevant for my present purpose.

The Space of Constructible Organizations

The starting point of my research efforts was the apparently innocent question of what organizations based on innovative use of information technology would look like. An effort to answer that question cannot build only on empirical evidence of past and present achievements, since we are only beginning to learn how to use computers. Rather, we must try to map out the space of possible organizational arrangements after the introduction of computers. We can now outline this problem more precisely.

As acknowledged above, organizations are shaped by a great number of factors. Not only the traditional contingencies apply. Clegg (1990), for example, drawing on a large, cross-cultural selection of studies, presents a convincing case for the way cultural, technical, economic, and other contingency factors can influence people to assemble their organizations in innumerable ways—and still operate them successfully, both domestically and when exposed to international competition. In addition comes the fact that organizations are constructed by real humans, exhibiting great variation in their dispositions and goals.

Building on this, we can say that the space of possible organizational solutions in any particular situation is determined by the *local mix* of relevant contingency factors at that point in space and time, including the normal range of individual characteristics of the members of that society, as well as their local social norms and arrangements. We can call this space the *local space* of possible organizations. Acknowledging our inborn limitations as humans, we can also safely conclude that there must be some absolute limits to what we can achieve, defined jointly by our biological nature and the capability of the available tools. These limits define what we might call an absolute space of all possible organizational solutions.

However, this absolute space is not constant, nor is it entirely defined by nature. I will therefore avoid the term "absolute space" and replace it with three concepts that reflect the mixed nature of humans: on the one side, we are biological creatures with a set of biologically defined characteristics, like other animals; on the other side, we have an extreme social and cultural plasticity and creativity, providing a potential for development that is utterly different and superior to that for any other creature on Earth; but even so, there are things we do not do, even if we could actually accomplish them.

The first of these concepts I will call the *primal space* of organizations. It is defined by man's biological characteristics and basic psychological and social needs—the possible organizations of the human animal, if you like. The second one I will call the *space of constructible organizations* ("constructible space" for short). It represents the expanded organizational space made possible by the tools, methods, and social practices developed by humans to relieve the limiting constraints of the primal space. The constructible space encompasses all existing local spaces. In fact, it is equal to the sum of all local spaces.

While the primal space is by and large constant (changed only by biological evolution), the constructible space is changing all the time. Generally, it also expands, since new technologies and the evolution of methods and customary practice tend to increase the number of alternatives. Of course, developments in social and moral attitudes will over time render some customary arrangements unacceptable (such as slavery and serfdom in our parts of the world), but such curtailments have so far not even remotely matched the increases in variation. The arrow has thus pointed largely in one direction, and only a major loss of technological, methodological, or social capability through a global catastrophe could possibly lead to a significant contraction of the constructible space.

The third concept is the *technical space* of organizations, which is defined solely by what should be possible given humanity's physiological capabilities extended by the existing technology and methods, thus excluding psychological, social, and cultural constraints. It will, of course, be larger than the constructible space, since it is always possible to imagine physically feasible organizational solutions that will not be psychologically feasible or socially acceptable in any actual situation, and thus impossible to realize within any local space.

My prime interest is the constructible space and how it is extended by information technology. However, as a step on the road, it is necessary also to try to outline the primal space, and the way the constructible space has grown with the development of tools and methods. Since many people in the computer business also show tendencies to equate the technical space with the constructible space, in blithe ignorance of the social and psychological needs and preferences of normal humans, it will also be necessary at various points to discuss some of the main differences between the two.

Defining the Boundaries of Constructible Space

What, then, defines the boundary of the constructible space? Obviously, the number of factors is large, and an exhaustive analysis is probably impossible. Analytically, at least, we can discern four broad classes of factors, hinted at above, which are the most significant:

- **Biological characteristics:** Obviously, we cannot build organizations that presuppose telepathy, unlimited human memory, or the ability to run at the speed of five hundred miles per hour.

- **Psychological characteristics:** As humans, we have a psychological makeup that limits what we can accomplish and tolerate in daily life. The limits here vary strongly with the circumstances. For instance, people are prepared to endure much higher strain in a crisis (such as a war or disaster) than in a normal work situation. Opinions also change over time—as for instance views on what kind of job conditions that are either harmful enough to impair an organization, or too harmful to be acceptable to employees. Indeed, to reduce the acceptable range of harmful working conditions has been a central purpose for the labor unions since their inception.

- **Social and cultural factors:** This class comprises social organization (including family systems), culture (including knowledge, norms, and laws), and social institutions in the fields of religion, economy, and politics. It is obviously of great importance to the definition of the constructible space. A special case here is the sphere of illegal organizations, like the Mafia and other agencies of organized crime, and organizations that defy commonly accepted norms, such as organizations of various kinds of dropouts. Insofar as they are fairly stable, de facto elements of most societies, they must clearly be viewed as being inside the constructible space: in fact, it is easy to show how they comply with the local mix of contingency factors in their particular sub-culture, and thereby define a viable local space. Borderline cases will be organizations such as the extermination camps of Hitler's Germany, the gulags of Stalin's Soviet Union, and the concentration camps of other, lesser perpetrators, which may be defined either as temporary, freak outgrowths of the constructible space or as a genuine part of the constructible space to which access is (fortunately!) normally hindered.

- **Available tools and methods:** Analytically, tools and methods can be viewed as two different classes of factors. However, they are so often intertwined that it seems more appropriate to group them together: writing is not possible without writing materials, nor is accounting; lateral filing requires special equipment; and so on. Sometimes it is also difficult to draw the line between a method and a social practice in association with a tool: the clock is certainly a tool for timekeeping, but is the practice of reliably reporting to work at a particular time every day (so necessary for certain organizational forms) a method or a social practice? Perhaps it is both—a basic instance of a method for coordination that has become an ingrained part of the social fabric of industrialized societies.

The example of the concentration camp underlines an interesting feature of constructible space: As one moves toward its boundaries, it becomes more and more difficult to actually construct and maintain an intended organization—sometimes because it pushes the limits of generally accepted norms, sometimes because it verges on exceeding the tolerances of human psychology or physiology, and sometimes because it stretches technology toward its limits.

If we were modern social physicists, then, we might endeavor to create field equations for the constructible space—and discover that there is a Great Attractor at its center, perhaps in the form of the rationalized myths of our societies (Meyer and Rowan 1977), which shape the organizations we build unless we consciously (and at the price of a considerable effort) go in another direction. Now, social physics is an antiquated approach, and field equations are hardly viable tools in the social sciences—but as a metaphor, they can be useful. All local spaces will have their own set of attractors in the form of traditionally preferred organizational forms, and it will always take vision, boldness, and energy to go against tradition and construct something new.

For an organizational form to fall within the constructible space, it is, of course, not a requirement that every particular instance of that form survives. It is, for instance, perfectly possible to set up a new organization in a market where the competition is too tough for most newcomers to make it; indeed, this happens regularly in open, market-oriented economies, as entrepreneurs often overestimate their chances and end up in bankruptcy. The point is that it is possible to set up that kind of organization at all. Environmental factors such as the number of existing firms in a market or the profitability of a certain line of business is therefore not a factor in defining the constructible space.

The Scope of this Investigation

The object of this investigation is to understand how and why information technology extends the boundaries of the space of constructible organizations. Obviously, it is impossible to discuss all possible permutations; to make a significant contribution without overextending my undertaking, I will have to concentrate on what I believe are the most important factors involved.

Our Biological Characteristics

As indicated above, I consider the first class of factors, our physiological characteristics, to be the most basic determinants of the size and shape of the constructible space. These constraints can also be assumed to be constant on the timescale of interest to us here. Proper training can improve individual performance, but our basic capabilities have probably remained fundamentally unchanged for thousands of years and represent the iron constraints that put absolute limits on human achievements. It is also these constraints that we have most eagerly attacked with the help of technology and methods—not only because they are so unyielding, but also because they are the ones most open to amendment by such means. I will therefore discuss these constraints in considerable detail, and base most of my analysis on the way they are alleviated by technology.

Our Psychological Characteristics

The basic situation is probably much the same for the second class of factors, our psychological characteristics. That is, they have been constant for a very long period of time. However, they are a lot more pliable than our biological capabilities, at least in the way they manifest themselves. The limits for the amount of aggression or compassion that can be expressed, for instance, or the amount of psychological stress a person can endure, are to a considerable degree determined by social and cultural factors. We do not find this kind of variation in talking speed or in the number of items that can be held simultaneously in short-term memory.

Since our psychological attributes seem to be both less limiting to our organizing abilities and less amendable by technology, they have received scant attention in the development of computer-based systems. The exceptions are, of course, the user interface, which has received much notice over the last ten to fifteen years, as well as methods and strategies for introducing computer-based systems in organizations.

Both of these factors as well as the size and vigorousness of the market for computer games and gimmicks such as cartoon-like screen savers, "eyes" that follow the cursor around, and so on, suggest that emotions and other nonrational parts of our psyche may be more important in our interactions with technology than normally recognized by computer professionals. Although the subject is somewhat elusive, I have found it difficult to leave it out altogether, especially since I believe emotions play a very important part in deciding the viability of a number of computer applications, not least in the "groupware" category. I have therefore included discussions on the role of emotions in several of my analyses.

Social and Cultural Factors

Social and cultural factors are, of course, even more malleable than our psychological characteristics, as we can see from the great variation found among the societies in the world today and in historic times. Their influence on the size and shape of the local constructible space is great but so varied that it constitutes a vast field of study in itself, challenging not only the discipline of sociology but almost all of the social sciences. This makes it impossible for me to incorporate social and cultural factors into my analyses—other than as examples to throw light on particular problems—with one very important exception: the tools and methods we use and have used to construct our organizations.

Of course, this does not mean that the present analysis is culturally neutral. Although I have strived toward a dissociation from my particular social and cultural background, I readily acknowledge the fact that a completely neutral stance is simply not possible for any human. My analysis will therefore obviously be most appropriate for the Western industrialized sphere. However, I also believe that humans have enough basic traits in common to make the analysis valid, to a large extent, even in other cultural settings.

Tools and Methods

Tools and methods are both creations of the human mind, and as such they are wholly constructed expressions of both knowledge and social values. A computer is indeed a cultural manifestation, and a mighty one at that.

Tools and methods also represent the most pliant class of factors with bearing on the space of constructible organizations, and is by far the class subject to the most rapid development. For the last several hundred years at least, the development of tools and methods have arguably outpaced all other patterns of change in human society, and the speed is not getting slower.

As I noted above, tools and methods can be roughly separated analytically, but in practice they are intimately connected and often intertwined, and will more often than not have to be discussed as combined phenomena.

This brings us back to an implication that was raised in the discussion on biological characteristics: it is, of course, a central question just *how* new tools and methods make their undisputed contributions to changes in social and cultural conditions (which include organizations). However, if we believe that the basis for the construction of the social fabric (and of organizations) is the individual actions of the members of that society, *it follows from our conclusions above that the direct influence of tools and methods must come from the way they change and enlarge the realm of possibilities for individual actions. And such changes must spring mainly from enhancements of our basic, physiologically defined capabilities.*

The main analytical thrust in this book will therefore remain *the augmentation of our natural, biological constraints by technological means (including both tools and methods), and what kinds of extensions to the space of constructible organizations these augmentations will allow.* To get started, then, we must first decide which of our abilities (or constraints) are most important to our ability to organize.

3
The Basic Preconditions for Organizing

> "I am certainly convinced that it is one of the greatest impulses of mankind to arrive at something higher than a natural state."
> **James Baldwin,** "The Male Prison," in *Nobody Knows My Name*, 1961

THE ESSENCE OF ORGANIZATION

I have stated that organizations, in my view, are constructed; like any other kind of social system, they are constituted through the actions and interactions of their members, both between themselves and with people in an organization's environment. I also said that the systems characteristics of organizations emanate precisely from these interactions and manifest themselves as a quality of the individual actions themselves. By enhancing the abilities and capacities of the individual organizational members, then, the use of tools will alter the systems characteristics of the organization as well.

Further, the most important systems effects must be those that arise from the types of recurring patterns of actions most common to organizations: the actions that aim to carry out their basic functions, and thus constitute what we may call their structure. To discover the main enabling qualities of new tools, we must therefore identify the human abilities and constraints that are most important to those basic functions.

When the Task Becomes Too Large for One

What, then, constitutes the essence of organization? What are the basic features and functions of organizations? When sifting through the literature on organization theory, one is struck by the fact that although nearly everyone complains about how difficult it is to define "organization," they still tend to end up stressing largely the same central features. Jay R. Galbraith (1977), contributes an intuitive definition, when he says that (p. 2): "...organization is that 'something' which distinguishes any collection of 50 individuals in Kennedy International Airport from the 50 individuals comprising a football team in the National Football League." Getting more formal, he stresses the need for a shared purpose, for division of labor and "information-based decision processes" (1977, p. 3).

Henry Mintzberg, on his part, starts his book *The Structuring of Organizations* (1979) with an illustrative story about the potter Ms Raku, who started out making pottery in her basement. She did everything herself, just like any ancient craftswoman—wedged the clay, formed the pots, tooled them, prepared and applied the glaze, and fired the pots in the kiln. She then marketed and sold the pots to craft shops. Everything went smoothly; there were no problems-except that demand outstripped supply.

Ms Raku then hired an assistant who was eager to learn pottery, and everything still went without hassle, even though Ms Raku now had to divide the work. The assistant wedged the clay and prepared the glazes, and Ms Raku did the rest—since the shops wanted pottery made by *her*. It required some coordination, but since they were only two, and worked in a small studio, this posed no problem.

Before long, however, Ms Raku was again outselling the production capacity. More assistants were needed and, even with three new people, coordination could be conducted informally. But as still more assistants were added, Ms Raku faced more serious problems. There were simply too many people to coordinate everything informally and without plans, and, besides, Ms Raku was now mostly away from the studio, spending time with her growing number of customers. The time had come for the first assistant to become studio manager and full-time supervisor.

Ms Raku's ambitions were limitless, and the company continued to grow, branching out into new product lines (even clay bricks) and new customer groups. Eventually, she was the proud president and owner of the large, divisionalized company Ceramico, with her office located on the 55th story of Pottery Tower. Ms Raku and her company had traversed the history of human organization in a couple of feverish decades.

Mintzberg concludes this introduction (p. 2, italics and bold in the original) by making the following observation:

> Every organized human activity—from the making of pots to the placing of a man on the moon—gives rise to two fundamental and opposing requirements: the *division of labor* into various tasks to be performed and the *coordination* of these tasks to accomplish the activity. **The structure of an**

organization can be defined simply as the sum total of the ways in which it divides its labor into distinct tasks and then achieves coordination among them.

To be recognizable, an organization must have a domain for its activity, and it must have a set of objectives and goals. There is great variation as to how consistent and explicit domains, objectives, and goals are, but it is difficult to envisage an organization completely without any kind of consciousness about a common domain and some common objectives; we would then really be confronting something that was more akin to Galbraith's accidental collection of 50 people in Kennedy International Airport. Next, an organization must have what Galbraith (1977) calls an *organizing mode*—a way of decomposing work into subtasks and a way of coordinating them for the completion of the whole task. This gives rise to a need for significant amount of communication and information processing, a need that grows with the level of task uncertainty and the pace of change in the environment (Galbraith 1977). To Galbraith, this strongly indicates that the required level of information processing will have a decisive influence on organization structure: The amount of uncertainty will dictate the amount of control and coordinative activities that will be needed, which again will require certain levels of information processing. He therefore ends up with an information processing model of organization as the basis for his design framework.

James G. March and Herbert A. Simon, in their *Organizations* (1958) also stress the high degree of coordination in organization behavior. In his foreword to the third edition of *Administrative Behavior* (1976, p. xvii, italics in original), Simon says that: "...the term *organization* refers to the complex pattern of communication and relationships in a group of human beings." To Simon, the organization is mainly a decision-making system—coordination and control for him therefore become synonymous with the communication of decision premises and decisions. He further emphasizes the importance of communication as "essential to the more complex forms of cooperative behavior" (1976, p. 106), and he is very clear about the need for stable, predictable cooperative patterns and communication channels if an organization is to operate efficiently.

Such definitions are what Scott (1987) would term rational systems definitions of organizations: they do not include either the informal communication and conflicting interests of the natural systems definition, or the relation to the environment of the open systems tradition—both of which are also vital parts of action and constructivist perspectives. However, the authors quoted here are aware of both aspects and discuss them in their books.

The views referred to above are also in close accordance with general systems theory, which claims to be a general theory of organization in physical, biological and social systems, and which has had substantial influence on organization theory for the last three to four decades. Both W. Ross Ashby (1962), Kenneth Boulding (1956), Walter Buckley (1967), and Ludwig von Bertalanffy (1973) define organization mainly in terms of communication.

BASIC ELEMENTS IN ORGANIZATION STRUCTURING

Most writers seem to agree on the basic features of organizations: the *division of labor* and the concomitant *need for coordination*. The coordination efforts in turn require both *information processing* and *communication*. Necessary exchanges with the environment and organizational adaptions because of environmental changes require additional processing and communication. Variations in the nature of these basic features should therefore have considerable influence on organizational structure.

The Division of Labor and Structuring of Work

The division of a greater, common task into smaller ones that are suitable for single persons is the defining feature of purposeful organizations. In principle, there are two ways of dividing work: Everyone can do the same in parallel, as when 50 people go together to clean up a beach and all collect litter in their own plastic bags, or the total task can be divided into specialized subtasks. Practically all purposeful organizations belong to the latter category, simply because there are extremely few of them that have tasks so simple that it is possible for every organization member to do exactly the same thing. Once the overall task is divided into more or less specialized jobs, it becomes a challenge to structure those jobs by grouping them (and thereby the people who execute them) in a way that ensures both that the organization's mission is accomplished and that the efficiency of the operation is sufficient to ensure the survival of the organization.

A basic determinant for organizational performance is the *grouping of tasks*. Grouping is necessary to establish a system of coordination and supervision, of resource sharing, and of performance measurement (Mintzberg 1979, Nadler and Tushman 1988). The basis for grouping can be either by activity, output, or customer. These three categories can be further decomposed—activity into function or skill, for instance, and customer into market segment or geographical region. Most often, different bases for grouping are used at different levels in the organization. For instance, top management may be grouped according to function (marketing, finance, production, etc.), the middle level according to market or product (or both), and production according to process or function. The reason is, of course, that different criteria for grouping may apply at the various levels.

The criteria used for grouping normally reflects the interdependencies that are seen as most important. Mintzberg (1979) counts four such interdependencies: *work-flow interdependencies* embraces all kinds of interdependencies between separate tasks or stages in functionally specialized organizations, *process interdependencies* refers to interdependencies within the separate stages themselves (note that "process" here does not mean the same as the "process" in BPR), *scale interdependencies* are simply about economies of scale, and *social interdependencies* denote social interaction and social needs.

When organizations are drawn between conflicting criteria, as they often are, they must either choose the one they deem most important or, if the conflict is too pronounced, try to accommodate it by creating various kinds of matrix organizations. The most common conflict is between product/market and function/process. A common solution is then to have one array of managers with responsibility for one set of considerations, and a second array for the other set. There are even examples of three-dimensional matrixes, with functional, product-, and market-oriented axes (Mintzberg 1979).

Coordination

Grouping is in itself the primary instrument for coordination. Usually, we (quite intuitively) try to group together those functions that seem to have the most immediate interdependencies. The reason is, of course, that physical proximity allows richer communication, and, generally, the richer the communication, the closer, swifter, and more flexible the coordination. The primary group, where coordination is effected through informal communication and where feedback is immediate, is the building block of all organizations.

However, while informal communication may be quite sufficient for the coordination of individual activities within the primary group, it cannot support the necessary coordination within and between the larger units in the organization. To accomplish this, the organization has to communicate and process large amounts of information across groups and units (Mintzberg 1979): *The information part of the work flow* (such as work documents and time sheets and even oral instructions), *control information and decisions*, which constitutes the main bulk of information associated with coordination (performance and problems upward; directions and plans downward), and finally *staff information* (operating data toward the staff, professional advice or plans and programming toward the line).

All of these information flows have to be taken care of in order to make an organization function properly, and this is where we hit the main challenge of organized work. Indeed, all the authors cited here view communication and information processing as the main bottlenecks for organized activities, although perhaps Galbraith expresses it most clearly. To him, information processing is the very focus of design; as organizations will seek to reduce the need for it as much as possible. They will group tasks with great care, they will preplan as far as the environment allows, and they will only maintain the flexibility that is needed to cope with the variations the environment forces upon them. If they can, they will in fact try to influence their environment to make it more stable, and if their competitive situation allows it, they may create slack resources in order to tolerate lower internal performance.

If this is not sufficient, an organization will have to increase its information processing capacity in order to cope. Two main alternatives are open (Galbraith 1977): Improving vertical information processing capacity (this is where Galbraith early on saw an important role for computers), or creating lateral relations. The information processing capacity of a hierarchy is bound to be quite limited—if it attempts to coordinate the activities of different units by communicating through the formal structure, the organizational hierarchy is easily overloaded. The development of lateral relations is seen as the main remedy. Both Mintzberg (1979) and Nadler and Tushman (1988) follow Galbraith closely here, and the prescription is what Mintzberg calls *liaison devices* and Nadler and Tushman call *structural linking*. They divide it into four basic types, ascending from *liaison individuals* (persons with a special responsibility to inspire cross-unit coordination by informing about certain aspects of their units' activities), via *cross-unit committees or task forces* (with the same purpose, but with more comprehensive participation), *integrating managers or departments* (similar to liaison individuals and cross-unit groups, but with a stronger mandate and more clearly defined responsibility), to the full *matrix organization*, where there are two (sometimes even three) intersecting chains of command. Mintzberg also argues that the organization's planning and control systems represent lateral linkages, especially action plans (Mintzberg 1979).

Another aspect of the struggle to coordinate is the question of centralization versus decentralization. If our capacity to communicate and process information were limitless, organizations could be totally centralized, with all decisions made by one brain, knowing all and directing everyone. Since this is impossible, no organization can be said to be totally centralized; however despotic the top manager, the majority of decisions will nevertheless be made by his or her underlings, although they will obviously try to cater to their master's tastes.

Decentralization, then, is a means to reduce the information processing requirements in the organizational hierarchy by spreading the processing throughout the organization—to engage more brains, so to speak. That will also reduce the amount of information that has to be communicated up and down the hierarchy. It is important to note that physical dispersal of services or facilities alone does not necessarily imply real decentralization (of decision-making power). It is quite conceivable, for instance, to run a bank with a network of branch offices and still have all loan applications sent to a central office for processing; indeed, that was what most banks did before the advent of computers and remote terminals.

Every organization also exists in a social, political, and technical context, and will always have a multitude of formal and informal relationships with both organizations and persons in its environment. These relationships may span the gamut from customers and suppliers to the Internal Revenue Service to the families of employees. To survive, the organization must maintain the necessary exchanges across its borders and be able to adapt to or resist changes in the environment to a sufficient degree to keep resources flowing. Both the daily exchanges as well as the necessary adaptions make heavy demands on the coordinative capacity of any organization, and the nature of the environment is therefore a very important parameter for organization design—to Mintzberg, it is even the most important determinant for organization structure. He describes (Mintzberg 1979) four basic types of environments (complex-stable, complex-dynamic, simple-stable and simple-dynamic), each of which correlates with one of his four basic coordinating mechanisms and thus also with one of his structural configurations.

The Linchpin of Organization

As a one-sentence conclusion of the discussion so far, I think a passage from Mintzberg's definition of organization quoted earlier in this chapter is perfectly suited (1979, p. 2): "*Every organized human activity—from the making of pots to the placing of a man on the moon—gives rise to two fundamental and opposing requirements: the division of labor into various tasks to be performed and the coordination of these tasks to accomplish the activity.*"

First of all, then, organizations above a certain small size (a few individuals) have a **division of labor**, since any single individual has a definite ceiling on his or her work capacity, be it physical or mental work. Single tasks must be made small enough to be fit for single persons. When you thus divide work among several people, it means that coordination between those tasks can no longer be effected within one brain, as when one person does everything. This sounds like a rather trivial conclusion (indeed a tautology), but the implications are far-reaching, because coordination of more than a handful of people involves most of what we know as organization.

Coordination among several individuals in turn implies **communication**, which may be either **routine** (proceduralized) or **ad hoc**. Without information flowing about what everybody should do and how they progress, coordination is impossible. Next, information about what is happening both inside the organization and in its environment must be **collected and distributed**, and the organization will also need to **process information** of this kind.

Communication and information processing also imply that the organization will need to establish some sort of an **organizational memory**— which in modern times usually means files and archives of different kinds, in addition to the vital information organization members carry around in their heads. (In preliterate times, people had to carry *all* the information around in their heads—a very constraining demand, as we shall see later.)

Further, there must be **accepted mechanisms for reaching decisions** on all levels, which also means that there will be a **power structure** of some kind (even in a small, egalitarian group, some people will usually have more influence on decisions than others). Finally, to secure permanence, the organization must fulfill a number of other conditions, which we have not discussed so far. If it is a normal public or private organization, it will have to **reward** its members in some ways, and provide the necessary tools, premises, and amenities for their work and well-being.

In my view, these propositions are as objective and well-founded as any social science proposition can be. Despite the great latitude of today's organization theories, and the enormous breadth of variation in actual organizations, it seems evident that organizations have some basic problems in common, and that *coordination* emerges as the crucial factor.

An analysis of the organizational contributions of any tool, including information technology, should therefore preferably be based on an organizational model built around the concept of coordination. To my knowledge, the best framework available that answers to this criterion are the structural configurations of Henry Mintzberg. The model presented in his *The Structuring of Organizations* (1979) also represents, in my view, the best attempt so far to meld the main structuring elements of organizations into one model. It has the added advantage of being well known both in academia and among professionals and managers. I will therefore use it as a workbench for my own analyses in this book.

Before we go on, however, I think it is necessary to take a second look at the subject of coordinating mechanisms, and I also think it will be useful to establish a taxonomy (Figure 3-1, p. 51), which we can refer to during subsequent discussions.

A Taxonomy of Coordinating Mechanisms

Even if Mintzberg's configurations and coordinating mechanisms are well known, I also hope I will have readers from professions and fields of research that are not acquainted with them. If you feel you need more background knowledge, I can only recommend you to go to the source itself (most complete in Mintzberg 1979, shorter in 1983 or 1989). There are no better expositions available. For the benefit of those of you who know them in principle but suffer from the same sneaking amnesia that I do, I will first provide a short summary of the main points before I discuss the coordinating mechanisms in more detail.

If a group is sufficiently small, says Mintzberg, both the division of work and coordination can occur naturally through informal communication between the group members. That is the secret of the small team's flexibility—everyone are constantly updated on the activities and intentions of all the others. Mintzberg (1979) terms this basic coordinating mechanism *mutual adjustment*. The corresponding structural configuration is the Adhocracy, a creative, project oriented organization living in a complex and dynamic environment.

However, mutual adjustment demands a high volume of communication. Ideally, every member of the group must communicate with every other member—or, at least, all the members must listen in on the group's shared dialogue, and contribute the relevant information about their own actions and needs. Obviously, when the group expands, the required volume of communication rapidly saturates human communication capacity, and coordination through mutual adjustment breaks down—just as Ms Raku in Mintzberg's example discovered when plant hangers started to take the wrong color and people began tripping over pots stacked on the floor.

At that point, someone must take the lead (either through appointment or common consent) and start planning and directing the work of the others. At its simplest, this takes the form of *direct supervision*. That is what Ms Raku resorted to when mutual adjustment ceased to work. She named one of her assistants studio manager, and divided her own time among planning, supervision, and customer relations. The corresponding configuration is the Simple Structure, a centralized organization (often a startup) in a simple, dynamic environment, with a strong leader who keeps the organization simple and informal, distrusts professionals and likes to interfere everywhere (because he or she "knows best").

Even direct supervision in its basic form breaks down fairly rapidly, however; since here is a definite limit to how many workers one person can continuously direct and coordinate. The actual number depends on the nature of the work, but even with the simplest and most undifferentiated work there cannot be more than a few tens at the most. However, direct supervision can be extended through delegation: the original leader can appoint a number of people to supervise a group each, and concentrate on supervising these subordinate leaders. In turn, they may again appoint leaders of still more groups, and so on. Theoretically, there is no limit to the size of such a hierarchy, but it is evident that lateral coordination must be achieved chiefly by channeling information and decisions up and down the hierarchy: to reach a decision involving two groups at the bottom, the matter must be brought up to the first common leader. The strain on individual communication capacities therefore increases toward the top, which is the only point where the communication lines to and from all the groups meet.

To avoid communication saturation, the need for coordination must therefore be reduced. Two avenues for action are open: the lower layers of the organization may be regrouped to create self-contained organizational entities that require a minimum of coordination, or the activities may be standardized in some way to reduce the need for supervision in the first place.

The first solution is what we normally understand as divisionalization, or the Divisionalized Form in Mintzberg's terminology. The complexity of day-to-day business is encapsulated within the division, corporate management will normally not meddle; and communication with headquarters can be limited to results, plans, and budget proposals upward, and appraisals, budgets, and planning directions downward. Such a company is often old and very large, and the divisions are most often organized as Machine Bureaucracies.

Standardization can take three forms: Standardization of work, standardization of outputs, and standardization of skills. Actually, divisionalization usually implies *standardization of output*: As noted above, corporate headquarters is primarily interested in a division's profit, not its internal workings. Even the work of individuals can be supervised in this way, as when factories employ piecework rates combined with standards for product quality, or as when Ms Raku tells the clay wedger only to deliver the clay in four-pound lumps, not how to wedge. However, as I will argue in a minute, standardization of output is really not a proper coordinating mechanism.

Standardization of work involves a direct specification of how work is to be done. It usually presupposes fairly extensive planning, to ensure that interdependent tasks are carried out in such a way that the necessary coordination between them is automatically ensured. On the other hand, it eliminates a considerable volume of supervision, and allow for a much higher ratio of productive to supervisory work in an organization. Ms Raku resorted to standardization of work when she hired a work study analyst to organize her first production lines. Mintzberg's standardization of work corresponds to Galbraith's preplanning, and is the defining characteristic of a bureaucratic organization, or Machine Bureaucracy as Mintzberg calls it. The Machine Bureaucracy is often large and old, it operates in a simple and stable environment and excels in mass production of products and services of a high and uniform quality.

Another approach is to build on *standardization of skills*. This is what vocational and professional training is all about. On all levels, from bricklayer to brain surgeon, the educational process equips craftspeople and professionals with a professionally certified set of solutions to common tasks, ready to be activated. When Ms Raku expanded, she hired assistants from the local pottery school, and they could immediately go about their work without further instructions. Mintzberg calls the organizations based on this coordinating mechanism Professional Bureaucracies. On the surface they may resemble Machine Bureaucracies, but they are normally dominated by one or more professions, and the rules that govern them are typically decided inside professional associations and educational institutions, not within the organizations themselves. Their environments tend to be stable but more complex than the Machine Bureaucracies. A hospital is the proverbial example.

Usually, an organization does not depend on only one coordinating mechanism; several or all will be used at some point and on some level. But often the organization has a defining mechanism that will serve as a basis for the main part of the work and contribute heavily to the organization's character.

Mintzberg later (1989) added another two configurations,[1] the *Missionary Organization* and the *Political Organization*, which are not so much complete configurations as images of organizations kept together by strong common norms or pulled apart by strong conflict, respectively. He also acknowledges that most organizations today are mixtures of configurations. He therefore now also represents them as forces acting on organizations. Circumstances decide which one of the forces will exert the strongest pull and shape organizational structure. For our discussions later, both the pure types and the concept of pulls will be useful.

---

[1] He has also changed the name of two of the configurations: the Simple Structure has been renamed the *Entrepreneurial Organization*, and the Adhocracy is now called the *Innovative Organization*. I use the original names here, since they are the most widely known.

Two Classes of Coordinating Mechanisms

As we noted, Mintzberg defines three main coordinating mechanisms, one of which has three subforms:

- Mutual adjustment
- Direct supervision
- Standardization:
  —of work
  —of skills
  —of output

Mintzberg also argues that these mechanisms create a continuum as one moves from simple to more complex work. Mutual adjustment gives way to direct supervision, which in turn must yield to standardization of some kind. However, if the level of complexity (especially combined with a high rate of change) rises even further, it will saturate the adaptive capacity of standardized coordination. Mintzberg then postulates a return to mutual adjustment as the only coordination mechanism that can handle really complex work with a lot of problem solving. However, it is clear (although he does not point it out specifically) that this is mutual adjustment on another level than in the small group working in Ms Raku's workshop. His example is NASA's Apollo project, which was extremely large and complicated, and where the adjustments had to take place in a "representative" system based on professional competence. He also sees a similar role for direct supervision, which may become the answer when an organization (or indeed a nation) in crisis appoints a manager with more or less dictatorial power.

If we take a closer look at these coordinating mechanisms, we see that they fall into two main classes: *the real-time ones* ("coordination by feedback," a term borrowed from March and Simon 1958), where coordination is continually adjusted as people observe the effects of their own and other people's actions, and *the programmed ones* ("coordination by program"), where coordination is effected through instructions or plans ("programs") generated beforehand. Both main types have two main variants (see Figure 3-1).

Real-Time Mechanisms

The real-time mechanisms are *mutual adjustment* and *direct supervision*, which are the same ones that Mintzberg defined.

With *mutual adjustment*, coordination is achieved by a continuous exchange of information among those who participate in the work. It is

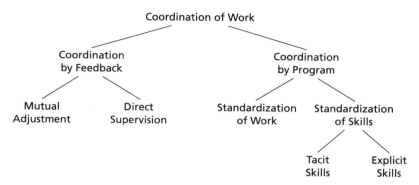

Figure 3-1: *A taxonomy of coordinating mechanisms.*

the coordinating mechanism best suited for complex problem-solving work with little standardization. In its pure form, there is no single person who continually directs or supervises the work, and it is therefore necessary for all organization members to have a sufficient understanding of their goal, the overall design of the work and how their different tasks fit together. They must also be sufficiently motivated to do their part voluntarily. Mutual adjustment is an inherently egalitarian coordinating mechanism, best suited for settings where people are on a fairly equal footing. Without compromises, it is impossible to extend it to organizations larger than the small group.

The reason for this is, of course, because mutual adjustment in its pure form requires everyone to communicate with everyone else. As the number of participants increases, the number of possible information links multiplies: with five people, there are 10 links; with 10 people, 45 links; and with 20 people, 190 links.[2] To use terms from network theory (Lincoln 1982): to employ mutual adjustment as the prime coordinating mechanism, a network must be very dense—and, since our communication abilities are limited, that means they will also have to be small. In large organizations, real mutual adjustment can take place only inside organizational units small enough to allow all-to-all communication, or between similarly small groups of managers or group representatives, acting on behalf of their departments or groups. Through an elaborate project hierarchy, it is thus possible to achieve a kind of layered mutual adjustment, but only with strong elements of hierarchy and bureaucratic control.

---

[2] The formula is $n \cdot (n-1)/2$, where n is the number of members in the group.

Direct supervision is quite different from mutual adjustment, since it presupposes that someone directs the others, tells them what to do (even how to do it), and monitors their actions during execution. While mutual adjustment requires all participants to know (and accept) the goals and task designs, direct supervision in principle requires only one person to know the goals, the overall design, and how tasks are meant to fit together. It is also inherently hierarchic, and therefore easily extendible through delegation of authority.

Programmed Mechanisms

Mintzberg lists three coordinating mechanisms based on standardization: *standardization of work, standardization of skills*, and *standardization of output*. In my view, only the first two of these are proper coordinating mechanisms, in the sense that they are used to coordinate the work of organization members in order to achieve particular patterns of action in an organization. Standardization of output does not involve any coordination of people or work at all, only a prescription for a certain result—usually in the terms of form of profit, although even total sales, or tons, or pieces of whatever one produces may be used. It is therefore of little interest for discussing the potential organizational ramifications of computer-based systems, even if it may represent a useful method for pacing work or for controlling the profitability of large and far-flung corporations.

I will therefore include only the two basic *programmed* coordinating mechanisms, standardization of work and standardization of skills.

With *standardization of work*, as Mintzberg describes it, coordination is achieved by specifying beforehand and in some (often considerable) detail how work is to be done. It is best suited for fairly simple work where tasks do not change very often, and can then be very efficient. Most large organizations use standardization of work extensively, especially Machine Bureaucracies.

While standardization of work may be said to represent the special program, developed for a specific collection of tasks in a specific organization, *standardization of skills* represents the general program—an education designed to enable one to tackle cooperation of a specific kind, unrelated to a particular organizational setting. I propose here that there are two kinds of standardized skills. For the set *tacit skills* I borrow part of the name from Polanyi's tacit knowledge; it is also related to Argyris's (1980) theories-in-use. It comprises the kind of internalized skills that are seldom or never made explicit, and which we may not even be aware of as distinct skills. The prototype of such skill sets is the standard social skills everyone learns during childhood and adolescence, which makes it possible to function as a normal member of society and perform the expected roles in everyday interaction.

The other set, *explicit skills*, includes the skills that are taught in schools or during apprenticeship, and which serve not only to teach the candidate a set of concrete skills, but usually also a code of professional conduct and a notion of the accepted level of quality. In larger organizations, this coordinating mechanism is best suited to fairly routinized but complex work (as in the medical professions).

Not only does this kind of education serve to standardize work processes on a professional basis, it also contains elements that are designed to enable coordination both within the profession and with colleagues from other, relevant professions. Mintzberg's example (1979) is the medical professions: the cooperation between the various specialists both among doctors and nurses during an operation is largely regulated by procedures learned during their education, and are usually not specific to a particular hospital. In fact, my own contacts with health personnel strongly indicate that the main stumbling block for organizational development in large Norwegian hospitals is the combination of standardized professional procedures and high staff turnover, which makes it excessively demanding for a hospital to introduce and maintain procedures different from those at other hospitals.

THE BASIC PRECONDITIONS FOR ORGANIZING

With the discussion in this chapter in mind, which of our abilities have significant bearing on our capability for organizing ourselves? Clearly, our capacity for *physical action* is pivotal; our limitations here is the reason we need to organize in the first place (apart from strictly social purposes). Further, as noted above, all cooperation presupposes *communication*, and our bottlenecks in this area are, of course, extremely important. Then there is our ability to *accumulate and retrieve information* and our capacity for *information processing*—what our brain can actually accomplish with the information it is fed. Finally, to carry on cooperation through time, the *reliability* of organization members also becomes an important issue.

Translating these five concepts into actual human faculties or properties, there seem to be six areas where we quickly run into limits restricting organization building:

1. **Capacity for work:** Obviously, both our need for organizations and their nature are strongly dependent on the nature and amount of work that we can carry out—on how much a single individual can accomplish. Although our capacity for physical work is of obvious

importance, our special interest is in the limitations we have with respect to mental work.

2. **Memory performance:** The basis for any intellectual activity, and crucial for accumulation of knowledge and for management of complex relationships. Both the storage capacity and the retrieval capabilities of our long-term memory is of vital importance. So are the limitations of our short-term working memory.

3. **Information processing capability:** Closely related to the question of work capacity, our ability for reasoning, problem solving, and decision making is directly related to the amount of complexity we can handle.

4. **Communication bandwidth:** This is the first of communication's two aspects. The amount of information we can absorb and disseminate per unit of time is of obvious importance.

5. **Communication range:** This is the second aspect of communication. How far and how fast we can communicate is also central, as are the possibilities of communicating not only over distance, but through time.

6. **Emotions:** The five properties above are derived from the rational activities in organizations. However, we are not entirely—maybe not even principally—rational beings. As the action, constructivist, and postmodern approaches to organization (among others) point out, emotions play a decisive part in our daily lives both within and outside organizations. We all have our secret aspirations, phobias, likes, and dislikes, and we all have to live with our basic, primate instincts and psychological makeup.

Some may find it strange to include emotions in the small number of basic human properties that are most important for organizing, especially when my expressed purpose is to analyze the interplay between organization and information technology. However, my purpose at this stage is not to single out the human faculties that will be most influenced by the use of information technology; rather, it is to decide which ones are the most important for the construction and maintenance of organizations—and I believe that emotions are extremely important, for the spirit that can develop in organizations, for the conflicts they harbor, and for their reliability as logical "machines." I also believe that emotions (used here as a collective term for the nonrational part of the human mind) and the social relations they foster have extremely important impacts on the use of technology, and often determine if a specific application will be successful or not—quite independent of its "rational" merits. My discussion of emotions will therefore differ from the way I treat the five other faculties listed above: the discussion will focus not so much on how emotions are "enhanced" or "improved" by information technology, but on how emotions will impact its possible use and thus influence the general development both of the technology itself and of IT-based organization.

It is difficult to ascertain which of these abilities or properties are most important, both in man's almost mythical "natural state" and in contemporary, industrialized society. It may even be meaningless to rank them, since they are so intertwined in real life. Most of the limitations we encounter can fortunately be ameliorated by tools (but to a varying degree), and through our history as a species we have amended our shortcomings in gradually more advanced and powerful ways. Both by material technology and with the help of techniques and methods of various kinds, we have considerably increased our organizing abilities. Those shortcomings that respond most readily to amplification by material means easily attract the most interest, of course, especially in a technologically mesmerized society like our own.

Information technology represents nothing more and nothing less than a new chapter in this history. It promises, however, to become an extremely important chapter, which we will be busy writing for a long time to come. In keeping with contingency theory, we may say that IT modifies and extends the technology contingency factor. This may seem innocent enough, but, in my opinion, computer-based systems modify this factor substantially—and in the process extend it from a matter primarily of the operating core to an important contingency factor not only for the rest of the organization, but for its exchanges with the environment as well. Through this, it may open up possibilities for new structural configurations and provide the basis for significant shifts in the fit between common configurations and the different kinds of business or task structures they can efficiently support.

II
Individual Capacity and Organization Before the Computer

In this part, my purpose is to establish a platform for the analysis of the possible contributions of information technology to the space of constructible organizations. I begin Chapter 4, *Confined by Physiology*, by looking at the six basic human preconditions or constraints (as listed at the end of Chapter 3) in more detail. I also discuss two of the most important methods we have always used to alleviate or circumvent some of these constraints (in addition to simplification), namely, imitation and the creation of mental sets.

In Chapter 5, *The Dawn of Organization*, I explore the problems of organization building in societies without significant tools for organizational purposes and try to determine the extent of the space of constructible organizations in such societies. The analysis is based on historical records and anthropological evidence from primitive societies, and focuses on the methods and techniques used to build and maintain organizations. The analysis corroborates the conclusion from Chapter 3 that coordination is the essence of organization, and it concludes with the basic principles of preliterate organization.

In Chapter 6, *The Power of Technology*, I discuss the nature of tools and the way the most important pre-computer technologies have alleviated our original constraints (preconditions for organizing), gradually allowing for extensions of the space of constructible organizations. The single most important innovation was undoubtedly the art of writing.

Finally, in Chapter 7, *The Modern Organization*, I try to assess the relationship between the development of these tools and the emergence of the modern organization. I conclude that the new forms of organization, especially the Machine Bureaucracy, were based on a new concept of coordination: the standardization of work processes in the form of explicit routines and automation. This allows a transition from direct to indirect supervision, which is vastly more efficient. However, I also propose that the emergence of the modern organization involved another breakthrough: the emergence of the explicit conceptual model and the concomitant explicit design of essential parts of the patterns of action that constitute organizations. This opened the door for conscious improvements and a rational approach to organization, as opposed to the traditional approach of oral societies and societies with a weak literate foundation. I end the chapter with a short discussion of the effect of culture on organizational forms, and the possibility of claiming any significant common ground in organization structure.

4
Confined by Physiology

"Man is a mind betrayed, not served, by his organs."
Edmond & Jules de Goncourt, *Journal,* 1861

The six areas listed at the end of Chapter 3 are all about restrictions ultimately rooted in our physiology. The limits to our capacity for physical work are the most obvious, but even the others reflect our biological capabilities at varying levels. Our capacity for communication, for instance, relies both on the physical bandwidth of our senses (chiefly the eyes and the ears), the strength and nature of our voice (relying on sound waves), the physical characteristics of our mouth and vocal chords, and the brain's capability for information processing. Processing, in turn, is dependent on extremely complex processes in the brain, of which we presently have very limited understanding. The same is true with our emotions, desires, and drives, and the irrationality they often give rise to. To understand the nature of organizations and the way tools empower us, we must therefore have a basic understanding of our fundamental capabilities and—most important—our limitations as biological creatures.

ONE THING AT A TIME

As any traffic authority can confirm, distractions while driving—from conversations to stereos—increase the likelihood of accidents. The reason is that we have to split our attention between driving and talking or pushing buttons. Even if driving is a more or less automatic activity for most of us, the simplest additional activities attenuates our attention sufficiently to slow down our responses to unexpected events on the road.

The fact is that we are quite single-minded animals, both with regard to physical action and intellectual activity. There are very definite limits to what we can consciously perceive and do in parallel. To achieve good control of any complex physical activity, for instance, we need to practice again and again until the control of movements is *automatized* (Ellis and Hunt 1989) and our conscious processing capability is relieved from the burden of coordination. That is why we need so much practice as children to walk and run with reasonable control. As grown-ups, we confront the same process again when learning to drive a car or to master new sports. Our conscious system is simply not able to handle the coordination of many muscle groups in real time. To achieve perfection in sports that require complex movements combined with high precision (like gymnastics), extreme amounts of drill are necessary—many hours every day, years on end.

It is fairly easy to understand some of the limits for parallel physical activity—in the end, we only have two arms and two legs. However, our possibilities for actual coordination of muscles seem to be restricted by the same basic mechanisms that limit our mental activities. Generally, activities (both physical and mental) that require our full attention preclude the possibility of doing something else simultaneously (Ellis and Hunt 1989, Barber 1988): we cannot carry on two conversations at once, or read a book *and* ponder a complicated problem at the same time.

On the other hand, it is possible to be engaged in one conversation and still keep "an ear" on a conversation close by. You can split your attention if you reduce concentration on the main task (Ellis and Hunt 1989). It is a common experience in the proverbial cocktail party: if you are engaged in a trivial conversation with someone, you will tend to notice the contents of the conversations around you, scanning for something more interesting. However, if the conversation you are engaged in is sufficiently absorbing, you will not notice anything other people say, except (possibly) if someone mentions your name.

Serious work, then, requires almost all of our attention and blocks other activities. If we are interrupted or attention drifts (shifts to a daydream or pondering a piece of news read in the morning paper), activity comes to a halt. The only exceptions are activities that are automatized to such a degree that we do not need to allocate much attention to them. If less common situations or problems occur, however, even normally automatized activities will absorb our full attention until a normal situation is restored.

Since there is no way of getting around the attention barrier (except for tasks that lend themselves to automatization), our work acquires a serial nature: we have to attend to one task at a time. We often do not complete it at once, but break off, do something else, and then return. In fact, this is the normal mode of office work. It may sometimes look like we do many things at once, but a closer look reveals that we are only switching back and forth—allocating slices of time to each task, as Mintzberg found managers do all the time (Mintzberg 1989).

If the number of such parallel "sessions" increase, we quickly approach information overload. Air traffic controllers in busy areas probably come close to the limit for human conscious control. Even when they are highly experienced, and have a level of automatization as high as this kind of mental work can allow, they are occasionally simply overloaded—sometimes with disastrous effects. Barber (1988) cites the evidence of an actual accident in the Zagreb area where two planes collided in mid-flight in September 1976 (p. 101):

> It was nearly two minutes before the DC-9 first communicated with the upper-sector controller, following the instruction to change to the upper-sector radio frequency. Meanwhile, the controller for that sector had been working without his assistant, having in effect been responsible for two jobs for some minutes. Moreover there were eleven aircraft in his sector, he was in radio communication with four other overflying aircraft, and he took part in a telephone conversation with Belgrade regarding two others. In that short interval he transmitted eight messages and received eleven. The task facing him seems to a lay observer to have been an unenviable one, and it is apparent from the working practices for air-traffic control (cf. Sperandio 1978[1]) that this is not a mistaken impression. Indeed the inquiry board were clear in their view that he had been subject to overloading. (He was subsequently prosecuted, held partly responsible for the accident, and was jailed.)

Our capacity for conscious action is thus limited by the serial nature of our mind. As additional work is piled upon us, we cannot compress our workload in time by doing several tasks in parallel; we have to increase the time available for work each day, thereby taking time away from eating, sleeping, family life, and socializing. This is a merciless fact, learned the hard way every day by millions of people in rich and poor countries alike. Taking our fairly modest physical strength into account as well, it comes as no surprise that most human endeavors require cooperation, and the amount of work or level of complexity does not have to be large before organization is necessary.

MEMORY

Memory lies at the very base of our nature as intelligent beings. Without memory, without any retained experiences or patterns to which we could compare sensory signals, we could not live. This is aptly reflected in archaic Greek mythology: Mnemnosyne, the goddess of Memory, was no less than the child of Earth and Heaven (Gaea and Uranus), and the

---

[1] Reference in original. The article is: Sperandio, J.C. (1978): "The Regulation of Working Methods as a Function of Workload Among Air Traffic Controllers," *Ergonomics* 21:193–202.

mother of the nine muses. Our memory is both wonderful, fascinating, and frustrating. It is also a very complex phenomenon. As Mishkin and Appenzeller put it in the introduction to their article "The Anatomy of Memory" (1987):

> Within the small volume of the human brain there is a system of memory powerful enough to capture the image of a face in a single encounter, ample enough to store the experiences of a lifetime and so versatile that the memory of a scene can summon associated recollections of sights, sounds, smells, tastes, tactile sensations and emotions.

Memory is indeed many-faceted; several areas of the brain are involved, and there is obviously a fair amount of specialization between them (Mishkin and Appenzeller 1987, Geschwind 1979). There are also various theories about how memory is structured logically, and whether different parts of memory functions according to different principles (Ellis and Hunt 1989). For our purpose, the distinctions here are not so important, and we can leave that discussion alone. The main divisions from a "user" standpoint are between the sensory registers, short-term memory, and long-term memory.

Sensory registers are simply buffer memories that store the raw data pouring in from our sensing organs for the very brief time (a few tenths of a second) it takes for our attention to select them for further processing and to transfer the result of the pattern recognition process to short-term memory for interpretation. Information *not* selected (by far the vast majority of it) is lost when the information in the sensory registers decays or is "overwritten" by new data. Even if we often find it irritating that information is lost in this way, it is in reality (as Weick remarks) a good thing (Weick 1979, p. 208). It is precisely the process of selection and interpretation that allows us to sense and function at all; otherwise, we would be permanently overwhelmed by unstructured information both from our senses and from our memory.

The *short-term memory* is the workbench of our active consciousness. There has been much theorizing about the similarities and differences between short-term and long-term memory, but the current view is that short-term memory is not so much a separate memory system as a work-space for information selected for transfer from the sensory registers, as well as for information retrieved from long-term memory when we want to use it in an active thinking process. For this reason, it is often termed *working memory* (Anderson 1990, Ellis and Hunt 1989). It can retain both sensory impressions (such as sights and sounds), numbers, words, concepts, and ideas. This working memory has a very limited capacity; laboratory experiments suggest that the normal range for humans is between five and nine elements or "chunks," with seven the average. It is thus probably not a coincidence that the number seven is sacred or prominent in religious conceptions in many cultures.

The "chunks" can be of any kind, size, and complexity—from single letters or numbers, to complex concepts (like "democracy") or objects (like "passenger airplane"). The very fact that we perceive them as chunks implies that we see them as organized entities, conceptually or physically, with certain main, defining properties that blend into a single representation in working memory.

The contents of working memory must be constantly rehearsed to be maintained for more than a few seconds. (Experiments indicate that, on the average, it takes us only 18 seconds to forget 90% of the contents in working memory if rehearsal is prevented.) However, with rehearsal, our access to its contents is fast and reliable, due to its high level of activation. We are able to compare, juggle and manipulate the items maintained in working memory.

Long-term memory, on the other hand, retains information for an indefinite period of time, once it is encoded. Indeed, most current theories assume that encoded memories do not decay, and that forgetting is just failure to retrieve (Ellis and Hunt 1989). There are a number of different explanations for why retrieval may fail. It has been claimed that we can recall even trivial childhood incidents under hypnosis, and experiments with electrical stimulation of points in the brain's temporal lobes have elicited forgotten childhood memories (Penfield, referred in Anderson 1990). It is, however, difficult to verify the correctness of such "provoked" memories, and they are generally not accepted as proof that we retain all memories.

There are likewise a number of theories about recall, building on different views of the organization of memory. We know, however, that we can remember things directly, recall the wanted item with the help of a cue, or slowly work our way toward the right information following chains of memories or associative paths in memory, uncovering new cues as we go along. Sometimes, we may even have to leave the conscious process alone for a while, to allow the wanted item to "drift" to the surface. Memories below a certain threshold seem to be impossible to recall under normal conditions, but experiments indicate that they are still present—number/ noun pairs once learnt but apparently forgotten seem to be easier to learn and remember later than totally new pairs (Anderson 1990).

Much to our chagrin, then, we seem to have limited control over what we can recall. Not only is it very often difficult or even impossible to remember the items we need, but what little we do recall is quite likely to be incomplete or even distorted, especially when it comes to details. Facts are not only selected, interpreted and accorded meaning during recording, but are subject to later selections, interpretations, and changes in a subtle interplay with other memories, as well as with preconceptions, desires, and hopes. It is not only the future that is unpredictable and open to conjecture; so indeed is the past. Anyone doubting this is referred to the daily affairs in our courthouses, where the dominating activity is the painstaking review of human explanations and physical evidence in order to establish plausible descriptions of past events. It is also precisely the fickleness of human memory that leads us to grant greater credibility to documents and pictures than to human explanations, even when there is no reason to suspect intentional misrepresentations. As Cohen (1980, p. 85) remarks describing the archaic Greek view of memory, "The hidden things of the past, no less than the future, have to be wrested from the gods. Recollection, therefore, becomes a species of retrospective prophecy."

In addition to the fuzziness that often mars our memory and makes us doubtful as to what actually took place or what the details of a conversation really were, our memory may also let us down in a more deceptive way: there may be errors in what we think is a clear and unequivocal memory. Sometimes we may even "remember" events that never happened, or remember as our own experience something told us by another. When it comes to early childhood experiences, for instance, it is often difficult to separate what we actually remember from what we have been told by parents, older siblings, or others. Our brain has no error detection and correction mechanisms that can alert us to such erroneous memories, once they are established.

There are thus clear limits to the amount of knowledge that any one person can absorb, remember, and, most important, *recall and use*, and with only our unaided memory at hand, we are therefore severely restricted when it comes to organization building; our memory deficiencies restrict the size of organization that can be run. It is difficult to keep tabs on large numbers of people, and the accumulation, transfer, and dissemination of knowledge is cumbersome. Moreover, information is continually subject to deterioration both in individual memories and during communication. The lack of permanent records precludes the accumulation of knowledge above a certain, rather basic level; social relationships spanning great distances are difficult to maintain, and trade is generally restricted to low-volume, direct barter.

No wonder, then, that organization in nonliterate societies tends to be fairly small scale (by our standards) and mainly tied to family relations— by far the strongest, most important, and stable social framework of societies past and present. Even personal connections outside the family line tend to be couched in family terms: for the aborigines of the Cape York Peninsula in Australia, for instance, trading partners in neighboring tribes were classified as ritual brothers (Sharp 1952). The relationship was considered so close to a real brotherhood that one of the men was always defined as elder and one as younger, with the "elder" brother having a perpetual advantage over the "younger" in the trading relationship, because a younger brother by custom had to show deference to an older one. Similar practices can also be found elsewhere in the world, for instance among the Lapps of Northern Scandinavia, and seems to be a significant characteristic of more complex nonindustrial societies (Pehrson 1964).

It is also noteworthy that some of the most successful nonliterate, expansionist peoples have been those with the most extensive family systems. The Bantus of Africa, for instance, had to their advantage a notion about a common forefather, implying that all Bantus are related. They also kept tabs on their lineage several generations back. If threatened, a Bantu could summon the assistance of his entire family line, down to the point where it merged with his opponent's. If the opponent was not Bantu, then he could call upon all Bantus. This enabled the Bantu tribes to amass superior forces in all instances when opposed by more fragmented tribes. In just a few hundred years, they swept southward from the North of Africa, eradicating weaker tribes in their way. Today, the large majority of the African population south of the Arab territories belongs to the Bantu group.

INFORMATION PROCESSING

Although we cannot handle more than one serious information processing task at a time; at least that process can be multidimensional—but only within narrow bounds, as our working memory quickly becomes saturated. There is a definite limit to how many variables or aspects of a particular subject we are able to juggle at the same time. To picture the relationship between cost, sales volume, price, and profit is barely possible, as long as the factors are stable and the relationship between them linear. If cost is production cost, however, with a nonlinear relationship to volume and time from order to delivery, and if the cost and effect of marketing and sales must be taken into account, as well as the size of different orders and the consequences of rebate schemes, then the conscious mind quickly bows out; the number of variables exceeds the amount we can keep in our working memory; they are simply not simultaneously available for processing.

The consequence is that we are not able to "see" all the different relationships and the effects of their mutual dependencies in one "picture." To work around our mental limits, we have to use time, ponder parts of the problem separately, structure it in subsets that can be treated as single elements, and so on. Sometimes, such long-time "submersion" in a complex problem alone allows us to organize it sufficiently to get an overall grasp on it and see a solution, but if the problem is complex enough, we need to commit intermediate thoughts and analyses to paper, use other tools (like computers!), or resolve the matter by dividing the task among several people.

Elements in Problem Solving

However, that is only part of the problem. In addition to the limits to our sheer processing capacity, there are many other constraints involved in problem solving as well. To examine them a little closer, we can use a three-stage model for problem solving proposed by Ellis and Hunt (1989, p. 219): understanding the problem, generating hypotheses about solutions, and testing and evaluating solutions. Since Ellis and Hunt refer mainly to laboratory experiments, they omit one stage that is very important in real-life situations, especially in organizations: the procurement of sufficient information. For real-life problem solving, we can therefore propose the following stages (stages 2 to 4 are adapted from Ellis and Hunt 1989, p. 219):

1. Procuring information
2. Understanding the problem
3. Generating hypotheses about solutions and selecting among the alternative hypotheses
4. Testing and evaluating the solutions

The logic of this ordered list of stages notwithstanding, as Ellis and Hunt emphasize, most problem solving is an iterative activity where we cycle through the different stages and even jump back and forth between them.

Procuring Information

While simple in the laboratory setting, where the experimenter furnishes you with the setup, the procurement of information is much more complicated in real life. Often, we do not even know exactly what kind of information we need, and if and when we find out, it too often turns out that we cannot obtain much of it. Procuring information is indeed a main organizational activity; there are entire departments devoted to it. The accounting department, for instance, has as its sole purpose to keep track of the economical performance of the organization, market analysts are occupied with collecting information about the outside world, production planners try to provide information about expected production schedules for both sales and management, and so on.

In addition, we almost always have a simplified (and sometimes quite wrong) perception of the problem itself and the causal relationships involved in it. We therefore often procure the wrong information set, and we also generally tend to believe that the information we have is more complete than it actually is. Elementary cognitive errors, such as misinterpretation of other people's behavior (including oral and written communication) may compound the problem.

Understanding the Problem

As Ellis and Hunt emphasize, "Before a problem can be solved, it must first be understood." Before we can start to seek out a solution, we must have a sufficiently clear picture of the problem. Research shows that an adequate mental representation of the problem is very important to finding a good solution, or even finding a solution at all (Ellis and Hunt 1989, Anderson 1990).

Understanding the nature of a problem may also involve understanding its causes. They are not always obvious, they are not necessarily objective in the sense that they seem the same regardless of perspective, and they are certainly not always unitary. When management rationalists Kepner and Tregoe (1965, p. 17) maintain,

> Here it should be pointed out that every problem has only one real cause. It may be a single event that produces the unwanted effect, or it may be a combination of events and conditions operating as if they constituted a single event.

they display an attitude that may be valid for simple engineering problems, but is grossly inadequate for the complexities of human life. Consider, for example, the editorial by Garrett Hardin in *Science* referred to by Weick (1979, p. 68), with the title "Nobody Ever Dies of Overpopulation." It treats the catastrophe that occurred when East Bengal (now Bangladesh) was hit by a cyclone in November 1970, and 500 000 people living on the low islands in the river delta were killed. A similar catastrophe hit in April 1991, with about 150 000 dead. Now, we may ask: What caused the death of these unfortunate people? Was it the cyclone, an unpredictable, natural disaster? Was it the lack of dikes that could keep the water out? Or the lack of cyclone-safe shelters? Or was it perhaps the fact (as Hardin argues) that overpopulation has forced people to live in places where even an ordinary storm constitutes a grave danger? And is it possible to devise a single best solution to ensure that such a catastrophe does not repeat itself in the future?

By choosing perspective, or problem representation, then, we also decide which information is relevant and what kind of causes will be allowed for consideration. By choosing evaluation criteria, we decide what kind of solutions will be considered "best."

Generating Hypotheses About Solutions

When we have acquired at least a tentative understanding of the problem space and have constructed a preliminary problem representation, we start the hunt for a solution, employing one of two main strategies. In some instances, especially when solving technical problems (involved in, for instance, the construction or computer programs), we will use an *algorithmic* strategy, which consists of a set of rules or procedures that *ensures* a solution. In everyday life, however, most problems do not have algorithmic solutions, and we have to use a *heuristic* strategy—a "commonsense," "rule-of-thumb" approach, a problem solving method that works and is used in practice, regardless of whether we know why it works; indeed, we may not care to know at all.

To illustrate the difference, Ellis and Hunt (1989, p. 220) use the example of locating a friend with the name J. Smith in a large city, where there are 41 J. Smiths listed in the telephone directory. An algorithmic strategy for solving this problem is to start at the top and call all J. Smiths in consecutive order until the right one is found. Normally, such a strategy will not appeal to us, however—it is much more likely that we will use our knowledge about his occupation and make an educated guess about where in the city our man is likely to live. This way, we can considerably reduce the number of people we need to call (if our guesses are about right, which they often are in everyday life). Everyday solutions, of course, often include both algorithmic and heuristic elements (Ellis and Hunt 1989, Anderson 1990).

Regardless of the strategy, the solutions we generate also depend on background knowledge, past experience (a problem that is unsolvable for most people may belong to the routine repertoire of an experienced specialist). Values are always of substantial importance, both during problem definition and in searching for a solution. A liberal left-winger and a Christian fundamentalist would almost certainly have very different problem definitions if their teenage daughters became pregnant without being married, and would quite likely arrive at different solutions—such as an abortion for the liberal, and a hurried marriage for the fundamentalist. Another very significant determinator for the generation and selection of solutions is what we know or believe about their consequences, including risk assessment.

Testing and Evaluating the Solutions

That brings us to the last stage in problem solving, which involves choosing the actual solution to be executed—a simple step as long as the problem and the possible solutions are well understood, and the criteria for judgment are clear. If price is the only criterion, for instance, it is simple to choose among the alternatives for a transatlantic flight presented by a travel agent. Unfortunately, however, the situation is seldom so easy except for simple and fairly inconsequential decisions. Important decisions tend to be complex and may involve both ambiguous problem definitions and solutions that are difficult to compare. They may also have consequences and benefits that are contested, or the criteria for judging the possible solutions may be unclear or have unclear priorities (or even both).

From Maximizing to Satisficing: Accepting Simplification

The picture that shines through this short discussion is not exactly that of a supremely rational being, analyzing all relevant facts, choosing the best among all possible solutions, and carrying it out flawlessly. And there are even many more cognitive pitfalls in the various stages of problem solving, especially when we operate under uncertainty (see, for instance, Kahneman, Slovic, and Tversky 1982). It is indeed *simply impossible* for humans to find the one best solution (given that such a solution exists in theory, which it often does not) for anything but the very simplest problems.

With what we now know, it seems preposterous even to suggest it. However, we need only go back 50 years to find this illusion widely accepted as fact, upheld both by the economists' image of "economic man" and by the "rational manager" of the management theorists. These concepts did not receive any real dents until the publication of Herbert A. Simon's *Administrative Behavior* in 1947, and even if they are now academically discredited, they linger on in the simpler parts of the management realm and flavor many an offering from the more archaic breeds of management consultants.

Simon's great, commonsense realization was that man operates with limited information and wits in an exceedingly complex world, and *perforce* has to simplify, to operate with a bounded rationality, to *satisfice*—not maximize (1976, p. xxviii, italics in original): "Administrative theory is peculiarly the theory of intended and bounded rationality—of the behavior of human beings who *satisfice* because they have not the wits to maximize." As a contrast to economic man, Simon defines administrative man, who "...makes his choices using a simple picture of the situation that takes into account just a few of the factors that he regards as the most relevant and crucial" (1976, pp. xxix–xxx). Simplification is indeed our basic weapon against complexity, and is used also when tools and organizational measures are brought into service. We simplify our models of the world quite simply because rich models are too complex to handle—and we then convince ourselves (and others) that there are actually just one or two or three factors that "really count."

Research on judgment under uncertainty is indeed rife with examples of how we make our judgments on the basis of information that is superficial, the most readily available, or easiest to think of, and how we are deceived by our intuitive interpretations of our immediate impressions of reality, even when we have solid theoretical and factual knowledge to guide us toward more correct solutions (Kahneman, Slovic, and Tversky 1982; Rachlin 1989). We also have a strong tendency to let concrete, immediate urges and experiences displace or overrule abstract knowledge about later, possible consequences—such as continuing to smoke even while acknowledging that it may lead to cancer at a later date, or driving our car very fast when late for an appointment, even though we know it increases the likelihood of a dangerous accident, with consequences that would be way out of proportion to the importance of the appointment in question.

Simplification is usually a combination of a conscious process (consciously choosing some variables over others) and an unconscious or intuitive one (just regarding some variables as "naturally" important or unimportant). The criteria in both cases can be questionable; for instance, it is not uncommon to have an over-representation of computable variables in organizational decision processes. Computable variables are convenient to handle and have the added advantage of appearing to be very objective and accurate, even when they are not—follies like market forecasts five years ahead reported to the tenth of a percent are routinely presented to credulous audiences in the most serious companies.

To be able to choose the right variables in real life, those that are really important, we need considerable experience with the problem domain. If we enter a new field of work or knowledge, or suddenly have to live in a country with a very different culture, we need a period of adjustment, until we internalize the essentials of the new setting.

As noted above, Simon's view of administrative man as satisficing rather than maximizing delivered the first real blow to the glossy picture of the manager as the supremely rational being presiding over tidy, rational organizations. Another strong blow was delivered by Henry Mintzberg (1973), who found that the old picture of the manager as a reflective, systematic planner was utterly false. He discovered that managers are interrupt-driven, strongly oriented to action, and dislike reflective activities. They prefer oral to written communication, and work chiefly through formal and informal meetings and telephone conversations. In addition to the simplification such informal work habits imply, another interesting way of thinking is suggested, which came to occupy more and more of Mintzberg's attention: unconscious processing and intuition.

Unconscious Processing and Intuition

In pursuing this line of thought, Mintzberg involved himself in a strong (but friendly) controversy with Simon, who held that even if man's rationality is bounded, we still talk about conscious rationality, and not about obscure subconscious processes. Simon also contended that human thinking is made up of programmed sequences, sufficiently similar to computer programs that computers can be used to describe and simulate them (Simon 1977).

The notion of unconscious processing and intuition is indeed interesting but still controversial. It may amount to the next step in the "derationalization" of decision-making that Simon started, and certainly deserves a discussion at this point.

As noted above, our conscious mind becomes bogged down fairly quickly as variables are added or as the relationships between them are made more complex. Our working memory does not suffice. Experience suggests, however, that subconscious thought processes can integrate and weigh a larger number of variables. A number of sayings and proverbs allude to this—we talk about "sleeping on a problem," about "problem gestation," about "digesting" information or dramatic experiences, and so on. Most of us have, for instance, probably experienced the anguish of having to face pivotal decisions about our lives or careers, and we know that we do not rely entirely on rational analysis in such circumstances. We "ruminate" on the decision until we have an answer that feels right "in our stomachs."

Incubation effects (more rapid problem solving after a period of thinking of something else) have been demonstrated experimentally (Anderson 1990)—especially for problems requiring *sudden insight* to solve (such as the problems presented in books or magazine columns on recreational problems and riddles). Subjects who had a break for some hours after studying the problem for a little while, and then resumed, had a higher percentage of success than those who did not have a break. Ellis and Hunt (1989) recommend such breaks to evoke the incubation effect as practical advice for problem solving, in spite of the fact that we do not thus far have a satisfactory explanation of why it works.

Many scientists have reported similar personal experiences when working with and suddenly solving particularly intriguing and hard problems—

problems they may have struggled with for long periods of time (Goldberg 1989). Kekule von Stradonitz's discovery of the molecular structure of benzene (which had puzzled chemists for many years) is perhaps the most famous example: He was dozing off, half-dreaming about strings of dancing carbon atoms. Suddenly one of the strings snaked back on itself, forming a ring—at which point he woke up with a jolt, the benzene ring clear in his head (Asimov 1975).

In his annual hour with the Nobel Laureates on Swedish TV, the host, Bengt Feldreich, always ended the program by asking the participants if they believed in intuition—and the majority of them invariably did, citing their own experiences with that sudden flash of insight. They all agreed that it feeds upon years and years of experience and knowledge accumulation, and that the problem-solving process is only partly conscious—the solution comes as a sudden culmination of a combination of conscious work and an inscrutable, subconscious process beyond inspection. This is in harmony with the views of most of the people who write about intuition, whether they think, like Simon (1989), that intuition is essentially a conscious recognition of established patterns, or, like Rowan (1989), that it is knowledge gained without rational thought: they all agree that intuition does not come totally out of the blue. Rather, it requires a solid foundation of factual knowledge and experience.

As a process not controlled by the conscious self, subconscious processing is of course subject to influence from all kind of facts, judgments, conjectures, desires, and other emotions that our mind harbors. Nevertheless, the intuitive insights that arise time and again from the depths of our mind are often worth more than weeks and months of "rational," conscious analyses. Indeed, as Simon (1989) notes, analysis is often an activity that experts carry out only to check the validity of solutions found almost instantly through intuition. In his now famous article "Planning on the Left Side, Managing on the Right" (1976), Mintzberg describes how such processes and their outcomes in fact seem more important for managers than conscious, rational analyses— even though managers and management consultants usually hold forth the banner of rationality both as an ideal and as a description of their way of working.

The more complicated the problem is, the more likely it is that the solution will not be found through rational analysis, but through "weighing," "digestion," and "sleeping on it"—mediated thorough informal discussions with people who also have "thick" information on the subject. The interest for intuition as a management device has since then spread, and is now definitely on the increase (Agor 1989), and new evidence is steadily surfacing (Weiss 1990).

Nowhere in the organizational world is the dependence on subconscious processes so apparent as in choosing main strategies for an organization. A common explanation for AT&T's miserable failure in attempting to enter the computer business in the last half of the 1980s, for instance, was that no one in the management had a "feel" for the special characteristics of the computer market. One may argue that they did not know the market, and the answer is both yes and no—they no doubt had the information available in reports, memos, and presentations. But, they had not *internalized* that knowledge—they had not been able to *digest* and *integrate* it, as only a submersion over quite a long time can bring about. Therefore, they did not have any *gut feeling* about the matter and could not come up with a vision or *sense of direction*.[2] In short, they lacked precisely what is generally acknowledged to lie behind Microsoft's phenomenal success: The longstanding, total submersion in the computer industry and the deep understanding of the technology that characterize Bill Gates, Steve Ballmer and the other key figures in that company. Strategy needs vision, and vision is not obtained through calculations—not even in business.

Of course, intuition may be wrong, just like rational analysis. If vital facts pass unknown, no amount of subconscious integration can make up for it. Combined with the process of groupthink it can keep a set of beliefs about the world alive in a group of people long after it has ceased to be true, blocking "unpleasant" facts and lead to decisions out of touch with the real world. Intuition is moreover easily influenced by our own feelings, hopes, and wishes. Its roots in the subconscious, its integrating powers, are thus both the source of its strengths and of its weaknesses. While it can no doubt be powerful for finding solutions to complicated problems, it is therefore not a viable tool for reliable execution and coordination of the everyday chores that also fill our lives. There, we have to rely on our limited, but still powerful conscious mind, and rather simplify, decompose, and distribute where the complexity of a task exceeds our powers.

The Delays of Deliberation

The time we need to reach a decision can vary enormously. If it is a question of a minor, recurring problem, we usually have the answer on hand, and a decision can be made in fractions of a second. If the problem at hand is totally new, of major importance, and involving a lot of parameters, we will often need to cycle repeatedly through the different stages of

---

[2] Note how all these common life expressions about problem solving and direction finding allude not to the conscious mind, but to instincts and the autonomous nervous system (which, among other things, runs our bowels for us).

the problem-solving process, and it can take a long time to reach a decision. A further reason for this is that we often like to obtain the "gut feeling" described earlier and convince ourselves that it points in the same direction as our rationally derived answer. In other words, we feel a need to bring our unconscious, integrating abilities into play.

These limitations clearly restrict the number and magnitude of the decisions that any one individual can handle, thereby constraining our freedom of organizing. They are of course compounded by our limited ability to absorb information, and are especially important as limitations for the centralization of control: In essence, you can only have first-hand control where you can decide yourself—decisions delegated mean control surrendered, even if you try to uphold control by orders, rules, regulations, or law. This is a basic dilemma known to every entrepreneur—expansion means loosing the total control you have as owner/manager of a tiny start-up.

OUR COMMUNICATION BOTTLENECK

Human beings have many senses registering information about both the world around us as well as our own states. Ordinarily, we count five, but there are many more: We sense temperatures, air pressures, acceleration, and the positions of our limbs, to mention a few. Our senses are capable of receiving and processing an astounding amount of information. In computing terms, our visual system processes raw data at the rate of hundreds of megabytes per second. Moreover, our additional ability to quickly scan the picture the cortex presents us with, and pick out and classify its important features in real time, is nothing short of an information-processing miracle. Simultaneously, our brain can also receive and digest information about the states of the muscles in the body, and coordinate their movements in real time with immense precision. It is only when we try to build walking, self-guiding robots that the prodigious information-processing capacities of the brain are really driven home to us. The day when a two-legged humanoid robot can compete with human downhill skiers in the Hahnenkam competition in Kitzbühl's notorious "Die Streif" track is indeed far off (but not entirely unthinkable—such a day may come).

However, the communication that builds organizations is first and foremost verbal. It is the spoken and written word. But our rate of acquiring and disseminating verbal information is painstakingly slow compared to our processing of pictures. The raw processing power of the aural system is only a fraction of the visual, and when we count only the factual information contained in speech, it is only a small fraction of that again. Of course, if we take into account the information contained in voice volume and inflection (which is frequently as important as the actual words), the amount of processed information in digital terms is much greater and perhaps similar to the interpretation of music.

Normal speech (and thereby listening) happens at a net rate of about 150 words per minute, not counting pauses for thinking, groping for words, etc. Very fast talk approaches 250 words per minute, but by then both speaker and listener will begin to experience problems. Sustained speaking for longer periods of time (for instance, a lecture) probably averages around 100 words per minute.

Reading is faster, but not so much—at least for factual prose. Most of us level off around 300 to 400 words per minute even when really concentrated and absorbed by what we read (like when devouring a really exciting novel). Taking into account our normal lapses in concentration when reading factual prose (with no plot or drama to capture our primate minds), it is difficult to average much more than 100 words per minute for longer periods of time (several hours). Assuming that the average word has 6 characters, that amounts to 10 characters or bytes per second (or 0.00001 megabytes). Even accomplished speed readers cannot go much beyond 1000–1500 words per minute (about 100–150 bytes per second, or 0.00010–0.00015 megabytes), and research indicates moreover that such reading is not very effective—it resembles most of all "skimming," giving an overview of the text without a concern for detail (Barber 1988).

Writing is the slowest means of verbal communication. Quite apart from the process of formulating the text, the physical writing process itself is a plodding activity. Until voice-recognition technology has developed to the point where a machine can reliably take rapid dictation and render it into text, the typewriter and the computer keyboard are the fastest devices we have available. An experienced (but autodidactic) 3–5 finger typist like myself typically enters text at around 25–30 words per minute, not counting error correction. An extremely fast touch typist can exceed 125, about the rate of normal speech.

The immense difference in speed between picture processing and verbal communication is the main reason for the efficiency of graphical presentation of data. Presenting data as pictures and graphs taps the enormous bandwidth of our visual system, and makes it possible to absorb both quantitative information and the interrelations between variables much faster and more accurately than through text and numbers. There is much research going on along these lines, not least for military applications. For fighter pilots being guided toward enemy aircraft or around enemy defenses, it will, for instance, be much easier to have the changing direction and altitude merged graphically into a curving tunnel on a screen (and then proceed to fly "through the tunnel") than to be presented with numerical data and compass bearings.

The extremely narrow bandwidth of verbal communication places serious limits to the achievable levels of organizational coordination and control. Every minute, large amounts of information are created or received in any organization, and to be acted upon much of it needs to be aggregated, processed, communicated, and presented. Much must also be stored for future reference. As the rates above indicate, such work is very labor-intensive—and the result is that only a fraction of the received information is ever processed, only part of the processed information reaches the people who need it, and they again will only acquaint themselves with a selection of what they actually receive.

The results are familiar for all who work in organizations. Decisions are made on shaky foundations, changes in the environment go unnoticed or are acted upon too late, coordination is often inadequate, there is much duplication of efforts, and different parts of the same organization may even be working against each other without realizing it.

As Mintzberg notes in his introduction to *The Structuring of Organizations* (1979), coordination is effortless only as long as the number of people that must coordinate their actions remains well below ten, and it is handled through continuous and informal communication. At that level, coordination is hardly noticed as a separate task—it just comes naturally. As soon as the number of people climbs into double digits and beyond, coordination and control becomes the most pressing operational problem, and a wide array of tools and techniques are brought to bear on it—schemes for division of labor, organizational structures, delegation of authority, coordination meetings, reporting, accounting, and so on.

Almost all of the planning, supervisory, and administrative work carried out in an organization is an expression of the continuous fight to stay in control of events and coordinate the various parts of the organization and its interaction with the environment. These coordination problems, rising from the limitations of our basic communication abilities, constitute one of the most iron-clad constraints on operational effectiveness and efficiency in all organizations above the minimum size.

THE CONSTRAINTS OF SPACE AND TIME

Parents who have tried in vain to call in children playing outside have no problem appreciating the fact that the unaided human voice has its limits. A conversation is difficult to keep going if the distance exceeds several meters, and even a primal scream does not go far on a day with normal wind and background noise. People living in mountainous terrain, like the Swiss and a few others, have devised rudimentary "languages" or code systems consisting of patterns of high-pitched tones or whistles that bear from hill to hill or across ravines, but even under exceptional conditions, their range is limited to a few kilometers. Our basic communication abilities thus allow for local communication only, mostly with one or a few persons at a time. Without special surroundings, such as an amphitheater (which has very favorable acoustic properties[3]), even a Stentor or a British sergeant major would have trouble addressing more than a few hundred people at a time.

Our vision does make it possible for us to receive information over great distances when there are no obstacles—after all, the naked eye can see stars trillions of kilometers away—but our means of replying are not on the same level. Some of the earliest techniques for communication tried to remedy this, by using visual aids—such as the smoke signals of the American Indians and the beacons of the Vikings—that can be seen from a great distance. In the century before the telegraph was invented, several European nations built national systems of semaphore lines. Their aural counterparts are the "talking drums" of certain African tribes.

Time is an even more merciless enemy of communication than space. Writers sometimes contend that one of their characters "left his/her words hanging in the air," but apart from this strictly literary storage mechanism, all unaided human communication must take place in real time. Once a word is uttered or a gesture performed it is also a thing of the past, and it may be remembered, distorted, disputed, or completely forgotten.

The fact that unaided human information exchange can only take place locally and in real time puts severe constraints on the possibilities for building and sustaining large organizations. The only means of communication over distance is then the dispatch of messengers, and the messengers have to rely on their memory to ensure that the message reaches its destination uncorrupted. The use of messengers also brings in the question of authenticity: When you speak to someone in person, you know immediately that the message is authentic. When you have to rely on messengers, you never know if the messenger intentionally or unintentionally is misrepresenting the words of his master. As Eriksen (1987) shows, history is rife with examples of messengers having decisive influence on historic events. The delay or liquidation of messengers can also have profound consequences. And when the messenger has to spend

---

[3] The amphitheater is actually a very advanced acoustic device. The ancient Greeks built many, and even in the largest, which lies in Epidaurus and can seat 22 000 people, the actors on the stage can be heard by everyone in the audience without any artificial amplification. The theater is still in use.

not only hours or days, but maybe weeks and months on the road to reach his destination, events unknown to him could already have changed everything by the time the information is presented to the receiver.

We must remember at this point that physical travel has been very slow all the way up to the middle of the nineteenth century, especially over land. In the year 1800, for instance, it took six weeks to go from New York to Chicago (Chandler 1977). Until the advent of large, swift sailing vessels, transport of cargo was also expensive and time consuming. Land transport remained slow and costly until the railroad revolution in the middle of the nineteenth century. Throughout most of our recorded history, therefore, long-distance trade has concentrated on high-value items, such as metals, spices, fur, and silk.

The strains on the communication system were prominent in every major empire in history, and large works were undertaken to speed the passage of messages. The Roman roads are well known (total length exceeded 300 000 kilometers and main roads were paved with stone), the Incas built roads as well, and the Mongols under Genghis Khan built a vast system of posting stations, where the Khan's express messengers could change horses on their breakneck journeys to and from the Khan's command posts. Communication technology has thus for a long time been a key factor in our ability to extend our organizations beyond the local community.

A striking example of the importance of enhancing our natural communication apparatus was demonstrated by the attack on Iraq on 17 January 1991. It opened with a massive air strike against radar installations, command and control centers, and communication lines. The rationale was that, if successful, orders for counterattack could not be given, information about the allied attacks and their effects could not be collected, and even consultation between different Iraqi command centers would be impossible. With only the real-time, local communication capabilities of the unaided human available, modern armies and air forces are instantly reduced to a fraction of their theoretical strength, even without any other material or human loss. The subsequent development of the war and the total collapse of the Iraqi army illustrate this point well.

WISHING, WANTING, AND FEELING

However sophisticated we have become, however much we hide behind our machines, our natural sciences, and our rational facades, we are still beings of flesh and blood, with complex minds, full of instincts, ambitions, hopes, fears, and desires. Some of our emotions are raw and basic, others refined and even noble, but the mixture is volatile and always prone to produce unpredictable effects. Our secret inner lives can be pretty wild and untamed. As the zoologist Desmond Morris noted in the introduction to his widely popular book *The Naked Ape* (1967, p. 9),

> ...in becoming so erudite, Homo Sapiens has remained a naked ape nevertheless; in acquiring lofty new motives, he has lost none of the earthy old ones. This is frequently a cause of some embarrassment to him, but his old impulses have been with him for millions of years, his new ones only a few thousand at the most—and there is no hope of quickly shrugging off the accumulated genetic legacy of his whole evolutionary past.[4]

Although each one of us (presuming a minimum of honesty) can confirm this through simple introspection, the importance—or even the mere existence—of emotions has to a large degree been ignored in the literature on organization, surfacing mostly in discussions of motivation, work satisfaction and stress (as noted by Hochschild in the preface to Fineman 1993). When you first notice this, it is a bit puzzling—when you reflect upon it, it starts to look like a very serious defect in organization theory and an embarrassment to organization theorists. As Fineman notes on the first page of his introduction to *Emotion in Organizations* (1993, p. 1): "Writers on organization have successfully 'written out' emotions, to the extent that it is often impossible to detect their existence. A scan of the indexes of recent texts on organizational behaviour reveals no direct entries under 'feelings' or 'emotions'."

This preoccupation with the rational side of organizing seems even stranger when you contemplate that there is indeed a vast literature on human emotions and their significance in social life. Not only can we look to the discipline of psychology; the study of history is also rife with examples of how emotions have decided or heavily influenced the outcome of social and political conflicts with far-reaching consequences.

Going still further, we can draw upon the literature of the world, or indeed the total body of art produced throughout human history, as a powerful witness to the sway that emotions hold over human actions. In stark contrast to the modern classics in the field of organization theory, which treat emotions either cursorily or not at all, Plato was very concerned with subject. In his three books *The Republic*, *The Statesman*, and

---

[4] Interestingly enough, today, we tend to describe this our emotional self as our "human" aspect—as opposed to our logical faculties, which we tend to perceive as machine-like: hence the contemporary fascination for the impulsive, emotional, expressionist personality, capable of loving and hating with equal intensity. People ruled by logic and reason are frequently depicted as cold and indifferent to other people's sufferings. This represents a turnabout from the time of the ancients, who looked at our emotions and instincts as something generally despicable that resembled animal nature, hailing reason and logic as our virtuous, "human" aspect—that part in us most resembling God.

The Laws—arguably the first books on organization ever written (around 2400 years ago)—we find that control of emotions, especially destructive emotions, is a central theme in the struggle to achieve justice.

Plato concluded that no one could rule justly without an understanding of what justice really was; in other words, the ruler must be so thoroughly trained in philosophy and so advanced in his thinking that he would be totally governed by reason, unmoved by all kinds of desires, always working for the best of his subjects and never serving his own interests. This view was initially presented in *Gorgias*, but received its full expression first in *The Republic* (where the philosophers are appointed rulers) and later in *The Statesman* (where rule is effected partly by law and partly by philosopher-statesmen) and *The Laws* (where an almost immutable set of laws is set to provide the rule that fickle human nature cannot).

Plato, then, who was much more uncompromising in his fervor for reason and logic as the governing principles for organizing than the modern classics of organization theory ever were, at the same time fully realized that it was the emotional side of human nature that was his worst enemy, and devoted large parts of his works to discussions of how the unwanted part of those emotions could either be eradicated, suppressed, or controlled. He certainly also realized (at least as he grew older) that his goals were utopian, and that the best one could do in practice was to enlighten prospective politicians as much as possible, hoping that this would moderate their behavior when in office. At least, that was one of the practical functions of his Academy, which attracted students from throughout the Greek world.

Indeed, then, as Fineman suggests, the time is long overdue for bringing the subject of emotion (back) into the discussion of organization, though the scope of this text does not permit a detailed discussion of the subject. However, I believe it is too important to leave out altogether, and all the more so because its importance seems to be grossly underestimated in the debate on the use of information technology in organizational settings. I will therefore include those aspects of emotions that I think are the most important in the following discussions.

As Flam (1993) points out, our emotional self is constantly interfering with the rational and normative parts of our mind.[5] Fear, for instance, which is the subject of Flam's discussion, can cause an individual to rationally plan and perform actions that are in direct conflict with the

---

[5] Flam herself contrasts this trichotomy with Etzioni's (1988) merger of norms and emotions. However, the division of the human consciousness into a rational, a normative and an emotional part is an old and established way of conceptually dividing human consciousness into partly conflicting selves. For instance, it roughly corresponds to Freud's *ego*, *superego*, and *id*.

normative self, and pride can cause an individual to obey the normative self even if it means death, thus overriding rational deliberations. As we all know, love and desire can also have devastating effects on rational behavior.

In a small hunter/gatherer band, our most probable "natural" state, the strong influence of the emotional self poses few organizational problems. On the contrary, organization in such a band is indeed structured around affectionate relationships, as well as real and ritual family relationships, myths, and religious conceptions—and emotions constitute a large part of the glue of such relationships. Emotions here ensure the stability and predictability of both structures and lines of authority, and can thus be said to constitute a fundamental human organizational tool.

That this basic mechanism is still very important can be seen from the fact that family ties continue to be of great importance in most societies of the world, both in private organizations (businesses) and in politics. Even in modern democracies, family ties continue to have considerable significance. Another class of emotional bonds, friendship ties, is also very important, and in the headlines of newspapers and newscasts we are constantly reminded of the immense power of tribal (ethnic) identification—both for the better (national unity in crisis or celebration) and for the worse (racial discrimination, war and ethnic cleansing).

As a tool for organization, emotions are definitely most appropriate in the small group—such as the hunter/gatherer band, where they probably awarded an evolutionary advantage. In larger organizations, however, emotions may give rise to problems such as factionalism, when loyalties and interests defined locally clash with those defined on higher levels or elsewhere in the organization.

Emotions also make us less reliable in many ways, and harder to predict. They often bend our memory, shift our focus of attention, create interpersonal tensions, give rise to tactical behavior and generally mess up our performance as organization members. Organizations become not only rational means to legitimate ends, but also, as Morgan (1986) shows, arenas for display of ambition, pursuit of individual goals and fights for control. They become instruments of domination and vehicles for status. Some of the most extreme demonstrations of this phenomenon are presented by the takeover kings of our modern market economies. Driving their aggressive manipulations are the same desires, ambition, and thirst for power and status that drove Genghis Khan, Alexander the Great and Harold the Fair-haired. Some of the modern warriors are no less ruthless than their ancient brothers-in-arms either, if judged relative to the accepted standards for chieftain conduct in their respective epochs and societies.

However, it is perfectly in line with the dual edge of our emotions that they sometimes make people extraordinarily reliable, as in times of war or other great danger, where, as already indicated, social bonding and emotional ties can induce people to remarkable selflessness and courage even in the face of torture and death.

COPING WITH REALITY

So, as naked animals, we have our limits. We have nevertheless been able to survive and prosper in a complex world even without our present sophisticated tools. Indeed, we still have to trust our basic capabilities for many of our activities. How do we cope with the complexities of life, with the avalanches of information of all kinds that hit us every minute, both through raw sensing and symbol interpretation? What about the innumerable large and small decisions we have to make every day—like figuring out which bus to take to work, what to eat for dinner, what to wear, whom to greet (and how), and so on? Why are we not permanently bogged down in decisions? If we had to analyze every new situation, every new challenge from scratch, we would be left in constant bewilderment—our brain would simply experience permanent overload. Luckily, we have some effective strategies strategies for coping. The two most prominent ones are imitation and the compilation of mental sets.

Imitation

Imitation is the most obvious of the two. It lies at the very base of human learning and has been discovered to occur even in infants only a few days old (Hofer 1981). The socialization process is nothing but a transfer and subsequent internalization of standard procedures and norms for everyday life in society. The standards are not immutable, but they normally show great resilience against sudden change. Much of what our great-grandparents considered proper conduct is still endorsed by the great majority. By accepting established norms, we can relieve ourselves of an enormous amount of decision-making—we greet another person without thinking about how to do it, we do our shopping without fussing about how to behave toward staff and fellow shoppers, we automatically behave differently in a funeral from during a rock concert, we know how to conduct meetings in our local residents' association, and so on.

In organizations, we learn the local mores as we go, internalizing their traditional way of conducting business. The importance many people accord to this organizational socialization can be judged from the fact that numerous organizations have adopted a practice of only recruiting managers internally—thereby avoiding the potentially disruptive consequences of putting people with deviant norms in positions of power. The downside of this approach is the risk of groupthink and blindness to alternatives, which can be very dangerous—especially in rapidly changing environments.

Organizational structures themselves are, as Stinchcombe (1965) convincingly argues, almost always imitations, most often of previously established organizations in the same line of business—copying organizational structure and business conduct from existing, successful operations. It is of course a lot more convenient just to roll out something one knows will work and is familiar with, than to use a lot of time and energy constructing something new and untried. Your financial backers may not approve it, either. On the other hand, you can also (as always in human affairs) find examples of the opposite: experienced people breaking out from a traditional operation to start a competing organization with a novel organizational approach as their main weapon.

In the same paper, Stinchcombe furthermore points out the conditioning effects of the prevailing social structure, which affects all contemporary organizations to a considerable degree. According to Meyer and Rowan (1977), organizations also tend to inherit formal structure from their society's institutional myths—often resulting in a formal structure that is out of step with the actual, day-to-day work procedures.

Imitation is a very economic way of building an inventory of responses to common problems and events, and it allows knowledge to accumulate and spread with significant speed.

Mental Sets

To a newborn baby, the world must be a bewildering chaos of light, patterns, and sounds. Although it can already recognize some sounds heard before birth (especially the heartbeat of its mother), it has few possibilities of understanding what it senses—it has no established pattern "library" to which to relate its impressions. Before it can recognize objects and sounds, it must build such a library, synthesizing similar, concrete, perceived patterns into generalized object classes, which can then provide the templates needed to recognize a particular instance of the class and ascribe the proper rules of behavior to it. It is exactly the class concept that allows us to recognize a particular car as a car, even if it is a model we have never seen before. We also know that we cannot expect it to stop on a dime—we assume that it will exhibit the general properties of its class, of which an approximate inertia and braking power are among the most important for pedestrians and drivers alike. The classes, their properties, and their relations to each other must be extracted from what we see and experience, and then stored in memory to allow later use. As Cohen notes (1980, p. 116), "If we are to be able to apprehend the world around us, this apprehension must be guided and shaped by our cumulative store of experience. In short, memory may be said to be the organ of perception."

Similarly Hofer (1981, p. 138–39) notes that "within the newborn's capabilities ... lie all the building blocks for the mind as we know it. The sensory plan by which certain information is selected, together with the related action pattern, may be referred to as a *schema* ... The essence of such processes is to form *inner representations* of the outside world and to make 'predictions' as to the outcome of actions directed at that world."

The speed with which the child advances in its early synthesizing efforts, its establishment of *schemas*, is a proof of the very powerful pattern recognition and integrating faculties of the brain. As the basic, physical patterns are synthesized, a child must also build the even more subtle models of the objects' properties, their normal behavior, the settings in which they occur, the relations between different objects, and so on. When it slowly realizes its own position as a separate entity with a certain free-dom of action, this exhilarating fact must be integrated with its views of the outside world. It must start to build its own implicit theories of action—its own *theories-in-use* (Argyris 1980).

As we advance from the concrete, physical level to the abstract and symbolic, the synthesizing process becomes more and more demanding. It takes many years to build an adequate set of schemas for understanding human behavior and the proper responses in different situations, and quite a number of people seem to have problems ever acquiring a suitable understanding of the intricacies of human interaction. Likewise, establish-ing an adequate understanding of a branch of science is no easy matter, and beyond the reach of many people. You get a renewed taste of this basic experience every time you enter a new field of knowledge: You are not able to judge what is important and what is not, or see what constitutes quality and what is more doubtful. You have to "get your bearings" first, to develop a "map of the terrain," a "feeling for the subject," so that you can judge and remember by relating to things you already know.

As we grow older, we build up an extremely rich complex of schemas covering the different aspects of the world and our lives, from the most minute details to a general world view. The schemas can relate to objects, persons, animals, acts, sensations, symbols, and so on, or combinations thereof. They tend to be organized in clusters, covering the totality of common situations. If we follow Goffman's (1959, 1970) analysis of human interaction and accept his metaphor of the theatrical performance, it seems natural to label these amalgamations of schemas as *mental sets*. A mental set defines the totality of the situation we confront and tells us what kind of objects, persons, acts, etc. are likely to occur, and which types of actions and responses that are appropriate on our part. It thereby guides our perception and decision processes, provides us with an arsenal of preconceived solutions, and makes it generally possible for us to scan and evaluate the avalanches of information constantly bombarding our senses, and react to it in real time.

Sets can exist on different levels. At home, one set is activated, covering our domestic activities. Engage in political or philosophical debate, and a more sweeping set may be invoked, called ideology. Join in scientific research, and you will soon discover the reigning set of that science— what Kuhn called its *paradigm* (1970). And while much of our set building is original, in the sense that we synthesize our own sets on the basis of original experiences, we also co-opt (imitate) sets or parts of sets built by others. That is especially true for the more abstract, symbolic sets— for instance, ideologies and scientific paradigms. As a student, only the foolishly self-confident or the true genius will dare to deviate from the basic set (paradigm) agreed on by the canons of the science in question.

The Constraints of Sets

Our mental sets are powerful and indispensable. Set building is a very efficient way of coping with reality, and we could literally not survive a day without them. But, like all simplifications (and they are indeed simplifications of reality), they are also constraining, because we tend not to perceive events or objects that fall outside our sets (or, if we perceive them after all, we are inclined to judge them irrelevant). Our thoughts and actions tend to occur inside the set and consider it given. In real life, breaking out of the set requires considerable energy, and will often be felt as disturbing and threatening. Thomas Kuhn (1970) has convincingly demonstrated this effect in the realm of science, but it is just as true in other spheres of action. Business history is full of companies going bankrupt because reality was changing, whereas the managers' mental sets were not, with the consequence that new, crucial developments were overlooked. You may as well talk of business paradigms as scientific ones.

Consider for instance the example of the Swiss watchmakers: their business paradigm was built around mechanical clockworks. They strived to become better precision mechanics. Unconsciously, they assumed that watches were in their essence mechanical devices. Accordingly, when a superior technology for timekeeping came along, they did not recognize it: electronics was not their business; it was not part of their paradigm. The customers thought otherwise, though, and electronic watches almost wiped out the entire Swiss watch industry. Their business was cut by two-thirds in just a few years, and the Japanese took over the hegemony.

The electronic revolution in timekeeping also tore the timekeeping function away from watches altogether, and we got timekeeping pens, calculators, and radios—even coffee machines! The business paradigm of the victorious Japanese watchmakers, however, was strictly a technological one—it did not contain the notion of a watch as a piece of apparel that happened to measure time. It took a shell-shocked Swiss to think of that, which shows that when a paradigm first breaks down, radical change in many directions becomes possible (indeed, for people who feel stifled by the old paradigm, its collapse is often experienced as a liberation). Combining the knowledge that people always like to dress smart with the low price of electronic watches, the stricken Swiss watch industry spawned the Swatch, and the ever-changing collection of funny, colorful watches soon swept the world.

It is also noteworthy that IBM almost did not enter the computer business, at least not as early as they did. According to Cuthbert C. Hurd, then a coworker of Tom Watson, son of the legendary Watson Sr and champion of the computer cause within IBM, IBM's planning department in 1950 vigorously opposed going into computers (Augarten 1984). "Because they could not imagine classes of problems different from those already treated by punched-card equipment," Hurd wrote, the planning department "told me throughout 1950 that no computer could ever be marketed at a price of more than $1000 per month."

At about the same time, Watson Sr is credited for saying that "the United States will never need more than twelve computers." Eventually, IBM delivered eighteen of its first computers, the 701, at a cost of $15 000 per month, and most of them to private corporations! Even after this remarkable success, the planning department kept repeating their "You can never sell a machine that rents for more than $1000 per month," now modified by the extension "except to scientists." They kept on resisting the construction of the 650 all the way to its release in July 1953, when it was an instant hit at around $3500 a month. Fifteen hundred machines were manufactured altogether before the 650 was phased out in 1969.

You may also speak of national or societal mental sets and paradigms. A contemporary example is the development in the newly liberated countries of Eastern Europe, where the communist paradigm has been officially discarded. The common mental sets created by this paradigm linger on, however, and are still the main obstacles for turning the economy around. Typically, those countries that fare best are those that experienced a period with a modern capitalist economy before they were occupied, and where capitalist/liberalist mental sets therefore still exist in the population.

As the communist sets slowly disintegrate under pressure of the new realities, chaos is threatening, as it is extremely difficult to build new sets shared by all in such a short time, even when there are obvious (and indeed identified) models to be found elsewhere. Most epochal of all, the paradigm of the Soviet Union as a strong, centralized empire broke down—not only the paradigm of communist party leadership, but the very concept of the union.

The breakup of empires is a risky business, and both revolutions and wars as well as other dramatic upheavals show us that we are not masters of the very complex—unintended consequences proliferate and surprises abound. Basic mental sets represent integrated knowledge, tested through centuries of unforeseeable incidences. We know they work in their proper settings; therefore, they provide us with much needed stability and predictability in human affairs. That is their strength but also their weakness, since stabilization also means a bias toward the status quo.

5
The Dawn of Organization

"My notion is, I said, that a state comes into existence because no individual is self-sufficing; we all have many needs."
Socrates, in **Plato**, *The Republic*, c. 380 BC

EVOLVING FROM THE PRIMATE STAGE

As naked animals, then, we humans are in many ways constrained in our organizational abilities, even if we far outperform all other animals. We cannot process important matters in parallel, we have a limited memory, and there are many important constraints on our capacity for problem solving. Our communicative capabilities are restricted by narrow band-width and short range, and our more basic, primate nature poses many obstacles to the rational behavior required for large-scale organizing, especially when it takes place outside the domain of the family or the local band.

What kind of organization did man then build in his prehistoric or "natural" state? To answer that question, we can either look to the studies of contemporary primitive societies, or we can consult historic evidence— or, preferably, both. There are a couple of problems, however.

First, if one wants to study preliterate organization, one confronts the same main problem as when studying preliterate history—there are simply no firsthand accounts available, because all written material must by definition be secondhand renderings of knowledge passed on from an oral tradition. What we do have preserved are myths and legends, such as folk tales, religious myths, and epics (e.g. the Iliad and the Odyssey). All is not lost, however. Although we know that myths are not accounts of historical facts, and legends are notoriously unreliable in details, both myth and legend preserve important background information about the societies that created them (Shotwell 1961). It is highly unlikely that myths and legends will operate with basic social and organizational patterns that are totally different from those of the societies that produced them, and archeological evidence can further corroborate the evidence they contain.

The myths and legends that have made it into writing, however, are largely the creations of the most advanced societies—those that made the transition to literacy. They therefore probably reflect social organization at a fairly mature stage. To gain insight into the conditions of man before what we call civilization, to grope for the very beginnings of human society, we are, as Wilson (1988) remarks, invariably drawn toward the simplest societies we know—the contemporary hunter/gatherer societies of the third world. This has its own problems, since the primitive societies that have survived to be studied in our own time may not be representative of man's prehistoric past—as Morris notes (1967), the tribes that still remained at the paleolithic level in the twentieth century were probably more representative of the dead ends in human cultural development than of the mainstream strains of creative, exploratory human societies.

However, everything we know about prehistoric man suggests he was a hunter/gatherer, and even if parts of the culture or environments of contemporary tribes have served to hold back their development, it is highly probable that they have enough in common with our (and their) distant ancestors that we can learn a lot about the conditions of prehistoric man by studying them. It is the closest we can get.

Present-Day Hunter/Gatherers

Hunter/gatherer societies—at least those that remained in the last half of the twentieth century—are extremely simple and small scale. According to Wilson (1988) the bands are small, consisting normally of 25 to 50 people, and they have no permanent place of residence. Neither do they recognize exclusive territories or formal boundaries. Although bands normally move within a geographically restricted region, the regions overlap, without this giving rise to territorial conflicts. There is nevertheless a definite association between the people and the territory, but it centers around features of the landscape rather than the stretches of land between them. Paths, tracks, water holes, and sacred sites are the landmarks of the hunter/gatherer bands, and serve them as base points for mapping their relative positions as they move about.

Because they are constantly on the move, they have no permanent settlements—they erect temporary camps that may last only a few days or weeks. Shelters normally take little more than an hour to construct, and in some cases they even live around the fire in the open. They live in very close physical proximity to each other, with almost no privacy as we know it. Not surprisingly, conflict management and control are well developed in these societies—conflict is disruptive and must be avoided. If things get too tense, the exit option is always there—it is perfectly legitimate to leave the band and join another.

This relaxed attitude to group membership seems to permeate hunter/ gatherer society. Wilson (1988) holds that modern research seems to bear out that hunter/gatherers have more flexible and fluid relations than conventional theory has acknowledged. Kinship ties are weak, says Wilson, even between parents and children. Pandam children, for instance, are free to leave their parents after the age of about six. Marital relations change, and people frequently change dwelling for what seem to be just desires and whims. The strongest criterion seems to be personal affection and feeling of friendliness, and kinship ties have significance only as far as they are reinforced by affection and physical proximity. Even for people in the same band, kin is generally not reckoned beyond the second degree of collaterals. At the third degree, people start to forget kinship ties. However, kinship still seems to be the most basic structuring mechanism. It can easily be overridden by affection, but in most hunter/gatherer societies, it always exists as an independent factor (the Pandam appear to be at the extreme end of the kinship importance continuum).

Above all, however, the hunter/gatherers seem to value independence— it is encouraged in children from the start. Dependence on others is looked down upon. The ideal is that everyone should be independent and self-sufficient. Sharing of food is nevertheless ubiquitous, especially the meat of larger animals. The bands are extremely egalitarian, and any attempt on the hunter's side (after killing big game) to boast about his skill is immediately put down by the others. Great care is also taken to avoid recognizing the lucky hunter as a benefactor, as someone to whom the rest should owe favors.

It follows from the fluidity of group membership and personal relations as well as the independence ideal that the hunter/gatherer bands have no real central authority structure. There is no chief in our meaning of the word, and the social order is upheld mainly through consensus and group pressures. People breaking the consensus are more or less ostracized— they are in reality forced to comply or leave the group.

The social structure is minimal and shows a definite resemblance to the roving bands of our relatives among the primates. Indeed, some of the apes have a clearer central authority (in the form of a dominant male) than a number of the bands described by Wilson. There is a degree of organization—common tasks are undertaken, food is shared—but on a very small scale, and based mainly on direct personal relationships reinforced by affection. The size and scope of organization is limited by the extremely low overall population density in hunter/gatherer territories, by the small size of the bands, and by man's intrinsic physical limitations.

There are, however, hunter/gatherers that have developed more advanced social structures—for instance, the aborigines of Australia. When Europeans first encountered them, they had been living undisturbed for perhaps as long as 30 000–40 000 years and had developed a richer culture and more elaborate organization than most of their remaining "colleagues" on other continents. But, even if they were more advanced socially than the Pandam, Naiken, Hadza, !Kung, and others described by Wilson, they were still distinctly "primitive" and without any trace of sedentism.

As Lauriston Sharp (1952[1]) described them, they lived a roving life in fairly small bands. They had domesticated the dog, but no animal that served as a source of food—foraging was their dominant activity. They did not know metals, and even their stone tools were primitive compared to the refined flint implements of the mature stone age cultures of ancient Europe.

Their social organization was structured along clan and kinship lines, and closely associated with their religious concepts and their perception of the world. Aboriginal belief divided time into two great epochs—the first a distant and sacred past, populated with mythical ancestors, and the second a new and more prosaic order comprising the present. The mythology held that everyone and everything present had a corresponding archetype in the mythical epoch, and that everything that happened today was just a reenactment of the actions originally carried out by the mythical ancestors. A man was a member of a particular clan because his alter ego among the ancestors was so, his name was the same as the ancestor's, he performed the same duties, married a certain woman from a certain clan because his ancestor had done likewise, and so on.

These relationships even transcended the local group, because of ritual and trade relationships between groups. In northeastern Australia, the most important items of trade were stone axe heads, coming from quarries in the south, and spears made from the barbed spines of stingrays, originating from the coast-dwelling groups in the north. This string of trade relationships may have extended up to a thousand kilometers, involving a large number of separate communities. The trade relationships between pairs of persons from different communities were defined within the ancestral system in kinship terms, although no actual kinship was

---

[1] Sharp's paper is about the Yir Yoront and their neighboring groups on the Cape York Peninsula in Queensland, Australia, in the 1930s. It has inspired several comments about the important interplay of technology, culture, and organization, for instance Peter S. DeLisi, "Lessons from the Steel Axe: Culture, Technology, and Organizational Change," *Sloan Management Review*, 3, 1990, pp. 83–93.

involved. Trade was carried out mainly during the great ritual celebrations in the dry season, which often attracted hundreds of people.

The aborigines had no conception of a future different from the present—their view of history was circular rather than linear. They believed that nothing new ever happened, that their total universe of people, actions, and artifacts was defined and laid down in the sacred epoch. No new actions or artifacts were in their view possible. This meant for instance that they did not use any form of boat or raft, even though their neighbors 70 kilometers to the North made and used bark canoes. They knew about the canoes, the materials were readily available, but they also knew, they explained, that their mythical ancestors never built or used canoes, and that was the reason why they lacked it. They assumed that the canoe was a part of the ancestral universe of their neighbors and regarded it therefore natural for them to have it.

The resilience of this system and was so great that even the account of a dramatic encounter with a party of cattlemen in 1864, where at least 30 aboriginals were killed, was effectively suppressed—not a trace of the event could be found in any of the stories containing the history of the group when anthropologists studied the group 70 years later. It was as if a collective suppression of the fact had taken place because it did not fit in their view of the world: None of the mythical ancestors had ever been attacked by white men and killed in scores by firearms. It is tempting to interpret this in the light of Morris's comments and the concept of mental sets described in the previous chapter: The Yir Yoront had developed a religious/cultural system and an accompanying mental set that blunted curiosity, blocked developments in knowledge and technology and locked them into an evolutionary dead end.

We may similarly question the extremely weak structures of the hunter/gatherer societies described by Wilson: Maybe it is their aversion to social control and obligations—a necessary complement to more permanent, close cooperation—that explains why they have remained at the hunter/gatherer stage.

Domestication

Ancient tribes similar to the Yir Yoront did not by any means exhaust the basic human potential, however. The evolutive process continued, and man settled down. Even if the hunter/gatherer society is mankind's starting point, the overwhelming majority of humans have been living in permanent settlements for the last 10 000–15 000 years. Historically, this has been the natural way of life for all important civilizations. When inquiring into the roots of human organization, we must therefore include some reflections on the changes wrought by sedentism—which we know fairly well both from archeological evidence and the study of simple sedentary people from the twentieth century.

When humans became sedentary, two important things happened. First, they began to build more sturdy dwellings, and second, the concept of property was extended. At the outset, it was not necessarily a question of individual property or the ownership of land or animals—many of the earliest known settlements were situated by the seashores or along lakes and rivers, and their inhabitants probably relied on fishing. But the village itself, at least, became the property of the community, as well as the increasing number of personal and family belongings such as tools and household utensils. Later, when horticulture, agriculture and domesticated animals became the economic basis for most societies, the rights to tillable land, herds, grazing areas, and tools became not merely important, but crucial for survival. Humans became fiercely territorial, defending what they had, and often engaging in war to seize new land.

When rights to land became established, kinship took on an important new dimension. The fluid arrangements of the hunter/gatherer bands were simply not adequate anymore, since kinship regulated the access to land— collective or individual. Land rights were inherited on the basis of kinship and village affiliation, and the exit option was not so easily available anymore—individuals could not simply leave their native village and expect to become a full member of another one. Leadership became more pronounced, either in the form of chiefs or councils.

There were (and are) many variations, however. The status of chief may be inherited, or a chief may be chosen. Councils may consist of family heads, elders, or combinations thereof. There is even evidence that the same societies may oscillate between the two forms, which Leach (1970) reports as a likely explanation for the existence of two parallel systems of authority among the Kachins of highland Burma: Some villages were hereditary chiefdoms; some were ruled by councils of family heads. However, the evidence suggests that chiefs who stretched their powers too far could be deposed and supplanted by a council, and a strong natural leader eventually emerging in a council could in his turn succeed in establishing a new hereditary chiefdom.

This new importance of kinship gave sedentary communities a much more permanent and substantial structure than hunter/gatherer society, a structure that was further elaborated and strengthened in societies that were systematically able to produce a food surplus. Surplus production of food made room for craftsmen, merchants, religious specialists, and ruling classes, and made large construction projects possible—some of which (like the extensive irrigation projects of the ancient civilizations in the Middle East) increased the fertility of the land further and thus contributed to the development of even larger and more complex societies.

Surpluses invariably lead to social stratification, an uneven distribution of property, and a more stable social structure. Again, we can turn to Leach (1970) for evidence: the Kachins, with their structural instability, lived in the steep hills in the highlands, more or less at the subsistence level. The villages could produce little or no surplus; there was simply no economic room for a class of landowners.

In the valleys, on the other hand, the conditions for agriculture were much better. The people living there, the Shan, had a more sophisticated culture and a stable social structure, forming feudal[2] states based on hereditary positions tied to the ownership of land.

This new, structured society imposed a much wider set of rights and obligations on people and developed a rich set of rituals and routines to enforce them. Unlike in hunter/gatherer society, routine is a hallmark of the sedentary community. Most of the day is spent doing programmed tasks that are necessary to fulfill one's obligations toward others or tending the land and animals that are the basis for one's subsistence. The social and political structure is thus cast in a stable pattern of actions that is constantly enacted and becomes thoroughly ingrained in people's minds. Periodical religious or other feasts and rituals contribute to this and give the status quo a more solemn blessing. Often, a period of religious training followed by initiation rituals becomes a part of the upbringing for all children.

When the development of human society reached this stage, technology and techniques had already started to make a difference. Domestication of the horse in many societies and the emergence of ships improved communication, and buildings were used not only for shelter, but also to encode information—especially information of a ritual character and with a bearing on the social structure. Mankind was approaching its first real technological revolution, the invention of writing—to which we shall return in Chapter 6. The rest is, literally speaking, history.

THEORY FOR SIMPLE ORGANIZATION

Most organization theorists are not very interested in simple organizations—in exploring the primal space of organizations. That is perhaps not so surprising, since organization theory as a discipline sprang from the problems experienced in building and running the complex organizations

---

[2] There are some nuances in how different people use the term "feudal." The most restrictive reserve the term for the political system of the kingdoms of medieval Europe, others think (as I do) that it is meaningful to extend the term to cover all hierarchical political systems where lineage and control of land are the main structuring elements.

that arose in the late nineteenth century and grew to prominence in the twentieth. Small-scale societies and simple organization have by and large been left to anthropology.

Another reason is probably the distinction between formal and social organization set up by the classical theorists. Organizational theory was restricted to the former—the latter, especially the family, was seen as something quite different. To me, this distinction is artificial. Organization lies at the bottom of human existence, and the repertory of behaviors that formed our societies from the earliest times are the same that underlies the more advanced formal organizations of the modern era—even if they have evolved considerably, and have come to depend in large part on tools not available to humans in the "natural" state. Even today, when formal organizations, voluntary organizations, and family life all have different "frames" (Goffman 1974), we are not able to separate them fully. Experiences and prescriptions from one frame tend to spill over into the others, and our situation in one of these domains always interacts with our situation in the others.

One of the few theorists who does discuss simple organizations is Henry Mintzberg (1979). His classification of organizations contains two forms that encompass small, simple organizations: The Simple Structure and the Adhocracy.

Of these, the Simple Structure is the intuitive small-scale organization with a strong leader, often charismatic and entrepreneurial, leading the organization through direct supervision effected through informal contact with its members (Mintzberg 1979, p. 306, bold type from original):

> **The Simple Structure is characterized, above all, by what it is not—elaborated. Typically, it has little or no technostructure,**[3] **few support staffers, a loose division of labor, minimal differentiation among its units, and a small managerial hierarchy. Little of its behavior is formalized, and it makes minimal use of planning, training, and the liaison devices. It is, above all, organic.** In a sense, Simple Structure is nonstructure: it avoids using all the formal devices of structure, and it minimizes its dependence on staff specialists. The latter are typically hired on contract when needed, rather than encompassed permanently within the organization.

Mintzberg gives the Simple Structure a much wider span, however—it ranges from the small entrepreneurial start-up, where everyone works in the same little room (which he calls the *simplest structure*), to the large, autocratic organization run by the iron-willed founder/owner. It also includes Thompson's (1967) *synthetic organizations*, ad hoc organizations

---

[3] The professional part of the staff, where you find the analysts who monitor and analyze the environment and plan and standardize the work that the others are doing.

set up to handle unexpected crises, such as natural disasters, and headed by strong leaders with comprehensive authority.

It is thus clear that many of the organizations falling into the Simple Structure category (the large ones) are anything but simple in administrative terms, and that they require sophisticated, technology-based infrastructures (such as paper-based archives and telegraph lines) to function. Prime examples are the large American trusts of the late nineteenth century, which Mintzberg classifies as Simple Structures because of their total dominance by single owners/entrepreneurs.

The Simple Structure, on a sufficiently small scale, has probably always been an extremely common organizational structure in human societies, as indicated by the foregoing discussion. This conclusion is also supported by recorded myths and legends. From the matriarchal queens of neolithic Europe to the nineteenth century chief and his tribe, to the master craftsman with his apprentices, and the patriarch with his family, the Simple Structure abounds.

But, as indicated earlier, other structures have also existed from time immemorial—from groups of cooperating hunters to more or less democratic villages and tribes with a council of elders or family heads as the supreme authority. The extremely simple bands of the Pandam, for instance, do not have sufficient leadership to qualify as Simple Structures. They can only be described as very loose Adhocracies. The more democratic variety of Kachin villages are a sort of a mixture, with family heads (Simple Structure) forming a governing council (Adhocracy).

With the term *Adhocracy*, Mintzberg mainly denotes innovative organizations with a high content of professionals and experts (Mintzberg 1979, pp. 432–33, bold type from original):

> **In Adhocracy, we have a fifth distinct structural configuration: highly organic structure, with little formalization of behavior; high horizontal job specialization based on formal training; a tendency to group the specialists in functional units for housekeeping purposes but to deploy them in small market-based project teams to do their work; a reliance on the liaison devices to encourage mutual adjustment—the key coordinating mechanism—within and between these teams; and selective decentralization to and within these teams, which are located at various places in the organization and involve various mixtures of line managers and staff and operating experts.**
>
> **To innovate means to break away from established patterns. So the innovative organization cannot rely on any form of standardization for coordination.** In other words, it must avoid all the trappings of bureaucratic structure, notably sharp divisions of labor, extensive unit differentiation, highly formalized behaviors, and an emphasis on planning and control systems.

This connotation is natural in the modern world of formal organizations. But the basic structural properties of the Adhocracy are found in the small, egalitarian human group, where problems are solved as they crop up, decisions are made by consensus, and coordination is taken care of by mutual adjustment. When society develops and grows beyond the limits of the mutually coordinating band, especially when it becomes sedentary, the Adhocracy evolves into the form seen in the Kachin villages, where the basic structure is the family, but where authority on the societal level is still created by mutual adjustment— now through the institution of the council. Following Mintzberg's terminology, we might well call this second-order form of the Adhocracy a *Councilcracy*.

If a strong natural leader emerges in a Councilcracy, it may change to a Simple Structure, but there may also be strong norms that inhibit such transformations (as in our own societies) or effect a return to Councilcracy when the leader dies, is deposed, or otherwise discredited.

*Looking at the anthropological and historical evidence there is much to suggest that those two configurations—the **Simple Structure** and the **Adhocracy**—are the two basic organizational configurations of the human race.*

In their simplest forms, they are also clean representations of two of the fundamental solutions to the problem of coordination (see Figure 3-1 on page 51): the Simple Structure achieves coordination by empowering one person to direct the others, and the Adhocracy by letting all the group members know what the others are doing at all times, thereby allowing each one to continually adjust his or her behavior accordingly. Coordination in the Simple Structure is thus focused on *directing work* and does not require that people are equally competent or informed (indeed, most leaders in such organizations will prefer that they are not). The Adhocracy, on the other hand, requires not only that everyone in the group knows the common goal, but also that they agree on it, have a common understanding of it, and are in reasonable agreement on the means. If not, their self-administered actions will simply not fit together. We may therefore say that coordination in the Adhocracy is focused on *sharing information*, and it requires that the participants are on the whole *equally competent* to act on that information.

The two other basic coordinating mechanisms delineated in Chapter 3, standardization of work and standardization of skills, did not give rise to separate organizational forms in preliterate societies, but they were obviously operative in rudimentary forms. As long as there have been humans, there must have been tacit knowledge and routinized ways of executing recurring tasks—indeed, as noted in Chapter 4, this is perhaps our main trick for surviving with limited cognitive capacities in an information-rich world.

Enlarging a Simple Structure is fairly straightforward, in the sense that the means are a part of an age-old human repertoire of social roles: if the organization becomes too large for the leader to oversee, he or she can *delegate authority* to trusted persons who are inferior in status and have clear loyalties. Insofar as such persons can be seen as direct extensions of the leader's own person and authority, the capacity for direction and control can be substantially increased, whereas the line of command is kept unequivocally intact. We shall soon see how that was done in preliterate societies.

The Adhocracy, on the other hand, is much more difficult to extend. In an organization where everyone communicates directly with everyone else, the members' communication capacity rapidly becomes saturated as the group grows, and all answers to this problem must compromise on the basic form to a much larger degree than for the Simple Structure. Because the only possible answer is to divide the growing group into subgroups, the all-to-all communication and direct, mutual adjustment is irretrievably lost. Even if direct mutual adjustment is preserved within the groups, coordination between them can be achieved only through group representatives. The method of representation then becomes an important parameter. The basic Councilcracy solved this by combining the Simple Structure of the patriarchal family with the Adhocracy of the council. The Greek city states evolved it into a combination of the town meeting and representative democracy (however, only proper citizens—free men who owned land—could vote), a tradition further elaborated to create our own modern representative democracies.

Adhocracy has not been a favored form of organization in more elaborate societies up through the ages. The reasons are probably mixed: in addition to the scaling problem, which is serious enough, the Adhocracy's democratic form could not survive in the authoritarian cultures that have dominated every large and sophisticated society until quite recently.

The Problems of Organization Building in Preliterate Society

There are three questions that seem especially interesting regarding organization in illiterate or semiliterate societies (societies where the art of writing is known, but where so few are skilled in it that most activities and organization building have to be conducted without its help): what are the domains of the organizations we find, how are they structured, and what happens when they hit the upper limits of human memory, communication, and information processing—when they become too complex to handle by mutual adjustment or by direct supervision (the commands of a single person)? How does a kingdom grow larger than the number of persons the king and his immediate helpers can oversee?

The Organization Domains and Their Structuring

The domains of organization in illiterate societies are few. The first and most basic domain is the family, then we have the society's authority structure—whether the boundary of the society is the village, the tribe or the state. In more advanced societies, there may also be specific religious domains with separate organizing, and even small organizational domains of a craft or commercial nature.

Some readers may balk at the idea of calling a family an organization. We are used to reserving that concept for formal organizations (see, for instance, the discussion in Silverman 1970). As I just said, I think this distinction is artificial. The formal organization, be it business or governmental, is a fairly new phenomenon. In preliterate society, the family was no doubt the main structuring element of society—indeed, even in Western societies, it kept this position until quite recently. In Taiwan, which has built a modern economy while retaining traditional Chinese values, the family can still be regarded as the main structuring element of ownership in business (Hamilton and Biggart 1988).

There are several reasons for this. First, the family was not only an informal group bound together by affection; it was a structure with very formal and material purposes: to uphold rights to land (or condemn to serfdom), and to channel political power. Rights to land—allocated through the operation of kinship, inheritance, and marriage, not through conveyance, contract, sale—were almost the sole source of economic and political power until trade became so abundant that a rich merchant class emerged (Nash 1966). Often, however, citizenship continued to be tied to the rights to land, as it did in the Greek city-states.

Second, the family structure was already there—an important feature in illiterate society, where the burden of retaining administrative information was formidable: everything had to be remembered by someone, and, preferably, by a number of people, should claims be contested. Family relationships were widely known and easily remembered and were therefore a convenient infrastructure for other purposes. Third, loyalty could best be counted upon from members of one's family, where both affective and economic ties were present. And, of course, let us not forget that ancient humans in all probability had the same kind of affectionate feelings for their family, especially their offspring, that we have. In a society without the social and judicial safety nets of modern industrialized nations, it is quite natural for people to protect and support their nearest and dearest first.

Circumventing the Barrier of Cognitive Capacity

The rule by family head, chief, or council is adequate as long as the family, tribe, or city is below a certain critical size. This critical size is not possible to determine in any exact way, because it varies according to contextual circumstances (geographical extent of domain, fertility of land, hostility of neighbors, etc.). However, as our assessment of man's cognitive capacities indicates, the critical size cannot be very large. The barrier must have proved a formidable one, and most prehistoric societies were probably small-scale structures, just like a large number of the primitive societies studied by anthropologists in our own time. The old Norse religious myths, for instance, tell us that all the gods, *æsene* (the Aesir), lived together in Åsgard, with Odin as their chief, and even if they all had their separate duties, there is no mention of a larger hierarchy based on territory.

But, somehow and sometime, such hierarchies emerged, and we can find evidence of this also in the myths, as for instance the Greek creation myths, where a Titan and a Titaness are placed in charge of each of the planets (Graves 1960). In the very old Mesopotamian epic of Gilgamesh, believed to be written down 1500 years earlier than the *Iliad* and the *Odyssey* (Sandars 1964), we can also find passages that indicate arrangements of a feudal character, as when Ishtar, Queen of Heaven, the goddess of love, fertility, and war, tries to persuade Gilgamesh to become her husband (p. 83):

> When you enter our house in the fragrance of cedar-wood, threshold and throne will kiss your feet. Kings, rulers, and princes will bow down before you; they shall bring you tribute from the mountains and the plain.

Even the myths of the Aztecs tell about how the supreme god, Omeyocán, divided the heavens into different regions and created a god to head each of them (Beals 1970). Further evidence of the general nature of this arrangement can be found in anthropological studies. If we return for a moment to the Kachins of Burma, a village was often part of a group of villages, and the local chiefs were subordinate to one supreme chief. The valley Shans, on their part, had a social structure that was even more distinctly feudal, where the local nobles were subordinate to higher lords and finally to the king himself.

In Africa, such structures were quite common in the kingdoms that existed when Europeans colonized the continent (Lloyd 1965). There were variations in the mechanisms by which the King appointed his subordinate chiefs, and the ruling class might be closed or open for upward migration from commoners, but the main principle was a division of responsibility by means of geography. Historic variations on the feudal structure have been the common political frameworks throughout the world, and these were probably developed to their most stringent and elaborate form in the kingdoms of medieval Europe.

The beauty of such a system—from a cognitive point of view—lies in the extreme economy it offers with respect to information processing, memorizing, and communication. Based on land rights and family lineage, it contains its own structuring information; information that is constantly enacted in everyday life and thereby reinforced in everyone's memory. By delegating to his vassals total authority over their fiefdoms and the people who live there, the king effectively encapsulates the information required to run the fiefdoms and shields himself from it. He now only has to worry about the loyalty of his vassals (often no small worry, however), the size of their tributes and their contributions to his army. The number of people with whom he must deal is drastically reduced. The king normally does not interfere in the way his vassals run their affairs, as long as they are sufficiently competent, loyal to him, and not so cruel or unreasonable to the people as to inspire massive uprisings.

It is thus a system that can exist without the help of writing, and, from an information processing point of view, there is no theoretical limit to the size of states built on these principles. However, we know of few large nonliterate states, and only one really large one: the Inca state overthrown by Pizarro in 1533. After extensive conquests in the two centuries preceding the Spanish invasion, it covered what is now Peru, as well as parts of Bolivia and Chile, an area of approximately one million square kilometers—about twice the size of France, or nearly one third the size of India. The total population of this empire was about 4 million.

The Incas' state organization was of a feudal type, and their expansion came almost exclusively in the coastal areas and in the hills where sedentary farming dependent on irrigation had already produced a society with feudal organization resembling their own. There they could rule through the established structure, through the old leaders, if these leaders agreed to submit to Inca rule (which they often did). The Inca king (or the Inca, as he was called) supplied the vanquished lord with a new first wife from his own lineage and in return accepted one of the new vassal's daughters into his harem. In such a way, the local lord was tied into the dynastic kinship system (Murra 1986). Note this prime importance of lineage as a structuring element. When such links were absent, they had to be at least formally established to foster loyalty and reestablish the customary congruence between lineage and political power.

Where the social organization stopped at the village level, and the villages themselves moved about, as in the semi-sedentary tribes adjoining their empire, the Incas had not managed to conquer and establish permanent control—the information economy of the feudal structure was not available and the task became too complex.

However, even if the Incas were not literate, they had a system for numeric records, called the *khipu*, to help them. It consisted of a bundle of knotted threads, where threads and knots of different colors had different values. It was primarily used for taxation, but as the empire expanded and the king's needs for soldiers, food and other goods and services came up against the limits of feudal organization, the *khipu*'s decimal organization started to be used also for organization purposes. Murra (1986) notes that, in the last years before the Spanish conquest, the Incas seemed to try out new local subdivisions based on numbers rather than on lineage and ethnic origin.

If there were other preliterate states of the same magnitude, knowledge of them has not survived to be written down. Judging from the empires we do know, we can only conclude that very large states seem easier to build and control when the rulers have access to a literate class of administrators—a conclusion that seems perfectly plausible. Maybe the Incas represent the extreme accomplishment in organization building for an oral culture. Judging from the great importance that the *khipu* had for their administration, we may even view them as a borderline case—not truly oral anymore, but not quite literate either. If left alone for another century, they might well have developed their own script as an answer to their pressing administrative challenges. After all, the Mayas and the Aztecs already had—in AD 50 and AD 1400, respectively (Ong 1982).

The Feudal Type Organization

The feudal system builds upon the rule of one, on the concepts of the family head and the chief. Because there is a hierarchy in the family (father–son, mother–daughter), this concept lends itself readily to build a hierarchical social structure as well. More democratic systems had no such blueprint to follow, and, anyway, it goes against the grain of democratic assemblies to delegate power upward. It is thus no accident that societies with a more democratic type of government have been less prone to build empires than autocratic states. When a Greek city-state founded a colony, for instance, it was at no point supposed that the new city should obey the authorities of the mother city (Kitto 1951). It was certainly considered distasteful to enter into conflict with the mother city, and her citizens usually enjoyed certain privileges when visiting, but the new city was by all parties considered politically independent from day one. Another indication of this can be found in the reluctance of the citizens of most EU-countries to move toward further political integration in the European Union.

From this perspective, it is also noteworthy that when countries in Europe managed to sustain colonial empires even when they themselves became democracies, they did so by basing their rule on ideas of racist and cultural supremacy. As soon as those concepts crumbled through moral debate and reflection in the ruling countries, the empires also disintegrated. The last example is the recent collapse of the Russian empire. Built by the feudal and imperialist czars, it was upheld and even extended by the Communist Party, which (though democratic on paper) ruled on the basis of their own supremacist ideology: the theory that only the party cadres were politically conscious and could understand the true interests of the people. By demolishing that ideology, the Soviet leadership destroyed the ideological basis for the union, and the republics and regions were bound to claim sovereignty.

How does the hierarchy of the feudal-type state fit into modern organization theory? It has certainly evolved from the Simple Structure, but it no longer belongs to that category. On the surface, it may seem, it is just a case of the universal hierarchical form, found today in military organizations and in the large bureaucracies of government and private business. However, there are in fact significant differences. Modern bureaucracies rely on advanced administrative technology, primarily the art of writing and its associated tools. They are specialist oriented, with each level and department having definite responsibilities that fit together in a complex task structure. Work flows through it in an orderly fashion, according to centrally administered plans and rules for execution. There are large flows of information both vertically and horizontally.

The original feudal hierarchies did not have the instrument of a written language at their disposal. They were not at all specialist oriented; on the contrary, the parts of a feudal state (on the same level) are by definition similar. Communication, both vertically and horizontally, was kept to a minimum. The whole point of the feudal structure was precisely to simplify complexity as much as possible, so that the unaided human mind could handle it—the idea was to *abolish*, as far as possible, the need for coordination in the first place.

If we can compare it to a modern form of organization, it must be what Mintzberg (1979) terms the *Divisionalized Form*. A division, in the original sense of the word, is a largely self-contained and self-sufficient part of the organization, with a broad objective (usually to serve a particular market) and a minimum interface with corporate management—ideally limited to passing general goals, budgets, and profit goals downward, and status information (mostly in the form of financial reports) upward. "In general," says Mintzberg (1979, p. 381), "the headquarters allows the divisions close to full autonomy to make their own decisions, and then monitors the results of these decisions." Not infrequently, the divisions are organized as separate legal entities (corporations).

The key elements, from our point of view, are the *separate objectives* of the divisions, the *duplication of operating functions* across them, their resultant *quasiautonomy* and *elimination of the need for interdivisional coordination*. Real coordination is not necessary, as evidenced by the use of *standardization of output*, which, as we concluded in Chapter 3, is not a proper coordinating mechanism, only a tool for controlling the level of performance.

The goal of this method of organizing is obviously to *limit the need for information flows across division boundaries* and thus obtain a *wide span of control* for top management. Viewed in this perspective, the Divisionalized Form is no more than the modern commercial version of a primordial *Feudal Form* of organization, which developed out of the need to build large organizational structures with minimal requirements for memorizing, information processing, and communication. In the Feudal Form, the subunits were fully independent from each other, answering only to the higher level, they had their own administrative apparatus, and their objectives, although usually similar, were separate in the sense that they did not depend on each other or require any coordination with other units on the same level. Finally, control was maintained through the use of established standards of output (with the size of the tribute or taxes and the number of men for the army as the most important) supplemented by the occasional royal command.

Except for the disagreement of the status of standardization of output as a coordinating mechanism, this is in no way in conflict with Mintzberg's definition. On the contrary, he emphasizes that divisionalization does not mean (1979, p. 381) "...a complete structure from the strategic apex to the operating core, but rather a structure superimposed on others. That is, each division has its own structure." He goes on to say that the Divisionalized Form tends to draw its divisions toward the Machine Bureaucracy configuration, but that it is not a necessary condition, since the focus of the Divisionalized Form configuration is on the structural relationships between the headquarters and the divisions.

Military Organization

Military organization is an interesting chapter in itself, and one that has undergone radical changes that are not (even today) fully acknowledged in the code of command.

At first, the military organization was only a mirror image of the feudal state, with a substitution of group (unit) for territory. There was little differentiation among the soldiers, and they were commanded by their feudal lords. The hierarchy was thus structured after the civil society, and, as the civil structure was fashioned to minimize information processing and communication, it also served the needs of war well: during battle communication is extremely difficult, and the need for it must be reduced as much as possible.

Even the feudal army was thus similar to the Divisionalized Form, with one important exemption: The King now needed to coordinate the actions of his subordinate lords, and he needed to do so in real time as far as circumstances would allow. In this respect, we may say that the feudal nation in war reverts partly to the Simple Structure by strengthening central coordination as much as possible. In preliterate society, however, it is not feasible to revert fully to the Simple Structure with a large army—the administrative load on the central command would then totally overwhelm its capacities. The modern, specialist, bureaucratic armed force with its abundance of communications equipment and its great capacity for detailed planning is therefore closer to Mintzberg's definition of the Simple Structure than the army of Genghis Khan was.

The small differentiation between soldiers that persisted up through history, even into our own century, also meant that an officer could successfully command almost any military unit, and it was from such a structure that the military code of command grew, whereby any officer had authority over all personnel below him in rank, regardless of unit. It was probably Frederick the Great of Prussia who really established this principle, through the standardized, elaborate training he mandated for all his soldiers.

Today, this tradition is rapidly becoming meaningless. The specialization in a modern armed force is just as extensive as in a modern corporation, and the notion of universal authority in war today makes no more sense than it would in industry—such as authorizing a vice president of finance in a manufacturing company to issue direct orders to a foreman on the shop floor about the way he should run his robotized paint line. In theory, the unity in military command is still in force, but, in practice, the sensible officer will always yield to the specialist knowledge of a subordinate.

The Basic Principles of Preliterate Organization

We have now explored what was defined as the primal space of organizations in Chapter 2. Before the art of writing permanently changed the premises for human reflection and human society, central planning and minute, standardized directives were not available as organizational tools. Preliterate societies had to use solutions with much greater information economy, structures that could rely on human memory alone, and that required an absolute minimum of communication between the levels in the hierarchy. The basic forms relied either on the rule of one or on a form of rule by consensus or council. For larger structures, where one ruler or one council could not manage the complexity, the iron constraints on human memory, communication, and information-processing capabilities forced a reliance on two principles: the *delegation of authority* and the *encapsulation of information*.

6
The Power of Technology

"It must be confessed that the inventors of the mechanical arts have been much more useful to men than the inventors of syllogisms."

Voltaire, "Philosophy," in *Philosophical Dictionary*, 1764

THE NATURE OF TOOLS

In many ways, this book represents an inquiry into the development and use of tools. Before continuing, I would therefore like to reflect for a moment upon the nature of tools—the implements we have invented to enhance our powers.

A tool is most often conceived of as something extraneous to humans—indeed, new and revolutionary tools are sometimes even seen as unnatural, alien and threatening. When talking about the natural state of humans, most people even today seem to envisage a primordial hunter/gatherer society, where man lives in peace with himself and nature—something like Rousseau's "noble savage." But even if hunter/gatherer society may well represent humanity in its primordial, natural state, such societies ceased to be typical representatives of our species thousands of years ago—and those that survived may represent no more than the longest surviving dead ends of cultural evolution.

As Morris (1967) argues, judged from an evolutionary point of view, the most successful and powerful human societies today are the modern industrialized societies of Europe, Asia and North America. In the course of their development, they have physically overrun and displaced other societies they encountered, like the Indians of North and South America and the aborigines of Australia. When they have refrained from doing the same everywhere it is mainly because of conflicts between themselves, their need to achieve viable balances of power and (not least) their own political and moral philosophical development. Today, most other societies do their best to become more like them. The culture of the

Western industrialized countries is therefore overwhelmingly successful in terms of diffusion and adoption.

It is also evident that cultural evolution has long since replaced biological evolution as the driving force in human development and competition—it probably happened when sedentism started some 20 000 years ago. Interestingly, the ecologists Robert Boyd and Peter J. Richardson (1985) argue that cultural evolution has many traits in common with biological evolution and follows many of the same laws—a fact that should perhaps not surprise us too much, given the basically systemic character of both spheres. Berger and Luckmann (1967) also argue along these lines.

Nevertheless, there seems to be a peculiar reluctance to acknowledge tools as something intrinsically human—especially advanced tools. But tools are not delivered by fate and do not spring spontaneously from lumps of raw material. Rather, they are conceived, designed, and crafted by humans; they are socially and culturally dependent *constructions*— material expressions of culture and knowledge (Bijker and Law 1992). Tools remain an intrinsic and natural part of human development, they are true expressions of the human mind.

If we accept that the physical and biological properties of the modern and the prehistoric human are not very different, there must be solely cultural reasons for the differences between hunter/gatherers and the modern industrialized societies—including the immense differences in size and scope of their organization. The basic preconditions must thus have been considerably augmented by knowledge, techniques and technology in the course of the last millennia, since we humans have totally transformed ourselves from intelligent apes, outwardly not that much different from their primate cousins, to beings with a knowledge and power that set us utterly apart from all other animals. In a mere blink of an eye on the evolutionary timescale, we have progressed from a position as unobtrusive members of the fauna, predators among many others and definitely no serious threat for any other species, to a position as the total masters of the earth and all large animals.

The developments of knowledge and methods on one side, and of tools on the other, are of course not separate processes. On the contrary, they are intimately linked—even more so than we normally recognize. Our intellect is not something that is suspended in a pristine, spiritual capsule; it has been and still is developed only in our ongoing interaction with nature and other humans.

The basic nature of this iterative, recursive process is aptly illustrated by Rachlin (1989, pp. 248–49) when he describes the opening sequence of a film about Picasso. Picasso is filmed painting, but the camera is set up to take single pictures about every other minute, compressing about a week's work into a few minutes. The picture starts with a few bold lines, but what follows is a constant metamorphosis, as Picasso tries one approach after the other: "A fish becomes a chicken. A bird becomes a woman. He keeps on working." After the week has passed, Picasso finally says, "Now I know what I was trying to do," and starts again-almost from scratch. Clegg, discussing the technical aspects of factory production, is on to the same phenomenon (1990, pp. 186–87):

> Technique is not simply a commodity to be bought, but a vital aspect of organization. This is clear in the sense that applied technique includes the human organization or system that sets equipment to work. Equally importantly the concept includes the physical integration of a new piece of equipment into a production process and its subsequent refinement and modification at the hands of the technically skilled workforce. Many manufacturers have come to grief on the belief that technical solutions can be bought pre-packaged. This is to ignore, precisely, that in operation these are always socio-technical solutions. What is at issue is precisely the "cultural" context in which these solutions have to work. Studies have shown that equipment users rather than makers develop major process innovations (thus stealing a march on their competitors) and that small, imperceptible "everyday rationalizations" account for the lion's share of productivity gains in an ongoing manufacturing business.

This is the basic human approach to discovery and innovation—to act, to try out, and then gradually modify until it is "right." In fact, this process is so basic that it is even reflected in the physical development of the brain. Experiments have shown that animals growing up in a complex and changing environment attain larger brains with more interconnections than similar animals growing up in extremely simple and stable environments (Hofer 1981). And it is important to note that this difference occurs only when the animals are allowed to engage in sensorimotor interaction with the environment, that is, merely living in a cage in a complex environment does not foster brain development; the animal must be able to move freely around, interacting directly with it, physically experiencing the changes and the complexity.

Our tools thus constitute our minds' projection into the physical world; they allow our minds to engage the complex world on a much grander scale and in a much more sophisticated way than our unaided hands and feet. The feedback our minds receive is correspondingly advanced, and it drives our thinking and investigations toward ever higher levels. The mind creates the tool; the tool allows us to do new things and shows us new constraints, thus posing new challenges and riddles to solve—both technological, scientific, and moral. This represents the essence of human progress—the concept of iteration, the endless number of small steps, some erratic, some successful, but always spawning new insights, new ideas, new experiments. The history of human development is therefore also the history of tools, and probably much more so than historians generally recognize.

The pace of this development is not even. Some inventions are more dramatic than others, carrying within them the potential for far-reaching changes and releasing spurts of rapid development. Other phases are characterized by the slow trickle of improved details. Astronomy, for instance, was clearly stagnating when Galileo set the stage for new growth by creating the first astronomical telescope in 1609. The revolutionary initial discoveries led to the construction of larger instruments to gather more light and resolve even finer detail. Development of telescopes was then gradually dampened by the law of diminishing returns, until we suddenly were able to lift them out in space, above the diffusion of the atmosphere, and start a totally new and exiting trail of innovations.

Pasteur, on his part, could not have developed his theories about bacteria without the microscope. On the basis of its new importance, the microscope was then subsequently developed to the limits of the resolving power of visible light. Further developments led to break-throughs like the electron microscope and later to the scanning tunneling microscope, which can resolve—and manipulate—individual atoms. Nuclear physics on its part rests heavily on the construction of particle accelerators, the king of which at the moment (and probably for many years to come) is the Large Electron-Positron Collider of the CERN laboratories near Geneva. Arguably the largest tool in the world, it is located in a ring tunnel with a diameter of 27 kilometers and a cross section of 4 meters, running from 50 to 150 meters below ground.

In practical engineering, the limitations of Thomas Newcomen's steam engine became the starting point for James Watt's improvements, sub-sequently leading to Richard Trevithick's high-pressure machine, the first really modern steam engine. (Watt, by the way, believed high-pressure engines would be too dangerous, and held back development until his patents expired in 1800.) In our own time, Shackleton's, Bardeen's and Brattain's crude transistor turned out to be the necessary stepping stone for the integrated circuits of modern microelectronics.

In business, we have seen the mutually dependent evolvement of modern communications and the modern industrial and retailing organizations from about 1850 (as described by Chandler, Beniger and others). And, to slip in a Norwegian example, one man's quest for synthetic saltpeter and another man's failure in building an electrical cannon led to the invention of an electric arc furnace for the manufacture of nitrogen oxide (the key to saltpeter synthesis), spurring a large-scale development of hydroelectric power, which in turn created the basis for a vigorous metals industry in Norway.

Indeed, even the development of moral philosophy is more closely related to our tools and material advances than generally acknowledged. Our ideas about war, for instance, have changed considerably the last 100 years, as we have developed modern weapons of mass destruction *and* experienced their effects. Before World War I, war, even between major nations, was much more readily accepted as a legitimate extension of politics. Even more obvious is the recent debate over the ethical implications of changing the genetic composition of bacteria, plants, animals, or even human beings. Before we actually had the tools and knowledge necessary to do it, it was not on the agenda at all—philosophers of previous centuries were not even aware of the possibility. The case is the same with global ecology—before human activities actually started to interfere seriously with nature, the question was not even raised.

Always, however, it seems to be easier and quicker to exploit innovations with a predominantly material and concrete purpose (like the steam engine) than innovations of a partly or predominantly intellectual nature—like writing. That should not surprise us, since manipulation of the physical world has been our main preoccupation and means of living for almost our whole existence as a species. All that we can see and touch is so much easier to comprehend, and dramatic developments may take place in decades. For matters of the mind, for the refinement of concepts, methods and social practices, we may need centuries.

Like writing, the computer is another invention that is partly material and partly intellectual. For the material part, the development races ahead at enormous speed, with hardware performance doubling every year or two—but when we strive to make good use of it, especially in the complex world of organizations, we obviously progress at a much slower pace.

Thus, our tools are our destiny, for better or worse. To paraphrase William Ralph Inge[1], man may never succeed in becoming lord of himself—there will always come a new tool, a new capability, a new insight that will tax our ethics and invite questionable actions. And we can never tackle the problems before we experience them; to think we need to be confronted with the physical world. Perhaps this is why so much of the discourse at our universities borders on the sterile, and why so many exiting things happen at their fringes—where intellectual curiosity and analytic power is more directly exposed to practical problems.

---

[1] "For better or worse, man is the tool-using animal, and as such he has become the lord of creation. When he is lord also of himself, he will deserve his self-chosen title of homo sapiens." William Ralph Inge, "The Dilemma of Civilization," in *Outspoken Essays: Second Series* (1922).

The Breakthroughs

The development of our tools as well as our knowledge and conception of work has gone through many stages, and some carry significantly more momentum than others. There may be several ways of classifying them and, conceivably, some disagreement as to their relative importance. For our purposes three breakthroughs stand out:

1. The invention of writing
2. The Industrial Revolution, with its sweeping developments:
   —abundant energy and mechanized production
   —new means of communication, from railroads to telephony
   —mass literacy, cheap printing, and the knowledge explosion
3. The invention of the digital electronic computer

In this chapter, we shall look at the first two; the third must wait until Chapter 8.

THE EXTERNALIZATION OF MEMORY

The Struggle to Remember

Cicero, in his *De Oratore*, tells a story about the famous poet and orator Simonides, who was having a meal with a number of friends (Eriksen 1987). The building they were in suddenly collapsed, and the diners were crushed to death under the tumbling stones. Just before the roof caved in, however, Simonides was rescued and brought outside by the gods Castor and Pollux. The only survivor, he was able to tell the rescuers who had been present, because he recalled exactly where they had been seated at the table. He then realized that much could be remembered if one located *pictures* at *places* in memory.

That was purportedly the wellspring of the classical mnemonic techniques so widely used from antiquity to the Renaissance, which involves building a permanent mental picture of a house with a number of rooms in a fixed order. For each occasion, the rooms can then be "filled" with objects or events that serves to recall a part of the speech. Advanced orators managed to build and maintain "houses" with a very large number of rooms, and was able to remember even very long speeches almost word by word.

However, mnemonics hardly originated with Simonides, who lived (from 556 to 468 BC) in a period when the Greeks had already started down the road to literacy, after the full Greek alphabet was developed from the Phoenician sometime around 700 BC (Havelock 1986). All nonliteral societies above the basic subsistence level of the simplest hunter/ gatherers must devote considerable time, effort, and ingenuity to keep the vital communal memory from fading, and would have had techniques for this. Both myths and religious conceptions aquire meaning in this perspective—adding pictures, stories, and emotions, thus making it easier to remember. Alternatively, memory may be kept alive by rituals and ceremonies, with role playing and drama. The Yir Yoront are a prominent example of both approaches. The rich pantheon of the aboriginal sacred epoch can from this perspective be interpreted as a mnemonic device, where the mythical landscape, figures, and events serve to visualize and thereby fix in memory the elaborate structure of aboriginal society. Their seasonal gatherings then served as opportunities to reinforce the myths by ritual acts.

Nevertheless, the life of nomadic hunter/gatherers did not lend itself to really elaborate social structures, and it was fairly well served by unaided memory. Sedentary life brought great changes, however, with property, larger communities and a much more complex social and economic life. The limitations of memory then became a much more important con-straint, and the new physical structures also took on a role as mnemonic devices—the house itself, for instance, became a powerful practical symbol, perhaps the most important one until the invention of writing (Wilson 1988). Both private houses and public buildings and monuments served as memory banks for common values and organizational systems. By learning to live in a private house and participate in the rituals and functions associated with public buildings and monuments, a child would also learn the basics about the reigning social organization and its own place within it. When property (especially the rights to land) became the subject of inheritance, either for the individual or the group, it simultaneously became the central structuring element in society, since persons or groups possessing more or better quality land than others were able to establish a permanent, superior position. The village itself, then, and later the town, the city, and the nation, created a rich and evolving set of anchoring points for social organization and stratification. Great engineering works (especially watering systems) allowed for even more intensive agriculture and larger cities, and technology proper became an important factor in the development of human organizations.[2]

---

[2] The architectural and construction technology of the ancient civilizations is impressive even today. Everybody knows about the pyramids, but there are other examples. For instance, 18 canals with fresh water went into Niniveh in Mesopotamia in the second millennium BC, the one best known was 20 meters broad and 80 kilometers long. It was built in only 15 months. Asphalt and bricks were used on the bottom, and in difficult passages the asphalt was covered with a foot of concrete, lined with stone tiles (Dahl, 1984).

Yates (1966) continues this discussion. She argues convincingly that the great cathedrals were designed along the lines of classical mnemonic theory—with their numerous niches and room dividers, their carvings, friezes, pictures and sculptures creating and furnishing the many "rooms" required to hold and display the entire common memory of Christianity. And, as anyone visiting national shrines like Westminster Abbey can witness, there was also room for conspicuous representations of the ruling elites and their historical claims to power. We might add that even modern churches, in all their stark simpleness, still contain works of art depicting central themes in the Christian heritage.

This tradition of encoding organization and the social order in buildings is in fact kept alive on a broad scale, from private homes to office buildings, churches, hotels and sports facilities. Parliaments in democratic countries invariably reside in buildings of prestige at the very center of the capital;[3] banks and industry erect pompous headquarters signaling their economic power; and hotels, the new cathedrals of the international elites, today represent the most daring and opulent architecture in the Western world. The encoding extends right through the interiors, and seldom leave you in doubt—for instance—about the relative rank of people you meet in their own offices.

Remembering must have put a growing strain on any society struggling to escape from mere subsistence. For instance, an inscription from Greece in the sixth century BC mentions the civic office of *mnemones* (literally, "remembrancers")—people entrusted with the task of remembering important public information, such as rulings, precedents, and other events worthy of chronicling. The office of mnemones illustrates well the iron-clad constraints of oral society. Keeping records of key public information required the dedication of many people's memories. Just memorizing the minutes of day-to-day affairs can be challenging enough, but then come affairs such as property rights, trade agreements, debts, and obligations, even kinship relations beyond the immediate family. As indicated in Chapter 5, from this perspective one can interpret feudal

---

[3] Interestingly, the Swedish parliament, in a fit of northern European rationalism, in 1971 moved out of its cramped building in the historical central part of Stockholm to a new and supremely functional structure in a more commercial district. The new building was very well suited to its purpose, but the representatives discovered (to their own astonishment) that they resented it—the symbolic value of its address, together with its businesslike modernity, collided headlong with the parliament's perception of its own position. It really signified that the parliament was not so important anymore, and that the power now resided in the cabinet and its departments, still located in its traditional quarters in the area the parliament had left. After 12 frustrating years in "exile," the parliament rectified the situation by moving back to its old building in the geographical center of power, now refurbished and extended through passages into adjoining buildings.

systems not only as power relationships, but also as mnemonic systems, which structurally defined and thereby fixed in communal memory large sets of rights and obligations.

The Art of Writing—an Administrative Technology

As the leading civilizations grew both in size and complexity, the limitations of memory became a severe constraint, blocking highly needed developments. Simple signs and representations of objects and numbers were not enough any more, a new tool was needed—one that could express and preserve complex information in an unequivocal way. And, it was administrative and commercial needs that spurred the development—all available evidence suggests that the first known script, the cuneiform of Mesopotamia (about 3500 BC), developed directly out of a need for economic records in the growing economy of what may be termed the world's first states—for private business, for public administration, and even for the economic side of the religious establishment (Goody 1986): the first use for writing in the temples of Mesopotamia was demonstrably not for recording religious material, but for temple administration. Discourse, recording of poetry, and recording of religious and scientific material all came later. *In my view, this innovation—the art of writing—represents the most fundamental, single technological breakthrough in the history of organizations—at least until now, when the ripening information technology may be able to equal or (given enough time) even eclipse it.*

We may not normally think of writing as a technology, but that is only because we are so used to it—it has become second nature to us, a complement to speech. Plato, who lived during the crucial transition from an oral to a literate society in Greece, thought otherwise—he considered writing an external, alien technology, in just the same way as many people today characterize the computer (Ong 1982). Its product is material (although with an immaterial message content), and to produce it, one needs tools (chisels, styli, pens, brushes, inkwells) and materials (stone surfaces, clay, papyrus, parchment, paper, ink).

So, writing is indeed a technology—a most formidable technology. It gave humans the immense power of absolute reminiscence and the ability to communicate across time and space without loss of content or accuracy. It made possible private records for business and personal use as well as public records about property rights, taxation, and compulsory services. In principle, there were no limits to the volume of information that could now be collected and preserved, although in practice, externalized information has *bulk*—it occupies space and is heavy to transport. Clay tablets, for instance, were the medium of early cuneiform. Technological innovations like parchment, papyrus and paper were therefore just as important to writing as the invention of magnetic disks and semi-conductor memory have been to computers.

The externalization of memory effected by writing was of course nowhere near complete—it offered no way of representing the full web of memories, with aspects such as sound, smell, vision, and pain, not to mention emotions—except, of course, as verbal descriptions. But the aspect that was covered—the ability to fix permanently any kind of verbal narrative and select pieces of verbal and (in due time) numeric information—was of such importance for our intellectual development and our ability to build organizations that it marked a true watershed in human history.

The Significance of a Shared Memory

The enormous significance of the written record does not only rise from the fact that it preserves information for an indefinite time, relieves the mind, and makes it possible to accumulate information on a grand scale. Even more important for the development of organizations is the fact that it creates a *shared external memory*, accessible by a large number of persons—in fact, by any person so authorized. An *active file* of written records allows many people to base their work on the same information, and an update made by one person is immediately available to the others and applies directly to their decisions. The revolutionary new information integrity inherent in the active file of written records provides therefore an *implicit coordination* of the people who work with it—because of their common basis of information, they are now able to act with considerable consistency without ever talking to each other. Since written records will not disappear with people who work with them, it also means that administration—public and private—can survive both normal and sudden changes in personnel.

The permanence and accuracy of written records made it possible to build much larger, more complex and more enduring organizations. Formal explication of rights, obligations, laws, and treaties added the necessary strength to relationships outside the bonds of immediate kinship and friendship, and made the partnership and the firm viable over time (Goody 1986). As Goody remarks (1986, p. 175), writing helps "to make the implicit explicit, and in so doing to extend the possibilities of social action ... by creating more precise types of transaction and relationship, even between trusted kin, that give these partnerships the strength to endure in more complex, more 'anonymous' circumstances."

Even if the the Incas proved that it is possible to build states and organizations of considerable size without the help of writing, it is also evident that once writing was available, much larger entities could be built and maintained. The great Arab and Asian empires, the Roman empire, the Roman church, and the Roman army were created and maintained by literate cultures, with their written codes and files, their reports and orders unequivocally committed to parchment, paper, or tablets. Even Genghis Khan, the warrior of warriors, who conquered his great empire by the brute strength of the sword and the horse, in the end had to rely on the delicate hands and minds of the Chinese mandarins to maintain and run it.

We also know that the riches, power, and reach of the Hanseatic League in Northern Europe increased many times over when writing was introduced as an instrument of business, allowing the merchants to direct their increasingly diverse and far-flung trading activities from their home bases, instead of traveling with their ships to manage the trading directly (Buckmann 1991). Wherever it was employed, writing also served to homogenize language and establish national or cultural identities.

The Importance of Numerals

The revolution did not only encompass letters—numerals, numeracy, and the development of systems and techniques for calculation have in many ways been just as important as writing, although they usually receive less attention (maybe because nearly all historians are men and women of letters rather than of numbers!). The use of numbers is a crucial aspect of our economic and scientific development.

The progress was very slow as long as Roman numerals were the only instruments. The Arab numerals and notation we use today (which are really Indian, and which did not become widely used in the Arab world until about 1000 AD) arrived in Europe around 1200 AD, but took several hundred years to become widely accepted. They met with much resistance—one of the arguments was that accounts kept with the new system were easier to forge, and in Florence, as late as 1299, a person could be fined for doing his accounts in the new system (Eriksen 1987). It nevertheless became popular with merchants, the fledgling bankers, and the money changers, since they appreciated its flexibility and efficiency much more than the theologically dominated scientists of the day.

When Roman notation was finally superseded throughout Europe in the course of the sixteenth century, development came rapidly, both in mathematical theory and mechanical tools. The crowning achievement in calculating techniques was the invention of logarithms, by the Scottish baron of Merchiston, John Napier (his *Mirifici Logarithmorum*

Canonis was published in 1614), and mechanical calculators[4] were also invented to relieve people from the drudgery of calculation. The new developments made it possible to carry out much more computing-intensive tasks than before.

Calculations remained labor-intensive, though, and continued to be a serious bottleneck both in engineering and science, even if mechanical calculators were considerably refined in the last half of the nineteenth century and the first half of the twentieth. It was only when they were superseded by the electronic digital computer that this constraint was really mitigated.

TECHNOLOGY TAKES OFF

The evolution of technology between antiquity and the Renaissance went slowly. It is not without its interesting moments, and there was much groundwork being done that would prove useful later. However, it is not possible within the scope of this volume to delve into the developments of this period, and it is certainly not necessary for our purpose, even if it is interesting in itself. We shall therefore go directly to a number of major developments from the Renaissance and onwards, and start with the first real mass production of identical products, preceding the Industrial Revolution by more than 200 years: the printing of books.

Printing and Mass Literacy

The invention of printing with movable type, unlike the invention of writing, did not have much direct effect on our possibilities for organization building. For instance, it did not affect the way most administrative records (both public and private) were kept—tax registers and general ledgers still had to be entered by hand. Correspondence was also still a manual affair. However, for society the consequences turned out to be momentous, since printing had a revolutionary effect on the economics of knowledge dissemination. By liberating it from the constraints of hand-copied scripts, printing had profound consequences for traditional structures of authority—both in society in general, and in some of its most central organizations, especially the Church.

When most people were illiterate, knowledge resided in handwritten books and a small number of persons. It could be—and was—controlled

---

[4] The first mechanical calculator was built by the German Wilhelm Schickard, not, as commonly believed, by Blaise Pascal (Augarten 1984). Schickard built his machine in 1623, the year Pascal was born.

by the hierarchies controlling the books. The Church was strong and unified because the priests were the only source of the scriptures and their interpretation. Dissenting interpretations could be suppressed by denying the perpetrators access to the pulpit, or simply by disposing of them.

Gutenberg's revolution meant that the written word became a mass medium and thereby escaped control. By printing a book, one could reach a much greater audience than by any previous communication method. There is little doubt that the success of the Reformation rests squarely on the printing press and Luther's understanding of its power. The Reformation and the printing business fed each other. According to Eriksen, only 40 titles were printed in Germany in the year 1500, and 111 in 1519. In 1523 the number had swelled to 498, of which an impressive one-third originated from Luther himself. All in all, 418 had to do with the Reformation! Not bad, considering only six years had passed since Luther nailed his 95 theses to the church door in Wittenberg.

So the scriptures were finally on the loose, and regardless of how much the Church deplored the new situation, it could not reverse it. It tried to stop unwanted books by banning and burning them, but the *Index Librorum Prohibitorum*, intended to suppress dissent, functioned more as a medium for advertising than anything else. Records show that a place on the index was the best guarantee for commercial success—and Eriksen concludes (1987, p. 115) that no Papal institution has contributed more to the promotion of science and general enlightenment than the Index! The paramount religious authority of the Church had received a deathblow, and it was clear that all monolithic political and scientific authority was in similar peril.

The printing press revolutionized society by effecting two mutually reinforcing changes. First, the printed book served as an extraordinary effective medium for the accumulation and dissemination of knowledge—scientific, political and, otherwise. Scientific treatises did not any longer have to circulate in a small number of handwritten copies, but were suddenly simultaneously available throughout the learned community as well as to the general public. Second, the sudden availability of (relatively) cheap books greatly increased the rate of literacy and pulled European societies through the transition from a predominantly oral mindset to a literate one. Analytic and abstract thinking became prominent in large segments of the society, notably the growing bourgeoisie, sweeping aside the Church's insistence on tradition and religious mysticism and preparing the ground for a widespread acceptance of empiricism, for new ideas and practical engineering—and thereby also for the modern organization.

As scientific discoveries and theories now spread much faster, the pace of scientific progress increased tremendously. Practical people (the engineers of their day) published directions for crafts and industrial processes, and the guilds began to lose their power. Innovation was stimulated, and new ideas spread rapidly. It is safe to say that the immense economic and intellectual developments of the centuries that followed would not have been possible without printing. It is equally true that the development of democracy owes a great deal to the dissemination of printed scientific and political knowledge, first to the bourgeoisie and then to the population as a whole.

The printing press also led to a further normalization of language and homogenization of national cultures. The later development of mass-distributed newspapers served to develop an even stronger sense of national unity and consciousness through the definition of national news and thereby the agenda for national concerns.

Organization of Records

Even if printing in itself did not make much difference to how organizations could be structured and run, there were innovations in record keeping as well. There is scant documentation to be found, but we can at least establish that elaborate systems for filing eventually were developed, with cards, folders, filing cabinets, and Rolodexes. Vertical filing was in its time seen as a substantial step forward (Yates and Benjamin 1991). The most monumental contraptions developed (in the twentieth century) were motorized filing cabinets, with storage bins in paternoster fashion and a height of several meters. The modern offshoot of this traditional filing technology is the microfilm reader, which greatly reduces the space needed. In principle, however, it is just another filing cabinet.

Cross-referencing and indexing systems were also invented along the way to help locate and retrieve recorded information. Information recording, storage, and retrieval nevertheless continued to be a very labor-intensive activity, and inventions such as the typewriter could not change that to any great extent.

But the crowning achievement of precomputer record keeping was of course the punch card reader. The idea of punch cards as information carriers probably originated in the textile industry, where the Frenchman Joseph-Marie Jacquard in 1801 invented a large automatic loom, controlled by punch cards, for weaving tapestries and similar complex textiles. (A demonstration program weaving Jaquard's own portrait in black and white silk needed 10 000 cards!). It was, however, Herman Hollerith, the son of a German immigrant to the United States, who put the punch card to practical use in record-keeping. His machines (with electrical sensors registering the holes) were first used in the American 1890 census, where they were a great success. They allowed for far more advanced statistics than manual methods, including filtering and cross-tabulation, and delivered the required information in a fraction of the time manual methods would have demanded. In a test arranged by the Census Office before the 1890 census, Hollerith's machines tabulated data ten times as fast as the two fastest manual methods. Even punching the cards went significantly faster than the manual registration (Augarten 1984). The reason for the success was twofold: both the mechanization itself and the new and much more *stringent structuring of the records* that became necessary to use the machines (Yates and Benjamin 1991).

Both public institutions and large private companies—notably in the service and utility sectors—invested in the new machines to ease the burden on their record-keeping departments. Punch card equipment represented a significant step forward, because it was the first invention that allowed mechanization of record keeping—the "industrialization" of an old craft. These systems also had many of the same properties as the first computer-based systems—indeed, for three decades, punch cards (based on the Hollerith cards) were one of the chief storage media for digital electronic computers.

In 1911 Hollerith's Tabulating Machine Company merged with three other companies to create the Computing-Tabulating-Recording Company (CTR), which was eventually restructured and, in 1924, renamed IBM.

Communications Revolution

The other great field of organization-relevant innovation is the field of communication. When memory was externalized and in principle no longer limited, communication quickly became the bottleneck for organization building. Communication has two aspects, both of which are important: physical transportation of people and goods, and communication of information. For a long time, they were (with very few exceptions) one and the same. Before writing came into use, the only way to send information over any distance was to send a person, a messenger. The advent of the written message made it possible to do without him, but the message itself was still a physical object. So, even though writing greatly increased accuracy, it did not necessarily increase communication speed. For some of the very oldest texts, engraved on rocks and large slabs of stone, the reader in fact had to come to the text rather than the opposite.

Couriers and Mail Services

Clay tablets were more handy, though, and we know that both the Egyptians and the Assyrians of northern Iraq were running regular courier services as early as about 2000 BC (James and Thorpe 1994). In the nineteenth century BC, the Assyrians had a dependable postal system operating between their homeland and trading bases abroad. Excavations of one of their merchants' colonies, at Kultepe in Turkey, uncovered a mass of correspondence, accounts and legal documents. The letters were small clay tablets, complete with clay envelopes inscribed with the name and address of the recipient. The service was even reliable enough for people to send money along with their letters. Chinese postal systems are known from around 1000 BC.

The development of papyrus paper and parchment made transport easier, and increased speed was sought by employing homing pigeons and horse riders. In Egypt, pigeons were used as early as the twelfth century BC, and regular, fast horse transport from about 500 BC. Cyrus the Great (550–530 BC), who built the almost 2600 kilometer Royal Road from Sardis to Susa, also organized a regular courier service with postal stations at regular intervals, and with relay riders carrying messages around the clock. The whole distance was covered in a mere nine days. A similar service, but much more extensive, was organized by the Mongols in China after the conquest by Genghis Khan. Marco Polo reported that Kublai Khan (AD 1260–1294) had 10 000 postal stations, with 300 000 horses employed on a regular basis (James and Thorpe 1994).

The great costs and extraordinary efforts involved in organizing these early communication systems only serve to underline the vital importance that communication has for large-scale organizations. Both Cyrus the Great and the Mongol khans no doubt viewed their courier services as vital for keeping grip on their empires, and they probably built on bitter experience.

However, none of these systems (with the possible exception of the early Assyrian system) had the capacity to serve as an infrastructure for mainstream organization building, and the beginnings of the first really comprehensive, public mail service only took place in Europe millennia later. France was first in 1576, followed by England in 1590 and Denmark in 1624. International postal cooperation was not institutionalized until 1874, when the world organization of post offices was founded. Before that, one had to rely on merchants, shipmasters, pilgrims, or other travelers if one was not wealthy enough to send one's own messenger.

Communications improved only at a very slow pace up through the millennia. The Romans and Incas built extensive road networks, and sailing vessels underwent a more or less continuous improvement. The improvements were nevertheless not revolutionary, even if they were considerable. The great clippers of the tea trade were very swift compared to their predecessors, but they still needed weeks to cross the great oceans. To cut travel time from, say, three months to six weeks was not enough to significantly change the basic constraints of organization building. International operations (the few there were), shipowners dispatching their shipmasters and nations their ambassadors still had to operate like the Roman emperor when he sent forth his governors: Choose reliable, sensible persons, give them general instructions, and pray they can tackle the problems challenging them on their own-since reports on critical events could not reach the headquarters until long after the matter was settled.

Railroads, Telegraphs, Telephones and More

The 1830s produced the first real communications revolutions in historic time: the railroad and the telegraph. The railroad got started first—it was officially "invented" when Stephenson built "The Rocket" in 1829, even if it has older roots (it developed slowly over about two centuries, starting with horse-drawn carts on wooden rails in the sixteenth century). The railroad revolutionized both travel and the transportation of goods. It is indeed a sobering experience for an IT buff of today to read about the development of the railroads in the middle of the nineteenth century. We like to think that we live in an age of unprecedented technological change, and that never before in history have such great changes taken place in such a short time. In a way, we are right—the pace of technological development is both breathtaking and unprecedented. However, the societal changes in the Western countries brought about by the combined technological developments over the last 50 years are hardly as great as those wrought by the developments of the railroads alone in the years from 1840 to 1890.

Consider the development of railroads in England: It "happened" almost overnight. In 1836 about 20 short lines were in operation, most of them concentrated in the Liverpool/Manchester and Newcastle/Middlesborough areas. The longest single line of rail was about 50 kilometers. In 1848, only 12 years later, the whole of England was covered with a surprisingly fine-meshed net of lines, connecting all major towns and scores of smaller ones. During the busiest year of "the railway mania" (as it was called), 1845, Parliament endorsed 623 new railroad projects, and more than 3000 kilometers of rail were laid that year alone (Dahl 1984).

In less than 20 years all major diligence lines were eliminated, the canal companies thrown from prosperity into financial difficulties, and travel times drastically reduced. Suddenly, small country towns that had been living a life in placid isolation were only hours away from the nearest big city, and large parts of Great Britain was abruptly brought within one day's travel from London.

In the United States, where distances were far greater and the pace of development was even more furious (even if it came a little later), the effect must have been still more revolutionary: In 1840 there were 4500 kilometers of rail; in 1870, 85 000 kilometers; and in 1890, 263 000 (Beniger 1986). That gives an average construction of 8900 kilometers per year from 1870 to 1890! This is quite impressive, especially when one takes into account that America's population in 1890 was only twice that of England's—or 62.6 million. In 1840 it had been only 17.1 million, about the same as England. The first American transcontinental link was opened in 1862, and within the span of 20 years, travel time from New York to Chicago was reduced from three weeks to three days (Chandler 1977). Now, *this* is change!

The telegraph spread just as rapidly after its invention in practical form in 1835. 1851 saw the first undersea cable between Dover and Calais; the first transatlantic cable (between Ireland and North America) came in 1866. Within a few decades, national telegraph networks were linked all over the world, and messages could be sped around the globe almost instantly. Semaphores, beacons, and drums notwithstanding, this was the first time in history that communication of information was truly separated from the transport of a physical message, and could take place reliably and routinely over long distances. In 1876 the telephone came, allowing people to speak to each other in real time irrespective of location. The invention of radio in 1896 increased the flexibility and range of telecommunications even further.

The first industry to profit from this double communications revolution was the newspaper industry, which in the second half of the nineteenth century turned a fairly exclusive phenomenon, the daily newspaper, into a mass product. But the telegraph also had impact on business and proved especially important for the growing railroad companies, notably because of safety considerations (Chandler 1977, Beniger 1986). Most lines were only single-track, and the movements of trains in both directions had to be closely coordinated. It was also necessary to monitor railroad cars traversing the different networks to offer point-to-point transport of goods without reloading. The telegraph was not fast or flexible enough to have really decisive influence on business, however. It was the telephone that really changed things. After its invention in 1876, it spread rapidly, especially in the United States, and played a crucial role in the growth of the great, national enterprises.

Of course, the communications revolution did not stop with the telephone and the railroads. The development of steam and motor ships speeded up sea travel; the automobile gave the individual the freedom of unrestricted, rapid personal transport; and the airplane gradually achieved primacy in the long-haul market, shrinking travel time to a small fraction of what even the swiftest train could offer. The telephone became ubiquitous; the telegraph was supplanted by telex; and radio provided even ships, airplanes, and remote communities with the benefits of direct, real-time communication. The printing press was supplemented by radio and TV broadcasting, records, and video.

The combined effects of these developments were quite significant. Indeed, it became possible to run large, international organizations as very tight ships, with strong control exercised from a central headquarters, for many decades before the computer became emerged as a widespread and significant tool. Harold Geneen, for instance, did not need computers to keep his legendary, 20-year iron grip on ITT—jet planes, telephones, and mammoth management meetings were quite sufficient (Schoenberg 1985).

Today, cellular radio and satellite technology is severing the last physical and geographical bonds of technology-mediated communication, at last giving us the capacity to communicate freely without spatial restrictions. From early in the twenty-first century and on it will be possible to reach and talk to people almost anywhere in the world without even knowing where the person in question is—as long as he or she has a cellular or satellite telephone and has switched on the receiver to signal availability.

THE TECHNOLOGY-AUGMENTED PRECONDITIONS

We have already noted a number of significant improvements in our organizing capabilities brought about by major technological innovations over the last 5500 years, beginning with the invention of writing in old Mesopotamia. However, before we can move on to look at the organizational fallout, we need to determine the extent of the improvements in more precise terms.

Memory

After the invention of writing, the amount of information that can be stored is in principle unlimited. In addition, it does not deteriorate over time, unless the physical medium itself deteriorates. Medium deterioration is of course a problem, especially for works of art, but important information can always be renewed. Information in verbal (written) or numerical form can even be renewed without any degradation or loss of content. The stored information is therefore accurate in the sense that what we get out is by and large equal to what we put in. The reservation expressed by "by and large" does not pertain to symbols themselves—the words in a book printed a hundred years ago are exactly the same today, the book has not "forgotten" any of them—but to their interpretation, which may change over time, and even change so subtly that we are not aware of it. Normally, it is not a serious issue, however. Pictorial information, on the other hand, remains problematic—photographs, drawings, and paintings can be copied, but information is invariably lost in the process, and there is a definite limit to the acceptable number of generations.

Even if there are no theoretical limits to the amount of information we can store, there are practical limits since externalized information has bulk. What we have in our heads we can easily carry around; what we store in books is another matter. Even paper-based information requires space, and there is a definite limit to the amount of information you can keep handy. Microfilm shrinks the physical bulk of information tremendously, but because of updating problems and cost, it has been practical only for special purposes.

Then there is the problem of retrieval—externalized information can be retrieved only when we know where it is. For limited amounts of systematized (indexed) information, retrieval is unproblematic. It does not take long to locate a card in a card file kept in a desk drawer, for instance, and most accountants will retrieve a particular bill as long as you can inform them of the approximate date. For large amounts of information, and information that does not lend itself readily to indexation, the problems are considerable. Filing systems, library systems and punch card equipment represent our best pre-computer attempts to overcome this difficulty, but even in extremely well-run (non-computerized) libraries or archives, one can only search by authors, titles and a very limited number of keywords. The necessary indexing systems are also complicated and very laborious to establish and maintain. So, even if we can store massive amounts of information, we encounter the same problem as with our biological memory: We can only access a tiny fraction of it. The difference is that the constraint on access does not reside in an inscrutable biological mechanism, but in the prohibitively long time it takes to search through large amounts of paper-based information.

Punch card equipment offer significant improvements in certain instances. If you want a single card (information on a specific customer) you still have to look it up manually (it will take much longer to run all your cards through a reader to locate it). However, if you want to send a letter to the 14% of your customers who happen to own cars of a particular make, then the card readers can sort them out for you in a small fraction of the time you would need by manual means. You can also count and produce simple statistics fairly easily—that is what punch card equipment was invented to do. But these improvements contribute little to change the preconditions for organizing. The main contribution of files and archives, the possibility for implicit coordination, is not significantly augmented by punch card equipment.

Information Processing

As noted in Chapter 4, the working memory is not able to hold the many variables of a complex problem in an active state simultaneously—its capacity is very limited. By providing an external memory that can hold and display a much larger number of variables, writing helps us extend our working memory and has proved to be a formidable technology for tackling complex problems. Strictly speaking, our internal capacity for problem solving has of course not been increased. But writing lets us utilize that capacity much better by relieving us of the task of memorizing all the information relevant to a problem.

We use writing extensively for all kinds of mental work—whether we write or sketch on a blackboard, a pad of paper, or a computer screen. This is both true for individual and group work—groups frequently use blackboards, whiteboards, flip-overs and overhead projectors to provide a common, external working memory to aid their processing. For groups, it also helps synchronize the minds of the participants and foster a common understanding of the problem at hand. In larger projects the more formal decomposition of tasks, with its problem definitions and job descriptions, serves the same purpose. In addition to serving as an extended working memory during problem solving, storing ideas and intermediate results, writing also allows us to do "preprocessing" by collecting relevant material, systematizing it, and thus creating a platform for analysis and decision making. Elaborate problems can be broken down into smaller chunks and distributed over time as well as between members in an organization.

Our processing is also helped by the phenomenally large vocabularies of written languages, allowing for great precision in descriptions and arguments. Ong (1982) considers this difference between an oral-only language and a language with a literate tradition so fundamental that he gives the latter a separate name: he calls the language of a truly literate society a *grapholect*, to emphasize its dependence on writing both for its richness in words and its style of expression.[5]

In the modern world, problem solving and decision making are most often part of a group process. We have already noted the concept of the common extended memory for groups, and even more important is the

---

[5] Oral languages can consist of as little as 5000 words. A rich literary language such as English now has maybe as many as 1.5 million (Ong 1982). Comprehensive English dictionaries contain several hundred thousand words.

ability to copy memos and reports and thus distribute them to everyone in parallel instead of circulating hand-written originals. This makes group work a lot more efficient. The real revolution, however, is found in the way writing lets us distribute large tasks among a large number of persons, synchronize and coordinate their activities, and communicate intermediate results between them. The ability to collect, systematize, and store information that writing confers upon us, and the way it allows us to distribute and synthesize problem-solving efforts, has totally revolutionized our capabilities and has made it possible to organize massive undertakings.[6] A literate society can therefore routinely tackle tasks that would completely overwhelm any illiterate society.

For really important decision-making groups, far more expensive solutions than whiteboards and overhead projectors have been devised. The mission control centers for manned space expeditions, for instance, bristle with technology and support personnel. The same is the case with the so-called situation rooms for military high commands. These rooms are equipped to handle the real-time conduct of major wars, when the chiefs of staff must communicate almost constantly among themselves and with their units, and at the same time be able to receive and have displayed vital information about their own and enemy movements. A few large, private corporations, where the leaders deem themselves to be in the economic and market parallel to war (the slogan "marketing is war" is an indication of this sentiment), have invested in their own "situation rooms," where top management can receive high-tech, graphics-filled briefings.

The situation room is an obvious advantage when it is necessary to monitor and respond in real time to complicated events unfolding rapidly. Whether the situation room is actually of any use in a corporate top management environment, or whether it just serves to enhance the prestige of the users, is open to conjecture. The closest thing to real, functioning situation rooms in commercial organizations are probably the broker rooms in banks and brokerages dealing in currency, stocks, or raw materials, and the control rooms in industrial processing plants and power stations.

---

[6] An interesting example of a really massive, pre-computer project is the Allied invasion of Normandy in 1944. Participating in the operation were hundreds of ships, thousands of aircraft, and more than a million soldiers, in addition to a large number of tanks and artillery units. This enormous force needed not only to be equipped and readied in the ports of southern England; when the attack had started, it also had to be managed. The efforts of all the services and fighting units had to be coordinated in real time, and there was no room for time-outs to collect one's thoughts. In addition, the invasion force had to be supplied with food, fuel, and ordnance, over provisional bridgeheads, and with constantly changing front lines. Over just one of the bridgeheads (on Omaha Beach), 15 000 tons of supplies and 15 000 soldiers were brought ashore *per day* in the most hectic period.

A more cumbersome operation is problem solving or decision making aimed at expressing the collective views of very large numbers of people. The basic technique developed over millennia is the method of representation, whereby a small number of representatives are elected or appointed and are conferred the power of deciding on behalf of the electorate. For political purposes, the basis of this method was developed by the ancient Greeks, and has since only been refined and modified to suit much larger electorates—where a recourse to direct voting in the town square has not been a viable alternative.

In organizations, the organizational hierarchy itself is supposed to support this process, but it is seldom adequate to serve all the different purposes and views present in a large organization. Often, organized labor takes over parts of the function (also using the method of representation), and almost always we find informal leaders and mediators who perform simply because a number of people trust them and see them as voices for their concerns. Shareholder democracy is also a graft of the old political metaphor into the realm of organizations.

We noted above that the development of democracy in Europe and North America was closely related to the invention of printing, the spreading of mass literacy and the growth of the newspaper industry. Mass media both informed and homogenized, and they provided the public, common event space for a national identity, a national agenda, and national leaders. They are also the channel for the representatives' communication with their constituents. The development of sampled polling provides another strong feedback mechanism, and although most would agree with the truism that an opinion poll is not an election, we can see that politicians are getting increasingly sensitive to results of such surveys—thereby acknowledging the fact that they do indeed represent a very effective short-term feedback mechanism.

In large organizations, some of the same technologies are brought into service to create a corporate identity and a corporate event space. Even a technique such as polling has gained a solid foothold in the organizational world. It is presently used by a number of consultancy firms to assess organizational health and provide a basis for proposing remedies.

Our inability to handle more than one conscious thought process at a time has of course not been modified by technology. However, the art of writing makes it possible to extend time slicing considerably and thus get a much better hold on complex matters. When intermediate results are committed to paper, we can leave the subject, do something else for a while, and then return to pick up where we left. We can thus keep many more parallel processes going than a person in an oral culture can, and with much higher precision.

Whether or not our speed of deliberation has been improved is really a matter of definition. There is no doubt that both writing and modern communications technology (both physical transportation and telecommunications) have speeded up parts of the total process. Information can be collected much more quickly, reading allows for more efficient information absorption, and consultations are much easier when one has access to telephones and rapid personal transportation. The reaction time for large organizations has therefore been considerably reduced, with notable consequences for innovation rate, the average lifetime for products, and so on. Strictly defined, however, that is not part of the deliberation process; it is a consequence of better communications, improved information retrieval, and more powerful tools for analysis. Deliberation proper is a process that is internal to our mind, and, as such, it has so far not been noticeably affected by technology.

The Development of an Analytical, Literate Mind

By liberating the mind from the task of remembering a numbing load of existing information, writing also set the mind free to work on contemporary problems. Its use slowly spread from the economic sphere to the recording of religious material; to the accumulation of knowledge; the creation of more widespread, detailed, and lasting systems of law; and to immortalizing verbal art and historic accounts such as poems, songs, and plays. It therefore had a profound effects on the human mind and the way people thought about things, effects that were just as important as the more immediate economic and political consequences, and a vital precondition for the Industrial Revolution and the developments that followed. "More than any other single invention," says Ong (1982, p. 78), "writing has transformed human consciousness." It is, however, only quite recently that we have become conscious about the magnitude of the difference between the oral and the literate mind. This new awareness really started in the 1920s with Milman Parry's groundbreaking theories about Homer's epic poems the *Iliad* and the *Odyssey*, but more widespread understanding was only established by the works of Walter J. Ong (esp., 1982) and Eric Havelock (esp., 1986).

What characterizes the oral mindset? First of all, people in oral cultures are predominantly concrete in their thinking. They think in terms of physical objects, actions, and events. Interpretations of things are always tied to their context of events and actions. A striking illustration of this is provided by A. R. Luria (Ong 1982) in his studies of illiterate, literate, and partly literate people in Uzbekistan and Kirghizia in 1931–32. In one of his experiments, he showed his subjects drawings of geometrical objects, such as circles and rectangles. The illiterate peasants would invariably identify them as representations of objects they knew—plates, buckets, mirrors, doors—never as abstract categories. Students from the same communities (under training to become teachers), on the other hand, immediately identified them by their abstract classifications. Likewise, when asked to eliminate one of the four objects *hammer, saw, log, hatchet,* that did not belong in the group, the fully literate subjects would immediately eliminate the log (which did not belong to the abstract class *tools*), whereas the illiterates would protest, saying that all the objects belonged together. Both the hammer, the saw, and the hatchet belonged to the *situation of working with logs,* which was their frame of reference. Ong refers to a particular peasant, who, when pressed, eliminated the hatchet, because "it doesn't do as good a job as a saw" (p. 51). Asked to explain what a tree is, a respondent answered: "Why should I? Everyone knows what a tree is, they don't need me telling them." The abstract definition of a class of objects named "trees" was simply not part of his mindset.

To us, this concrete, contextual orientation seems backward and even childish—a patronizing view that is a product of our literate bias. That we compare oral people to children is not surprising, since young children are themselves oral people, living in a partly oral community with other children. The process of acquiring a capacity for abstract thinking and symbol manipulation, which we normally regard as part of the natural maturing process of the child and the young adult, in reality represents a forced, culturally determined transition from an oral to a literate mindset, a transition necessary to become a fully functional member of a modern society.

The action- and context-centered state of the oral mind is easier to understand if we consider the nature of the spoken word and the way it differs from the written word. The spoken word is an event—it happens when spoken and heard; immediately disappears and lingers on only as a fleeting trace in the memories of the people present. It is also a social event, since an exchange of words requires at least two people. Talking is action; it happens in a social context. To be remembered, the spoken word must be forceful; it must tie meaning to actions and events that are easy to remember. Rhyme and rhythm is often added. The bard in an oral society is not primarily an entertainer (although he is also that): he is even more a living memory bank, storing both the chronicles of important events *and* the social code of moral conduct, all embedded in the stories that make up his repertoire. His memory, however, is neither infallible nor incorruptible; he subtly edits his songs to suit the audience, especially people of power and riches. Oral memory is therefore unstable, and accounts of past events are often changed to suit the present.[7]

Because the volume of information that can be kept in memory and wilfully retrieved is limited, accumulation of knowledge in our sense of the term is not possible. An oral society will therefore be hesitant to pursue new information and will stick to tradition, to proven knowledge. Since knowledge and experience accumulate only in the living memories of the relatively few people who survive to an old age, oral societies normally also hold their old members in great respect: They become—like our libraries—repositories for society's accumulated knowledge. If they die before they have transferred their knowledge to others, *that knowledge is irretrievably lost.*

It is probably no coincidence, therefore, that old people love to tell the same stories again and again, and that small children are equally enthralled by the hundreth repetition of a favorite tale. It is not unreasonable to claim that these complementary characteristics of children and old people constitute an important evolutionary advantage for oral societies, and that natural selection has favored families with this trait.[8]

The written word, on the other hand, is an unchanging thing; it has an existence of its own, and reading and writing it is something one does in isolation—if not physically isolated, at least mentally so. It is normally not part of a collective experience. There is a literally a world of difference between 300 people gathered in the village fête grounds to hear a visiting bard relate the latest news of the king's exploits, and 300 students sitting in a large reading room, all of them absorbed by their own particular book.

By eliminating memory as the prime storage for information, writing also eliminated the need for oral mnemonics. The heroic personalities of oral narratives, the narrative itself; the bonding between pieces of

---

[7] The myths of the Yir Yoront also had some of this flexibility, although only in details, and Ong (1982) provides further examples of the flexibility of religious doctrines in oral societies. It is interesting to reflect upon this in view of how present-day religious conservatives get locked into the particular wording of the scriptures—as the Vatican in its view of contraceptives. Mainstream Protestants and other liberal Christians have solved this and similar problems by abandoning literal interpretation of the scriptures in favor of a symbolic approach. Christian fundamentalists, however, remain prisoners of the fixed scripture, and will appear increasingly archaic as the world changes and our knowledge grows, just as their counterparts in other religions with immutable holy books (such as Islam).

[8] In this connection, it is also interesting to note the speculations by deBeer, mentioned in Anderson (1990), on the reasons for the extraordinarily long time a human needs to reach adult stature—about 15 years, or around one-fifth of a normal life span; deBeer argues that the reason for the slow physical development of human offspring (lagging far behind that of the brain, which is almost complete at the age of 5) is the evolutionary advantage of prolonged dependency on the parents, guaranteeing that the children do not leave before they have had time to acquire all the knowledge necessary to become a competent adult.

information and descriptions of actions or concrete properties; the rhymes, the rhythm, and the reinforcing redundancies (*copia*) of oral accounts became superfluous in the written text. A written text is its own memory, it is always there for reference. It fosters linearity in presentation and argument, as well as precision and clarity. Distancing itself from the boisterous vigour of oral dialogues, the written discourse grew cool and analytic.

The surviving texts from the classic period in Greece provide an illustrative example of the transition from an oral to a literate state of mind. After the first spurts to record oral material, such as the *Iliad* and the *Odyssey*, the Greek mind slowly started to explore the new tool. Its expressions became less and less epic, more and more analytic. Language became separated from man, it acquired an independent existence, and Greek philosophers started to exploit and study the analytic and epistemological properties of the language itself. Even Socrates (470–399 BC) demonstrated an analytic approach that was clearly marked by a developing literacy (Havelock 1986), although his dialogues retained an oral unaffectedness right through Plato's writing.

It is noteworthy that Socrates did not write down his thoughts himself, even if he lived more than two hundred years after the invention of the Greek alphabet—we had to wait for Plato (427–347 BC) to write "the first extensive and coherent body of speculative thought in the history of mankind," to quote Havelock (1986, p. 111). Plato himself struggled with the transition. Despite his distinctly literate, analytical discourse, he laid out his text in the form of dialogues; he extolled the virtues of the dialogue as the supreme pedagogical instrument but banned the poets from his city-state in the *Republic*, because they appealed to the emotions alone and not to reason (Ong 1982, p. 80). Plato's pupil Aristotle (384–322 BC) brought the transition to its conclusion in his lucid, analytical prose and his foundations of formal logic.

After Aristotle, the literate program was firmly established: an analytic approach, a linear account, a concise prose, and a context-free language separated from its author and the collective listening experience. Free from the oral mind's constant load of memorization of precious private and collective information, the literate mind could allow itself to collect new knowledge, to compare new with old, and to speculate about new theories. With an infallible, extended working memory, it could tackle much more complex problems than the oral mind, present them for large audiences, and preserve them for posterity.

A truly literate society therefore tends to be much more oriented toward new things than toward tradition, and is much more prone to invent and develop. It takes fewer things for granted, and has great confidence in its abilities to understand, change and improve.

Communication

The area of communication has been one of far-reaching innovations in most aspects. If we look at physical transportation, *travel time* (and cost) has shrunk enormously, especially in the last 150 years. Paleolithic man could travel at most a few tens of kilometers per day and normally did not stray outside an area he could traverse in a few days. Today, it will not take more than 48 hours to go from almost any major city in the world to almost any other. Travel between capitals seldom requires more than 24 hours. From Oslo, I can go to New York, have a meeting, see the town, and get back in less time than it would have taken my grandfather to make a return trip to Bergen on Norway's west coast, and his grandfather again to go one-way from Oslo to Lillehammer—the venue of the 1994 Winter Olympics, some 180 kilometers to the north.

The increase in speed for the transportation of goods is just as great if one is willing to pay the price. Books, machine parts, flowers and fresh fish is speeded around the globe in airplanes, and a salmon can be served in a Tokyo gourmet restaurant as little as 48 hours after it is snatched from its enclosure off the coast in the south, west, or north of Norway.[9] But even for less perishable and costly goods, intercontinental transport takes a matter of weeks, or maybe a month or two at the most. Mail services are universal, and even if the distribution speed varies from country to country, two places in the world are seldom more than two weeks apart. Courier services offer considerably faster delivery. These improvements in transportation make global trade and global organizations eminently feasible, especially when paired with the advances that have been made in the communication of information.

For the developments in global transportation pale when compared to the strides taken by the communication of information. Our *range* of communication has been extended to interplanetary proportions, and the *speed* to the speed of light. For most practical, earth-bound applications, we talk about instant, real-time communication regardless of distance. This holds both for one-to-one (telephone) and one-to-many communication (radio and television broadcasting). In addition to the electric and electronic media, mass distribution of books, newspapers, and magazines has made possible a *massive exchange* of information. *Return channels* such as sampled opinion polls and "letters to the editor" make leaders aware of prevailing opinion, and even make people aware of what other people think—in itself a very important precondition for opinion formation.

---

[9] Such rapid transit (with its concomitant high transport costs) is not the usual—most of the salmon requires three to five days to reach its destination. Only the most experienced experts will note the very slight difference, as salmon packed in ice keeps very well.

For organizational purposes, the telephone became of great importance, and numerous effects have been noted (Pool 1983). One of the first of major importance was the support of a physical separation of plant and office. Until then, it had been common to house the office in a building adjacent to the plant itself, to ensure sufficient communication between administration and production. The telephone allowed the office functions not immediately connected to production to move to the central part of the cities, closer to customers and finance institutions.

By making the physical separation of different parts of the enterprise more feasible, the telephone in fact supported centralization of decision-making while allowing physical dispersal of organization units. The control provided by the telephone convinced managers that they could locate major business units far away from the main office, and put greater emphasis on proximity to major markets or sources of workers, energy, or raw material.

The telephone also had great effect on the speed of many types of transactions, from banking to the ordering of goods—especially perishable goods. Pool cites a 1906 article in *Scientific American* on "The Sociological Effects of the Telephone," describing how oyster barge men were put out of business because restaurateurs could phone their orders directly to the oyster planters. "In general," Pool notes, "the greatest business use of the telephone has been in finance, commerce and where complex logistical coordination is required." Even the railroads, after much hesitation, converted from the telegraph to the telephone for train operation. As Pool goes on to say (1983, p. 68),

> It permits coordination of pieces of that complex clockwork which is the economic system. It is used millions of times a day to control production, shipping, recording, and selling. It permits the operation of a complex division of labor. All of that was recognized from early on.

With the new transportation infrastructure for information, goods, and people in place, it suddenly became feasible to build efficient distribution networks, to trade reliably over great distances, and to exert a degree of control over branches and subsidiaries in remote locations that had been impossible up until then. In retrospect, it is evident that the telegraph and later the telephone went a long way toward easing the constraints on organizations spanning great distances, and the improved physical transport offered by the railroads took care of much of what was left.

Among the predictions recorded by Pool, some are more notable than others. One prediction in particular should have a familiar ring for proponents of electronic mail and video conferencing: that the telephone would reduce travel. This was attributed both to the use of normal telephone calls and to telephone conferencing, which was easy to set up in the first decades of telephone service because of the flexibility of the manual operators. Then, as now, it was difficult to discern any reduction in travel as a result of the improved telecommunications, but it is of course impossible to say what the volume of travel would have been without them. After a long period when mechanical exchanges made telephone conferences all but impossible, they become a viable service again in the last decades of the twentieth century, when computer-based switches were introduced. The jury on travel reduction is still out.

The telephone has obviously made group work easier, has probably made a number of meetings unnecessary, and has made it more feasible to organize work groups without co-locating the members. Experience tells us, however, that it cannot fully replace face-to-face meetings. The telephone is very useful for questions, informal discussion, and general conversation between two persons, but most people experience telephone meetings as awkward and rate them as clearly inferior to "real" meetings. Reports about regular use of telephone conferencing almost invariably involve small, close-knit groups of people who have been working together for a long time and know each other well. The most common exceptions are training and sales conferences, which more have the character of broadcasting (Johansen 1988).

The videophone, or "picturephone" as it was originally called, was envisioned as the next step in telephony, and it has prematurely been predicted at regular intervals. It was also expected to reduce travel significantly. Pool quotes a 1914 article in *Scientific American* in which it was argued that something soon had to be done to check the congestion of the city, and that the fundamental difficulty seemed to be the necessity for close proximity when transacting business. The telephone and the picturephone were expected to change that. Since the late 1960s, conference television has been an available instrument in a number of countries, but it has met with limited enthusiasm. The main reason may be the high cost or poor quality involved so far (generally, you have had to choose one or the other), but people also feel that it is "artificial" (Johansen 1988). Even here, the most successful use has been in training and sales, where the broadcasting aspect is strong.

The telephone even eliminated jobs—most notably, the position as messenger boy. This was far from inconsequential: there were considerable numbers of messenger boys employed in every large city, giving many a poor family a welcome extra income. The advent of the telephone left them bereft of their jobs, but, on the brighter side, it therefore allowed them to stay in school.

It is irresistible to end this discussion of the telephone with another quotation related by Pool, showing how established mental sets can prevent an otherwise knowledgeable person from perceiving and understanding the portents of a new technology: in 1879 (three years after its invention) Sir William Preece, then the chief engineer of the British Post Office, told a special committee of the House of Commons that the telephone had little future in Britain, even if it seemed to be a success in the United States (Pool 1983, p. 65):

> There are conditions in America which necessitate the use of such instruments more than here. Here we have a superabundance of messengers ... The absence of servants has compelled Americans to adopt communication systems.

The Iron Constraint on Information Exchange

Unfortunately, the revolutions brought about by the externalization of memory and the development of communication technology has not had any parallel when it comes to our personal interfaces with the real world: our basic capabilities for information *input* and *output* have not been changed much by technology. Yes, we can now instantly connect to and talk with a person sitting halfway around the globe, but our information exchange can still not exceed 250 words per minute—in fact, because of the slight deterioration that always follows transmissions through the telephone, we cannot even talk as fast as when sitting in the same room. True, we may now watch events taking place on other continents on TV in full color and in real time, but we cannot absorb the televised information any faster than information reaching the eye directly.

The invention of writing helped somewhat, because we can read a little faster than we speak (and thereby listen). Written material is also more generally accessible (it is physically separated from the originator) and thereby allows us to devote more hours per day to information intake. The typewriter has likewise made writing a little faster (and the result generally more legible), but the increase in speed has not been dramatic and has not made any real difference for our organizing abilities. The slow speed at which we can absorb and output information continues to be a source of frustration, and it remains an iron-clad constraint on our organizing abilities.

Much energy has been expended through the centuries trying to alleviate this shortcoming, and we are still striving to cope: from the perspiring student poring over his books the last weeks before the exam to the distressed CEO spending even Saturday and Sunday reading reports, memos, and magazines, desperately trying to catch up with the information constantly pouring in. No breakthrough has yet been achieved, and the measures we employ are still the tried and tested ones.

The first main remedy is **selection**—ferreting out the most relevant pieces of information. It is typically a demand placed by managers on their subordinates. Many top-level managers set a limit of one or two pages on memos, contending that what cannot be presented on one page is not worth knowing. Selection is also standard procedure in the news media. The problem with selection is that, to obtain a good result, the selector(s) must know exactly what is relevant for their masters/customers, which they of course do not do—at least not fully. Managers are normally aware of this, and seek out alternative information sources as well. Nevertheless, we all have to depend on others doing selections for us, and we never know in which way they are biased—and, too frequently, we are not concerned. Only professional investigators and researchers routinely question the reliability and completeness of the information they receive.

The next countermeasure against information overload is **concentration**—presenting the information in as compact a form as possible. The copywriters in large newspapers are infamous for this—reducing the lavish prose of a proud journalist to a few close-cropped sentences. Television news and advertising are also arenas for extreme compactness.

Concentration is not only achieved through expert editing and economy in words, however. Numbers are more readable if presented in a systematic layout such as a table, and the information they contain is even more accessible if presented as graphics. The brain's capacity for pattern recognition and visual processing is massive, and any information that can be presented in pictorial form will be grasped much quicker than the corresponding numbers. We must still conclude, however, that our capacity for absorbing information has not been dramatically enhanced in general, and is lagging far behind the huge increase in our storage and communication abilities.

When it comes to information dissemination, the picture is mixed. In face-to-face communication, our capacity has not increased. If we extend the concept to letters, typewriters (and later, word processing computers) have marginally increased our rate of output, but it is nothing to brag about. Our capacity has increased beyond all measure, however, when it comes to one-to-many communication. The printing press, radio, television, records and tape of various kinds have totally revolutionized the human capacity for addressing others. Of course, it is an intrinsic property of the concept of mass media that channels are not open to everyone—but in principle (at least in an open society) they are open to *anyone*. The powerful nature of the mass media's communication capacity is reflected in the exertions made by totalitarian regimes to control them, and in political parties' efforts to use them.

For organizations, the new media mainly allow for easier communication from organization leaders to their subordinates and for more efficient information distribution to customers or other organizations in the environment. Even fairly small organizations have their internal circulars, and larger organizations often have elaborate internal newspapers or magazines. Mailing lists are kept for many purposes, and almost all commercial (and many public) organizations advertise. Indeed, mass media advertising is one of the prerequisites for the formation of large companies building their business on national or international brand names. By dramatically enhancing our capacity for one-to-many communication, mass media technology has also significantly enhanced our possibilities for organizing and sustaining large organizations.

Serial Mind, Parallel Action

While our minds remain serial, and refuse us to divide attention, we have for some purposes overcome our limited ability to do things in parallel: We have built automatic machines. An automatic machine mimics the work of humans—either directly, as with mechanical arms gripping objects and moving them from one place to another, or indirectly, as when car bodies are painted by electrophoresis as they move through large chemical baths.

Automation has to a certain extent made it possible for us to transcend both our innate problems of coordination and of attending to more than one task at a time. Pure mechanical automation, which started in earnest in the middle of the eighteenth century, has made great strides, and quite complex products can be manufactured with a minimum of human intervention. Through the programming laid down in the mechanical design of machines and tools, a variety of tasks can be carried out in perfect coordination, and with a good number of parallel sessions per human operator. In addition to greater speed and precision, an automated system wastes no time making decisions—the decisions have been made once and for all through its design.

Automation, then, can be viewed essentially as canned action, as the enactment of previous design. The machine is, so to speak, a set of crystallized decisions, the result of an extensive information-processing undertaking, ending with a carefully choreographed set of movements and work operations. It represents a total externalization of a plan for a specific production process. Once forged in steel and powered by steam or electricity, the automatic machine can repeat its designed actions again and again. And once designed, it can also easily be replicated, and our canned actions can finally be carried out in parallel by a large number of similar machines.

This is quite different from using power to increase our physical might, as we do, for instance, with bulldozers. A bulldozer allows a single individual to move hundreds of times more soil than he or she could with a shovel only, and thus increase his or hers productivity hundredfold. In principle, however, it is no more than a power shovel. The automatic machine, on the other hand, replicates on its own certain productive aspects of the human organism. We cannot really say that such a machine is processing information, since all it does is to repeat a sequence of movements. But, just as much of the human work in an organization, those machine movements are carefully planned and designed.

Even pure, "old-fashioned" mechanical automation is thus a powerful expression of collective information processing, and it can be viewed as a part of the organization—just as humans are. This aspect of automation becomes even more evident when we cross the threshold into the world of information processing, which opens up new areas for automation. Before the advent of computers, for instance, there was scant automation in the realm of administrative work. The most advanced examples were mechanical calculators, bookkeeping machines, and punch card equipment.

By harnessing external sources of physical power and multiplying our physical operations, automation has become the main basis for our phenomenal growth in material wealth. It has made it possible for us to produce goods in volumes that are many orders of magnitude greater than before. At the same time, however, it has forced standardization. For even if automation of physical operations is very efficient, mechanical automation also results in a rather inflexible production apparatus. Machines all have their very definite purposes and ways of operating, and their repertoire can normally only be changed by physical modification. It takes considerable time and effort to externalize decisions in the form of a machine. Mechanical automation is thus conducive to mass production of standardized products, but generally extremely sluggish in its response to changes in consumer preferences.

Emotions

Can technology "augment" emotions? It may seem preposterous to ask such a question, but we must consider the evidence. Control of raw emotions has always been of great importance in human societies, and it still is. We should therefore expect efforts to improve it by tool development. As Wilson notes (1988), even a hunter/gatherer society such as the bushmen of the !Kung San "dread the prospect of tempers flaring out of control," and place much emphasis on the control and management of emotions. This is also the case for the Innuit Eskimos. In general, it seems that societies in which people are forced to live very close to each other develop strong norms demanding tight control of emotions and encourage mental training and the development of techniques for this purpose. Both China and Japan are famous for this, and India is the home of yoga and other mental techniques.

In industrialized societies, handling of emotional problems and aberrations has typically enough been professionalized and has become the subject of scientific research (psychology and psychiatry). And, as wizards of the material world, we have not been content with techniques and "empty talk." The development of psychopharmaca has proceeded from the narcotic herbs of tribal society to a broad array of modern medications. Even if we are not counting the more exotic (and even illegal) drugs, both sedatives and stimulants are routinely used by a large number of people every day. Hochschild (1983, p. 54) even reports that nurses in the medical department of AT&T "gave out Valium, Darvon, codeine, and other drugs free and without prescription" to help employees cope with stress and boredom on the job.

If we follow Morris (1967), we may also include much literature, photographs, and movies/TV as emotion-controlling technology. Morris notes that our innate interest in sexual activities outside the pair-bond is strong but socially denounced, and that the solution is sex by proxy, from the innocent romantic to the hard-core pornographic. A similar case may be made for our bent toward adventure and heroism, especially when young—it feeds the movie industry like nothing else. The movies and the corresponding books may provide a much-needed cathartic effect for postmodern youth trapped in a society where the challenges of life are increasingly abstract, and where physical excitement and adventure is channeled into sports that are themselves ever more regulated and loaded with safety precautions.

Our basic emotions and desires have not changed, then, but we have learned to *control* them to a certain degree both through mental techniques, the use of social norms, projection (the use of proxies through literature, pictures, or movies) and (in some instances) medication. The basic techniques of self-control and the instrument of social norms are nevertheless very ancient indeed, and it is doubtful whether (for the purpose of organization) the differences between modern man and his Paleolithic ancestors are really significant in this respect. Our emotions are still among the major sources of organizational conflicts, disturbances, and failures.

CONCLUSIONS

The discussion in this chapter has shown how our technological achievements from the advent of literacy and up until the invention of the electronic, digital computer has greatly improved our potential for organization.

We may point to three periods in particular: the slow development of literacy in the great Eastern and Western civilizations in the long period from about 3500 to 600 BC, the development of modern numerals and mathematics from about AD 900 to 1600, and the development of automation, physical transport, the telegraph, and the telephone from about 1800 to 1945. We can safely conclude that this pre-computer technology vastly improved our storage and communication capabilities, and provided a solid augmentation of our basic problem-solving and

Memory	Unlimited amounts of information can be stored outside the brain for indefinite periods without loss of content. *Main constraints: Large amounts of information require considerable physical storage space, retrieval becomes problematic when volume increases.*
Processing	Greatly improved by better preprocessing and storage of intermediate results. Far better monitoring of complex events. Much better possibilities for distributing tasks over time and between many persons, as well as for coordination and cooperation over distance. A literate mindset that is more analytical and more interested in change and improvement. Vastly improved capacity for parallel actions through unlimited replication of "canned" processes with mechanical automation. *Main constraints: Externalization of information processing still not possible. Processing capacity per se not significantly increased.*
Communication	Physical transport revolutionized, communication of information doubly so—information can be transmitted instantly regardless of distance. Mass media allow information dissemination on a massive scale. For individual information absorption and dissemination, however, there are only minute improvements in speed, although accessibility is greatly improved. *Main constraints: High cost of large volume point-to-point electronic communication and low social "bandwidth" of the affordable channels, the iron constraints of our own input/output limitations.*
Emotions	Some improvements in control.

Table 6-1:   *Main technology-based changes in preconditions.*

decision-making abilities—especially when it came to groups and large undertakings. However, its effect on our "processing" was almost totally indirect—it supported problem-solving and decision making only by storing, arranging, presenting, and communicating information, and could not augment our processing capacity directly. The key points are summarized in Table 6-1.

These were the main, technologically based changes in the preconditions for organizing that allowed the great changes in organizational appearance and functioning that took place in the nineteenth and twentieth centuries.

7
The Modern Organization

"Everywhere in the world the industrial regime tends to make the unorganized or unorganizable individual, the pauper, into the victim of a kind of human sacrifice offered to the gods of civilization."

Jacques Maritain, *Reflections on America,* 1958.

INTO THE MODERN AGE

It took a long time to discover and exploit the new organizational possibilities opened up by the evolving technology. The state continued to be the chief domain for organization on a significant level, and the feudal structure remained the main organization type. Religious hierarchies were also modeled on the feudal state, with divinely sanctioned offices corresponding to the nobility's secular positions based on lineage and inherited rights to land. The administrative technologies provided by literacy were only used to support already existing organization practices. Literacy was limited to a very small part of society—the ruling elites, a number of their servants, the religious establishment, and a few others— and so the information economy of the feudal structure was still necessary to manage large states and large religious or military organizations. Economic organization remained small-scale, mostly of the Simple Structure type—either with one owner/manager, or with a small number of partners dividing the managing role between them. (A partnership may also be viewed as the commercial variant of the Councilcracy.) The structure provided by family ties was almost always there as the dominant pillar.

This situation lasted for a long period of time—more than 2000 years, if we count the time from the more widespread development of literacy in the Mediterranean until the start of the Industrial Revolution in England. There were of course important developments taking place in that interval, but by and large they were all variations and refinements within the scope of the organizational forms discussed in Chapter 5. Not even the considerable growth in literacy that followed the development of printing in Europe and the United States from the sixteenth century onward produced any significant developments in organization—with the possible exception of the slow but steady growth of representative democracy in England. The revolutionary changes in the preconditions for organizing that were provided by the invention of writing were simply not exploited. This fact can serve to remind us that new capabilities do not force development in themselves—they remain potentials until they are actually discovered and explored.

The best explanation we can provide for this failure to take advantage of available administrative technology is that the material needs for large organizations besides the state, the armed forces, and the Church were simply not there. The vast majority of people all over the world still worked the land, the traditional organizational structures were quite adequate, and the preeminence of the land-holding nobility in the body politic of the feudal states was in harmony with this state of affairs. The craft-based production of material goods still did not achieve a volume where production needed more organization than the direct supervision provided by a master or a "foreman." The same was the case with trade—as long as transportation was slow and fairly expensive, volume was low and could easily be handled by the traditional merchant and his few assistants. Chandler (1977) describes how this was the case in the United States right up to the 1840s. Even in Europe, where both the scientific revolution and industrialization started, there was little innovation in organization before the middle of the nineteenth century.

But, as we now know, a revolution was brewing in Europe and the United States, where a long and slow accumulation of knowledge and development of new tools now accelerated. The application of external power (especially steam) and the construction of machines for manufacturing boosted the output of the growing factories, whereas the advent of trains, swift sailing vessels, and later steam ships provided cheap, rapid transport. These developments cleared the field for business ventures many orders of magnitude larger than before.

The new opportunities, however, could not be realized through the traditional, small-scale business organization. Building commercial organizations capable of handling much larger numbers of people and spanning much greater distances than before thus became one of the major challenges of the new entrepreneurs.

The Growth of Complexity

The Starting Point

Prior to the Industrial Revolution, work tended to be holistic in character—one person usually carried out a complete set of tasks. This does not mean that there was no specialization at all—even hunter/gatherer societies show some rudimentary differentiation of roles, and medieval society displayed a rich set of specialized occupations, notably in the crafts. Even so, work was usually quite varied. A craftsman, for instance, would do almost all the work on an object, from obtaining raw materials to the finishing touches and even the delivery to the customer. Apprentices and journeymen would often take care of the more tedious chores, but the craftsman was always in control of what happened—coordination took place by means of informal communication and mutual adjustment, intuitively and without significant formalized structure.

Farmers likewise carried out all the different tasks associated with their position, and merchants would usually have a very personal relationship not only with their customers and suppliers, but also with the different work processes required. They might hire laborers to handle the goods, and clerks to do various administrative work, but there was not any great degree of specialization. By and large, business was a family affair or a partnership—where the partners worked largely in parallel with similar tasks, rather than dividing work according to functional specialization (Chandler 1977). You may well say that this is the spontaneously natural way to work for a human—it has dominated all the way from hunter/gatherer society up until the spread of industrialization.

If there was a hierarchy in the business, it would typically be of the *task-continuous* type (Clegg 1990), in which a person at a certain level would master all the activities of lower levels. The owner, mastering all the tasks in the business himself, would usually be very competent to coordinate all the activities.

The importance attached to such mastery is illustrated by the fact that it was usually considered obligatory for the owner's heirs to work in subordinate positions for many years, with all the different tasks, before being considered ready to take part in the direction of the business.

Scaling Efforts

The first steps toward industrial production and modern organizational forms consisted of a more intensive exploitation of traditional approaches. Entrepreneurial artisans increased the number of apprentices and journeymen in their shops; in some trades, such as building and shipbuilding, masters increasingly took on total contracts and then put together teams of the necessary craftsmen to complete the job. But even this extended approach was kept within the Simple Structure model—the workforce or team was usually not larger than the number of people the entrepreneur himself could oversee.

Another approach to expanding the production of goods was the "putting out" method, whereby a master or a merchant contracted out work to households or independent craftsmen. This method of production was extensively used in Europe, and one merchant could have more than a hundred such contractors working for him. None of these practices were new, however—according to Goody (1986), they were already routine in Assyria more than 3500 years earlier—in 1900 BC!

People working under the putting-out system had considerable freedom in their daily life; they could to a large extent decide their own working hours. To illustrate this, Chandler quotes the historian Blanche Hazard (Chandler 1977, p. 54):

> The domestic worker had enjoyed all the latitude that he needed or wished. He sowed his fields and cut his hay when he was ready. He locked up his ten footer[1] and went fishing when he pleased, or sat in his kitchen reading when it was too cold to work in his little shop.

Descriptions such as this make us reflect on what we have lost through industrialization—and it is no wonder that the first factories had great trouble getting skilled persons to show up regularly for work every day. They still tended to go fishing or swimming when the weather was good, and to be absent the day after a particularly intense celebration. Such privileges are not easily surrendered, and we may ask if not some of them are now in the process of being restored under the banner of teleworking.

In the struggle to find suitable new ways of working, old practices were stretched in yet another way, even as the trend toward specialization and factory organization was becoming more pronounced. Building on traditions from craft shops and contracting, *internal contracting* became a fairly widespread way of organizing production—especially where specialization was not too extensive (Chandler 1977, Clegg 1990). In this type of arrangement, the factory owner negotiates a contract with a number of subcontractors specifying the quantity of goods to be delivered over a certain time period, usually a year. The factory owner would typically provide floor space, tools, raw materials, and so on, and pay the subcontractor a lump sum, possibly with the addition of a minimum

---

[1] A common term for the small workshops such workers usually put up as annexes to their homes. A length of about ten feet was the usual size of these shops.

foreman wage. The subcontractor would then hire his own people to do the work, pay their wages from his own contract money, and supervise their work himself.

Another form of internal contracting developed later as a result of the merger waves in the last half of the nineteenth century (Chandler 1977, Clegg 1990). The new amalgamated companies were too large to be managed by traditional means, and administrative techniques for large-scale, task-discontinuous organizations were still not fully developed. The former owners were therefore often asked to continue, but now as internal contractors, with lump-sum payments for providing agreed volumes of their goods or services within the larger whole. As Clegg says, such arrangements to a large degree reconstituted the task-continuous style of management in pockets within the larger companies.

Internal contracting had the same advantages in information economy as the feudal structure: It effectively encapsulated the production process within the work group or the acquired firm and relieved the top management from worrying about the details of the daily work process. They only had to manage their contractual interface to the subcontractors. These advantages have helped such arrangements to survive to the present day—even in advanced industries in the leading countries of the world. For instance, you will find that Japanese car factories are surrounded by entire districts composed of small, family-owned workshops (Clegg 1990), barely surviving in a harsh contracting system that can be viewed as a combination of internal contracting and putting-out.

The growing intensity in the use of practices such as contracting and putting-out that marked the immediate preindustrial period in Europe and the United States can definitely be interpreted as a sign of stress on the old order. Technological progress was accelerating, and the craftsmen and businessmen of the day were feverishly trying to accommodate the changes by scaling up their traditional work processes and organizations.

However, their traditional organizational practices could not be scaled up to exploit the fine-grained specialization that was now developing, with its accompanying needs for rigorous planning and detailed control of activities. In the internal contracting system, coordination between the subcontractors was mostly handled on an informal basis, and it was often less than optimal. Top managers had little information about real costs and waste in production, for instance. A closer coordination of the entire production process and more direct supervision and control of costs and quality was difficult to achieve with the traditional approaches, and the concept of centralized planning and total coordination of production gained ground. Even among traders and transporters, the increasing volumes of goods and raw materials required new approaches.

The Birth of the Machine Organization

The New Needs

As we have already noted, the most pronounced features of industrialization were the use of increasingly sophisticated fabricating machinery and the mechanization of transportation, both accompanied by growing functional specialization. In their turn, these developments invited factory production on an ever larger scale. To coordinate the efforts of large numbers of specialized workers, new work practices and organizations were needed.

There were probably two main reasons for the development of functional specialization: one was the growing pressure toward increased productivity, the other the scarcity of skilled workers (craftsmen). The limited availability of craftsmen and the several years needed for training one represented a serious bottleneck for industrial growth. Extensive specialization thus became a prerequisite for the rapid growth the industrialists pursued: it allowed them to hire unskilled laborers and train them only in their particular narrow tasks—a process requiring maybe only days or a few weeks at the most. In addition, such workers were much easier to control and command than the traditionally quite independent-minded craftsmen.

The decisive advantage of specialization, however, was its impact on productivity and the way it supported mechanization. It was specialization and mechanization together that brought us the productivity revolution of the nineteenth century. The roots of specialization are certainly older and can be found in early attempts to organize craft production in larger units, as in the tenth century English textile "industry" mentioned by Mintzberg (1979). However, until the advent of the mechanized factory, it played no important role.

One of the first descriptions of thorough specialization was Adam Smith's famous example of the trade of the pin maker, presented in *The Wealth of Nations* (published in 1776), where he identified 18 different operations involved in making pins. He also observed that this specialization resulted in a productivity far superior to that of a traditional, holistic approach. Although the pin-making process primarily represented an elaboration of the craft approach, it clearly pointed toward a new era. It was not until the nineteenth century, however, that functional specialization became widespread, was supported by mechanization, and ushered in a new type of organization.

In the United States, extensive specialization was first implemented in the manufacture of small arms early in the nineteenth century, coinciding with an advancement in the precision in manufacturing to the point where parts became interchangeable, allowing products to be assembled without the extensive adjustments of the preindustrial and early industrial era. Eli Whitney, the inventor of the cotton gin, was the first (in 1801) to demonstrate publicly the assembly of guns from piles of standard parts (Morgan 1986); the American Springfield Armory is generally reckoned to be the first factory to achieve such production on a large scale (Chandler 1977). In Britain there was evidence of specialization in the organization of Boulton and Watt (the steam engine manufacturers) as early as 1830 (Hollway 1991).

Specialization subsequently spread to other industries, but the development did not really accelerate until after 1850, developing into what was known through the latter part of that century as "the American System of Manufactures" (Pine 1993). This approach to work organization requires much more emphasis on coordination and control than the craft shop approach and its derivatives. As Koolhaas remarks (1982), it entails splitting all the problems of design and production—an integral part of the craftsman's work—away from the worker. Those tasks must now be carried out by specialists on design and planning, and the workers are only required to carry out their ordained tasks, which become more and more specialized and narrow as mechanization and automation progress. This process was accelerated when industry made the transition to the second generation of mass producing systems, pioneered by Henry Ford.

The responsibility for coordination is now removed from the workers and shared between the central planners and the plant supervisors. To ensure that the throughput at each step in the production process matches the total process, and that the quality of each worker's output satisfies the standards required for the assembly of parts into working products, stringent measures for quality and production volume become necessary. Specialization in production therefore also calls for a much more sophisticated approach to information processing and communication and, consequently, to organization. It cannot be fully realized within the framework of a Simple Structure, and it is also easy to see that it is impossible (above a very modest scale) without writing. Indeed, the analysis of the 18 operations of pin production presented by Adam Smith is a typical example of the literate mind at work—you would not find this kind of analysis in an oral society.

Clegg (1990) is talking about the same processes when he points out that the growth of large organizations with extensive functional specialization constituted a decisive break with the task-continuous organization. It was no longer possible for any one person to master all the specialized tasks in the organization, and the direction and supervision of activities on lower levels had to be indirect and based more on formal standards—also dependent on writing.

Even if writing provided the necessary tool for handling large amounts of information and building complex organizations, however, literacy had to be widespread to be really practical for large-scale administrative purposes. That was exactly what happened in the eighteenth and nineteenth centuries, which saw the development of mass literacy and an unprecedented spread of knowledge through printed books and newspapers. In addition, the new communication technologies—the rapid physical transport, the telegraph, and the telephone—made it possible to build not only complex and large organizations, but organizations that spanned great geographical distances.

Within a short period of time, then, many of the traditional constraints of human physiology were considerably amended by new tools. The simultaneous changes in the preconditions for production and organization combined to open vast new territories for human industriousness and ingenuity, and development finally surged ahead. It changed forever not only the commercial sector of society but also the political one, at least in Europe—the fast-growing European bourgeoisie did not in the long run accept the political monopoly held by the king and the land-owning nobles.

The Transition to a New Organizational Form

Nowhere did the new developments take stronger hold than in the United States. This is reflected in the rapid growth of the mass-producing American industry and in the fact that both the most influential theoretician of functional specialization and the man who applied it most successfully were Americans.

The man who developed this line of thought to its natural conclusion was Frederick W. Taylor, and the man with the greatest practical success was Henry Ford—who, after the introduction of the moving assembly line, managed to manufacture cars at close to half the cost of his nearest competitor, all while paying his workers the highest wages in the industry *and* getting immensely rich himself (Chandler 1977). When he introduced the assembly line in his Highland Park plant, the amount of labor expended to make a car dropped from 12 hours, 8 minutes to 2 hours, 35 minutes. Six months later it was down to 1 hour, 33 minutes. This breakthrough inaugurated the transit from the first generation of mass production systems, such as the American System of Manufactures, to the second—the Fordist systems (Pine 1993). The first-generation systems still incorporated a lot of the qualities of craft production, and primarily achieved higher productivity by moderate specialization backed by tools that augmented the workers' efforts. They thereby retained much of the flexibility of craft production and could turn out quite varied products with small retooling costs. The second-generation systems developed specialization further, increased the dependence on machines, and introduced automation to a much greater degree. Productivity increased dramatically, but flexibility was correspondingly reduced and the cost of retooling for new products increased.

As both corporations and public institutions grew to staggering new dimensions, the necessary administrative workload also grew, and the sheer volume of it became much more than one or a few individuals working in a fairly unstructured manner could handle. According to Chandler (1977), the need for extensive administrations first arose in the rapidly expanding railroad companies, where the administrative tasks grew with each new line, each new car, and each new locomotive.

The men who faced the challenge of establishing the first major, private administrative apparatuses had few models to learn from. Their major source of inspiration must have been the fantastically successful new methods for material production—whether it was in mass production of industrial goods or in the large construction works of the time. These new leaders were all civil engineers, and there is reason to believe that they (as most people will do) tackled the new problems with methods from their existing repertory, rather than from, for instance, the military model (Chandler 1977). There is no doubt, however, that at least some of them were acquainted with military organization, since the military academy educated some of the best civil engineers. Morgan (1986) thinks the military did indeed provide an important model for organization; he gives special mention to Frederick the Great's reorganization of the Prussian army in the middle of the eighteenth century—which preceded the great railroad and manufacturing companies by about 100 years. But Frederick the Great and the first large-scale industrialists may have had a common source of inspiration: Frederick the Great was especially fascinated by automatons and mechanical toys, and through elaborate drills, increased specialization of tasks, and standardization of weapons and uniforms, he wanted to shape his soldiers into the human equivalents of mechanical toy men (Morgan 1986). Behavior and equipment should be standardized to allow easy replacement and interchangeability in war, and the men should learn to fear their officers more than the enemy. As an eigtheenth century Danish-Norwegian regulation for officers stipulated for the attack: "In the rear follows the non-commissioned officer, with drawn sabre, driving his men forward with blows and harsh words."

But even if Frederick the Great increased specialization in his army, a military force at that time did not have very extensive specialization. Planning capacity was also limited and information economy was still very important. We should not be confused by the fact that there were great numbers of soldiers, or that the hierarchy of command was very elaborate, because when they battled, they all did more or less the same in parallel. Rather than being a model of the emerging industrial corporation, the military still built on feudal roots and was in many ways more like a massive replica of the preindustrial artisan shops.

The enormous success of the mass-producing factory and of engineering must have provided both a more immediate and a more powerful model for the organization of all kinds of activities than military organization. Taylor himself believed that his principles were equally valid for clerical work, and he was not the only one. Henry Ford, for instance, also believed in the general applicability of the principles of mass manufacturing. It was no wonder, then, that the functionally specialized, procedural work model was adapted even for routine administrative work and clerical production from the very beginning. The trend toward imitation of the factory grew through the 1920s and 1930s, as new office buildings were constructed with the explicit purpose of facilitating the flow of paper among office workers, who were no longer given separate offices, but housed in factory-like halls (Sundstrom 1986). Some offices even used conveyor belts to carry papers from one operation to the next!

At about the same time, Max Weber delivered another strong impetus in this direction through his analysis of bureaucracy and his deep conviction that it represented the ultimate in rational information processing. And the crucial tool was writing—to Weber, it was the key that made everything else possible, coupled with the superior skill developed by the well-educated, specialist bureaucrats. Specialization and hierarchical supervision (documents could be passed on), impartiality (decisions could be audited, and they could be contested and appealed to higher authorities), and the application of rules and regulations (they could be written down in unequivocal form).

However, writing was not only a tool for increasing efficiency and impartiality, it had its greatest potential as a tool for managing complex work and large organizations. It was the information storage and communication capacities becoming available in the wake of the growing literacy that opened for the decisive transition from the Simple Structure to the archetypal large organization of the modern era—the Machine Bureaucracy.

Writing also led to a depersonalization of coordination. In non-literate society, complexity had to be kept to a minimum, and authority relationships were strictly personal—building on recognized power relationships between particular individuals. Enlarging a Simple Structure necessitated extensive delegation of power from one individual to another, bound together by personal loyalties and dependencies—often reinforced by family ties. Information flows had to be kept to a minimum.

In the new paper-based, functionally specialized organizations, a large part of the practical coordination effort was shifted away from the direct, personal relationships of nonliterate organizations toward files, written plans, instructions, rules, and regulations. One still had real persons as superiors, of course; their presence was undoubtedly very important, and in some parts of the organization (notably in the bottom layer of manufacturing or construction organizations) authority and coordination would still be very personal. But, as complexity and organization size increased, the growing and strongly regulated flows of work, control information and staff information (Mintzberg 1979) carried a larger and larger part of day-to-day coordination. For many employees, the human face of direct, personal authority was to a great extent replaced by the rule of written plans and regulations.

The principle of functional specialization that was the hallmark of these new organizations was further reinforced by the nature of paper-based information storage itself. A filing cabinet—perhaps the single most important element of pre-computer administrative technology—had the very constraining property of being accessible in only one physical location, and if a person did not work on the premises, there would be a number of tasks that he or she could not easily carry out. The account of a bank customer, for instance, could only be read or updated in the main office or (if the bank had decentralized account administration) in the branch office that kept the account.

Another constraint of paper-based files is that they normally have only one index—if you have a file of persons, for instance, you must choose whether you want to organize it by name, by date of birth, or by address (to mention the three most common keys). Cross-referencing paper-based files is extremely time-consuming, and really only viable for historical (and thereby unchanging) information. When paper-based files grow really large, their monodimensional nature tends to favor a procedural, specialized mode of administration. Files kept in the form of punch cards and processed with the help of card counters and sorters were of course more flexible, but not sufficiently so as to create a fundamentally different situation. These practices of organization and information processing formed in the nineteenth and early twentieth century still have a very strong influence on the way we work.

The Limits of Monolithic Bureaucracy

As they grew, the functionally specialized organizations became increasingly unwieldy, since they did not have the mutual coordination of the total work flow that is inherent in the holistic approach. Coordination had to be handled through planning, written communication, and hierarchic management—tier upon tier of managers, finally converging in the president's office. The larger the organizations became, the more energy had to be devoted to the coordination of their various functional departments.

Of course, the formal structure would always be somewhat alleviated by informal horizontal links facilitating daily operations, but functionally specialized organizations are nevertheless inherently difficult to manage—they require large management resources and are slow in responding to changes in the environment. As Williamson noted (1975), reports (upward) and instructions (downward) are liable to interpretation at each organizational level, and therefore tend to become more inaccurate for each level they pass through. If there are too many levels in the hierarchy, this "control loss," as Williamson terms it, can isolate top management from reality. When a certain size is reached, such organizations simply threaten to atrophy.

The most monumental example of the failure of large-scale functional specialization is perhaps the collapse of the communist economies in eastern Europe. It was not only the absence of competition that made those societies rust out, it was also the serious breakdown of coordination that was a consequence of the attempt to organize whole societies as monolithic, functionally specialized corporations. In the former Soviet Union, for instance, a country with about 290 million inhabitants, there were numerous examples of important product classes where production had been allocated to one large, specialized facility only.

One is reminded by this of the fact that Frederick W. Taylor's ideas were well received by the Bolsheviks in the young Soviet state (Morgan 1986). According to Clegg (1990), they were in fact introduced by Lenin himself. Braverman also notes the enthusiasm and quotes (1974 p. 12) Lenin as saying that "We must organise in Russia the study and teaching of the Taylor system and systematically try it out and adapt it to our ends."[2] It is quite evident that Taylor's extreme emphasis on planning, control and rational behavior corresponded very well with central Marxist-Leninist dogmas as they were practiced in the Soviet Union under Lenin and his successors. It is in fact tempting to suggest that the Soviet Union in many ways represented a monstrous attempt to create the largest Tayloristic factory organization ever.

What we can learn from this experiment is that monolithic, functionally specialized organizations do not scale well—they may work quite perfectly up to a limit, but then gradually crumble under the sheer weight of the required coordination. The total work flow of a whole society is orders of

---

[2] Braverman's reference is V.I. Lenin, "The Immediate Tasks of the Soviet Government" (1918), *Collected Works*, vol. 27 (Moscow, 1965), p. 259.

magnitude too great to be coordinated within a single hierarchy—it is indeed much to complex to be deliberately coordinated at all. All the successful economies of the modern world have in common a large private sector evolving according to principles resembling Darwin's "survival of the fittest." As organization ecologists have pointed out (see for instance Hannan and Freeman 1977 and 1984), there are many parallels between an open economy with independent actors and nature's ecological systems—today's free-market economies have achieved effective large-scale mutual adjustment (increasingly at a global level) only through each unit's independent exploitation of its immediate environment.

There is of course considerable disagreement about how unfettered the actors in such an economy should be, and judging from the relative successes of, for instance, the American, Japanese, German, and Scandinavian approaches (both in economic and social terms), the optimum degrees of freedom in the economy are by no means obvious—but few people dispute the basic soundness of the principles.

It is also interesting to view this in the perspective of information economy. In the free-market economy, the complexities of operation are encapsulated within independent companies, minimizing the amount of information that has to cross organization boundaries. The resulting simple interface to the world (mainly product properties and prices) makes organizations interchangeable and permits the competition and dynamic, continuous adjustments that are the hallmarks of an open economy.

But let us return to the corporate dimension. As we just noted, the growing organizations of the early twentieth century were coming up against the limits of the available administrative solutions. Remedies had to be found. In the corporate world the honor for creating the major new model is most often bestowed upon Alfred P. Sloan Jr, one of the managers of General Motors during its turnaround in the early 1920s (Chandler 1977, Williamson 1985). Pierre du Pont took over a controlling position in GM after the company's near bankruptcy during the collapse of the automobile market in September 1920 (Chandler 1977), and he brought Sloan in to help him with the cleanup.

They quickly realized that the sprawling empire of companies assembled by William C. Durant needed much closer attention than Durant had given it. However, they decided against creating a centralized company organized in a single tier of functional departments. The company's activities were, in Chandler's words (Chandler 1977, p. 460), "too large, too numerous, too varied, and too scattered to be so controlled." Such a configuration would also have swamped the top managers with daily administrative tasks and prevented them from devoting their time and energy to the tasks du Pont saw as the most important ones for top management: strategic planning and business development.

Du Pont and Sloan's solution was to establish within the company autonomous operating units, called divisions. Each division was given the responsibility for a particular price bracket, and was given complete control over all the resources and functions necessary to manufacture and sell its own cars. The total work flow of General Motors was thus divided into several self-contained work flow domains. Separate financial and advisory staffs kept close tabs on the development in the line divisions, constantly reviewing their performance according to plans and forecasts and continually revising budgets and forecasts not only according to past performance, but also with an eye on the national income, the state of the business cycle, seasonal variations, and the expected market share for each line of products.

Top management in General Motors was consequently relieved from its position as the crowning apex of day-to-day administrative chores, and could concentrate on long-term development. With fewer levels of coordination, the divisions also became more nimble actors in their respective markets than GM could have been if managed as one integrated company. This represents the *Divisionalized Form* in Mintzberg's classification.

In our perspective, however, divisionalization was not an innovation at all. It simply represented a recourse to the fundamental administrative principle of feudal type societies—simplification by encapsulation of complexity—and for the same reason: to achieve the information economy necessary to manage within the constraints of the available administrative technology. From their vantage point, Sloan and du Pont converted the organization from a vast array of tiered departments into a small number of operating and staff divisions, which they controlled chiefly through sales targets, budgets, and profit rates, just as the feudal king used tributes and quotas for military contribution as his main instruments of control. We may say that Sloan and du Pont simplified GM by encapsulating the complexity of car manufacture within the divisions, "hiding" it from their view as general managers, thus reducing the information flow between the divisions and company headquarters to a trickle. Each division was of course still a complex, hierarchical, procedural organization full of functionally specialized departments. But, being much smaller than GM as a whole, and with simpler objectives, the divisions were easier to manage.

In this connection, it is also interesting to note that the railroad company generally considered to be the best run in the United States in the last part of the nineteenth century—the Pennsylvania Railroad—deviated markedly from the monolithic organization of its competitors. Even more of a structural parallel to a feudal type state, it was organized into five self-contained, geographically delimited units (Chandler 1977). They were in their turn composed of smaller geographical units with a great degree of independence in operations, but with the same kind of tight, central control of key performance parameters later developed at GM. The central management and staff handled external strategies for expansion and relations with connecting roads; they determined and supervised technical standards, and closely monitored the financial performance of the different units. There was also a centralized purchasing department.

So the final verdict may not only be that divisionalization was no more than a revival of one of our oldest administrative techniques, but also that it was Pennsylvania's president from 1852 to 1874, Edgar J. Thomson, and not Alfred P. Sloan Jr, who should be awarded the honor for reinventing it as an organizational tool for large corporations.

The principle of encapsulation can become the basis for modifications at lower levels in the organization as well. Instead of a functionally specialized organization covering several markets and/or delivering many products or services, one can for instance organize a department or organizational unit responsible for a specific market or a product/service, or even for a certain product in a certain market. This ensures increased responsiveness to the environment, by reducing the number of organizational layers that need to be activated to arrive at decisions concerning product strategies, customer service, or manufacturing methods.[3]

Very few organizations are consequent in following only one pattern, however. Different structures will often be applied at different levels, and, even within one main level, there may be numerous exceptions—usually as a result of ad hoc responses to pressing challenges from the environment. A bank handling loan applications by passing them along through a functionally specialized organization, for instance, might react to a sudden surge in application volume or increased competition by forming a separate loan department to process applications faster and more efficiently.

As already indicated, the development just described was both strongest and most consequent in the United States. But not even there did the organizational forms portrayed here—in Mintzberg's terminology the

---

[3] While facilitating coordination and responsiveness, market-based, or product-based organizations may suffer from disadvantages when it comes to economy of scale and sustaining necessary expertise, however. Creating several independent production units requires the duplication of many functions, which can lead to higher overall costs. If the decentralized specialist groups become too small, specialists may find them less attractive places to work, since they think a certain number of like-minded colleagues is a prerequisite for maintaining and developing their skills and knowledge.

Machine Bureaucracy and the Divisionalized Form—replace all others. Even as late as in the 1990s, 90% of the six million businesses in the United States had less than 20 employees, and it goes without saying that they were not organized like Machine Bureaucracies. The situation is just the same in other industrialized countries. In Norway, for instance, about 80% of even the industrial firms have less than 20 employees. If we include companies between 20 and 50 employees, the figure rises to 90%, employing close to 35% of the total workforce in Norwegian industry.

Consequently, the older organizational forms, such as the Simple Structure and the Adhocracy, are obviously thriving. The Simple Structure is, among other things, still a natural form for the small shop and for an entrepreneurial startup driven by one individual's vision. The Adhocracy has survived as the preferred structure for many knowledge-based companies (such as consultancy and law firms) and organizations dominated by research and development—even organizations so large that they would otherwise be candidates for bureaucratic organization.

For the organization of really small companies, the technological innovations of the Industrial Revolution have not meant too much, since specialization is generally limited and coordination anyway depends on close, informal contact. Moreover, most small firms have local markets and relatively simple logistics. The dramatic effect for craft-type firms came first and foremost from the competition many of them suddenly faced from standardized, mass-produced goods marketed on a national or even international scale. That was the change that drove scores of them out of business.

The new preconditions, however, as we have just seen, made it possible for entrepreneuring people to build much larger and more complex organizations than before. For those larger companies, which tried much harder to routinize tasks, the effects of functional specialization and the limitations of available administrative technology combined to make the Machine Bureaucracy the dominating organizational structure and divisionalization the main remedy for handling complexity too great for a monolithic structure.

A NEW CONCEPT FOR COORDINATION

The Bureaucratic Advantage

We have already concluded that the bureaucratic organization could both grow larger and operate more efficiently than earlier organizational forms, and we have also said something about the reasons for this. To fully understand the nature of the change, however, it is necessary to take a closer look. And it is all the more worthwhile to do so, since the development of the bureaucratic organization also contains the seeds of a new intellectual tool—*the explicit, conceptual model*—that will not fully come into its own until our use of computers matures in the twenty-first century.

As noted earlier, Weber's main explanation for the bureaucracy's effectiveness was the superior skill of its clerks. They are well educated and highly specialized, and they continuously polish their proficiency through their work, following the guidelines laid down by their superiors. He compares the bureaucracy to a machine—it functions in much the same way as a modern factory producing goods in a very efficient, partly automatic manner—and attributes its efficiency to the increased productivity and quality at each step in the production process (see, for instance, Weber 1968, pp. 973–75). If we generalize this argument for both manufacturing and clerical organizations, we may say that it is *specialization*, the concomitant *superior skills* of the employees and their *improved tools* that do the trick. And the arsenal of tools includes not only the "hard" tools and machinery of material production, but also office implements such as files—extremely important through their capacity for implicit coordination.

This is not a sufficient explanation, however. Specialization and improved skills may indeed increase quality and efficiency at each step in the process, but there is still the challenge of coordinating the work of the multiplying ranks of specialists—making it possible to build and run large organizations while preserving the advantages achieved for each individual task.

A more comprehensive explanation is provided by March and Simon (1958). They recognize two basic methods for the coordination of large organizations with high internal interdependence among tasks—that is, organizations with a high degree of internal specialization, requiring careful and extensive coordination to operate efficiently. The first one is *coordination by plan*, which is based on preestablished schedules, the second *coordination by feedback*, which relies on continuous transmission of information about the workings of the different parts of the organization.

Coordination by feedback requires open lines and fairly intensive communication between the coordinator and the coordinated. It corresponds to (and encompass) Mintzberg's direct supervision and mutual adjustment, which began as the two basic (intuitive) coordination methods used in small-scale, oral societies. However, the heavy communication load of coordination by feedback becomes a severe penalty when the organization grows. Relying on coordination by feedback alone, the effort needed to coordinate an organization will grow much faster than the organization itself, and, without some kind of simplification scheme, an organization would not have to become very large before coordination would break down and confusion reign.

There are two main ways to solve this problem. One is to abolish the need for coordination as far as possible, which was the essence of the encapsulation of complexity inherent in the feudal system. This "evasion tactic" was the only available method in preliterate societies, and it was later revived in the form of divisionalization. It can only work, however, when there is no need to coordinate persons or processes across different subunits.

The other solution is what March and Simon (1958) terms *coordination by plan* (termed *coordination by program* in Figure 3-1 on page 51), which requires much less communication and thus emerges as strikingly more efficient (March and Simon, 1958, p. 162):

> As we noted earlier, it is possible under some conditions to reduce the volume of communication required from day to day by substituting coordination by plan for coordination by feedback. By virtue of this substitution, organizations can tolerate very complex interrelations among their component parts in the performance of repetitive activities. The coordination of parts is incorporated in the program when it is established, and the need for continuing communication is correspondingly reduced. Each specific situation, as it arises, is largely covered by the standard operating procedure.

The efficiency of the bureaucracy, then, both in its blue collar and white collar versions, is also to a large degree based on the fact that work is standardized and the coordination of work is *preprogrammed*. The various tasks are first analyzed in considerable detail, and prescriptions for carrying out work and solving the most common problems are specified. Once they have learnt those prescriptions, the workers and clerks are able to execute most of their work without further instructions.

We can clearly see how this is a direct continuation of central principles behind coordination in the Simple Structure (discussed in Chapter 5). The *focus* is exactly the same: both in the Machine Bureaucracy and the Simple Structure the necessary coordination is achieved through *directing work*, as opposed to the *information sharing* of the Adhocracy. But whereas the Simple Structure relies on *direct supervision* for its coordination, the Machine Bureaucracy relies on *indirect supervision*: The role of the physical supervisor is assumed by the standardized work rules (the *program*). Mintzberg (1979) clearly builds on the passage from March and Simon quoted above when he describes the coordinating mechanism of the Machine Bureaucracy—in fact, he quotes briefly from it himself (Mintzberg 1979, p. 5)—and his *standardization of work processes* is roughly equivalent to March and Simon's coordination by plan.

The ultimate in preprogrammed work is of course the automatic machine, which represents a carefully designed program forged in steel, repeating its designed actions again and again without further human guidance. It is also worthwhile to note that the impressive efficiency of the automatic production line does not only reside in the speed of each particular operation, but just as much in the perfect, automatic coordination of those operations.

We can then extend the taxonomy of coordinating mechanisms presented in Chapter 3 with two new variants, both dependent on technology (Figure 7-1). The first one I propose to call *explicit routine*, the other simply *automation*. The explicit routine is the "program" you end up with when you consciously design an organization. In larger organizations it will usually contain both organization charts, overall process descriptions, and job descriptions. It will normally be based on a planning process involving at least a basic level of explicit modeling and design.

In addition to these two extensions, the era of organizational tools also opened up for a development of mutual adjustment, where considerable extension is possible if the adjustment is mediated not by direct information exchange, but by indirect communication through a common information repository. To be practical, this common repository needs technology for externalizing memory: Although it is conceivable that implicit coordination could be used with a person's memory as repository, it is hard to see how it could be of real importance. The written record, however, created exactly the kind of information repository needed. Records kept together in a file made it possible for many persons to base their work and decisions on the same information, and changes introduced by one would apply for the work of all the others, without

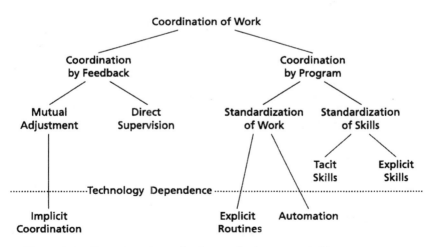

Figure 7-1:   *Taxonomy of coordinating mechanisms extended by pre-computer technology.*

any need for meetings or other forms of personal communication. This made possible what I prefer to term an *implicit coordination* of the people who worked with it: a coordination that is an implicit, automatic effect of working from a common base of information, eliminating the need for extra communication and direct supervising efforts.

At least within a narrow area, then, a fairly large number of people can coordinate at least part of their activities by working with the same files. By relying on this continuously updated, common kernel of information, they directly modify each other's actions by mutual adjustment without ever meeting face to face, extending the use of this mode of coordination to a significantly larger number of people than was earlier possible. For a bank clerk, for instance, it is not necessary to notify all the other clerks about a change in a customer's account balance; it is only necessary to post it in the books.

Although implicit coordination works by effecting mutual adjustment through common information, it is sufficiently differentiated to be considered a separate coordination mechanism. As such, it became the first technology-based coordination mechanism, and thus marks a watershed in organizational history. Its use, however, was limited before the development of large private and public organizations in the nineteenth century.

What about direct supervision, then—did it, too, receive a boost from the new technologies? Some will perhaps argue that the developments of communications technology in the nineteenth century, especially the telegraph and telephone, have indeed made a difference and allowed direct supervision to be used over much greater geographical distances. This is of course true: The geographical reach of direct supervision was greatly extended by pre-computer communication technology, and larger organizations spanning greater distances could be kept under close control. The space of constructible organizations was thus extended, but I will maintain that this did not imply the creation of any new coordinating mechanisms: It was still one person giving orders to others. While implicit coordination represents something genuinely new (coordination not via direct communication, but indirectly via a common, external information repository), direct supervision via telephone or letter represents little more than an amplification of the principal's voice.

I have not included here any extensions to the two mechanisms subsumed under standardization of skills. *Tacit skills* are by definition unchanged in their nature, although modern mass media have greatly expanded the sources for the kind of information that contributes to the formation of tacit skills. This is precisely the reason for many parents' dislike of certain kinds of TV-programs, films and records: that they may tend to instil unwanted norms and tacit skills in their children. The teaching of *explicit skills* has of course been strongly enhanced by the development of literacy, but although the textbook certainly made it easier to teach the same skills to many people, it did not change the mechanism per se: The way coordination is effected is not related to the medium for the original knowledge transfer.

Explicit Design and The Emergence of the Conceptual Model

Both methods of coordination by standardization (of work and of skills) have old roots and have been used in nonliterate societies, for example, in craft and trade. In their old versions, however, these coordination methods were largely implicit in tradition and customary ways of working and organizing. The circumstances of their use did not involve formal planning or written documentation. Consequently, they did not contain explicitly designed work programs; rather, they grew out of customary practice and were transferred from generation to generation as part of the continuation of a craft, a trade, or the social order.

As we have already seen, however, there is a definite limit to the level of complexity that the unaided human mind can handle. The new organizations, with their elaborate interdependencies, were far too complex to be conceived and run within the framework of an oral tradition, and by unaided memory alone. Both their manufacturing and clerical parts required detailed and explicit analyses of the operational requirements and the interdependencies of the different steps and levels in the process, to be followed by careful and detailed design and planning of operations. Writing was an indispensable tool for this work, as well as for the design and construction of the new tools and machinery that were so important for the new developments.

Following Ong (1982) and Havelock (1986), there is also good reason to believe that a mature literate tradition, a developed *literate mindset*, was a necessary prerequisite to this new analytical approach to work and organization. People from oral cultures seem to have trouble using and manipulating the symbols and abstract categories used for complex analysis and planning. The oral mindset is concrete and person oriented, and it correlates with the basic organizational structures (relying on personal authority) that we explored in Chapter 5. The literate mindset is abstract and role oriented and correlates well with bureaucracy, where work is specialized and authority is tied to positions, not particular persons.

In the modern organization, then, work is no longer organized in accordance with custom and tradition, but according to a *conscious* design based on an explicit analysis of the desired outcome and the available means. In my view, this represents the decisive break with the past and marks the transition to a new paradigm for the organization of human work. *The old paradigm, developed in an oral world, was characterized by a reliance on tradition, tacit knowledge (Polanyi 1967) and theories-in-use (Argyris 1980), and was focused on personal relationships, family ties and holism in work. The new one, born in the first fully literate societies, builds on conscious analysis and explicit design and focuses on the coordination of interdependent, specialized tasks. It will almost gleefully break with tradition when that is instrumental to improvements in effectiveness and efficiency.*

If we look at this from the perspective of action-oriented organizational theory (as discussed in Chapter 2), we can perhaps express it more clearly. Within the oral paradigm, the organizational patterns of action more or less *emerged*. Because they were based on tacit knowledge and theories-in-use, they were seen as an inevitable part of the social fabric, as a part of the natural order of things. However, the explication of design that forms the basis of the Machine Bureaucracy meant that patterns of action were *consciously constructed* for a specific purpose, partly separated from the larger society and constantly open to inspection and improvement. The road to greater efficiency seemed always to go through greater sophistication and thoroughness in design. Indeed, the most efficient production is achieved through automation, which builds squarely on a total, conscious design of recurring patterns of action, or—to comply with the tradition of reserving the term "action" for human activity (Silverman 1970)— recurring patterns of machine movements.

The Machine Bureaucracy, as we have described it, then, is a production and coordination "machine" with a specific purpose—it is consciously designed to accomplish certain tasks or solve certain problems. It is designed on the basis of a detailed analysis of a set of purposes, tasks, and relevant environmental factors that its creators deem relevant to its success. This set we may call its *problem domain*. The designers need to have not only a knowledge of the features and events in this problem domain, but also a set of postulates—a theory— about how those important features and events relate to each other. To use a systems term, we may say that the design is based on an at least partly explicit *conceptual model* of the problem domain.

What is a conceptual model? It is a representation of a part of reality, just like the physical models we use to comprehend and test the behavior of complex artifacts and phenomenons—by, for instance, placing an airplane model in a wind tunnel. Conceptual models are used for the same reason: to establish an understanding of reality that is sufficient for initiating sensible, effective actions toward the part of reality represented by the model. The only difference is that the representation of reality is *conceptual*, not physical—it consists of words and drawings on paper, on a screen or in the mind. An organization chart, for instance, is a simple conceptual model of an organization, representing its formal decision-making hierarchy.

In general, we can define a conceptual model as a conceptual representation of a limited (bounded) part of reality, that part which we are interested in for our particular purpose. The model is of course a simplification of reality and will most often only describe the features that the designers judge to be sufficiently important, and not self-evident. It is, however, crucial that *all* the aspects of reality that are important for its purpose are represented in the model—objects, phenomenons, the relations between them, and their static and dynamic properties. The organization designers can then use this model—which represents their best understanding of the problem domain—to work out the details of the division of work, organizational structure, task formation, work instructions, and the like.

I do not mean to say that the pioneers in organizational design used the term "model" or were aware of the concept of modeling as a tool. Even today, the use of this term in connection with organizations and organizational design is by and large limited to the fraternity of systems analysts and designers. However, even if the people who work out the designs and task structures of organizations do not use the term and are unaware of the concept, the descriptions and plans that form the basis for their designs are conceptual models nonetheless.

We may well say that even the traditional organizations of oral cultures built on conceptual models of their problem domains. But those models were not made *explicit*—they existed only as theories-in-use (Argyris 1980). They were therefore *not* open to inspection or conscious elaboration and could *not* serve as a basis for innovative design. To develop and design the modern organization—with its intricate interdependencies and its new approach to coordination, with its drastically reduced control and communication needs—an explicit model was needed: A model developed on the basis of a conscious analysis of the problem domain and documented on paper.

In contrast with models implicit in theories-in-use, the new, explicit model was wide open to inspection and improvement and could therefore support the steady improvements in operational planning, automation, and work procedures that characterize the modern organization. It could also be used to establish a necessary minimum of consensus throughout the organization regarding important goals and operating principles, another condition for making large organizations work. It was thus the combined development of programmed coordination and explicit modeling that constituted the foundation of the new organizational paradigm, which we may simply call the *literate paradigm*—after the technology that made it possible.

The Constraints of Standardization

Compared to older organizational forms, the Machine Bureaucracy offers great economy in coordination and information transfer and is very efficient in turning standardized inputs into standardized outputs. However, the penalty is inflexibility: it can only handle inputs and deliver outcomes that are defined in the underlying conceptual model. Because the actual formulation of both the model and the standardization rules necessitates analyses and planning procedures that are exceedingly laborious, changes in the model and the "machine" are very expensive and take a long time to accomplish.

Therefore, Machine Bureaucracies are slow in adjusting their behavior to changes in their problem domain. In very dynamic environments, they simply cannot keep up. That is why one has to revert to more flexible coordinative schemes for highly unstable problem domains: if the environment is simple, direct supervision will be close at hand; if it is complex and especially if it requires knowledge in multiple fields, mutual adjustment will be preferred, at least at the most crucial levels. In war, for instance, the chiefs of the different services will work very closely together, and during large and important combined operations they will usually spend most of their time in the same room, conferring continuously while adjusting the actions of their respective services in real time. (That is what war rooms are all about.)

What this means is really that to use standardization of work as a coordination method, and to reap the great rewards it offers, it is necessary to have models and a modeling capacity that can keep up with changes in the environment and operating conditions. In other words, there is a need for a professional staff to analyze change requirements; design the new routines, rules, and/or machine combinations; and then manage their implementation. The great savings offered by automation and the new organizational form thus also carries a penalty, which is greater cost for maintenance and change.

If the cost of updating the model becomes too great, or if there is a need for change too often, the organization is forced to adapt a coordinating mechanism that needs less analysis and planning but craves more resources in daily operation. There are very real tradeoffs to be made here, and organizations that straddle the crossover point or experience significant changes in the dynamics of their environment very often run into huge problems trying to adapt their structures and coordination methods to the new realities of life.

CULTURE REVISITED

In Chapter 2 I concluded that the influence of social and cultural factors on the local constructible spaces was too varied to incorporate into my analyses of the enabling powers of technology. I still hold that they are— but the natural question then is if this variation represents a problem for the validity my analysis.

The rather neat account of the growth of modern organizations given in this chapter is to a large extent in accordance with Chandler's (1977) interpretation. Chandler explains the rise of the modern corporation (and thereby the Machine Bureaucracy) by the driving forces of the technological developments of industry and transport *and* the concomitant development of a national mass market for industrial products in the United States. Companies grew because their internal coordination was more efficient than the market-based coordination of small, independent firms, and because the larger firms had much more power for market penetration and domination. It was the large, homogenous national market in the United States, Chandler argues, that caused the large, multi-unit firm to flourish in the United States before it became a decisive factor in European business. He acknowledges that legal and cultural differences also had a role in delaying the development in other countries, but he does not doubt that the American experience will sooner or later repeat itself everywhere else, when the local economies reach the proper development stage. This is a view shared by Williamson (1975, 1985), who argues forcefully that the logic of *transaction costs*—the cost of exchanging goods or services between people and across organization boundaries—eventually will prevail, and foster similar organizational solutions everywhere.

However, many other scholars have pointed to the fact that the Industrial Revolution originated in what is now loosely referred to as the Western industrialized world, and the first large, private organizations were accordingly products of those societies. Many of the organizational traits we used to take for general principles may thus be no more than artifacts of our own particular culture. Chandler and Williamson, who concentrate most of their arguments around developments in the United States, may easily be unduly influenced by American peculiarities.

Does this criticism, then, undermine the validity of the analysis we have made in this chapter about the ways technology has extended the space of constructible organizations?

Important instances of the criticism against the convergence theories of Chandler and Williamson are Granovetter (1985), Hamilton and Biggart (1988), and Clegg (1990). Granovetter discusses the tendency of theories of economic action to offer explanations that are either *undersocialized* (fail to take into account social factors, as the classical and neoclassical "rational man" theories of economics) or *oversocialized* (picture humans as more or less passively succumbing to the prevailing social forces, as in orthodox Marxism, where class properties and class distinctions take preeminence over individual characteristics). For instance, while Granovetter acknowledges that Williamson's focus on institutional and transactional considerations differs from neoclassical theories, he maintains that Williamson's theories are still clearly on the undersocialized side, paying too little attention to sociological, historical, and legal arguments.

As Granovetter points out, undersocialized and oversocialized theories ironically both end up by robbing us of most of our humanity and discretion—the undersocialized theories by making us mere slaves of a rather narrow logic, the oversocialized by making us robots programmed by our environment to merely enact prevailing norms. Granovetter argues that economic action is thoroughly embedded in both the actor's social environment and his or her personal values and goals. Rationality cannot be judged on the basis of narrow slices of a person's life only. Organizational politics may for instance make it subjectively rational for an individual to behave in ways that are economically irrational for the firm. And history and traditional authority structures may heavily influence company organization without determining it. Many aspects of organization may be imported from abroad, or may even come as a result of the idiosyncrasies of powerful organization members.

Hamilton and Biggart (1988) attack both the market-based theories of Williamson and Chandler and the theories that explain national differences in organizational structure on the basis of culture. To test different approaches, they look at firm structures in three successful countries in East Asia: Japan, South Korea, and Taiwan. If economic factors alone determined organizational structure and practice, then Asian enterprises would be quite similar to Western (especially American) enterprises, and they would not show great internal differences. Similarly, since the three countries are strongly related culturally (all of them drawing heavily on Chinese culture and tradition and having intertwined histories), their organizations should not differ to much among themselves, even if they differ from Western firms. Economic organization, however, differ markedly in the three countries, and all of them are different from the United States and Europe. To explain these substantial differences in organization, Hamilton and Biggart conclude that the preexisting authority structure (which was distinctly dissimilar in the three Asian countries) is the key variable.

The arguments presented by Granovetter as well as Hamilton and Biggart agrees with that of Clegg (1990)—and Clegg also draws on their work. His key issue is precisely the paramount importance of embeddedness, institutional frameworks, and modes of rationality, and his criticism of Williamson (and a number of others, including Chandler) goes along the same lines. Drawing on a broad selection of empirical material, he shows both how structures differ between cultures and within them, and how they may vary considerably even within countries, markets, or enclaves that are homogenous in most other aspects. Clegg concludes that the diversities offered by contemporary organization forms cannot be interpreted in terms of any single, decisive factor—be it economy, culture or authority relationships. He mandates a more complex explanation, encompassing a wide variety of contingencies, and in this he seems to be much more in tune with the central theme emerging from the last 30 years of organization research: that there are a large number of contingency factors which have been shown to influence organization structure. Summing up the arguments, he says (1990, pp. 162–63),

> ... organization forms are human fabrications which agencies[4] will structure using whatever discursive rationalities[5] they can secure. These rationalities will vary in their institutional location, drawing not only from occupational identities, or from the regulatory framework of law, accounting conventions and so on. In addition, they will also draw on whatever resources find expression in a particular context, local resources which are particular for that context.

I believe we can conclude that the structure of modern organizations vary, and that there are many important factors on different analytical levels that contribute to that variation. It only serves to underscore one of the basic tenets of general systems theory: the concepts of equifinality and multifinality. As Crozier (1964) remarks, when analyzing the reasons for the fact that the French economy lagged behind the British from the start of the Industrial Revolution until after the World War II, the most baffling fact is *not* that some countries in the industrialized world lag a little behind others, but that the differences are not greater.

Of course, the examples of the communist countries in Europe, of Argentina (one of the most developed and economically advanced nations in the world around 1900) as well as the divergent development trends in Asian nations show that there are indeed limits to this equifinality—you cannot succeed by *any* mix of means—but the fact remains that there are no single prescription for success, and no single pattern of development and organization that is destined to percolate through the world and gradually make all organizations and societies similar. And there is no such thing as technological determinism—a particular technology or set of

---

[4] In Clegg's sense, an *agency* is an entity that makes thing happen. It can be an organization, a part of an organization, or an individual.

[5] Rationality as it appears to the agent under the full (and dynamic) set of circumstances under which he operates.

technologies does not invariably lead to the same organizational solution. Using whatever material we humans have found in our environment and in our own minds, we have together created a panopticon of practical solutions that shows great leeway for variation.

Nevertheless, the iron constraints of our biology and our tools are still there, and no member of the human race can operate outside them. Complex technology and large-scale production of goods and services require organizations much larger than the artisan shop, and, in this sense, the technology of the nineteenth and twentieth centuries had a deterministic streak: to exploit it for the creation of increased material wealth, we *had* to build large organizations. Further, all large organizations *have* to tackle the challenges inherent in the coordination of large numbers of people. If we look at large organizations around the world, we will therefore find a lot of common ground.

However different the authority structures in such organizations may be, for instance, they all *have* an authority structure. Despite major variations in job definitions, in the proportion of workers that are skilled, in job rotation schemes and distribution of authority, all firms above a certain (rather small) size still *have* job specialization. And, because of this, they all have planning functions, coordination needs, and extensive internal communication. Even the light-footed Taiwanese manufacturing firms, relying more on their ability to adapt fast to changes than on forecasting future market trends, have to plan their production at least a month or two ahead.

In oral societies the constraints of human physiology will keep organization at a fairly simple level, and people will depend to a very large degree on their own immediate work and actions for their survival and well-being. In a developed, literate society, on the other hand, one of the key aspects of human life is the extent to which the citizens as individuals are constantly dependent on the extensive collective information processing taking place in innumerable large and small organizations. This information processing is really pervasive. Even in organizations established to produce material goods, information processing is often the major activity if measured in work hours. Its level of complexity is also orders of magnitude greater than the collective processing of even the most advanced oral societies, and is extended further through the use of advanced automation.

I discussed this at some length in the preceding chapters and concluded that the constraints on human communication and memory are the basic problems in the control and coordination of organizations, and that control and coordination are the most pressing operational problems of all collective human undertakings. The subject of organized, collective information processing has therefore risen to a much more prominent position in modern societies than in preindustrial civilizations. The preoccupation in both public and private enterprises *in all cultures and societies* with subjects such as formal and informal organization structures, lines of authority, communication channels, job designs, and management styles, as well as the fervor of the discussion, is a clear expression of the universally perceived gravity—and the universal validity—of the problem.

So far, the development of the *Divisionalized Form* represents our best effort to harness this complexity within the bounds set by the modified preconditions that has emerged from the technological development of the last 3500 years. It is reasonable to assume that the possibilities awarded by these preconditions have largely been exhausted in this period of time, as millions of attempts to create and run successful organizations throughout the nations of the world have employed a great breadth in innovation and angles of attack. To evolve distinctly new organization schemes, we will therefore need new technological developments, such as the emerging information technology that is the ultimate subject of this book. Only they can modify the preconditions further and thereby enlarge the realm of the possible. It is, however, up to us to explore the new frontiers—it is people who discover, invent, and act, new developments do not come about on their own just because they are feasible.

This is in good accordance with the framework of the present study, which builds on the notion of *physical and cognitive preconditions* for organization building, defining the limits of the possible in the organization domain, and how the development of tools has changed them. Within the limits set by these preconditions, which amounts to the total *space of constructible organizations*, other constraints will also operate—cultural constraints, the traditions of power arrangements, of markets and competition—to define the many *local spaces of constructible organizations* one will find around the world.

Within the spaces defined by these constraints, within their innumerable nooks and crannies, human beings maneuver, motivated by a diverse mixture of basic drives, dreams, and emotions, as well as more elevated considerations. And, as we all know, such individual mixtures vary enormously, and they are not determined by the environment alone (as the oversocialized theories imply). Not infrequently, they will come into conflict with established social values, leading to breaches both of trust, custom, and law. That is what makes the study of human action both so frustrating and so fascinating, and why theories explaining human action and social evolution from just one perspective always remain inadequate.

III

IT and the Preconditions for Organizing

The four chapters in Part II have tried to show how human limitations have constrained the development of organizations and how we have developed a succession of tools to alleviate or circumvent these limitations. The foundation is now in place for the analysis of information technology and its contributions. Before we move on, however, it could be useful to sum up the conclusions from Part II.

Chapter 4 (*Confined by Physiology*) began by looking at the six basic human preconditions in more detail. The fickleness of our memory, our limited information processing capacity, and the very short range and limited channel capacity of our natural means of communication are the main factors delimiting our natural capabilities for organizing. The chapter also noted that we are only partly rational beings and that our actions are strongly influenced by emotions, rooted in the deeper and more archaic parts of our brains.

Chapter 5 (*The Dawn of Organization*) explored the problems of organization building in societies without significant tools for organizational purposes, and tried to determine the extent of the space of constructible organizations in such societies. I suggested that there were two basic structural configurations, the Adhocracy and the Simple Structure, building on the two primeval coordinating mechanisms—mutual adjustment and direct supervision. For larger structures, where one ruler or one council could not manage the complexity, the iron constraints on human memory, communication, and information processing-capabilities forced a reliance on two principles: the *delegation of authority* and the *encapsulation of information*.

Adhocracies do not scale well, but the Simple Structure can easily be scaled up by encapsulation and delegation, preferably with geography and lineage as structuring elements. Such a system provides an extreme economy with respect to information processing, communication, and memorizing. Based on land rights and family lineage, this feudal type organization contains its own structuring information; that information is constantly enacted in everyday life and thereby reinforced in everyone's memory. At any level, the number of people the ruler must deal with is thus kept within manageable limits. It can be viewed as a forerunner of the Divisionalized Form.

Chapter 6 (*The Power of Technology*) discussed the nature of tools and how the most important precomputer technologies alleviated our original constraints, gradually allowing for extensions of the space of constructible organizations. The single most important innovation was undoubtedly the art of writing, which made it possible to externalize memory and thus lifted many of the constraints placed upon us by our limited recall. Even more important for the development of organizations was the accessibility of written information for large numbers of persons. The emergence of *implicit coordination* of people who work with an *active file* marked a watershed in organization history. There was also a gradual development of a literate mindset, characterized by abstract and analytical thinking and extensive use of symbols, finally extended to the vast majority of the population through printing and mass education.

The other great field of organization-relevant innovation concerned communication—which quickly became the bottleneck for organization building when the memory barrier was lifted. Communication has two aspects, which for a long time were one and the same: physical transportation of people and goods, and communication of information. Even if we know of regular courier services as early as 2000 BC, communication technology capable of serving as an infrastructure for mainstream organization building had to wait for the Industrial Revolution. However, the bandwidth problem remains: regardless of channel capacity, we can still only absorb 250 words per minute, and output even less than that.

When it came to information processing, the ability to write down intermediary results and collect written information made it possible both to process much more complex problems and to time-slice (work on many problems more or less in parallel) much more easily. The real revolution, however, was the way writing let us distribute large tasks among a vast number of persons, synchronizing and coordinating their activities and communicating intermediate results between them. A literate society can therefore organize massive undertakings and routinely tackle tasks that would completely overwhelm any illiterate society.

Finally, mechanical automation helped us overcome our limited ability to carry out physical operations in parallel. The machine is, so to speak, a set of crystallized decisions, and it represents a total externalization of a plan for a specific production process. Thus, even coordination is automatic in an automated production line—that is one important reason for its phenomenal efficiency. However, even if a steady succession of tools has enhanced our capabilities, important parts of the basic limitations have prevailed—notably in our abilities to communicate and process information.

In Chapter 7 (*The Modern Organization*), I then tried to assess the relationship between the development of these tools and the emergence of the modern organization. The most significant developments did not appear until the needs of the growing firms during the Industrial Revolution outgrew the capacities of traditional organization. The key concepts here were specialization and mechanization, which required much more emphasis on coordination and control and entailed splitting the problems of design and production methods—an integral part of the craftsman's work—away from the worker. This called for a much more sophisticated approach to information processing and communication, and, consequently, to organization. The Machine Bureaucracy was born.

The development of the Machine Bureaucracy depended on the emergence of a new concept for coordination—indirect supervision by the means of standardization of work processes—which resulted in two new coordinating mechanisms: explicit routines and automation. Both these new coordinating mechanisms depended on writing; automation required additional technological advances. With the addition of implicit coordination, there were now three new, technology-dependent coordinating mechanisms available that supported the development of very large and efficient organizations.

The new organizations also represented another decisive break with the past: They required detailed and explicit analyses of both the operational requirements and the interdependencies of the different steps and levels in the process, to be followed by careful and detailed design and planning of operations. The patterns of action constituting the new organizations were thus *consciously constructed* according to a *conscious* design based on an *explicit* analysis of the desired outcome and the available means. Explicating analyses and design and committing them to paper, the new organizers also created (unknowingly) the first explicit conceptual models of organizations. By lifting the models out of the subconscious world of tacit knowledge, and literally spelling them out, they also opened them up for conscious inspection and improvement. This is the foundation of the modern organization. The chapter concluded that it is reasonable to assume that the possibilities awarded by these preconditions have largely been exhausted by countless trials and errors, and that we will need new technological developments to evolve distinctly new organizational schemes.

It is now time to proceed to analyze these developments more precisely. The approach from now on will be more detailed, and divided into three parts (Part III, IV, and V). Part III will delve into information technology itself and the way it helps us relieve main limitations above and beyond what earlier tools have done. Part IV will move on to discuss the new organizational opportunities that information technology opens up. Part V will return to the subject of structural configurations, now with information technology as a prerequisite.

Part III starts with Chapter 8 (*Information Technology Characteristics*), in which I try to assess the state of the art of the technology and the likely achievements in basic performance improvements during the next decade. Chapter 9 (*The IT-Based Preconditions*) will proceed to analyze how information technology can improve the capabilities of the individual over and beyond the contributions of earlier technology. Following the conclusions in Chapter 2, that organizations are constructed and that their system properties derive from the qualities of the actions performed by individual organization members, this discussion really represents the foundation for the analysis of possible new organization forms and practices. To balance the fairly technocentric discussion in Chapter 9, which mainly explores the basis for the technical space of organizations, Chapter 10 (*Emotional Barriers and Defenses*) will end this part by discussing emotional barriers and defenses against technology-based changes—problems which are, in my view, generally underestimated and ignored by the industry.

8
Information Technology Characteristics

"O that a man might know
The end of this day's business ere it come!"
Shakespeare, *Julius Caesar*, 1599–1600

NEEDED: A REALISTIC ASSESSMENT

One of my more cherished computer memorabilia is a graph produced in 1986 by IDC (one of the big players in the market analysis and forecast arena), forecasting the developments in market shares for the "Primary Operating System Environments" of the next ten years (through 1996). Among a number of lesser mistakes, one stands out: Microsoft Windows, the increasingly dominating environment in 1996, is not mentioned at all, and the top slot is awarded to OS/2. This is not so strange, since Windows was not really introduced until 1987, when Microsoft's own Excel spreadsheet was the first application to take advantage of it. However, it should teach us to be humble before the task of predicting developments in this industry, where the achievements have been so impressive since the first experimental steps were taken in Britain, Germany, and the US during and just after World War II. The basic price/performance level of computers has improved more rapidly than for any other technology we have seen, and the rate of adoption has been very high, especially since the PC made computers affordable for almost any budget. Already, much has been achieved that has irrevocably changed the preconditions for human work and organizing.

Even if we know this, it can easily fall into technological myopia's double trap: at the same time becoming too conservative in short-term judgements and wildly futuristic in medium- and long-term judgements. When thinking about one's own business, where the details are well known—the installed technological base, the budget for upgrades and new systems, the people in the organization, the products, the competition—it is easy to get caught by the present level of technology and the present practices, and fail to take into account the dramatic and steady improvements in basic technological capabilities and price/performance levels. Stepping outside the immediacy of our everyday frame of reference, however, it is just as easy to get swept away by bold predictions about how a galloping information technology will soon stand society on its head and totally transform our lives.

This is not a new phenomenon. All great new technologies have had their heralds and their prophets promising all-embracing changes, while countless businesses have simultaneously been swept aside because the proprietors did not see the short-term changes wrought in the basic pre-conditions for their existence. It is tempting to stick to the telephone as an example—as we have already noted how the chief engineer of the British Post Office in 1879 explained to the House of Commons why the telephone had little future in Britain. About 20 years later, General John J. Carty, then chief engineer of AT&T, was more bold, extolling the peace-making qualities of the telephone (Pool 1983, p. 89):

> Some day we will build up a world telephone system making necessary to all peoples the use of a common language, or common understanding of languages, which will join all the people of the earth into one brotherhood.
> There will be heard, throughout the earth, a great voice coming out of the ether, which will proclaim, "Peace on earth, goodwill towards men."

This was written at about the same time as an eminently practical man, the Japanese general Oyama, pioneered the use of telephones in warfare—his troops strung telephone wires behind them as they advanced against the Russians in the Russo–Japanese war in 1905, connecting all the regiments along a 100-mile front to fifteen regional headquarters, three group headquarters, and finally to the general himself, sitting in his head-quarters ten miles behind the front line with an excellent grasp of the unfolding events—in contrast to his Russian counterpart, who had to rely on orderlies. Oyama's victory was squarely attributed to this innovative use of the telephone (Pool 1983).

Some of the visions are even recurring ones—presented anew for succeeding generations of technology. A persistent vision in this class is the idea that we all will end up as high-tech couch potatoes, working, living, and entertaining almost solely by means of the wall-sized screens (or even three-dimensional holograhic display units) in our living rooms-cum-offices. Now, drawings of such rooms were presented as early as a hundred years ago (Dahl 1984)—the only difference was that movie screens, telephones, and printing telegraph receivers (for continuous news services) took the place nowadays reserved for computers, videophones, and fax machines. And, come to think of it, has not the Internet also been heralded as a a peacemaker, because it will connect, on an equal basis, people of all nations, creeds and political convictions? Repression is no longer possible, we hear, because the Internet is impossible to censor. Indeed it is, but physical access is still needed, and sufficiently determined regimes will have little problem controlling physical access for the masses. Let us not underestimate the ruthless ruler—history shows him always able to turn any new technology of value to his enemies into a tool for himself as well. As we shall briefly explore in the last pages of Chapter 14, information technology is actually an eminent tool for gifted dictators.

What we need for our purpose in this book is an assessment that avoids this double trap—avoids visions of indeterminable future states, and avoids getting caught up with contemporary products. We need an analysis that uncovers the basic characteristics of the technology while preserving a realistic view of its deep development trends.

This is not an easy proposition. The properties of computer systems are multifaceted, and the products that are brought to market represent a bewildering array of tools and gadgets, with market lives of a few years at the most—some as short as a few months. Often, they are so complex that the average user never utilizes more than a fraction of the functions available. This profusion of products, often presented through high-strung marketing blitzes, and extensively covered in the media, makes it difficult to distinguish the important from the insignificant, and the truly revolutionary from the superficially sensational. We must nevertheless try to do precisely that—to ferret out the most important development trends without being led astray by marketing hype and general excitement.

Since the virtues and deficiencies of specific products are of no consequence for our purpose, I believe it is possible to make such an assessment. What *are* important are the general capabilities of the technology, the capabilities that allow the products to be created in the first place. These developments constitute the *deep trends* of the industry, and they have fortunately proved to be extraordinarily stable over a period of several decades. As long as we keep to them, we stand a much better chance of being largely correct even for predictions stretching a decade or two ahead. As an example, we may return to the IDC forecast just mentioned: IDC was wrong in predicting that OS/2 would lead in the market in 1996, but it was wrong for the right reasons. Their forecast built on the belief that rapidly increasing price/performance ratio of PCs would make them proliferate (which they did); that a multitasking, graphically oriented, windowing environment would win in this new market (which is what happened); and that this environment would thereby rise to the top slot in market share (which it did). However, it was not OS/2, the obvious candidate at the moment, that succeeded, but the soon-to-come Microsoft Windows. This substitution, however important to business analysts, is only of marginal interest in the greater picture of computer utilization. The interesting point in that perspective are precisely those where IDC hit the bull's eye.

Three Basic Characteristics

Before we go on, it is necessary to establish just what constitutes the basic characteristics of computers and computer-based systems. And, even if the multitude of computers and computer-related products on the market exhibit great variations in performance and capabilities, a closer look at systems past and present will reveal that all their capabilities and functions can be related to three basic properties or characteristics.

First of all, computer systems of all kinds *process* information—they operate on it in some way or other. This capability has two aspects of equal importance: The first is the actual operations on information (for instance, adding numbers together); the second is the program—the specific instructions deciding the way the physical logic of the processor itself shall operate. Next, computers also *store* information, usually both programs and data, but at least a program of some sort. Third, they *communicate*—data and program must be put into the computer in the first place, the results must be presented to the user, and information is often transmitted to other systems, either for further processing, storage, or presentation.

The decisive underlying technology here is of course the representation of information and programs alike in *digital* form—in 1s and 0s. All digital information is thus represented by absolute values that can be copied, manipulated and transformed indefinitely without degradation, unlike the progressively attenuating amplitudes of analog technology. Without digital representation of information, the computers and applications described in this and later chapters would largely be impossible. (For an account of the ramifications of the principle of digital information representation that is both entertaining and enlightening, see Negroponte 1995).

THE EXTERNALIZATION OF PROCESSING

In many ways, ENIAC—traditionally recognized as the first electronic computer—was not a genuine, multi-purpose computer. It was a special-ized calculator, more like an electronic version of the Jacquard loom, optimized not for weaving, but for solving mathematical equations of a certain kind (ballistic trajectories for firing tables). However, in important respects, it was also very different from the loom. It could punch intermediate results on cards that could later be fed into it for new rounds of calculations, it could loop, repeat subroutines, and do conditional jumps—that is, branch the execution of the program in one of several directions based upon the results of previous calculations. It already exhibited the tree basic characteristics of computers, and it was more adept at solving equations than any other machine before it. But, it was not very flexible—it was programmed by setting physical switches and plugging cables in something that resembled old-fashioned, manual, telephone switchboards, a maddening task that took considerable time. It was the stored-program computer (of which the first one—the Manchester Mark 1—was built at Manchester University in England) that unleashed the real power of digital computing.

When the program escaped physical wiring and could be entered in a rewriteable, electronic memory, it could both become more complex, it could modify itself while running, and it became easily interchangeable. It is this almost unlimited programmability that makes the modern computer so different from a traditional machine, with its extremely limited programming logic (that quite literally has to be forged in steel). However, in one very important respect even the computer remains a classical machine: It cannot go beyond its set of design objectives; it cannot do anything that has not been spelled out in painstaking detail in a program on beforehand. Even with self-modifying programs, the rules for the modifications are given by the programmer, and programs that can "learn" from "experience" also obey preordained rules. The instructions may not always be conscious—there will be errors and ramifications the programmer was unaware of—but instructions they are.

Since programs are immaterial, the room for complexity is almost infinitely large compared to physical automation, which is limited by material restrictions. The result is that even small computer programs (and even the programming that is inherent in the circuit designs) are immensely more complex than mechanical automation can ever aspire to. The computer therefore allows us to build logical "machines" that are many orders of magnitude more complex than any physical machine we could conceive of. Electronic processing is also infinitely faster than the movements of wheels, levers, pistons, valves, and other actuators can ever be.

What does this really mean, then? What is the main contribution of the electronic, digital computer when it comes to human work and organizing? I have argued earlier that the main gift of writing was the externalization of memory. Looking back over about 5000 years, this conclusion is uncontroversial today. Some may think it premature to proclaim already the main contribution of the digital computer, but I believe that our experience during the decades since its first appearance demonstrate this beyond reasonable doubt: it is no less than the *externalization of information processing*—the possibility, for the first time in history, to process information outside the human head. As such, it represents the first tecnological innovation that matches the importance of writing. It might of course be said that externalization of processing has some modest roots in mechanical automation and computation devices, but the new frontier was not opened up in earnest until the advent of the programmable, electronic, digital computer—the first truly Universal Machine.

Just as the externalization of memory, the externalization of processing is of course not in any way comprehensive—it does not cover the whole, broad range of human information processing, with its rich web of logic and emotions. Computers can only mimic certain *aspects* of the human mind. But this must not fool anyone into thinking that those aspects are inconsequential or unimportant. Experience has already shown us that computers excel in performing logical operations; in information retrieval, selection, sorting and monitoring; and in number crunching and quantitative conversions (such as converting information from numbers to pictures)—types of processing that are extremely important in administrative work, material production, science, and in all kinds of information analyses.

This is a kind of processing, then, that we can externalize—that we can offload to computers, and it is when we exploit them to multiply our capacity in these areas that we really experience dramatic changes in productivity. Indeed, computers already allow us to perform tasks that would be impossible even in theory with human brainpower alone—no matter how many persons the project employed. There are simply not enough people on earth to carry out all the calculations involved in, for example, the modeling of the atmosphere that lets us study global warming or produce ten-day weather forecasts—and if there were, you would surely not be able to organize them (let alone pay them!). And, as the processing power of computers increases, the multiplication factor for our externalized processing only grows.

The development of the digital computer was incremental, with a lot of different persons contributing with a large number of small steps. It is debatable whether any of those steps involved a shift of paradigmatic magnitude; a transition from one kind of machine or tool to a fundamentally different one. It may even be debated whether the computer indeed is different in principle from previous machines—or if it just a very powerful kind of self-regulating machine (Wiener 1954).

However, even if the computer at the outset did not constitute something principally new, the quantitative changes it has undergone since its inception add up to a decidedly qualitative difference in relation to other kinds of machines. To draw a parallel, we may well say that both the earth and the smaller asteroids are lumps of rock circling the sun. But there is, literally, a world of difference between the earth and a small asteroid, rising from their different size and relative positions. The modern computer has a complexity, flexibility, information-processing capability and storage capacity so immense compared to any other machine that it constitutes a totally new class of devices. The possibilities it opens up are in many areas profoundly different from those that arise from traditional machinery, and they are all rooted in its paramount characteristic: its programmability.

Trends in Processing Power

When it comes to processing, speed is obviously important, and it has grown to become more important than we originally thought. If you had described the processing power of the modern PC to a computer engineer or computer user in 1955, he (it would surely have been a he) would have wondered how a single person could possibly utilize more than a fraction of that capacity. The users of today, with PCs strained by the demands of the latest version of their office suites, know better. In fact, as we enter the new world of pervasive IT, of graphical user interfaces, of multimedia and giant databases, our thirst for increased processing power is more acute than ever before. Will we never be satisfied? There is no reason to believe that the annual increases in power that we have grown accustomed to will slow down in the foreseeable future. The predictions for the years through 2010 are fairly safe, since we can even maintain the present rate of progress simply by the gradual refinement of existing technology. There is also every reason to believe that we will be able to continue the improvements even after the present approaches come up against final physical limits (like quantum effects when chip details become too small).

If we look at the most familiar processors for the average user at the time this book was written, the Intel 80 × 86 processor family (up to and including the Pentium II/III[1]), Intel was able to increase the processing power by a staggering 50% every year in the 20-year period 1978–1997[2], while at the same time reducing the price for one MIPS (unit of processing power) by 25% per year. This adds up to a 2000 times improvement in

---

[1] The Pentium III is only a "media upgrade," it is not a new processor at all. It is a Pentium II with a new set of multimedia instructions, produced by an improved production process.

[2] Figures are based on data compiled from articles and advertisments in numerous issues of *Byte*, *PC Magazine*, and *Scientific American*.

processing power, and a 300 times improvement in price/performance in just 20 years. And it still goes on.

Today, data processing has come to mean more than numerical calculations. Computers process not only figures, but text and graphics as well (including live video). They store and retrieve vast amounts of information. At the bottom, however, it is still just binary number crunching, and the speed of the processor is of course directly dependent upon the speed of these basic calculations. In modern, complex computers the speed of the primary and secondary memory (mass storage devices), the capacity of the transfer channels between the processor and the memory, and a host of other factors are of course also of great importance for the total performance of a particular computer.

The key to the incredible increase in speed and the impressive reduction in price we have seen, decade after decade, lies in the constant refinements of the integrated circuit. The number of discrete components that can be put on a single chip has increased tremendously, both because the size of components have shrunk and because chip size has increased. The first integrated, one-chip microprocessor (Intel's 4004, launched in 1971) had a mere 2300 transistors. The Intel Pentium II/IIIs of 1997–99 had 7.5 million (including on-chip Level 1 cache memory). That is an increase in the number of transistors per chip of roughly 35% every year for 27 years—almost a doubling every second year. We can expect this trend to continue for some time yet, and remain confident that new approaches will be found when needed.

The increase of power at the chip level does not automatically translate into corresponding gains in power at the system level. But, rather than being less, the gains in system power are in fact likely to be even greater than the gains in processor speed, as new, parallel architectures are perfected. The gains will come for systems on all levels, from the most humble PC through database servers and high-end transaction-processing machines, as well as workstations and supercomputers for technical and scientific applications. Moreover, an increasing number of specialized processors are added—such as graphics processors, communication processors, I/O processors and sound processors. An average user will have a multitude of superfast processors working for him or her—allowing for much more sophisticated software and greatly improved user interfaces.

If some of the basic problems of parallel processing are solved, standard processors may become even more commodity-like than today and fall into a pattern resembling the one we now have for memory chips: extremely high volumes, low prices, and liberal use. This will allow not only for new qualitative jumps in user friendliness, but also for the use of substantial processing power in the most trivial circumstances. Not that many years ago, people joked that even toasters would have processors in the future. Today, some toasters *have* processors, which help them toast the bread to the same degree of crispness regardless of whether the slice comes from a freshly baked loaf or from the freezer.

Together with the advances in storage media and communication, the increases in available processing power will also usher in the inclusion of high-quality sound and pictures, including live video. Multimedia PCs are already swamping the marketplace, but their capabilities will increase dramatically in the future (without significant price hikes), and many forecasters (beware!) predict the demise of the "dumb" TV.

It is tempting here to stray a little from the realistic assessments we are after in this chapter—for more than any other tool, the computer is becoming an expression of the human mind rather than of the human hand. Indeed, the hardware can be viewed as a kind of materialized spirit—its power coming not from physical force, but from its speed and accuracy in carrying out logical operations. And the logic content of computers is increasing all the time, in step with the miniaturization of electronic circuits. Whereas ENIAC was a 30-ton agglomeration of rather crude matter, with a very modest logic content, a modern microprocessor, several orders of magnitude more powerful, is almost immaterial—weighing less than one gram without its protective coating. Even a complete computer, with screen, mass storage, power supply, and keyboard, can now weigh less than 300 grams, and the weight of these "palmtops" is still going down.

Today, microelectronic chips are the medium for this logic, but there is no necessity in this—it only means that such chips are the most economical and convenient carriers at our present technological level. Other technologies will take over later, and, in a not too distant future, logical operations may be carried out by the manipulation of single electrons and photons. With intangible logic thus contained in almost immaterial quanta of energy, one realizes that the old philosophical debate about mind and matter is not nearly over yet.

In fact, if we look further ahead than the timeframe we otherwise adhere to, the evolvement of the computer may give this debate a new fervor, a new perspective, and a whole new set of arguments in the twenty-first century. I have always been a skeptic when it comes to the question of computers eventually attaining the same level of complexity as the human brain—partly because the brain is so exceedingly complex, and partly because our knowledge of its intricacies and operation is so limited, that we could not even use this processor complexity if we could produce it. However, if we consider the strides made in the few decades since the completion of ENIAC, versus the more than 300 million years that have passed since mammals and reptiles evolved from their common ancestor (and the development of the brain started even long before that), I am not so sure anymore. We have just discussed the power of computers in the near future. But how powerful will they become further down along the road? In the February 1996 issue of *Internet World*, science fiction writer Vernon Vinge points to the fact that if the current trend in processing power improvements continues, computer hardware processing capacity will actually reach what we now estimate to be the level of the human brain already between the years 2030 and 2040. What about the situation a hundred years after that? Five hundred? Two thousand? Will we be able to develop software that can take advantage of this tremendous processing capacity and create entities with higher total processing capacity than ourselves? If so, what will the consequences be? Who knows—but one thing is for sure: the computers of the more distant future are going to be incredible indeed when judged by today's standards. As Arthur C. Clarke used to say, any technology sufficiently more advanced than the one we know will always look like magic. So would the computers of the distant future seem to us, if we could catch a glimpse of them today.

The Future of Software

Processing power is useless without programs. In many ways, the development of computers, or at least the use of computers, is a matter of software improvement. To say something about the future of software, however, is the most difficult task of all. The number of companies and people engaged in software development is so large and the latitude for creativity in that area so great that almost anything can happen—as far as it satisfies a need (real or imagined) in the user community. What we can say is that, as more powerful computers can take on ever heavier software loads, programs become more comprehensive, more complex and increasingly incorporate very computing-intensive components, not least at the user interface (such as graphics, video and sound).

Standard packages are moreover becoming more and more flexible, due to an increasing number of functions, options, and open parameters. Programming languages, on their hand, are increasingly equipped with libraries of subroutines and other basic program elements that increase programmer productivity. Organizations therefore have a rich set of options to choose from when they need new systems.

Working against the variety in main application areas is an increasing globalization of software. Since the costs of changing software is considerable and generally increasing, people will put great weight on the business prospects of their vendors—especially for mission critical applications. To ensure the best possible compatibility and interoperability between software packages, there is also a strong tendency toward choosing the market leader even if smaller competitors offer better solutions. In some product classes, notably word processing and a few other office products, we are actually coming close to a de facto monopoly on a global basis. The number of serious players in the database market is also rapidly dwindling. However, the major products are now so rich in functions that they already represent a significant degree of overkill for the average user, and most organizations are not anywhere near of getting full mileage out of the systems they already have.

In fact, the bottlenecks of software development are rapidly becoming not the programming itself, but the processes coming before and after. The mounting complexity of the analyses and planning needed to create really large software systems is now taxing the skills and intellectual capacity of both users and analysts, and is not infrequently defeating them—leading to aborted projects or software with major deficiencies. After a system has been completed, the intricacies of the new software and its organizational ramifications often require such skill and knowledge to really take advantage of them that the software is poorly employed at best, and a prolonged period of trial and error is needed before operations stabilize.

STORAGE

My first job after I finished my MA in sociology was in the personnel department of a shipyard in Oslo. The shipyard was old; it was started as an engineering workshop in 1841, and moved to the sea front and turned into a shipyard in 1854. It eventually evolved into a modern yard, building some of the first semi-submersible oil drilling platforms used in the North Sea. Countless workers had passed through its gates since its inception, and a succession of devoted personnel clerks had scrupulously kept the files for all who left, probably in case they should return later (which was quite common—many alternated as sailors). In the 1970s, when I worked there, the personnel office had complete files for more than 100 years of employees. What a treasure trove for a sociologist! But, alas, the information was written on thousands of individual cards, the only indexing scheme was alphabetical by name, and the effort required to extract even a fraction of the data these files contained was prohibitive. So, although the information was physically there, it was not accessible in practice. Had it only been in a database! Then, analysis would have been comparatively easy and cheap—and of great interest—not only for scientific purposes, but also for the company.

The database, however, is an even more recent phenomenon than the computer. Computers were invented to make calculations, not to store information, and storage was not exactly their strong point during their first decades. ENIAC could store only twenty 10-digit numbers in its internal accumulators while running—a meager 800 bits—apart from the program, which was "stored" in wiring and switches. Data was fetched number by number from punch cards. Because of its limited ability to store intermediate results internally, more complicated calculations usually meant that intermediate results had to be output to punch cards, which then had to be loaded for the next sequence of computations. The first stored-program computer, the Manchester Mark 1, had a CRT-based internal memory of between 6144 and 12 288 bits, but still had to rely on paper tape for secondary storage. The first UNIVAC computer represented something of a breakthrough with its internal memory capacity of 84 000 bits (10.5 Kb in today's language) and its magnetic tape secondary storage with megabyte capacity (up to ten tape units storing more than one megabyte each). After a period with quite exotic memory devices, like CRTs and glass tubes filled with mercury, the magnetic core memory in the 1950s became the first practical way of equipping computers with a reliable and comparatively large memory. However, we had to wait for the semiconductor and the integrated circuit to make it both really large and affordable—and allow computers to shrink to desktop size and price. The first practical microcomputer, the Altair, appeared in 1975 with a basic capacity of a tiny 256 bytes (2048 bits), but soon 4 Kb add-in boards were available. When Apple II was launched in 1977, it had 16 Kb of memory as standard (expandable to 64 Kb, as the Altair).

Still, limited memory capacity for a long time represented a serious bottleneck for computer performance, since the size of the memory decides both the size of the program modules running at any particular time, as well as how often the computer must access its secondary (and much slower) storage medium for reading and writing data. Especially when sorting and indexing (common database operations) the size of the available memory has a very decisive influence on execution time.

The low capacity and high price of secondary storage likewise limited the computer's role as an archival device for a long time. The first mass storage devices were punch cards and paper tape. Then magnetic tape came along, but even if it represented a great improvement in speed and capacity, it was still a sequential medium—to get at a piece of information in the far end of the tape, one had to spool it from one reel to another. The first random-access medium was the magnetic drum memory of the late 1940s and early 1950s, but a satisfactory solution was not found until magnetic disk memory was introduced by IBM in 1956 and used in the IBM 305 RAMAC computer. The disk in IBM's first unit was 24″ (61 cm) in diameter, had 50 platters stacked on top of each other on the one shaft, and stored 5 Mb of data.

Today, the situation has totally changed, and it is still changing fairly dramatically from year to year. Storage capacity, both in terms of primary memory and secondary storage, is becoming ever cheaper, even when measured in relative terms against the increasing demands from new hardware and software. Although there are still some problems at the extremes, especially in high-end graphics processing, ample storage is now increasingly taken for granted.

Trends in Storage

Since the early 1970s, semiconductor memory has ruled the market for primary memory, and the price performance ratio has improved steadily—even for memory chips, the number of components per chip has increased by about 50% per year, and still shows no sign of leveling out. The cost per megabyte has been reduced by 35% every year since 1975, when it was $20 480 (chips only).[3] Because of the geometrical regularity of the design, memory chips can be much more densely packed, and have a much larger number of components than processors. At the time of writing 64-million cell chips (each cell consisting of one capacitor and one transistor) are in volume sale, and one-billion cell chips are planned for. Such a gigabit chip will be able to store (with an 8-bit character standard) about 134 million characters, the equivalent of about 65 000 pages of text like this one—more than some people will read in their whole life.

With the gigabit chip, we will approach the limits for further improvement of the venerable silicon memory chip. Larger chips may be manufactured by increasing chip area, but continued shrinking of transistor size will come up against the emergence of quantum phenomena—the chance jumping of electrons across the insulating barriers. Because of the unpredictable nature of these quantum jumps, they will destroy the reliability that is so important for computer memory. It would be foolish, however, to suppose that this signifies any permanent barrier to further improvement in the price/performance of computer memory. Other technologies are already on the horizon, and even newer ones are bound to appear further down the road.

For several years now, the increase in memory price/performance has been faster than the increase in need for memory capacity. This trend seems to continue, and we have already started to use memory freely, without bothering too much about the cost. This will have significant

---

[3] Figures are based on data compiled from articles and advertisements in numerous issues of *Byte*, *PC Magazine*, and *Scientific American*.

consequences for how computers will look and operate in the years to come.

When it comes to mass storage, disk development has relegated magnetic tape to a position as a medium for backup and archival purposes. An increasing number of gigabytes can be stored in surprisingly cheap miniature disk drives (3.5″ and smaller). The development has followed the same pattern as for processors and memory, and has been just as stable. I have only seen data from 1983 onward, but for the 12 years through 1994, the price per megabyte of magnetic disk storage fell by roughly 38% per year—from $100 to 50¢. After that, it has fallen even faster—in 1997 storage costs on cost-effective magnetic disks fell below 5¢ per megabyte, only a fraction of the cost for storing text on paper, if printing and storage shelf/cabinet costs are counted (around $15 per megabyte). With the present development, paper is even losing its cost advantage for graphics storage. Disk storage is actually becoming "free" for all but the most extreme storage needs, and even better performers for very high-volume storage are in development—among them holographic storage of information in light-sensitive crystals. This holds the promise of a new revolution in storage with both higher densities and far higher speed than conventional media, although progress has proved to be slower than anticipated (Parish 1990, Baran 1991, Psaltis and Mok 1995, Thompson 1996).

The biggest drawback of magnetic media is that they lose their data gradually over the years and must be refreshed from time to time (tapes in archives are usually refreshed every two or three years). For archival purposes, certain types of optical disks are therefore preferred, which—according to conservative estimates—will retain their data uncorrupted for at least 60 to 100 years (Harvey 1990).

Whatever mass storage technology wins in the future, however, we can be quite confident that we will have available abundant capacity at very low prices, enough even for the storage and real-time playback of high-definition video movies. This will mean that digital storage media will become the most economical and compact alternative *for all types of information storage*. As Nicholas Negroponte has pointed out (Negroponte 1995), this will put a significant pressure on the traditional media and possibly reduce their roles considerably.

Pillars of the Memory Revolution

However, the large available volume is not the most significant aspect of computer storage. Indeed, the theoretical space available for information storage does not even increase as we make the transition to digital storage. This may seem surprising, since data already takes up so much less space on disks than on paper—but the earth is pretty large, and there is always a blank sheet of paper or a new file card available. We should also remember that microfilm is *not* a child of the electronic computer, and microfilm density can be quite respectable—especially for ultrastrips (which is, literally, microfilmed microfilm). Even if the new digital media now have overtaken microfilm as well, it is only when their extremely compact and cheap storage is combined with the *access, search and retrieval capabilities* of the computer that we achieve something truly new.

Like written files, digitally stored information is also in principle available to all and anyone. But, compared to the written file, which requires that you (or someone else on your behalf) physically walk up to it to retrieve information, digitally stored information is so very much more accessible. Anyone with a terminal connected to the system, directly or through a communications network, can access it, regardless of geographical location or time of day. It is, moreover, *simultaneously* available to a large number of users—how many is determined solely by technical factors such as system capacity and the number of communication ports, and the limits here are steadily and briskly being pushed upward.

If we envision future computer systems—of, say, several decades into the twenty-first century—with extremely powerful parallel processors, holographic mass storage and direct fiber connection to a fiber-based telecommunication network, their transaction capacity will be several orders of magnitude greater than the most powerful systems available today, and they may serve global communities numbering hundreds of thousands, even millions, of simultaneous on-line users. Even the largest multinational corporations would then easily be able to consolidate their operational databases into either one unified virtual base (distributed among many physical sites) or one central physical base. The actual solution chosen would depend on the level of integration required in running the organization and its business activities. The idea of a central database for a multinational corporation may seem preposterous at this point in time, but I am not so sure it will look that way in a couple of decades.

Vast amounts of information are of no use, however, if you cannot retrieve the items you need when you need them—and to retrieve them you first have to find them, just as with written information. Luckily, the fact that digitally stored information can be read by a computer also means that the computer can search for us, as long as we can provide relevant search criteria. The computer can also index, cross-index, sort, and compare with enormous speed. It can retrieve one record from among millions in a small fraction of a second, and, just as quickly, store it back again after it has been changed. It can select groups of records on the basis of certain properties and sort them according to various other properties, it can count them, and so on. The computer's outstanding ability to search vast amounts of information in an incredibly short time, and extract, combine, and concentrate data, makes for a momentous difference between computerized and paper-based files.

When we talk about records, we mostly mean information that is precisely defined and put into a strict format, like accounting data for a bank or customer information for an insurance company. The items of information and the form they are going to be stored in are decided on beforehand, and for each item a corresponding field is defined in the database. The field is normally designated at least as numerical or alpha-numerical, and will usually have a maximum number of positions, or even a mandatory number of positions (as with dates and article numbers). There are also usually a number of other design options for each field.

The advantage of storing information in this highly structured form is that it can be easily retrieved, counted, and classified; numbers can be used in calculations; names and addresses can be used to produce mass mail-ings; and so on. It is simply a prerequisite to automatic processing: The programs must "know" exactly what kind of information they shall retrieve, where it is stored, on what form, and exactly what to do with it and where to put it afterward. It is structured databases such as these that lie at the bottom of almost all the familiar success stories about profitable use of IT that circulate in the business world (and in the realm of public administration, for that matter).

There is quite a lot of information that is impossible to accommodate in a structured database, however. In fact, even these databases will often contain a "comment" field, wherein unstructured, textual information can be entered—information that is too important to be left out but too special to be defined in advance, or simply too varied to be included in a classification scheme.

The first attempts to use computers to store and retrieve more "soft" information were just a few years behind the applications focusing on structured data. As early as the second half of the 1950s, 20 years of headnotes of design patent law cases had been entered into an IBM 305 RAMAC (the machine with the world's first magnetic disks). At the same time, what was probably the first full-text "database" came into being when Professor John F. Horty of the Health Law Center of the University of Pittsburgh used the university's computing center to solve a practical problem: the actual implementation of a bill passed in the Pennsylvanian legislature to replace the term "retarded child" (and all its permutations) with "exceptional child" (and all the corresponding permutations) in the state's health statutes (Bing and Harvold, 1977).

After two consecutive tries with groups of students reading the statutes and substituting terms, and with too many errors still remaining, the complete text was registered on punch cards—and the substitutions left to the computer. Horty then found that the machine-readable text could be exploited in much more exciting ways as well, and he went on to develop what was probably the world's first full-text search and retrieval system.

The benefits are here already—just think about the full-text databases now offered by many leading newspapers around the world, or the improvement in literature searches provided by computerized book and journal catalogues—not to mention the rapidly expanding jungle of both serious and oddball databases accessible through Internet. Of course, no search is perfect, as everyone with some experience in database search will agree (and will probably never be), but with some experience, computer searches are already vastly more effective than anything before. Although they will not find all the relevant information, and often not even the majority of it, the catch is always much more complete than with manual searches, and exceedingly fast in comparison. The performance of computer-based systems is simply so much better than the old, paper-based ones that they can only be compared in principle.

In real life we may often encounter practical obstacles to information retrieval—such as incompatible storage formats, inflexible database structures, inadequate application software, and the like. However, they all represent temporary technological shortcomings or are the results of the vendors' commercial considerations. They are not consequences of the technology's inherent properties, and can thus always be overcome—even if it may cost a lot of money sometimes.

COMMUNICATION

From Artifacts to Waves and Current

Communication has always involved both physical transportation of goods and people and transfer of information. Except for marginal technologies such as semaphores, drums and the proverbial smoke signals, transfer of information over almost any distance before the telegraph was equivalent to physical transportation, since it invariably involved people (messengers), tablets, paper or paper-like materials. The telegraph, and, later, the telephone, radio, and television, changed this and established information transfer as a separate category—the symbols of human communication escaped from the world of paper and parchment and became embodied by radio waves and the current in telegraph and telephone wires.

Computers do not change this in any basic, physical sense. Electronic mail and telefax are much more efficient than the telegraph, but they still rely mostly on electrical signals traveling along a wire—in some instances probably even the same physical wires that earlier carried the telegraph traffic. Even the introduction of satellite communication and optical fiber do not change anything in principle—it is still a matter of transmitting symbols instead of physical objects, even if the capacity of the carriers probably has increased beyond the wildest dreams of both Bell and Marconi.

The context of communication has also broadened to include not only communication between human beings, as was the case with all the pre-computer communication technologies, but also direct communication between computer systems. Of course, one may always claim that it is only a matter of mediated communication between humans, since there is always a human somewhere downstream and somewhere upstream. Both are often so far removed from the direct effects of the communication, however, that I would maintain that system-to-system communication is a separate category that merits its own considerations.

When it comes to physical transport, the consequences of information technology have been mainly indirect: The ship, the airplane, the train, and the automobile are not inventions of the computer age; neither are the steam engine, the diesel engine, the petrol engine, the jet engine or the electrical motor. But, of course, there are important contributions that improve the performance of our physical transportation systems, both with respect to design, operation and administrative support. Modern jet liners, for instance, could not have been designed and built without computers, they could hardly have been flown without computers, and computer-based navigation and air traffic control systems allow traffic regularity under almost all weather conditions. Routing systems for railroad cars are computer-based, trucks are directed with the help of computer-based systems, and computer systems keep track of each single package transported by express freight companies and courier services. Electronic customs systems, as Norway's TVINN,[4] speed the transport of goods further by eliminating delays at the border. The contributions of information technology to physical transport are marginal, however, compared to the improvements originally brought by the development of the prime movers of goods and persons: ships, trains, cars and airplanes.

Basic Input and Output

Communication is a many-sided thing, however. Most basic is the communication between the computer itself and its users and programmers.

---

[4] TVINN was the second or third such system in the world when it went into regular production in 1988. (New Zealand was first, and Singapore came along about the same time as TVINN.)

Some may puzzle over the fact that I include both input and output of data under the heading "communication," but both constitute information transfer, and will increasingly include direct data capture from sensors, data interchange through common database access and messaging between computers. That way, they become inseparable from what we normally think about as computer communication. But let us start with the basics.

For any piece of data to be processed, and any program to be run, it must of course first be loaded into the computer. As we have seen, loading data and programs into the first computers could be quite demanding. Being able to load programs from fast disks or over networks, we are far better off today. To enter data we still often have to use keyboards, however—even if it is increasingly captured directly from sensors, bar code readers and other automatic means of data capture. Data can of course also be generated internally in the computer as a result of transformations or processing of original data. Once registered, data is stored in a mass storage device like those discussed earlier.

Keyboards have not changed much since the *qwerty* keyboard was devised a hundred years ago, proving the enormous inertia of established standards. Although more efficient keyboard layouts have been devised (for instance, the Dvorak keyboard, with the most frequently used letters in the middle), it seems that the old standard is going to keep its dominating position. Keyboards are still our main instrument for communicating with computers (complemented by mice and tablets of various kinds) and will remain so for many years yet. Both speech and handwriting recognition have repeatedly been prematurely announced, and all commercially available systems so far have had serious limitations.

The problem is that both speech and handwriting recognition belong to the difficult field of pattern recognition, where humans excel and machines are so far ineffectual. Reliable recognition of continuous speech with normal vocabularies from arbitrary persons is exceedingly difficult for a computer, and requires both more sophisticated software and a lot more powerful hardware than we have had available so far. Recognition of natural, flowing handwriting from arbitrary persons is even more difficult, and will probably take more time to solve than speech recognition. However, with the rate of improvement we have grown used to in processor power, there is little doubt that both will become available in the foreseeable future. Whether speech recognition will succeed in the marketplace is another question, but those who prefer to talk to their PCs will eventually have the opportunity of doing it for a very small extra cost (if any). When general handwriting recognition eventually comes, it is difficult to say if it will meet with success outside a number of niche markets—especially since it will only appear after general speech recognition has become an affordable reality. However, it may be a preferable interface for taking notes and for editing and making corrections in text entered by dictation or by keyboard.

Direct data capture by way of sensors is rapidly becoming more important, however. It is no longer only a question of lab data or temperature and pressure in processing plants. Increasingly, our shopping is registered automatically by light pens or label scanners, payments (for goods, bus tickets, and pay phones) effected by card readers communicating with smartcards, toll road passage certified by machines reading chips glued to a car's windshield, and so on. Because of the huge savings in labor hours it normally represents, there is a very strong impetus for increasing the extent of automatic data capture, and we will see even more of it in the future.

After input and processing follows output. When ENIAC produced an answer, it communicated it to its users by punching cards. Its successors rapidly learned to address their users through screens and teletype printers. Printing rapidly became the method of choice, as it allowed the user to read at his leisure without tying up precious processor capacity. When processors became less costly and more powerful, and users more craving for the direct responses of interactive computing, screens became increasingly important, and are today the predominant medium.

Printing is still very important, however, and paper is easily the preferred medium for final output and presentation. It got a real boost during the 1980s by the development of the low-cost laser printer—an incredible improvement over the clattering one-page-per-minute typewheel printers of yesteryear. At first, it lacked color, but there is no doubt that the price/performance equation even in this field will improve to the point where high-quality laser color printing becomes economically attractive for "the rest of us." For ink jet printing, it has already happened. Color is of course intrinsically more complicated than black and white, and should therefore invariably cost more, but in a mass market, it does not always turn out that way. Consider photography. Even if color film and prints are intrinsically more expensive than black and white, color costs (a lot) less for the average consumer—simply because all the big consumer-oriented labs as well as the small automatic developers only do color, thereby reducing black-and-white prints to handicraft work produced by your local photographer. Market penetration decides the price.

Printing also has a wider role in communication. The fax machine has been a runaway success, and the reasons are obvious: It is low-cost and very easy to use; utilizes existing telephone connections (and thereby addressing conventions); transmits the output from any program and printer, including one's *pen*; and accepts graphics as well as text. Electronic mail will definitely win in the long run, but the fax machine has, at our present level of technological sophistication, provided a very simple and elegant solution for rapid communications. With a fax-capable modem and appropriate software, you computer can use fax machines as remote printers. With cheap color printing and faster modems (or ISDN), an improved fax standard could allow you to output directly to a printer halfway around the globe with decent speed, normal print quality and faithful reproduction of any fancy letterhead at the receiving end.

One of the main reasons for the heavy reliance we still place on paper— perhaps *the* main reason—is the shortcomings of present screen technology. Whereas all the other vital parts of a computer system have enjoyed a very rapid and sustained increase in performance, screen development has been sluggish. To do away with paper, we need screens that are large enough to show us a lot of information simultaneously, so we can work the way we are used to, with several information sources available concurrently. The screens must have good contrast, high resolution and provide good reading comfort. Preferably, the viewing position should be easy to change, to let us keep our normal habit of shifting back and forth between positions when reading a report or a book. None of the commercially available screen technologies today can fulfill this.

Really large displays are extremely bulky as well as expensive, and you simply cannot buy the big, high resolution screens necessary to really do away with all the paper on that desktop. To do so, you need full square meter screens or larger—flat screens that are part of our desktops or even constitute the desktop, preferably tiltable, and with a detachable panel for comfortable reading. With adequate resolution and contrast, screens like that would really take a bite out of the paper market—we would not need printouts for that final control, documents could be distributed electronically, and the receiver might prefer to view the information on-screen instead of printing it out. Even the hour of the CD-ROM-based magazine might finally come, and the fax machine would at last feel the competition of screen-fax and global electronic mail. Unfortunately, such screens will not be available in the short run. There are potential technologies under development, but they will need considerable time to achieve the sizes and prices necessary (Chinnock 1997, Sobel 1998). However, I believe we can be confident that such screens will appear in the not too distant future.

Electronic Mail

Not long after computers got screens and text editors, entrepreneuring programmers and users found a way of connecting computers over ordinary telephone lines. The first first crude standards for message exchange between different types of computers was probably the protocols developed in the ARPANET project around 1970 (the forerunner for

Internet). This computer-mediated messaging was based on the computer's ability to store data and to forward and receive messages automatically. Thus, a new medium was born with the almost instant transfer of the telephone coupled with the asynchronous nature of the letter. It has proved to be a great combination, and its double nature shows in the fact that email language tends to be much more informal than the language in old-fashioned letters—it is almost oral in character.

Up to quite recently, email suffered because of a lack of standardization regarding address formats, message formats, character encoding, and mechanisms for attaching files to messages. Even if there were pioneering standards available quite early, most of the different computer companies had their own proprietary mail systems, and there were even competing international standardization schemes. As late as in the early 1990s, the process of standardization seemed slow. Then the sudden and phenomenal growth in Internet use rapidly established de facto standards in all these areas. There are still problems, but the market pressure on the vendors has increased dramatically, and those who want to survive must converge toward a common set of solutions fairly rapidly—since the users will flock to the solution that ensures them the most painless communication. As a result of this, we are experiencing a dramatic increase in the use of email, and the use of file attachments has already become a viable alternative to fax and remote printing. An offshoot of email is *computer conferencing*—where electronic mail is put in a storage area where all the conference participants can read it and respond to it. It then remains in storage for later reference or is deleted at the discretion of the conference moderator (more about conferencing later).

Telephones and Videophones

In an earlier discussion of the way technology has enhanced communication, we touched upon both the telephone and video-based communication. The further development of both has for many years depended on microelectronics and computer technology. Telephone switching has already become a task for specialized computers (digital switches), telephones themselves are increasingly chip-based, cellular phones are crammed with microelectronics, and the whole transmission system is now in the midst of a change from analog to digital signaling (ISDN and ATM[5]). There is also a movement toward one or a few digital

---

[5] ISDN stands for Integrated Digital Services Network, ATM for Asynchronous Transfer Mode. ATM is a second-generation standard for digital communication that will allow transfer rates several orders of magnitude greater than ISDN. ATM is already available on a limited basis in many countries and is expected to eventually supersede ISDN.

standards for cellular telephones, which means that we will eventually get truly international networks allowing the owners of standard cellular phones to place and receive calls from their own sets regardless of which country they are in. In the high end, there will even be fully global satellite-based services with handheld receivers about the size of normal cellular phones. Other notable developments in telephony are voice mail—really only an auditive parallel to email—and the self-service switchboard, which represents an attempt to automate switching, access control, and simple direction-giving.

As we have noted earlier, the videophone has been one of the chief recurring sensations of the twentieth century. The limiting factor has always been the excessive cost associated with the high-capacity lines needed for the transmission of live video. Considerable progress has been made in compressing video signals, however, and the prices of channel capacity have also been falling at a steady rate, not least because computer-based technology has made it possible to transmit far more information over existing copper wiring than anybody thought possible as late as in the 1980s. This means that we can finally see the day when this turkey will mutate into a bird with a more pronounced ability to fly. With the present development, high-quality video telephony and conferencing is bound to become available at affordable prices, even before the public telephone networks are fully rewired with optical fiber into every home and organization.

The days when we seriously considered the need versus the cost before placing an intercontinental telephone are by and large gone, and the same thing will happen with video. Combined video and computer conferencing—with simultaneous viewing of screens and exchange of comments and data—will become cheap enough to allow widespread use. And there are even more exotic alternatives on the horizon: research has already started on the possibilities for holographic displays, allowing for three-dimensional representations. Work done at MIT's Media Lab (among others) indicates that it will be feasible some time in the future. If so, it will give an entirely new twist to video conferencing and make simulated presence almost as good as being there. However, it is definitely outside the frame of realistic assessment we adopted at the beginning of this chapter.

System-to-System Communication

Email is really built on the ability of computers to communicate with each other automatically and without direct human intervention. In this case, the messages are directly originated by and intended for humans, but the mechanism behind can also be used for other purposes—such as communication between applications running on the same machine as well as communication between systems residing on different computers. It was pioneered already in the 1950s, and the SAGE computers (the core of the first American early warning radar system) were linked when they were deployed in the late 1950s.

Basically, information interchange between application or between systems can be effected in two different ways: Either you can share the data by common database access, or you can have the applications or systems send messages to each other. The common database approach is really the computerized parallel of the concept of the active file—a unified collection of organized information for administrative purposes. It is often the natural solution inside an organization, or at any rate for those parts of an organization that have to work intimately together. The messaging concept will most likely be the right answer for communication between organizations and between various parts of a large organization, where shared databases are not a convenient solution.

Common database access means that information captured or keyed into one application or task module[6] can be accessed, processed, and presented by other applications or modules. Data registered through a production control system, for instance, can thus be immediately available for the sales support system, keeping sales representatives continually updated on the status of individual orders. The same data can then be directly utilized by an inventory control system (ordering replenishments for parts or raw materials that are running low), and a transport scheduling system (supporting the shipment of finished products). An order entry system may in its turn supply input data for the production control system, possibly by way of a separate or integrated system for production planning and scheduling. An executive information system may cull data from all of the various systems, presenting a coherent and continuously updated picture of the main activities in the organization.

This is not yet a description of the common situation in user organizations,[7] but it should gradually become so. Common database

---

[6] The boundaries of applications tend to follow the boundaries between task clusters in the traditional organization—general ledger, for instance, or order entry, inventory control, or payroll. The different applications in their turn consist of a number of task-oriented modules, usually organized around specific screens. The modules can in many ways be viewed as applications within the application, and in less traditional future systems, they will probably be grouped differently (and quite a number of them may even be eliminated). The distinction is therefore somewhat arbitrary.

[7] In most organizations the various systems (and few organizations will have systems in all these areas) will most likely be of different origin, use different databases and formats, and even run on incompatible machines from different vendors. In some industries (notably, the automobile industry), integration has become fairly advanced, but, even there, much remains to be done.

access is bound to become a cornerstone in administrative computing. Going external, however, messaging becomes necessary, and message transmittal in the form of automatic data transfer irrespective of application or computer type is not trivial. It is not necessary here to describe the many layers of communication protocols needed, but I will point out that communication on the application level requires a considerable amount of standardization, both between vendors (equipment and software) and between users (data formats). If an order is to be dispatched automatically by a inventory control system and directly received and processed by an order entry system in another company (running on a computer from a different and incompatible vendor), even the number and definition of the data fields, as well as their size and content must follow strict standards—otherwise, the receiving computer may mistake an order number for an amount to be shipped, and the name of an article for a company address. Such standardized definitions must be established for all the different types of "documents" required.

This standardization is really what such messaging, or *electronic data interchange* (EDI) is all about. Several standards have been created through the years—national standards, industry standards, and even company-based standards (large companies are able to dictate their suppliers and strongly influence their customers)—although none of them have been really comprehensive. Today, there is a broad effort underway to create a truly international standard—or, rather, set of standards—for commercial applications. The work is carried out under the auspices of the United Nations. The UN/EDIFACT[8] effort aims at establishing a definite international standard for all main types of documents used in international business, regardless of industry. It has been underway for a number of years; the first standards have already emerged, and more will follow in the years to come. There is also work underway on standardization of drawings and graphics, an important area for the manufacturing industry. Creating standards involving so many nations, agencies, and industry associations is a promethean effort, and it is destined to take a long time. Indeed, it will never be completed—there will always crop up needs for alterations and new standards. But the main groundwork and the standardization of the main document groups are well underway, and the rewards for its accomplishment are so great for all parties involved that it is also an effort destined for ultimate success.

In addition to this basic standard, we can expect supplemental conventions to develop at many levels—within organizations and between trading partners and manufacturers and their suppliers. The net result

---

[8] United Nations Electronic Data Interchange for Administration, Commerce, and Transport.

will be a lot less keying in of information, with concomitant savings in labor hours. The consequences may prove much more profound than simple savings, however, a subject we will return to in later chapters.

AN ESCAPE FROM PAPER?

Information Presentation

In Chapter 6 we discussed the transition from orality to literacy, and the fundamental changes it wrought. In addition to all this, it also brought us a physical format for information presentation—the written word is a material product with both design and packaging, both with an interesting history we unfortunately cannot detail here. Suffice it to say that after centuries and even millennia of tablets, scrolls, and various other formats, the sheet and the book gradually became the preferred solutions. Sheets are easier to manufacture than scrolls, and books have the advantage of being random access devices—you can open them on any page.

That sheet of paper, the page, has been with us ever since, and it is today the principal setting for all kinds of textual information: almost everything has to fit a page. Even as I write this, thin dotted lines appear from time to time on my computer display, telling me that I have reached the end of the current page—yet there is no such thing as a "page" in a computer text file. The creators of my word processor, however, knew full well that the intended product of my keyboard efforts would be stacks of pages from the laser printer down the hall, and therefore provided me with that unobtrusive cue to help me with my formatting.

In the beginning, computers were not at all slaves of this paper paradigm, but as soon as printers entered the scene, their output was brought under page control. Even if it has an interactive nature and can display varied information, the traditional computer screen is treated largely as "reusable paper"—information is displayed in an orderly, serial format that resembles a paper-based presentation as much as possible. For office support systems the ideal has always been to make the screen look identical to the prospective paper output, even to the extent that black letters on a white background are preferred—in spite of the fact that this combination is not necessarily ergonomically preferable.

The paper paradigm can be traced further in software design, from the on-screen, visual index cards of archiving systems and simple databases, to the drawers, folders and document icons presented by the latest in office support systems. The reasons are twofold: first, most of what we compose on the screen is finally destined for output on paper, and must therefore be designed to fit the page format produced by the printer. Second, the software designers all seem to think that the friendliest computer is the one that provides the user with an emulation of his or her paper-based past, and thus attunes itself to the user's established mental set for office work. How could it be otherwise? As both Ong (1982) and Havelock (1986) note, it takes an oral culture generations to pass from an oral form of expression (with formulaic style for mnemonic purposes) to a truly native, literate (chirographic, written) style. We have more than 5000 years of chirographic tradition behind us, and with only a few decades of computer experience, we are doomed to mimic the past—we need time to adjust, to enter into a working relationship with the new technology, to iterate our way toward more *computerate* manners. As the systems become more powerful, however, and (not least) the screens bigger and more comfortable to read from, things are bound to change.

The evolvement away from the paper paradigm can be traced in the development of user interfaces. We have now largely left the green-phospor character-based screens, and are immersed in paper-mimicking graphical interfaces. A growing number of features point even further, though. Some of the controls are distinctly nonpaper, for instance, buttons and sliding controls. Even if they are borrowed from well-known mechanical and electrical appliances and thus do not represent "native" computer innovations, they show us that the computer can do more than simulate pen and paper.

Hypermedia

More exciting still are the developments in the direction of object orientation, hypermedia, and "hot links" between applications. Such a higher-order object consisting of chunks of text, spreadsheets, and graphics is nevertheless little more than a compound document, a collection of pages, and it will still print neatly. The next step is to have a document that merely contains pointers to where the different information chunks are stored. When any of the chunks is modified, this modification will then also automatically apply to all the compound documents that contain pointers to it. Such documents can still be printed without problems, but version control now becomes more important.

However, such links can also be made conditional—like an electronic footnote. A word, a picture, or a table can be marked as a button, and when you activate that button, the link will come to life and retrieve the supplementary information. This is the basic idea of "hypermedia," an idea that has also inspired the principles behind the World Wide Web. A "document" with such buttons would be harder to print, but it could still be done, if it were acceptable to convert the buttons to footnote markers and the supplementary information to footnotes.

But hypermedia (and the WWW) goes further than this—it can easily be nested. The supplementary information can contain its own buttons, pointing to even more information, where you will find still more buttons, and so on. This is what hypermedia is really about—a three-dimensional information structure where you can establish both factual (providing explanations or supplementary information) and associative links, building an information structure that will be totally unprintable. Some of the information chunks may consist of live video or sound, which is even less representable on paper.

Hypermedia links can have many properties. They can be *bidirectional*, meaning that you can not only point to a reference like in a footnote, but you can also, from the reference, be able to trace all the works referring to it. The links can also have different granularities. A link can point to a book, paragraph, or word; a picture or a section of that picture (possibly even a single pixel); a passage in a piece of music (or even a single beat); and so on. There can also be different types of links, with different access levels, and you may be able to establish filters, showing you only the types of links you are interested in. A distributed hypermedia system could also have "document sensors" that constantly monitor documents or parts of documents, carrying out certain actions when triggered—for instance, notifying the original author if someone else updated a piece of information.

Advanced hypermedia systems should make it possible to establish "living" information bases, where revisions are automatically accessible to all links, and where the revisions themselves can trigger messages to those who have referred to that information. Full version control will be possible, and it should also be possible to backtrack revisions and reconstruct the original document. If write-only storage media are used, such a system should make it possible to operate without paper even in highly formal environments, such as government offices, because of the audit trail left in the system.

The idea of a hypermedia system was first presented by Vannevar Bush in his famous 1945 article about the Memex (Bush 1945). However, since the computer was yet in embryo, he was thinking about a microfilm system. The hypermedia concept was brought into the computer world by Theodor H. Nelson, whose brainchild, the Xanadu hypermedia system, was designed with the idealistic goal in mind of providing an engine for a world-wide hypertext publishing network (Nelson 1988). The network should store a particular piece of information in only one location, while allowing it to be incorporated in any "document" on any server in the network via links. Despite the somewhat grandiose aim, Xanadu became a real piece of software, with 30 years of development work behind it. It never succeeded in the marketplace, but it was well known and admired in the inner circles of the software community and can undoubtedly be nominated the mother of all hypermedia systems.

Today, the baton has been handed to the Internet's World Wide Web. The Web is still primitive in principle compared to Xanadu, but the size of the amalgamated information bases you find there is already staggering, and is growing every day. It represents the first real step down a very interesting road.

Multimedia and Animation

Multimedia, for its part, is only possible when we leave the paper paradigm. To really come into its own, however, it, too, will depend on the advances in display technology—even without paper, there will still be so much text around that affordable screens with good reading comfort will be necessary. If we think about the possibilities offered by holographic or other three-dimensional displays, they are truly staggering.

Holographic displays would also add a new realism to the three-dimensional (3D) CAD and modeling systems already in use in engineering, architecture, design, and science. These systems are also leaving the paper paradigm behind. While they once started out as drawing tools mimicking the original paper-based drawing process, they are now increasingly able to generate full-bodied three-dimensional models of the drawn objects—models that can be rotated, exploded, and enlarged to reveal detail. If the object is a house, the system allows you to do a walk-through on screen, studying how the light flows through the windows and the effects of different forms of interior lighting schemes and color options. A model of a processing plant can reveal any conflict between the positions of various equipment. The models on screen can now also be reproduced as physical models in what almost amounts to an "object printer," where a thin beam of UV light solidifies layer upon layer of polymer.

Computer models can in turn be animated, to simulate, for instance, production processes, thereby bringing the design process one step further. Numerical simulation is nothing new, of course, even old ENIAC was involved in that. But when we leave the printouts behind and couple simulation with animated models showing the result of the simulations in real time, our comprehension of the outcomes is brought to an entirely new, more sophisticated level. Instead of struggling with reams of data, taxing our working memory to the limits and beyond trying to visualize the effects, animations can bring the vast capacity of our visual system into play, improving our understanding many times over.

The windowing interface is thus a product with a Janus face, straddling the fence between the old and the new. But there is no doubt which side is growing fastest, and there is a large number of efforts underway to develop it further. The Internet marketplace is perhaps the strongest force today, but interesting work is also being done on totally new user interfaces in laboratories such as Xerox PARC in Palo Alto—the birthplace of the original graphical, windowing user interface (Clarkson 1991). When really large, affordable screens with good reading comfort become available, the movement away from the paper paradigm will experience a surge in development and demand.

Structuring Information

We noted above that the paper paradigm can be traced in the way information is represented on the screen. But the matter runs deeper than that. If we look at how information has been structured both in storage and processing, we will find very strong influences from the administrative practices developed during the growth of modern organizations since the middle of the nineteenth century. The protocol and the file were the established hallmarks of administration, and it was no wonder that the budding systems analysts and programmers were caught up in the reigning paradigm. Just note the vocabulary: computers still store their data in "files," the collection of data belonging to one entity is called a "record," and the individual pieces of information are located in "fields." Information is located through "indexed" keys.

First of all, computer files came to mimic the paper-based files and punch card equipment they replaced, and they were designed and used more or less as electronic filing cabinets. Information items were put in fields collected in records, which were direct descendants of the file card. One located a particular record through a *key* (normally, a name, address, or some kind of unique identification number), just as in a manual file. The database was really nothing more than an elaboration of this scheme, allowing several indexes as well as pointers relating records through connecting fields. Early databases only allowed predetermined pointers that were part of the application program code, and were thus extremely inflexible. In effect, they even required all the report formats one would ever want to be part of the program specification—a hopeless task in a changing business environment. To establish new relations between data elements, you would have to modify the program code, and the old pointers and definitions could well be hidden within algorithms deep down in the program. That is why any functional change (including the creation of new reports) used to cost so much and carry the risk of creating new errors and inconsistencies. Later databases became more flexible, but at the price of more complex software and a much heavier work load for the computer.

As electronic filing cabinets, the computers fitted quite nicely into the existing work flow. And, as programs evolved to support existing routines, it was just natural that they, too, were structured basically in the same way as traditional office work. The main determinant for this structure is the way large tasks decomposed into the basic tasks people actually perform when they work. As we have noted earlier, the classical model for administration was molded on the mass-producing factory and reinforced by the characteristics of large, paper-based files. It prescribed functional specialization, fixed procedures, and detailed rules and regulations. Routine tasks were decomposed into separate steps or operations, similar to an assembly line, and often described in detailed manuals. Job design was procedure oriented: It specified who would do what to which piece of information and in which order.

The Functional Approach

Computer programs, following the well-trodden paths of 150 years of administrative work, were also viewed as procedures, decomposed into single steps of operation on the various data files. Systems people call this method of decomposition *functional* (Coad and Yourdon 1991) or *algorithmic* (Booch 1991), and the resulting design and programs *structured*. Another vital characteristic of this approach is the distinction between program and data. *Data* are viewed as given, something you analyze to design a suitable database. The program contains the operations you want to perform on the data, and to design the program you analyze *functions*. Or, to use the language of systems theorists; traditional, structural analysis is based on the assumption that reality is composed of *entities* and their *states* on the one side, and *functions* on the other.

Functional or algorithmic decomposition and structured programming as a method was also reinforced by the very nature of the computers themselves, since they all complied with the basic scheme devised by John von Neumann in his famous "Report on the EDVAC" in 1945.[9] A von Neumann machine (as all computers following his basic principles are called) is characterized by serial processing—it has *one* central processor, fetching and executing *one* instruction at a time. Almost all computers

---

[9] EDVAC (Electronic Discrete Variable Computer) was the direct descendant of ENIAC and was also conceived as a project for the Army Ordnance Department—the same organization that financed the construction of ENIAC. The report was the first outline of a design for a stored-program computer, but the project had many delays, and EDVAC was not completed until 1952.

to date have been von Neumann machines, even if computers based on parallel processing are now becoming more common.

Because systems based on functional decomposition and structured design are built like trees of specialized routines, there is a great degree of interdependence between different parts of the system. Changes in one subroutine may require changes higher up in the system, which in their turn have consequences for many other subroutines. As such systems get larger, they therefore become very complex, and the interdependencies very difficult to keep track of—which means they also get increasingly difficult to change. However, needs always change over time and force modifications of the system. Since the cost for altering the main structure of a system based on functional decomposition is usually very high (it is often tantamount to developing a new system), changes tend to consist of ad hoc patches and additions crisscrossing the original logical structure. This further increases complexity and makes the system less and less comprehensible, until one reaches a point where it becomes unstable, because its procedural labyrinths are no longer fathomable. Changes may suddenly have unpredictable consequences in unexpected parts of the system, and one is faced with the choice of using it as it is without further changes, or discarding it completely to build a new one.

The Object-Oriented Approach

The complexity and inherent inflexibility of systems built on functionally decomposed designs made reflective systems people look for ways to simplify things, and from their work grew the object-oriented approach. It, too, has interesting parallels in the organization domain— such as the feudal type state and the divisionalized enterprise. The under- lying principles of the object-oriented approach to systems analysis and design are exactly the same as those applied to achieve maximum information economy in organization, and which we have analyzed earlier: the reduction of complexity by way of modularization and encapsulation.

The basic metaphor for the object-oriented model is the modularity found in human cognition and natural hierarchies—for instance, the hierarchy *organism–organ–cell* (Booch 1991). A cell manages its own internal processes, and the fact that all the cells in the organism do so in parallel relieves the central coordinating organ (the brain in an animal) of an impossible burden of coordination. Indeed, it also makes feasible organisms, such as plants, that are without any central coordination at all. For organisms that do have central coordination, such as mammals, the brain does not exert any direct control over intracellular processes;

rather, it controls cell behavior by broadcasting chemical messages that trigger local processes in the appropriate cells.

This is basically the same concept that lay behind Sloan's and du Pont's management of GM's divisions by sales targets and budgets—leaving the internal workings and initiatives in the divisions for the division management. The pure organizational example would be an organization consisting of self-managed teams. It is also the principle behind the capitalist, free-market economy, where independent companies ("objects") chart their own courses and cooperate through the exchange of "messages"— contracts, money, goods, and services. As history has shown, this is a superior coordination method for very complex organizations, such as large national states.

If we return to the organismic metaphor, a cell—for instance in the liver—is an example of an *object*. It would belong to the *class* "liver cells." The liver itself as a complete organ would constitute a higher-order object, containing both liver cells and other objects (e.g. the gall bladder and blood vessels), and belong to the class "livers," a subclass of the main class "organs." The organism would be our problem domain if we were only interested in its internal composition. If the area for study included the organism's interaction with its environment, including other organisms, the complete organism would in itself be an object of a still higher order than the liver, and a member of its own class—for instance (if it was a mouse), the class "mice."

Like an actual cell or team, an object (in the data-processing sense) has an internal structure—it stores its own data, or states, as well as the rules pertaining to those data and their representation. Its internal structure is thus encapsulated and hidden from the environment—the environment only "sees" the object as the messages it can receive and send and the behavior it can display. The class defines the properties that are common for all the objects in it, and the objects in their turn "inherit" them. Changes in the class description therefore instantly apply to all the relevant objects. An object communicates with other objects through messages, and the receiving object "knows" what to do when it receives a message. No master program is thus needed to direct the detailed processes within each object, and any object is interchangeable with any other object having the same 'message interface.'

The focus of object-oriented decomposition, then, is not the functions and procedures found in the problem domain, but the *items or entities of interest* for the system in question (Booch 1991, Coad and Yourdon 1991). Since those entities are generally much more stable than particular procedures, object-oriented systems are less susceptible to need major changes as business requirements change. The changes that are required will also be easier to implement. Object-oriented systems are moreover able to handle greater complexity than functional systems, through their use of encapsulation and hierarchies of objects and classes. They will also, in most cases, offer better abstract representations of reality than functional systems.

Object orientation represents a break with the old link between the paper paradigm, functional decomposition, structured systems, and functional organization. It shakes information structuring loose from the file cabinet and the procedure, and returns it to the main avenues of human cognition. For, objects and object classes are indeed the pillars of human cognition: we cannot even comprehend the world until we have established notions of object classes (e.g. "houses"), their properties and their relationships to other object classes. The object-oriented approach is therefore much better suited to analyze the domains of human work and cognition and to create systems that are compatible with human thinking and human work.

9
The IT-Based Preconditions

"Memory is like all other human powers, with which no man can be satisfied who measures them by what he can conceive, or by what he can desire."
Samuel Johnson, *The Idler*, 1758–60

We have now established a reasonable understanding of the central properties of information technology: Computer-based systems *process* information, they *store* information, and they *communicate*. And, the key to the power of computers, to all of their capabilities, is their *programmability*—the possibility to have immensely complex sets of logical operations executed automatically. Both hardware and software have undergone rapid developments, and new classes of organizational tools have been developed, as we have just discussed in Chapter 8.

We must now try to assess how these new tools enhance our own capabilities over and beyond the contributions from earlier technology, since this is the key to understanding possible extensions to the space of constructible organizations. This follows from our analysis in Chapter 2 and the conclusion that organizations are constructed: Only changes in the abilities or available options of the individual organization members can give rise to fundamental new possibilities for organizational design.

In this chapter, we shall only assess the basic enhancements. Their organizational ramifications are too diverse, and will have to wait for a detailed analysis in the four chapters in Part IV. The attempt at synthesis will then follow in Part V.

MEMORY

The externalization of memory provided by the art of writing had profound consequences for our administrative capability, our problem-solving ability, and our capacity for knowledge accumulation. All of these improvements were not only important for our ability to build organizations; practically all our advances in knowledge and technology—that is, the very foundation for our present material prosperity—rest squarely on the invention and exploitation of writing.

However, except for a certain refinement of the material means for filing and archiving (such as the invention of more elaborate classification schemes—e.g. library systems—and, eventually, the punch card), very little happened to the basic efficiency of information management up through the centuries—and our biological memory has hardly improved noticeably either. The usability of stored information (externalized memory) has also been severely constrained by several factors: the need for physical access to the storage media (files, books, etc.), the large amount of work involved in the search and retrieval of information items, and the slowness of the human input/output process (reading and writing).

The computer is now changing this—we are in the middle of a revolution in memory tools that will still roll with considerable speed for several decades, and perhaps bring changes as fundamental as those brought by the introduction of writing itself. This new revolution is built on the fundamental improvements it offers in storage economy and accessibility.

We can already hoard immense amounts of information almost anywhere, and the prices are swiftly falling to a point where cost will be irrelevant as long as the information is even remotely useful. This will allow us to accumulate all kinds of information produced by our own computer-based information systems, and have it instantly accessible on-line for reference, monitoring, and analysis. As the price of the storage medium falls, the limiting factor will in the end be the price of the information itself—either the price of purchasing it, as in the case of commercially available information, or the cost of producing or capturing it (and then organizing it for storage and retrieval), as with information indigenous to the organization or available through partnerships or other business relations.

Access to this information has moreover been separated from physical access; an extremely large number of people can access the same piece of information simultaneously, and it possible to locate, retrieve, sort and compare information with great speed and accuracy. Access is of course not as swift as the recall of something we remember clearly, and the ripples of association will also still flow faster in the brain. But for the vast volumes of information we cannot even hope to remember, and, even more significantly, all the information we have never heard about at all before our new tools find it for us, we will have an access that is many orders of magnitude faster and more exhaustive than before. Less time will be spent in search activities, and the yield of relevant information will be much greater. It should allow our own information processing to draw on a much larger set of facts and viewpoints than before. In fact, the limiting factor will be our own innate capacity to absorb and digest the information.

This new memory technology is not like our own memory, it is an external memory just like the traditional filing cabinet—but it is also much more than a filing cabinet, or a bookshelf, or a library—so much more that it deserves a new name. To keep in tune with the trend-setting term "artificial intelligence" (AI), we may call it *artificial memory* (*AM*). This term is not entirely new, Simon (1976) refers to it as already in use— but it has up to now been used to denote all kinds of records outside human memory, chiefly libraries and paper-based files. However, since it has been used so sparingly and since it matches the now thoroughly established term "artificial intelligence" so well, it seems easier and wiser to change its content rather than to coin an entirely new term. It will still fit Simon's (1981) definition of the trichotomy natural–synthetic–artificial.

Of course, not all information of interest to us is available in digital form. Much is still found in books and journals, in looseleaf binders, archives, even piles on desks and shelves. The all-encompassing informa- tion bases we have been alluding to remain a potential, not a fact. Nevertheless, the information used and produced in the organizations of the world is rapidly becoming digitized, as computer-based systems are introduced to take over or support one after the other of their work processes, and the structured database is becoming the new linchpin of organizational coordination.

This is perhaps the core of the greatest revolution of digital storage—the tremendous boost it gives to implicit coordination. No longer is the effect of this extremely effective coordinating mechanism limited by the physical access restrictions and puny volume of traffic associated with paper-based files—in the comparatively near future, hundreds of thousands of simul- taneous users all over the globe can be served by a single database, and thereby achieve strong, instant coordination in selected aspects of their work. In a more extended perspective, volume restrictions will for most practical purposes cease to exist.

We shall explore this new revolution in more detail later (in Chapter 13). Let us finish for now by noting that the number and quality of available information bases are also rapidly growing, thanks to the standardizing effects of Internet. Whereas the various database services up till quite recently displayed ample variation in log-on procedures and command languages (and enjoyed limited commercial success), Internet has in a few short years completely taken over as a gateway, and the www browser has established the standard for information retrieval and presentation. The chief obstacle today is a reliable and simple mechanism for pay-as-you-go information retrieval, but it will soon be cleared away. New software will also come to assist in the process of finding what you seek—both search engines that "learn" from your searches as well as "agents" who crawl the net on your behalf, returning periodically with their catch, have been proposed so far (Stein 1991, Negroponte 1995). Interesting products are bound to come along here, even though it usually takes longer to perfect this kind of AI-based software than the proponents initially believe.

This is not so important for our purpose, however, since there is little doubt that it will only be a matter of time before most of the information we need in the course of our daily work will be accessible through our workstations, with very capable search-and-retrieval tools available— probably even tools that will be able to continuously (and in the background) build and maintain links and search profiles from the factual and associative jumps we make during our normal search activities. Such tools will apply both to external and intra-organizational information bases.

When that happens, our active information repository will become vastly larger than it is today. Comfortable, speedy access is critical for information to be used, and scarceness of time and economic resources will always tend to severely limit our search. A lawyer I once met summed it all up in what he called *the law of arm's length*: "You know, 99% of the time, you make do with the information you can reach out and grab without leaving your desk chair." Which is, of course, the reason why people keep private copies of central files, why they buy books that are available in a library three blocks away, why they make copies of everything that may come in handy at a later stage. It also means that 99% of the time we make do with the information we *remember that we have and know where to find*, and even the information in our offices is liable to get lost within a meter or two of our desks, as long as we do not index anything and everything. IT will place a vastly larger volume of information within "arm's length"—which is what much of the current excitement about the Internet and the so-called "cyberspace" is about.

PROCESSING AND CAPACITY FOR WORK

Before writing, our only available strategy for alleviating the limititations of our processing capacity was simplification—singling out a few variables for concern and forgetting the rest. Writing greatly enhanced our overall processing capacity by providing a second-tier working memory with storage of intermediate results. We accumulated knowledge, kept records, and expanded our vocabulary to allow more precise expressions. We achieved a vastly superior understanding of nature and of causal relationships. Writing also made it much more feasible to decompose complex tasks and distribute them both over time and between many persons. It greatly improved the possibilities for coordination over distance. The telegraph and telephone further reduced the significance of geography. Finally, the development of mechanical automation made it possible for us to multiply our capacity for physical labor. What do computers provide over and above this?

First of all, we should note that the time we need to think through a problem, to mull over likely and unlikely consequences, to weigh the preferences of possible solutions is still an internal process of our minds. As such, it is no more augmented by information technology than by writing. We are still also serial processors, and can only concentrate on one problem at a time, and information technology does not change this any more than previous inventions have done. No matter how advanced the workstation on your desk, when the telephone rings, you will still lose the thread of your work, and the conversation will effectively block any other serious mental activity. Combined with the restrictions of our working memory, this one-trackedness of our mind will still put a limit to the number of variables we can handle simultaneously.

What the computer does offer is the opportunity to unload some of the information processing itself. Further, computer-based support tools may make task switching even easier than written notes and records could, and increase precision by organizing information better. At the personal level a properly equipped workstation can keep parallel work processes going—such as sending and receiving faxes in the background, sending and receiving voice messages, calculating large spreadsheets—and even do database selections and sorts while a person works on other tasks. There is also the prospect of "intelligent agents" that can take care of more complex tasks, but, for the present, such agents represent little more than a gimmick. What the distant future will bring is of course impossible to foretell, but in my lifetime I do not expect to see computer systems that can effectively emulate humans on an overall basis—research on neural networks and artificial intelligence notwithstanding. Computers and humans are simply too different to make that an early success. We should reserve for our own minds the tasks where we excel, and exploit computers for the tasks they master—and where we can profit from their great speed, accuracy and untiring work. The computer's potential for automation and processing of quantitative information is thus in my view much more important than its role as an office assistant.

However, if we look at the whole process involved in reaching decisions in organizations, including the collection of relevant information and consultation with others, considerable improvements are possible, mainly in the area of information collection and communication. McKersie and Walton quote an example from a high-tech organization (1991, p. 252):

> During my last weekend in Washington, an important issue arose late Friday that required an official written agency position Monday morning. A few phone calls locked in the key experts (five different states) for an electronic brainstorming session on Saturday. I got initial thoughts from everyone on electronic mail Friday night (ideas were iterated once or twice) as well as access to information and graphics from local databases with comments and proposed rewrites or reorganizations with appropriate rationale. Three iterations were completed by 5:00 P.M. and a draft was electronically forwarded to three senior managers at their homes for approval. After incorporating their revisions, the position paper was approved and printed for an 8:00 A.M. meeting Monday morning with the head of the agency.

There is no doubt that the position paper could have been produced by Monday morning even without computers, relying on telephone and possibly telex or fax. But it is equally clear that electronic mail and remotely accessible databases made it much easier to produce the required document, and with a better result. Further developments in software (discussed in more detail in Chapter 11) will help to speed up the decision-making process even more. Just like writing, computer-based systems thus provide a set of tools that make it possible for us to exploit our innate processing power to a larger degree than before.

The Quantitative Revolution

However, the main contribution of information technology towards mastering complexity is without doubt the way it allows us to manipulate quantitative information—information that can be expressed in numbers and categories. This sounds rather narrow at first, but when you look into it, you will find a vast array of applications where the computer has greatly enhanced our ability to handle complex tasks. The computer's ability to handle numbers, and to present them graphically on the screen, has meant a revolution that is, in my opinion, at least as great as the original contribution of written numerals. The reason is twofold.

First, even if it was possible to develop advanced theory in mathematics, physics, and engineering without computers, much of that knowledge was simply impossible to use in practice because of the enormous burden of calculation. Cheap and powerful computers now allow almost any scientist and engineer to routinely carry out calculations that were simply unthinkable 50 years ago. For instance, finite element analysis is now a practical, everyday tool of engineering—not merely an exotic, theoretical possibility. Chaos theory was not even discovered before the computer was available, since the nature of the regularities in chaotic systems were too complex to comprehend without it (Gleick 1988).

Second, the computer is capable of tracking causal relationships—and not only between a few variables (as in a simple spreadsheet model), but also between exceedingly large numbers of them (as in a weather model for a 10-day forecast). The computer works as an automatic preprocessor, combining a large number of predefined causal relationships into a few aggregate ones that we can comprehend and manipulate in our own minds. It can even do so in real time, as in trading systems, process control systems and flight and weapons control systems on modern military aircraft—which let the pilot control and coordinate tasks that would have demanded a sizable crew just a decade or two ago.

The advancement of artificial intelligence can also contribute. Heller (1991) describes, for instance, a system for routing trucks developed by Carnegie Mellon University and DEC. Incorporating rules developed by interviewing experts in the trucking company, it has allowed the same experts to reduce the company's continuous-mileage transport costs by 10%—not because it "knows" more than they do, but because the system is able to take all the rules into account every time, even when time is scarce. AI also has the potential to become an important tool for real-time monitoring of complex technical installations, where it is essential to maintain a continuous overview of main events.

Automation

As we have already noted, automation is our only way to achieve the capability of working on many tasks in parallel. Simple automation can be seen as an enhancement of the capacities of the individual operator only, more sophisticated automation replacing scores of workers of many different trades must be seen as a tool on the organizational level. We shall return to this last (and most important) aspect of automation in Chapter 12. At this point, we shall only discuss the main differences in principle between mechanical and computer-based automation.

In the classical machine the "program" governing its movements is contained in the physical shape of its different parts. Since one part can only have one particular shape, its information content is low, and to make a machine with a relatively high information content (able to do complex operations or different types of operations), one must use a very large number of parts, making the machine expensive to manufacture and less reliable (one of the main concerns of mechanical engineers is always to reduce the number of parts as far as possible). Mechanical automation has nevertheless been developed to a very high level of sophistication, where even highly delicate operations, such as the manufacture of light bulbs, have been fully automated (Bright 1985).

Another area of importance to automation concerns linking sensor input to operations. Some such links are simple to establish by mechanical means; the best known is probably the classic thermostat with a bimetallic switch. But, even in this field, the complexity achievable without the help of computers is limited, and despite much ingenuity, automation could not proceed beyond certain limits—witness the control rooms of precomputer power stations or factories in process industries, where a considerable number of operators would walk around, all the time reading dials, turning wheels, pulling levers, and flipping switches.

Now, to automate by computers, we still have to plan and describe in painstaking detail every action to be carried out. The material difference is that the information, instead of being embedded in the physical shapes of parts, is simply lodged in software and hardware logic. What was earlier impossible to change or required new parts or rebuilding can now be done by changing parameters or code lines in software—a much simpler and more economical alternative. This difference translates into an enormous divergence in the level of complexity we can operate with and the speed by which the embedded information is processed.

As the processing power of the controlling computers is increased, the scope for automation in production and control is therefore drastically widened, and no final limits can be seen. Computer-controlled systems can collect and analyze very diverse and sophisticated signals from a broad variety of sensors, can direct all kinds of machinery, and can be equipped with an array of responses covering almost any conceivable eventuality—also error conditions and accidents. Any process that can be precisely defined can in principle be automated. This is not to say that we do not experience limits today, but it is very difficult to determine which ones are fundamental and related to basic constraints in the nature of computers and computer-based systems, and which ones are simply due to the present immaturity of our computers, our software and our theories of computers and their use. I suspect that very few of the constraints we have experienced so far are of the fundamental kind.

Computer-based systems are also very reliable when we consider their enormous complexity. This may sound strange in the ears of the average computer user, regularly frustrated by inexplicable error conditions and just as indecipherable error messages. Considering the number of discrete electronic components contained on the chips in an average PC, however, and the number of code lines in the software employed, we might be more surprised by the fact that it works at all than by the relatively few errors that occur. If we count each separate component on the processor chip, the memory chips, and all the other chips for a separate part (which it really is, even if it is miniaturized beyond normal comprehension), and do likewise for every line of source code for the programs normally run on the average business PC, that PC consists of several hundred millions parts, and will soon be in the billions. How reliable, for instance, would a machine with 300 million mechanical parts be? A modern airplane, such as the Boeing 777, has approximately 3 million parts (excluding computer components!)—and needs extensive, regular servicing to operate within acceptable safety limits.

COMMUNICATION

All the great breakthroughs in the history of human communication—the written word, printing, the telegraph, the telephone, radio, and television—were developments of the pre-computer world. Even the telefax is an old invention from the nineteenth century, although microelectronics was needed to make it cheap enough and provide the necessary document quality to really make it popular. Computer technology has so far not provided breakthroughs of a similar magnitude, and its ability to do so in the near future is in my view generally overestimated—despite the advent of several interesting technologies: electronic mail and conferencing, cellular phones, videophones, and, of course, the modernized fax.

Our Very Own I/O Bottlenecks

The reason for this is simply that communication is not only a matter of transporting symbols from one person to another. There is also the problem actually *absorbing* incoming information, and *disseminating* the information we intend for others (the human input/output, so to speak)—a problem that represents a far more formidable problem than increasing the bandwidth of long-distance information transfer. Actually, there is even a third important aspect of communication, which we shall not discuss here: the question of how well *meaning* survives the encoding/decoding processes involved in human communication.

Although bandwidth is an interesting issue, then, it is definitely not the only issue. Electronic communication as well as digital storage and computer-assisted search and retrieval certainly allow us access to vast information resources. But even if we can unearth mountains of relevant information, how can we absorb it all and really use it? Information must still be read off the screen or off paper printed out by the system. The cry is in fact already going up in corporations worldwide, from overloaded managers and professionals: What we need is not *more* information, but the *key* information. We do not even find time to absorb the day-to-day business data that is already there. As Long remarks (1987, p. 45), "By providing a manager with the capacity to call up more and more analyses, there will be an implicit pressure for him/her to do so."

Simon (1976) reflects on a new computer system installed by the U.S. State Department for receiving the 15 million words received per month from its 278 diplomatic missions throughout the world, and with the ability to print out 1200 lines per minute (the old teletypes could only manage 100 words per minute). He remarks wryly (1976, p. 284): "A touching faith in more water as an antidote to drowning! Let us hope that foreign ministers will not feel themselves obliged to process those 1200 lines per minute just because they are there."

The sad fact is that our innate capacity for information absorption remains the same as before, as does our capacity for disseminating information. Our eyes, ears, and mouths are the same as our forefathers', and even if some people from time to time speculate about the possibilities of interfacing computers directly to the brain, we can safely rule that out as a useful option in the foreseeable future.

In particular, the computer has not done very much to improve on our ability to express ourselves. It has made it possible to compose text somewhat faster, but that is about all. Of course, we can now produce much better-looking material than before; our presentations can be studded with graphics and nice fonts. But it still takes the same old time and effort to present the result of our thought processes to others. Where the computer *can* help is when it can concentrate or transform information in such a way that it speeds our perception. However, both the challenge and the remedy vary according to the nature of the information—that is, if it is verbal, pictorial, or numerical.

Verbal and Pictorial Information

Information embedded in text or pictures is intrinsically resistant to automatic concentration. Text can be condensed by rewriting and the creation of summaries, but both are labor-intensive tasks that will require human processing in the foreseeable future. For film, still pictures and sound the possibilities are likewise meager. The only significant advantage computers offer is the fact that computerized searches should return information with a higher content of relevant material than we can obtain through manual searches. That is, even if it will not help us to absorb more information, the information we ingest should be more relevant.

Apart from the improvement provided by the basic capabilities of search engines, work is also being done on other kinds of tools intended to concentrate the information presented even more. Associative searches and hypermedia links have been mentioned, and experiments are also made on structuring tools (Winograd 1988) and programmable filters for electronic mail and conference contributions (Robinson 1991).

In addition to this, new ways of information presentation and representation should make it possible to get a somewhat better overview of complex textual and pictorial information, especially with the advent of larger screens. However, our absorption of this kind of information cannot be improved dramatically—at the very most, we are probably talking about a doubling, not orders of magnitude.

Numerical Information

Numerical information is quite another matter, however. Since numbers very often lend themselves to graphical representations, we can tap into the very powerful visual-processing capacity of the brain. There is no doubt, for instance, that a pie, column, or line chart conveys information much more quickly than the tables they are based on. Three-dimensional charts add even more information (if used correctly).

Graphical representations are nothing new—scientists and economists plotted graphs long before the advent of computers. What *is* new is the speed and ease with which the conversion can now happen, and the forms the graphs may now take. Graphs used to take a long time to produce, even simple ones, and only the most important or complex information was the subject for such VIP treatment. Today, with a modern spreadsheet or statistical package, graphs are almost a free lunch to be had once your data are registered. Software packages for administrative purposes also increasingly have capabilities for graphical output, and spreadsheets steadily improve their capacity for extracting data from other applications for further analysis. Indeed, spreadsheets are now evolving into all-purpose tools for reports and analysis.

A quite different example is found in the new naval navigation systems, in which the combination of satellite navigation and electronic maps lets the helmsman follow the ship's position continuously on a screen showing both the map and a representation of the ship. The small ship on the screen moves as the ship moves, and the map rolls continuously in the direction of movement. For fast crafts operating in narrow waters, such a system is much safer than traditional navigational aids.

The most sophisticated visual representation systems today are found in engineering and scientific data processing, where information is presented not only as static graphs, but also as animations. Especially impressive are simulations based on numerical models—be they of new airplanes, waves generated by projected boat hulls, car suspensions, cloud development, or cosmological events. Animation in particular can concentrate numerical information to a very high degree and present us with clean and comprehensible representations of enormously complex data. Such tools have up to now been very expensive because of the large computational power required. But, because of the ever decreasing cost of raw computing power, this fascinating class of tools is now rapidly becoming available for almost any purpose.

Animated simulation is in my view a branch of software with a great future. It will not only help in designing physical objects (e.g. factory production lines, cars, or houses) but also aid in all kinds of data analysis. Even social science survey data can conceivably be animated, with moving planes and shapes visualizing the mapping of multivariate distributions and correlations. In business, animation should be able to provide very interesting tools for analyzing and monitoring key variables (budget and real)—in production, sales, and accounting—and, not least, in *combinations* of these areas. I believe such tools will be applied in all areas where there is a need to analyze or monitor complex numerical relationships. The managers of a retail chain, for instance, could get sales for various product groups or products presented as animated columns on a map with all their locations—one column for each location. By presenting 20 days per second, the whole year could be played through in 15–20 seconds. Interesting overall patterns—such as seasonal variations and geographical variations—could be spotted at once, and greater resolution applied to the graphics for more detailed analysis.

The New Channels

Although our innate bottlenecks for information absorption and dissemination largely remain in place, the channels for information transfer have seen significant development on all levels—from the physical (from copper to fiber, from earthbound radio to satellites) via basic representation (from analogue to digital) and bandwidth (including multiplexing) to presentation (application level). What are the implications?

Electronic Mail and Conferencing

The most touted aspect of computer-mediated communication is electronic mail (email). There has been (and still is) much excitement over this new medium, and the growth of the Internet in particular has raised the spirits of many journalists and salespersons to exuberant levels and fostered visions of a world of unrestrained communication. Electronic mail is also much used as an entrance point to computer use for managers and is therefore often somewhat oversold as a productivity tool.

What electronic mail provides is simply the ability to transmit written material instantaneously and have it stored for later presentation in case the recipient is not present. Good email systems also make it very convenient to answer, by automatically applying the address of the sender to the reply, posting a reference to the original message, and so on. At its best, therefore, email functions as something of a cross between letters/ memos and telephone conversations—it has the speed of the telephone but does not require the sender and the receiver to be simultaneously available at their respective terminals. It can therefore be very efficient for people who are away from their desks a lot (especially frequent travellers) and can significantly reduce the number of unanswered telephone calls. It is particularly useful for communication across time zones—especially for intercontinental communication, where time differences can be so large that there is no overlap of working hours—and for cooperation on documents.

Developments are also under way for "screen sharing," where two or more people can both see the same screen picture and have access to it. There is work going on both on systems for meetings where the participants are in the same room (when the common screen typically will be projected onto the wall) and for meetings/conferences where the participants are in different geographical locations. It is too early to assess the impact of such systems, but they will clearly facilitate cooperation over distance, particularly in small groups.

Ordinary conferencing systems, on the other hand, are really just an elaborate form of email systems, where exchanges are open to all participants in that particular conference. Conference systems are useful for spreading information fast to many people ("bulletin board" function) and for conducting group-oriented work.

Experience shows that we intuitively perceive email as a new medium with a new set of properties: The casualness induced by the easy, instantaneous, and paperless transmission of messages; the ease of replying; and the absence of the formalism associated with paper combine to make email messages much more "oral" in their form than ordinary letters. Because of its informal character, email can also function as a valuable feedback channel for managers. It tends to elicit comments more in line with what the manager would get through an informal chat with a subordinate, while preserving the time-saving, asynchronous nature of the written memo. Through conscious use of electronic mail, it is therefore possible for managers to appear more accessible to a larger number of their subordinates. The informal and private character of an email system, however, also makes it conducive to gossip and slander—it is in many ways a new and much more efficient office grapevine.

Electronic mail is not the panacea that some people seem to think, however, and many of the predictions about email and conferencing have a lot in common with the generally euphoric predictions made about the telephone around the start of the twentieth century. We therefore have good reason to maintain a relative calm.

The main point is simply that email does little to speed our comprehension. We may *transmit* messages more easily, and, yes, it is somewhat easier to compose them. Email messages also tend to be terser (and thereby more efficient) than other written messages. Word for word, however, they still take the same time to read as other written material, and the same time to ponder as information in any other guise. Because it does not enhance our basic communication capacity in any dramatic way, email will therefore not represent the revolution in communication that many predict. We already spend a fair amount of our time communicating, and to increase our use of email we must spend less time on other channels. To fulfill the predictions of some of the most eager proponents of email and conferencing, we would have to forgo all or most other tasks, and that is just not going to happen. Many users in organizations with electronic mail networks even now receive 100 messages or more per day, which is probably already taking them to the limits of their capacity. "We believed e-mail was a way of saving time," begins an article about email in *Svenska Dagbladet*,[1] one of the major Swedish broadsheet dailies. "But the truth is that we are about to become slaves under the new communication medium. Many people spend several hours every day answering electronic mail." In the article, Professor Jacob Palme of Stockholm University says his research shows that it takes an average of 30 seconds to read a message and 4 minutes to answer one (see also Palme 1995). If 100 messages is received, 20 of them answered and 5 new ones written, a simple calculation indicates that this will on average take 2.5 hours, or a third of a normal working day.

Mitigating remedies for overload will no doubt be found—indeed, some are already available (such as filtering and automatic prioritizing based on keywords) and more sophisticated schemes are under development. That is not the point, however. The crux of the matter is that we have about the same limit for output and input of verbal information as our forebears of hundreds and thousands of years ago, and with the size of the nozzles thus being relatively constant, we gain little by increasing the diameter of the hose, or by connecting more hoses.

Although distance education can make teachers more effective by saving them travel time, I always wonder when I hear proponents of

---

[1] *Svenska Dagbladet*, October 16 1998. My translation.

distance education extol how PCs and modems will also make it possible for so many more students to achieve direct contact not only with national experts, but even with leading international academicians. I keep getting this vision of a poor professor, already straining under the effort required to keep a decent dialogue with the students physically present at the department, one day receiving the joyful message of a sudden availability, through electronic mail, to 10 000 new students nationwide and 5 million more worldwide! Telecast lectures and remotely accessible text bases is one thing, that will work; unlimited return channels are something entirely different, and will not work.

Telephones and Videophones

The telephone is definitely a pre-computer invention. Computers do not change them very much, except for sharply reduced communication costs and the feeling of freedom associated with the cellular phone—the illusion that we may now roam the sea, the forest, the mountains, or the prairie while remaining in touch with the office and the world that brings in our money. The cellular phone does not entail any real revolution in our communication abilities, though. Combined with a modem it will make a real difference for people who need to conduct their business on the go, but, for the majority, it will only afford a number of conveniences and a marginal increase in efficiency. It will not usher in really significant, broad changes in organization.

A part of the new telephone environment is voice mail. It has largely the same kind of advantages and disadvantages as email, with the added advantage of the extra information contained in voice inflection, and the added disadvantage that it is not text and thereby not as useful in our predominantly chirographic work environments. Some managers like the way their messages to subordinates get a more "personal" touch when delivered in their own voice. There are examples of systematic use of this effect. One of the most well-known ones is Debbi Fields' use of voice mail to communicate daily to the store managers in her chain of Mrs. Fields cookie stores (Walton 1989). The voice mail system also allowed the store managers to send voice messages to her, which they often did. For Debbi Fields it was mainly an instrument of control, but also a channel for informal feedback. It consumed a considerable amount of her time every day, but it gave her a very direct channel for influence, and the store managers, a feeling of direct contact. It did this while preserving her power to decide when to listen and when to speak, and she could still keep command of her schedule.

The slow but steady progress toward affordable videophones is probably of far greater interest. But even videophones will not increase our capacity for information absorption—their contribution will be that they may reduce the need for travel and make it possible to have a close working relationship without meeting in person too often. We do not know for sure yet, since the high cost of videoconferencing up to now has precluded widespread use, and the necessary facilities have not been suitable for desktop installation—making it inconvenient to use even in those organizations where it has been made available.

However, the videophone is already on its way to become an add-on card that can be integrated into the PC or workstation, or even just a feature of the graphics adapter, and the larger screens gradually becoming the norm ($17''$–$21''$) should allow us to conduct small video-meetings (up to seven or nine participants) on our desktops as soon as the video equipment and transmission itself become cheap enough. The even bigger screens that are bound to take over as soon as technology can provide them at a reasonable cost should be able to display pictures of an even larger number of participants, as well as a common working space for sketching, writing, and presentation of pictures or output from various programs.

The arrival of affordable desktop videoconferencing could make a really significant difference to cooperation over distance. The added information provided by the picture could make the videophone an instrument for comfortable conferencing—good enough to replace "real" meetings in many instances when travel (short or long distance) is involved. It is therefore likely that video conferencing, within the scope of a couple of decades, will finally provide the necessary means for reducing the need for "physical" meetings significantly. Whether this will actually happen, however, depends not so much on the technology itself, but on people's preferences—they must actually *prefer* video meetings in instances where they would previously have traveled. It is still too early to tell, but we might guess that most of the really frequent travelers will welcome the opportunity to spend less time on the road or in airports, whereas those who make only a couple of trips a year will want to hold on to what they experience as a welcome escape from the daily routine. Several studies support this view (Long 1987).

A significant catch, of course, is that if desktop video conferencing really reduces the perceived threshold for holding meetings and becomes popular, it could well increase the total number of meetings. This is reported in a study quoted by Long (1987). About half of the respondents reported an increase in the total time used for communication after the video-conferencing system was introduced, whereas the other half reported no change. Such an increase in meeting activity could be productive in some instances, but not necessarily always. A reduced threshold for meetings (through video conferencing) also means that the threshold for follow-up meetings with superiors will be reduced—something that could once again reduce the independence of geographically dispersed organizational units.

Video conferencing will not eliminate the preference for colocation for groups working really close together, especially groups doing creative work where cross-fertilization is important. No electronic channel can yet replace the richness of informal, personal dialogue, the chat in the door of an office you were passing while you were really heading for the copier, the chance meeting by the coffee machine, or the inspired but unplanned discussion during a break in a late-night dash to meet an approaching deadline. As a manager I once talked to said: "It's so much easier when you meet people in the corridors." The attempts to recreate such avenues for unplanned, informal communications by electronic means have had scant success (Johansen 1988). We may also suspect that problems of a more intricate or delicate nature will lead to travel no matter how widespread video conferencing becomes. Indeed, another study quoted by Long (1987, p. 58) found that some corporations experienced that their "travel costs have increased as better communication with distant operations reveals problems which require in-person appearances of top-level executives."

But, for more routine administrative work, for coordination, following up on work in progress, and for sorting out the daily problems cropping up in every organization, video conferencing should be adequate in many instances. It could therefore make geographically dispersed organizations more feasible, especially if they are otherwise advantageous— for instance, because of market considerations or the availability of energy, raw materials, or suitable personnel. It may also be very useful for bringing cooperating, but otherwise independent organizations closer together.

Better Hoses, Same Nozzles

To sum up: Computer-based systems provide a couple of new "hoses" for information transport, and significantly improve some of the old ones. The "nozzles" at both the transmitting and receiving end have not changed very much, however. Our basic capacity for input and output of verbal information (be it oral or written) still puts the same iron constraint on our communication process. We already use so much time for communication (especially if we include the time used for reading printed material) that we can hardly increase our total communication volume very much, except for using the time now spent on travel and unanswered telephone calls. Increased use of new channels will therefore normally entail a reduction for old ones.

A SUMMARY OF THE MAIN IMPACTS

Computer-based systems usher in a revolution in the performance of our externalized memory. That revolution is built on three pillars: *compact and cheap storage; universal access;* and *automatic search, retrieval, and registration.* The most important application is the *database.*

In contrast to the written file, which requires that you physically walk up to it to retrieve information, digitally stored information can be accessed by anyone so authorized, regardless of geographical location or time of day. It is, moreover, *simultaneously* available to a large number of users. Just as important, digitally stored information can be indexed, sorted, and compared with enormous speed. The computer's outstanding ability to search vast amounts of information in incredibly short time, and extract, combine and concentrate data, makes for a momentous difference between computerized and paper-based files. This is especially true for information in highly structured form, but, even for text and other information items stored in free-form databases, accessibility is dramatically increased.

However, the greatest achievement effected through the digital computer is the *externalization of processing.* The fact that we can now have information processed outside the human head will prove to be at least as important as the externalization of memory brought about by the invention of writing. But the computer can only mimic certain aspects of the mind—notably, logical operations, especially all kinds of calculation. The narrowness of the computer's proficiency must not fool us into believing that it is inconsequential, however. It allows us to manipulate vast amounts of quantitative information very cheaply and quickly, something that translates into a revolutionary ability to handle a great number of complex matters—from budgeting to finite element analysis. It allows us to keep track of a vast number of variables and their interrelationships—complexity on a scale that we were not even able to approach before—and through this it will also allow us to develop automation to a level of sophistication that will completely overshadow all that mechanical automation has ever achieved.

The great breakthroughs in human communication were all developments of the pre-computer world. Computer technology has so far not provided breakthroughs of a similar magnitude, and its ability to do so in the near future is in my view generally overestimated. The reason is simply that communication is not only a matter of transporting symbols from the desk of one person to the desk of another—there is also the problem of the actual *absorption and dissemination* of information, which represents a far more formidable problem. However, the computer can be of great help in transforming information for faster absorption—notably quantitative information, which can be represented through graphics and animations. The possibilities are far less promising for verbal information, which is one of the reasons why email and computer conferencing will have limited impacts. The bottleneck is still in our heads; and the nozzles there remain the same size, no matter what the width of the hoses leading up to them.

Videophones and video conferencing will definitely become common when quality transmission becomes cheap enough, but the effects are uncertain. So far, telecommunications (which we have had for more than a hundred years, even internationally) have not led to any measurable reduction in physical travel—but the technology has perhaps contributed to more meetings overall and stronger centralized control in organizations.

10
Emotional Barriers and Defenses

"Men live but by intervals of reason under the sovereignty of humor [caprice] and passion."
Sir Thomas Browne, *A letter to a friend,* 1690

In Chapter 6 it was briefly noted that technology and scientific methods are indeed used to affect emotions—from drugs and psychotherapy to movies. IT does not seem to bring much new in this respect, except for making existing products more sophisticated. We may, for instance, observe that Morris' remarks about our need for sex by proxy can be extended from literature and movies to computer-based systems. Just as in video, the sex industry has been among the pioneers in multimedia, something that can be ascertained just by browsing the back alleys of the World Wide Web or looking at the last few pages of the classified ads in *PC Magazine*. Indeed, according to frequent reports in the media, pornography downloading is so widespread that it is periodically straining the capacity of coporate communication networks. If we are to believe the more easily excitable journalists in the trade press, virtual reality is the next frontier—although I have an inkling that it will be harder to provide adequate feedback than the enthusiasts seem to believe. Reading such speculations, one is reminded of one of the bleak worlds described by Olaf Stapledon in his 1937 novel *Starmaker*, in which broadcast brain-stimulation had advanced to a stage where simulated experiences became more important than reality. Ultimately, this civilization developed the possibility for their citizens to retire into a completely vegetative, simulated existence: lying permanently on a bed, connected to life-supporting machinery, one could indefinitely immerse oneself in broadcast simulations. Seemingly, the broadcaster networks have been working hard toward this goal ever since.

Some may feel it inappropriate or at least not very serious to draw such matters into the discussion. However, the immediate and widespread exploitation of new technology for sexual purposes can serve to remind us that our basic drives and emotions are with us still, and in no small way either—if the fervor of the development efforts reflects the size of the market. We are not intellectual beings with rational purposes all the time, and raw emotional cravings can easily override even strong rational criteria and organizational as well as social norms—on all organizational levels. Emotions are an issue in organizations whether we like it or not, and the whole range will be present, from the despicable to the noble.

So far in Part III, technology and the rational use of it has had the whole focus. Before we go on to analyze the rational use of technology in organizational contexts it seems therefore highly appropriate to consider some emotional issues as well.

ORGANIZATIONAL EFFECTS ON EMOTIONS

That emotions were something that affected workplace behavior was not generally acknowledged in the modern era until after World War II, and the first significant impetus in this direction only came after the Hawthorne studies (the experiments were conducted between 1927 and 1932) established it as a fact of social science (Hollway 1991). Hollway quotes Roethlisberger and Dickson[1] (Hollway 1991, p. 72), describing the early experimenters at Hawthorne as

> ...carrying around in their heads the notion of "economic man", a man primarily motivated by economic interest, whose logical capacities were being used in the service of this self-interest. Gradually and painfully the experimenters had been forced to abandon this conception of the worker and his behavior...they found that the behavior of workers could not be understood apart from their feelings or sentiments.

Since the Hawthorne studies were published, the scope of work psychology has been both broadened and deepened through human relations, organizational development, and the concept of organizational culture. Practical efforts have focused not so much on job content and design as on selection and motivation building, which is far less intrusive with respect to work processes and organization design. The modern emphasis on organization culture can even be interpreted as a return from a focus on organization and job content to the more pure motivational effort of early human relations (Hollway 1991), and the proliferation of psychological testing could indicate a preference to fit persons to jobs rather than the other way around.

---

[1] From Roethlisberger, F. J., and Dickson, W. J. (1939): *Management and the Worker*, Cambridge, MA, Harvard University Press.

I am not sure if this can be said to represent an advance in work psychology. It could well be that the development of the modern organization poses new challenges to our basic emotional apparatus, which it is poorly equipped to cope with, and which a recharged motivation only can serve to gloss over. It seems reasonable to believe that our emotions co-evolved with our physiological abilities to cope with the challenges of a life that for perhaps 95% of our existence as a species[2] has been life in a hunter/gatherer band, and for the rest (save the last 200 years) a life of subsistence farming and simple crafts.

Physiologically (genetically), we are therefore probably best equipped to do physically varied work of a routine character, interspersed with limited amounts of problem solving and crisis management. During the last 200 years, however, an increasing number of people have entered into jobs that consist mainly of problem solving and crisis management, and the problems have grown increasingly complex and abstract. Quite a few of these problems may even be impossible to solve in a satisfactory manner. Moreover, many jobs are also such that the people doing them cannot easily see their significance either for the organization or for any particular end product, and they are deprived of the inherent meaning we find in work that is whole and with an immediate bearing on our own or our family's survival—as is the food foraging and tool making in a hunter/gatherer band.

It would be understandable if such situations generated considerable stress and emotional problems—which they seem to do. In a survey conducted by an American insurance company in 1991, 46% of American workers felt that their jobs were very or somewhat stressful, and nearly 27% reported that their jobs were the single greatest source of stress in their lives (Quick et al. 1992). Factors such as high work pace, repetition of work, lack of control over work and work situation, quantitative overload (too much work), and qualitative overload (too difficult work) are reported to be among the chief sources of occupational stress (Ross and Altmaier 1994).

Growing complexity is, in fact, an increasingly prominent characteristic of modern society as a whole—and an increasing number of people find it difficult to understand how it works, what their options are, and how they can claim a meaningful place in it. Even everyday life requires a growing sophistication in abstract thinking and symbol manipulation, from filling in forms to using computers and other electronic devices, and many people probably feel that society is closing them out.

---

[2] *Homo sapiens*, which has existed for about 300,000 years. If we count in the whole genus *Homo* (about 3 million years), we talk about more than 99% of our existence.

Many jobs are also much more monotonous than any we would encounter in our "natural" state, and probably produce a strain on our emotions. Finally, many modern service jobs demand a significant degree of "emotional labor" (Hochschild 1983, Putnam and Mumby 1993)—the effort exerted when "individuals change or manage their emotions to make them appropriate or consistent with a situation, a role, or an expected job function" (Putnam and Mumby 1993, p. 37). Typical examples are the consistently smiling attitude of the McDonald's salesperson or the airline hostess, and the professional consolation of the cancer ward nurse.

We should be careful, however, not to think that our emotional situation has necessarily deteriorated as a whole. Small peasant villages pose their own emotional strains, as does life in the extended family. The work of the serf or the tenant farmer could be harsh and monotonous enough, and serfs as well as servants have always had to do emotional labor to please their masters—who up through history have had considerably more gruesome sanctions to apply than the sack.

Emotions and Organizational Constraints

Our emotional apparatus was shaped in small groups and tuned to the needs of a life in the roving band. It might easily have dysfunctional effects in larger organizations, especially organizations built on the rational model. As we made the transition to modern society, emotions became a double-edged sword.

On the one hand, positive emotions bring social bonding and cohesiveness and oil the inner workings of organizations. Emotions are vital for producing the *esprit de corps* and individual motivation that makes organizations flourish and that can bring about success even in the face of what seems like insurmountable problems. They also provide us with many of the spices of organizational life.

On the other hand, as we noted, emotion-based social bonding functions (in line with our primate nature and hunter/gatherer origins) primarily within the local group—the people we meet in the flesh and interact with on a daily or almost daily basis. Although it is extremely useful for building cohesiveness in small organizations, this trait is just as likely to bring divisiveness in large ones—pitting departments against department, and work group against management.

This mechanism works on many different levels, not least geographical. It is quite common, for instance, in large multiplant companies, that the different plants exhibit strong, even fierce, independence and view company or division headquarters as a remote and largely irrelevant entity, only noted for its "interference" in local affairs. Clearly, such strong plant loyalty can be an asset in the efforts to improve locally, but a liability when it comes to achieving close cooperation and coordination in a larger organization. Building the necessary minimum of loyalty among people and organizational units who are geographically dispersed and who seldom meet requires strong, persistent efforts, and considerable energy is necessary on a continuous basis to maintain it.

In the world of humans, however, almost any difference can serve as a basis for divergence in culture and loyalty—not only geography, but also product affiliation, profession, status, and age, to mention some of the important ones. The natural preeminence of such local cultures and loyalties over an identification with the organization as a whole probably constitutes one of the most serious constraints on the size an organization can attain and still operate effectively and efficiently, and successful large companies devote considerable resources to foster common, company-wide sentiments. Especially in multinational companies, the problem of fragmentation is one of management's main concerns, and a driving force behind their demands that prospective managers circulate through several countries and companies during their career buildup (Bartlett and Ghoshal 1989).

All organizations experience emotion-related problems, and much energy is daily spent coping with them. From time to time they may become serious and require considerable attention and effort, and sometimes an organization will encounter conflicts so severe that it simply goes under—is dissolved, taken over by others, or simply goes bankrupt.

IT AND EMOTIONS

If it is correct that the increasing complexity of society as a whole and of many work situations does not match our emotional predispositions, the situation is hardly improving. Based on the rapidly increasing use of computers and ever more complex tasks, the tendency toward greater complexity and abstraction in work is continuing. A steadily growing number of jobs are performed with computer-based systems as the only tool or as an important support tool, whereas simpler jobs are eliminated in large numbers.

This is not unproblematic—after all, why should our emotions be better adapted to computer-based work than our bodies are to screens, keyboards and mice? If we contrast the tools provided by information technology and their possible use with the life situation that has formed us, we will easily see a number of areas where the exploitation of the new tools in the name of logic and reason will clash with older parts of our psyche. These main areas seem to be the *increasing abstraction and complexity* of work, the inherent *relentlessness* of a tireless technology built on logic and an unwavering demand (and capacity) for preciseness, and the *social isolation* that can grow from screen-based work.

Abstraction and Complexity

The process of abstraction is fundamental to the use of information technology—you always interact with a *representation* of the thing or process you work with, not with the real thing itself. Even in word processing, you leave behind the paper and work on a virtual document. This means that you must be able to understand the relation between the representation and the thing or process behind it, and you must learn to relate to unfamiliar cues and impressions. Usually, complexity also follows abstraction; the ability to manage more complex tasks will often be one of the main reasons to use IT.

Zuboff (1988) has described and named some of the most important changes that have happened to our everyday work in the course of this process. She has done so by exploring two central concepts: (a) the qualitative changes in the required set of skills as we make the transition from *action-centered* to *intellective* skills, which we will discuss here, and (b) the *informating of work*—the deepening of the understanding and responsibility that increasingly sophisticated control systems thrust upon us—which will be discussed in Chapter 14.

From Action-Centered to Intellective Skills

In Zuboff's terms, then, we are experiencing a transition from a reliance on action-centered skills to an emphasis on intellective skills. Action-centered skills are the skills of manual labor and of the direct control of machinery. They are, so to speak, the skills of the body— acquired through extended hands-on experience, and relying heavily on tacit knowledge (Polanyi 1967) and theories-in-use (Argyris 1980), even intuition. In many ways, action-centered skills correspond to the oral mindset. This correspondence is also noted by Zuboff. Explaining the transition to fully computerized process control in a paper mill she studied, she quotes a manager (1988, p. 71): "You need a new learning capability, because when you operate with the computer, you can't see what is happening. There is a difference in the mental and conceptual capabilities you need—you have to do things in your mind."

The transition here is even more dramatic than the passage from an oral to a literate mindset. Not only does work in a control room involve the acquisition of a set of abstract symbols and categories that describe the machinery and processes used in production (artifacts and events in the real world), it also requires the ability to understand what is happening in the production process through the nature, values, and interrelations of those symbols. On top of that, the operators must also be able to exert precise control over the production process (real-world artifacts and events) through a highly abstract, symbol-based interface, without any physical contact with the actual process at all (with the exception of some error situations).

Evidently, the abstraction of work—which is one of the outcomes of this transition—represents quite a dramatic change in the work situation. It therefore seems reasonable to expect emotional problems to crop up, both because of the changes in the individual work situation and as a result of the concomitant (and inevitable) changes in organization roles. There are probably many people who will find it difficult to adapt to this kind of work, and to a situation of greatly increased personal responsibility and the loss (at least partially) of the protection that has traditionally been built into workers' collective culture and bargaining (Lysgaard 1961).

Responsibility and Role Conflicts

As we shall see later (Chapters 12 and 14), the new computer systems not only force an abstraction of work, but also impart a deeper understanding of the processes they are used to manage and increase the possibilities for improving the performance of that part of the organization—or even the whole organization, as in the case of the control room operators in the paper mill Zuboff studied. With such an increase in understanding and control follows a corresponding increase in responsibility, which means a transition from a relatively simple job with a limited and stable set of rather concrete problems to tackle, to a job where a lot more time is devoted to problem solving, and where the problems are more complex, more abstract, more varied, and more difficult. This change is noted also by Walton (1989).

To cope successfully with the new job, people have to make deep changes in traditional attitudes to work, turning away from the old tenet that one is not responsible for anything outside the narrow frame of one's own job. A change here will in turn undermine old peer group identifications. If you start to feel (and respond to) responsibility for a larger part of the organization (or the whole organization), your identification is already shifting out of your peer group and is becoming more like the attitude formerly exhibited only by managers. This can cause considerable problems and conflicts between long-time fellow workers, with serious emotional fallout, as reported by Zuboff (1988).

But computers do not only tend to make work more complex and more oriented toward problem solving. The changes described are also often accompanied by a greater emphasis on teamwork and flexibility, which, for many people, can be another source of stress and insecurity, since such demands can also easily be perceived as resulting in less autonomy. Instead of carrying out well-defined tasks with a mutually recognized, limited set of responsibilities, one is suddenly at the mercy of events over which one has little control. Problems crop up and demand solutions, and one never knows what one will have to do next. Zuboff quotes an operator reflecting on such a job situation (1988, p. 405):

> They say the new technology will require a flexible system, you have no choice but to go where they send you, when they send you. You can get to earn high pay, but you have no choice about what your job is, and you can't have your own job. You never know what to wear to work—do you wear your good Levi's or do you wear your greasy ones?

Rigidity and Relentlessness

Then there is the issue of the untiring nature of computer-based systems, their inherent craving for precision, and their narrowness in only responding to and reporting information types that have been defined beforehand. Taken together, these characteristics can easily translate into rigidity and relentlessness, if special care is not taken to avoid just that. Zuboff (1988) describes several examples. An interesting case is the Work Force Supervisory System (WFSS) of what Zuboff calls Metro Tel, a part of a large telecommunications company.

Prior to the introduction of that system, each worker was a member of a crew assigned to a particular electronic switching station (ESS) and headed by a foreman. The crew was responsible only for the maintenance of its local ESS, and the foreman decided job priority and assigned individual workers to tasks. When error detection and analysis were centralized to switching control centers, each covering an extended geographical area with many ESSs, a new situation arose. Because error detection and analysis were no longer local, tasks did not have to be locally assigned either. That meant that maintenance workers did not have to be "wedded" to one particular ESS; they could be dispatched from the center as the need arose, with precise instructions for each job.

With this new angle of attack, there was suddenly a need for a considerable new bureaucracy to manage the queue of tasks and assign them to capable workers, and the situation quickly approached a mild chaos. There was also the new problem of supervising workers working in isolation in the (now more or less deserted) ESSs.

The WFSS was designed to solve these problems. From a work identification number, it prioritized tasks and automatically determined the time they should take to complete. Then it assigned jobs to the individual workers that put together should match the priority listing, match the worker's skill level, and give each worker a workday lasting the prescribed 8.5 hours. Instead of reporting to the foreman at their ESS, the workers now reported to the system each morning, receiving a description of that day's work. Of course, they also had to report back to the system each time they completed a task, and this information was available to the centrally located foremen—giving them a very accurate view not only of each worker's progress through the day (or night, for this was a round-the-clock operation), but also of their accumulated productivity. Failures to meet the calculated repair times would show immediately.

For the workers (and even for the foremen) this represented a dramatic change. Under the old regime, they lived in a traditional work organization, with ample human contact, and with all the ambiguities and flexibility of normal human interaction intact. With WFSS, they could work for days without any face-to-face contact whatsoever.

Initially, many foremen favored the new system, since it gave them an unprecedented overview of their subordinates' work. As two of them said (Zuboff 1988, p. 331): "It is beautiful now. I can track my people's work. All I have to do is type the craft's initials in and see how he is progressing and see what his total workload was. What is his productivity? Before, we had to judge people more on hearsay. Now we have it in black and white."

The workers, however, quickly perceived the system as rigid and unrelenting—it was no longer possible to negotiate tasks and times, and it was hard to gain acceptance for extra time if unforeseen difficulties cropped up. When management started to use the system's efficiency ratings to evaluate workers, even many foremen cautioned against it. Among other things, they pointed to the fact that the best people tended to get the most difficult jobs (the system was biased to do just that), jobs that often required more than the calculated time to finish. That would not show up in the statistics, and the best people could therefore end up with the worst ratings.

The foremen also discovered that they lost touch with their old people, and knew next to nothing about new hires, whom they only met as numbers in the system. They started to lament the loss of flexibility, of joint problem-solving, and the circumstantial but important knowledge that only diffuses through personal contact—such as if anyone had problems in the family or any other legitimate reason for receiving lenient treatment for a while. After some time, the foremen also learned that the system was being used to rate them as well, and they were beginning to feel the same sort of misgivings as the workers about the omnipresent monitoring the system represented. As a former worker, recently promoted to foreman, said about the WFSS system, also reflecting the feelings of the majority of workers (p. 352): "I hated it. It was too close. I could no longer hide anything. Management could monitor me hour by hour, and that was kind of scary."

After a while, the system was being widely experienced as too precise (in quantitative terms), too rigid, and too unrelenting to live with—it left no room for human judgment or for the pockets of privacy, ambiguity, and personal relations that human emotions crave. The outcome should have been predictable: to reclaim some of their lost room for maneuvering or to correct what they perceived as distorted reporting, people started to cheat the system—feeding it false information, ignoring some job assignments and claiming they had never received them, and so on.

Cheating the system can of course be interpreted as a manifestation of bad discipline and general irresponsibility among employees—after all, we know that discipline in such matters is, to a large extent, an acquired quality. The development of industrial culture through history as well as the differences between national cultures today testify to that. But, for most of us, there also seems to be a final threshold, beyond which we cannot be pushed without serious consequences. We all need a sphere of privacy, a certain room for maneuvering, a minimum of slack. That men are not machines is generally regarded as a truism, but sometimes we seem to forget that truisms are in fact true. Our basic emotions are not rational, they cannot be eliminated, and systems that encroach too much on them are bound to cause problems.

The Significance of Design

The objection can of course be made here that the WFSS system mirrors a rigid and inhumane management philosophy more than features that must necessarily be a part of computer-based systems, and that other design decisions could have produced a system with quite different characteristics. That is true to some extent, and a lot of people working with systems design and development have been quite concerned about this and sought ways to build "humane" systems (a good approach is presented in Eason 1988). The WFSS system could, for instance, have been designed not to schedule work and calculate necessary time automatically, but only to provide foremen with information as a basis for their decisions. It could have provided fields for comments and other unstructured information. It could have provided the workers with some latitude in choosing the order and priority of tasks.

However, computer-based systems are in their very nature based on logic; their strengths are first and foremost the storage, retrieval, and automatic processing of structured, preferably numerical, information. Therefore, they have an inherent tendency toward rigidity and relentlessness, especially in environments where increased efficiency is highly valued (which includes most places in today's industrialized societies). To escape the worst outcomes, it is especially important to avoid machine-paced work and detailed surveillance, and to position computer-based systems primarily as tools, not as automated managers.

Social Isolation

Humans are social animals and generally dread social isolation—*loneliness* is indeed a very negatively loaded word. Isolation is also a traditional punishment, and extreme isolation has always been a central instrument for those who want to break someone down psychologically.

Common sense would imply that isolation in the workplace is generally no more desirable, and research seems to bear this out (Sundstrom 1986), although Sundstrom remarks that "isolation and its effects have apparently not been systematically studied in work places" (1986, p. 295). Isolation is reported to be more tolerable if the work is interesting (Sundstrom 1986), but even then a certain level of social contact is preferred—there are few people who do not venture out of their offices for a chat a few times during the day.

Technology-induced social isolation is nothing new. Noise and machine layout in factories have often created jobs where it is impossible to talk to or even have eye contact with fellow workers, and, as mentioned earlier, it was not until after the Hawthorne studies that feelings and social relations really started to be acknowledged as important factors in the workplace (Hollway 1991). Social contact has been a consideration in factory layout since then, but it is impossible to tell how strong the impact has been across industries and national cultures.

As with older forms of technology, the introduction of information systems can easily produce social isolation for workers and professionals alike. If information is stored in databases and channeled through computer systems instead of human contacts, if email replaces a significant part of all telephone calls, and video conferencing does the same for travel and face-to-face meetings, our social interaction at work can be reduced significantly both in volume and quality[3] if steps are not taken to avoid it.

Social isolation was one of the complaints raised against the WFSS at Metro Tel, but it can be more pronounced in other situations. The obvious

---

[3] To me, it is obvious that a reduction in "bandwidth" means a reduction in quality of social interaction. Being there is better than video contact; a live voice is better than letters on a screen.

case is the caseworker supplied with a terminal giving him or her a total set of tools and all information necessary for completing work. In addition to the isolation produced by the systems themselves, seclusion is often intentionally maximized to eliminate chat and increase productivity. A benefit analyst is quoted by Zuboff (1988, p. 139):

> We used to be able to see each other and talk. Sure, sometimes we just talked about what we were going to make for dinner, but we always worked while we talked. Most of the time, we talked about something related to a claim. Then with the new system, they put in two filing cabinets between us, because we weren't supposed to see each other anymore. But there was a small space between the two cabinets, so she could still turn around and look at me, and we would talk across to one another. Well, one day a manager walked by, and I was asked who left this space there. I said that was how they left it when they put the cabinets in. The manager had them move the cabinets together because they don't want us talking.

Most of the workers who were affected by this system reported sharply reduced satisfaction with their work, both because of the isolation they experienced as well as the monotony of screen-based work and what they felt was the relentless tempo of their new, system-paced work situation. It represents another example of heedless exploitation of the technology's strong points.

In addition to the negative effects that such isolation has on the individual worker, it seems fairly obvious that it is detrimental to any efforts in the direction of improving employee morale and building an enthusiastic corporate culture. It may therefore run counter not only to employee well-being, but also to the total interests of the organization. If there is no social interaction at work and if the work situation is experienced as stressful and socially impoverished, loyalty is bound to drop and corporate culture will suffer.

Emotional Barriers to Virtual Organizations

A popular theme of the last few years has been the prospect of "virtual" teams and "virtual" organizations. The meaning is seldom clearly defined, but a "virtual team" generally implies that the people in the team work in at least two different locations. Often there are more locations, or one or several team members may be traveling most of the time. The defining feature is that the team members use one or more electronic media, such as email, computer conferencing, video phones/conferencing, common calendars and common information bases as their main communication channels, and they have little face-to-face contact.

"Virtual organization" usually has two main meanings: It may (a) either designate several more or less conventional companies working very closely together (even fronting the market as one organization) with electronic channels or even common systems as communication medium, or (b) an organization where a large number of the organization members use electronic channels as their main (or even only) medium for contact with each other and with the rest of the organization, thus forming the virtual teams that carry out the work and represent the main organizational structure.

Today, many seem to believe that the virtual organization is the main candidate for the title "organization of the future." I think that is a superficial judgment with a very weak foundation. We shall return to this question in connection with a discussion of groupware in Chapter 11. Here, we shall consider how emotional aspects may act as barriers or brakes on the establishment and success of virtual organizations—at least of the latter type, where the organization members use electronic communication channels only (or mainly) for their interaction.

True to our heritage as humans, we tend to achieve closest contact and build the most durable trust and loyalty toward the people we meet most often and over extended periods of time—whether they are (originally) involved in our work or not. We like to look people properly in the eyes to assess their worth. Face-to-face contact is the richest communication channel we have, and *any* electronic channel is significantly poorer—even top-quality video equipment cannot measure up to physical presence, let alone the barren dialogue of email. Of course, our extraordinary flexibility (Berger and Luckmann 1967) will allow us to build human bonds by the help of very narrow channels, such as email (or even through old-fashioned letters, as some people actually continue to do), and some people may even build very strong relationships that way—just like people earlier have done by writing letters. Indeed, the first Internet marriage (where the couple met and courted on the Net) has already taken place—although, undoubtedly to the chagrin of true cyberspace devotees, the bride and groom chose to appear before the parson in (physical) person.

My assertion is that, given our basic psychological makeup, the richer channel will in general produce the stronger bond. And, if this is true, it stands to reason that organizational loyalties in a virtual organization, where members' face-to-face contacts mostly involve people outside the organization, will be significantly lower than in a more conventional organization where people meet physically almost every day. The chances that organization members will be tempted to let their ideas and initiatives take off in other directions should also increase. It should also be much more difficult to build a strong organizational culture and a corporate identity that people can identify with when the organization is virtual and offers few opportunities of normal social encounters.

A virtual organization, then, should normally not be able to display the same cohesiveness, resilience, and endurance as a "physical" organization, and should therefore experience a handicap that must be outweighed by other factors. I therefore doubt that the fully virtual organization—without a physical location and built fully on electronic communication—will become a common form. Flexibility in structure and personnel is good up to a point, but extreme flexibility may all too easily translate into instability, disloyalty, and inefficiency. I also suspect that if a *really* important problem cropped up, the responsible person(s) in a hypothetical virtual organization would still pack their suitcases and go—to bring into action the intangibles that are impossible to convey by electronic means: the sensing of an atmosphere, of a handshake, or the intimacy of a lunch or dinner conversation.

A New Gender Gap?

In an age where the equal status of women in society is a very important issue, and their victories often must be defended for long periods of time before they become ingrained features of social life, it is not without peril to talk about differences between the sexes. However, it is probably not too controversial to point out that there seems to be a difference between men and women when it comes to social abilities and the need for deep personal relations and rich dialogue. Men are generally acknowledged to be less interested in personal matters, to pay less attention to feelings, and to make do with a terser dialogue. Women get more involved in social relations, seek out more personal information, and generally try to build more complete relationships.

If this is true, it follows that women will find virtual organizations and electronic communication channels less satisfying than men, will be less ready to enter into such more narrowly based interactions, and thus prefer conventional organizations to a larger degree than men. This could lead to a new kind of gender gap in working life. It could also offer at least a partial explanation of why there is such an overwhelming majority of men in IT-related occupations (normal office use excluded). The human-machine dialogue could simply be more to the male liking, devoid as it is of emotional content.

Information Technology as an Emotional Booster

After all these reservations, it is necessary to point out that information technology can also help to strengthen both organizational loyalty and culture in situations where colocation is impossible for old-fashioned reasons, such as the need to locate close to markets or sources of raw material or energy. One of the main problems in national or international organizations is just to build and, not least, to maintain a sense of organizational unity. Elkem, for instance, one of the organizations that has sponsored this study, has a number of smelters both in Norway and in the United States. Many of them started as independent enterprises and were later acquired, and many of them are located in small, otherwise rural communities—a long distance from company headquarters or even the division headquarters. These plants are by tradition fiercely independent and often resent "meddling" from corporate management. In addition, the company has the Atlantic divide to overcome. Forging a sense of organizational unity in such an organization is not easy, and the lack of a community feeling is perhaps the single biggest obstacle to organizational streamlining in this type of organizations.

Even in organizations with less geographical and historical distance to overcome, the task of building company identification can be formidable. Some of the energies bound in the social identifications at the primary and secondary level (team/department and site/plant) must be transferred to the higher levels. Mature international organizations have established a lot of practices to achieve this, especially at the management level (Bartlett and Ghoshal 1989). Mandatory temporary relocations to one or more foreign sites as part of a career track is but one of them.

In such organizations, electronically mediated contact is of course better than no contact, and email and conferencing (particularly video) can build a sense of community, especially among like-minded people. It can therefore be an interesting tool for building coherence and cooperation among experts of the same trade who are spread out among different sites, as well as for cooperating units at different sites.

A General Caveat

Industrialization and the emergence of large organizations have brought us far away from the content and conditions of our primeval work conditions. IT will most likely transform our work further. We should therefore take the opportunity from time to time to remind ourselves that, in our discussions of technology, systems, and structures, we must not forget that people are what both society and organizations are about.

Even if they have a rational side that interfaces well with the technology, people are also living humans with a profoundly emotional nature that must be taken into account and that has great value in its own right. When discussing matters like the subject of this book, it is easy to forget that economic efficiency is not an end in itself and should not be pursued to the detriment of basic human values. In a competitive world, many people have a tendency to regard such a view as a luxury one cannot afford, and it is indeed often difficult to harmonize with a realistic attitude toward pressing economic realities in organizations fighting for survival. We can only hope that the steadily increasing material prosperity in industrialized societies will gradually lead to a more relaxed attitude and a greater interest in using the increased productivity to improve our lot in a broader sense. We should remember the words of Blaise Pascal (from *Pensées,* 1670): *"The hearth has its reasons which reason does not know."*

IV
Extending the Space of Constructible Organizations

In Part III of this book, we discussed how computers have delivered another quantum jump in the history of organizational tools. In my view, information technology already ranks on the level of writing itself, and it leads to profound changes in some of our preconditions for organizing. The most important improvements over pre-computer technology, as analyzed in Chapter 9, are:

- Computers allow, for the first time, the externalization of processing, and certain kinds of work that previously required the attention of human minds can now be offloaded to machines. A potentially limitless source for these categories of work has been created.
- Processing of quantitative information is presently most important. Computing tasks that seemed impossible to carry out 50 years ago are now routine.
- Computers vastly extends the scope for automation and elimination of tasks in both manufacturing and administration. The potential of computer-based automation is so great compared to mechanical automation as to be unfathomable.
- Computers can concentrate quantitative information enormously by presenting it in graphical form, especially when combined with animation. By thus exploiting the large bandwidth of our visual system, information technology allows us to absorb such information much faster than before.
- Computer processing also greatly enhances our insight and understanding of complex matters and improves our ability to handle complexity. It significantly extends the coordinative reach and power of one person or a single team.
- Artificial intelligence and embedded rules and information can support work, both in time-critical and in knowledge-intensive activities.

- Computers also usher in a new revolution in memory. The database offers an improvement over paper-based files so large that it is of a quantitative as well as qualitative nature.
- Structured databases are so far the most important, with vastly improved implicit coordination achieved through global reach, enormous capacity, and blistering speed.
- Free-form databases (text, sound, and pictures) are interesting and have important economic potentials but are considerably less important for organizational purposes.
- Computers increase available communication bandwidth by several orders of magnitude. The most important aspects are direct system-to-system communication and remote access to databases.
- Of less but still significant importance are email, computer conferencing, video conferencing, and other team support tools.

When we go on to discuss what kind of new possibilities these advances open up for organizing human work, however, we must remember that not even information technology can cure all ills, and that a number of important constraints remain in force:

- The human input/output capacity is basically unchanged, with the exception of quantitative information that can be represented graphically. All information in verbal form must still be read or heard, written or spoken, and this iron constraint shows no sign of yielding.
- This constraint still also puts absolute limits on the number of people with whom we can maintain a meaningful two-way communication—all new electronic media notwithstanding.
- The usability of databases, especially free-form information bases, is also severely constrained by the limits of human input/output and processing capacities. Simply increasing the amount of available information is not necessarily beneficial.
- Just as with previous technology, human internal processing and deliberation are not speeded up, even if our ability to handle complex work and parallel work processes is greatly enhanced.
- The limits of our own mental capacities now manifest themselves in a new way. The recent (and imminent) advances in information technology, especially in hardware, place such storage and processing capacities at our disposal that the main constraint for building more sophisticated and complex systems has become our own ability to first adequately analyze and understand the problem domain, and then design and install the intended systems.
- Neither our physiology nor our emotional makeup is adapted to the kind of highly abstract, problem-oriented work that fills an increasing

part of our workdays. The result is often physical and mental strain that can lead to reduced morale, reduced performance, and even injuries.
- The preeminence of face-to-face contact in the establishment and maintenance of primary group identification may reduce the viability of virtual organizations. This constraint may affect women more than men.

Part IV attempts to establish how this new set of preconditions will allow us to extend the space of constructible organizations. The first chapter discusses the individual and team level—because they represent the primordial elements of organization as well as the fundamental building blocks of larger organizations, and because there are a number of application types (among them some of the most hyped-up ones) that apply first and foremost to this level.

Then I will move on to discuss the core of the matter: the larger organizational context and the tools and potentials that apply to the organization as a whole. This discussion is centered on the three themes that I think embody the most important potentials provided by information technology for organizational change and improvement.

Each theme is treated in a separate chapter. The first is "Routines and Automation," which will continue to represent an extremely important contribution to the development of modern societies, allowing enormous increases in productivity—something that will have a number of interesting side effects. Computer-based automation also includes automatic routines at various levels, which is a very important prerequisite for the two other themes. The second theme, "Coordination by Default," is about how the use of databases can contribute to the age-old problem of coordinating the work of all organization members, both improving on existing arrangements and providing new ones. The third theme, "Comprehension and Control", is about how information technology is used to procure previously unavailable information and to make information more accessible, thus improving our understanding and control of both our work and the organization. This has clear implications for organization structure and the way organizations can be run.

At the end of each of these three chapters, I will discuss the possible extensions that the examined aspect of information technology may offer to the space of constructible organizations.

11
The Individual and the Group

"One man may hit the mark, another blunder; but heed not these distinctions. Only from the alliance of the one, working with and through the other, are great things born."
Saint-Exupéry, *The Wisdom of the Sands*, 1948

In Chapter 9, we discussed how information technology can improve individual capabilities in those areas that are most important for our ability to organize. In accordance with the view of organizations as constructed and constituted through individual actions, these improvements represent the foundation for any IT-induced change of a systemic nature.

However, there is another side to these improvements: they also improve individual productivity. In this chapter we shall discuss these possible improvements and try to assess whether they can in turn induce organizational changes and improvements. We shall also discuss the group level before moving on to the subject of larger organizations in the next chapters, since the small group has, throughout human history, represented a basic level of organization with its own distinct needs and priorities.

THE INDIVIDUAL LEVEL

Support Tools

When talking about gains in personal productivity from computers, people mostly think in terms of increased efficiency for standard office work—for example, faster production of documents, budgets and related calculation chores, presentations, and communications. Even though these "Office Suit" applications have driven much of the investments in computer systems from the late 1980s and onward, their potential impact on organization is in my view limited; it may represent no more than a significant reduction in the number of typists—a contribution to the general trend of eliminating routine work. Such tools provide mainly what we might term *bounded improvements* in productivity—local improvements within the confines of the jobholder's usual set of tasks and responsibilities. A typical example might be the salesperson who can complete a few more customer contacts and dispatch a few more letters and offers every day with the help of a PC-based sales support program and a word processor.

We will find the same effects in the realm of science and engineering, such as systems for statistical analysis, computerized equipment for chemical analysis, and CAD (computer-aided design) systems. They generally deliver much higher gains in personal productivity than the standard office tools mentioned earlier, however—simply because they tap much deeper and more directly into the numerical processing power of the computer. The combination of simulation and animated graphics alone has been extremely advantageous. Just imagine the difference for an engineer designing the front wheel suspension for a new car. Before the computer, it meant trial and error supported by time-consuming and rudimentary manual computations; in the first three to four decades of computing it meant poring over computer printouts, trying to envision what the numbers really implied. After the advent of cheap and powerful workstations, the simulated behavior of the new suspension can be *seen* in real time on a computer screen as it travels over various simulated surfaces.

As long as they are isolated systems, however, just supporting the work of the individual professional, even engineering and scientific workstations do not have any more impact on organization than office tools do. Their main effect has been a significant reduction in the number of draftsmen and calculation assistants (a parallel to the decimation of typists). The really exciting processes do not start until the systems are linked into design databases or planning and production systems, but, then the systems become more than personal support systems.

In the ordinary office environment, there is always the danger that increased productivity will be eaten up by increased output of material of low significance or through unnecessary embellishments such as fancy layout and presentations laden with ornamental graphics. It takes both a conscious approach and good management to really make savings stick.

Cell Automation

In organization terms, some of the same can be said about isolated automation of single tasks—what we might term *cell automation*. In both offices and factories, automating single tasks can increase local (cell) output per employee many times over. In an office it can, for instance, be used for address selection and printing; in a factory, for computer-controlled machine tools.

In both instances the computers provide not only greater speed, but also much greater flexibility than previous automation efforts, because of the almost infinitely greater complexity computer programs will allow. However, unless the automated cells are linked into some sort of department- or organization-wide system, traditional coordination methods and organizational structures will most likely prevail, and the bounded productivity improvements will not translate into significant changes on the organizational level.

By this, I do not mean that bounded improvements in productivity are unimportant. There are significant (in some instances even spectacular) savings to be had, especially in science and engineering, and as the price/performance ratio of processors continue to improve, processing power that used to be reserved for multimillion dollar supercomputers is invading the desks of rank-and-file engineers and scientists. This opens up for dramatic increases in productivity and an ability to tackle problems with a complexity many orders of magnitude greater than before. The demand for processing capacity is rising fast, and, in many areas of science, extensive use of very powerful computers is greatly accelerating the pace of progress.

Increasing the Span of Competence

Are there, then, any personal support systems that support significant changes in organization? I think there are—and that the key notion is the attainable *span of competence*. The area of interest here is the degree of specialization, and the amount of coordination and information transfer it necessitates.

When we discussed the emergence of functional specialization in Chapter 7, it was attributed both to the resulting increase in productivity as well as the need to reduce the time used for training. But there is of course also another and more fundamental reason for specialization, rooted in both the limitations of human memory and our low rate of information absorption: it is simply not possible for anyone to become proficient in everything.

This is of course not a barrier for the narrow, repetitive jobs of mass-producing industry, but it becomes an important constraint and a determinant for the design of organizations or parts of organizations where more complex tasks dominate. Typical examples are thoroughly professional organizations like universities, research laboratories and hospitals, but most organizations (and every large one) will have jobs where the limits to a person's effective, attainable span of competence become a design parameter. In a travel agency, for instance, no one can give a customer expert advice on travel in every part of the world. In a large bank, no clerk can advise you on all aspects of the bank's services. In a government department, no single person will have the necessary knowledge to carry out more than a fraction of all the varied tasks falling within the department's responsibility.

This is not to say that all specialization in such organizations is based on the natural limits in the diversity of knowledge that humans are able to maintain—on the contrary, in most organizations, there is considerable room for broadening the area of responsibility for individual employees without the need for recourse to new tools. My point is only that it is not possible to broaden jobs indefinitely without coming up against fundamental human barriers, and risk a rapidly decreasing quality of the work in question. This is undoubtedly the cause behind a significant part of the functional specialization in modern organizations. Computer-based systems, however, do have the potential to expand our effective span of competence through *artificial memory, artificial intelligence* and *embedded knowledge.*

Artificial Memory

Even with present text retrieval systems, it is possible to offer much easier and more comprehensive access to laws, regulations, precedents, guidelines, policy handbooks, solutions to previously encountered problems and so on than when relying on printed or written media alone. Future systems will improve this further. With the fast and exhaustive information retrieval provided by advanced computer-based systems, it should be possible to support decisions and problem solving for broader fields of work than we can safely master without such assistance.

Artificial Intelligence

Artificial intelligence clearly also has the potential to help stretch our span of competence. It has already been demonstrated that expert systems can improve decisions. Rasmus (1991), for instance, reports how an expert system introduced by Southern California Edison incorporated the company's policy for computer purchases and allowed the departments to configure their own PC purchases in adherence to the central guidelines without assistance from the DP department. DEC's XCON system and the successor XCEL is well known (Walton 1989, Heller 1991). XCEL helped DEC's salespeople to arrive at the best systems configurations for their customers. The pace of development here has been slower than predicted, however—even for XCON, perhaps the most extensively used expert system and certainly one of the most widely reported successes—as it was deemed necessary to have a human expert check each and every "decision" (Long 1987). Nevertheless, there is little doubt that such systems will play an important role in the future within particularly well-defined problem domains.

Embedded Knowledge

Embedded knowledge is not the same as an expert system. It simply means that a computer-based system may have "knowledge" embedded in it as a part of its data structure and its functions. A simple system for computing annuities, for example, has embedded in it the rules for such computations. A bank clerk with access to a system like that can advise a customer on the size of his annual payments for a particular loan without knowing anything about how to compute annuities himself. All computer systems have such embedded knowledge to a greater or lesser extent, and many computer systems are therefore able to extend the span of competence of their users.

One interesting problem turns up as more and more knowledge and rules are embedded in systems—both in this simple sense and in connection with the rule-based inference engines of AI programs. Work rules, regulations and even the substance of laws may end up as embedded information in computer programs designed to support office work. The problem is particularly important in the government sector, where an increasing number of regulations and even law clauses are embedded in systems used for administrative purposes.

When this happens, it becomes more difficult not only for the public to fully understand how the laws and regulations are applied, but also for the lawmakers to control whether their laws are actually represented correctly in the systems. Experience has shown that you cannot always trust programmers to render law into code and carry the lawmakers' intentions through unscathed. We can therefore anticipate a growing need for *system auditors*, people who can scrutinize systems and see if the embedded rules are in accordance with the regulations or laws they are meant to express. We may even see laws passed demanding that all systems with laws or government regulations embedded (which will include accounting systems) *must* store all rules pertaining to those regulations or laws in separate tables (and not have them "hard-coded" into the body of system code) for easy auditing. In my view, such legislation is long overdue already.

Embedding laws in systems may also make them harder to change, because of the limits of the systems they reside in, and simply because nobody may have a complete knowledge of the systems involved. There are already stories circulating about how proposed changes in taxation have had to be abandoned or postponed because the necessary changes to the internal revenue service's computer systems demanded rewrites too extensive to meet deadlines.

I have no doubt, though, that such problems will be overcome and that systematic use of all the tools available–both artificial memory, artificial intelligence and embedded knowledge—will make it possible to broaden the range of tasks people can carry out with an acceptable level of quality, in some instances considerably, and thus make it possible to eliminate even more coordination and control activities.

Another aspect of this combination of support tools is that it will make it possible to improve the quality of professional work overall. Appropriate systems built on this technology should allow physicians to make better diagnoses, judges to pass sentences that are more consistent, and caseworkers to achieve greater consistency and quality in their work—in short, to help most professionals to adhere more closely to professional standards. Viewed in this perspective, this collection of tools should provide us with a much improved version of Mintzberg's (1979) coordinating mechanism standardization of skills, which is defined more narrowly to standardization of explicit skills in Figure 3-1 on p. 51. I suggest the name *system-supported skills* for this new, computer-dependent coordinating mechanism (see also the extended taxonomy of coordinating mechanisms in Figure 13-1, p. 315).

Response Assistance

Finally, systems based on the concepts behind artificial intelligence should be able to help by suggesting responses in complex operative situations, especially during cognitive overload or when time is a critical factor for other reasons. The systems could even be designed to take action without "consultation" with the human operator if the time allowed for response is so short (as it may be in an emergency) that the human operator cannot be expected to react fast enough. Such systems could probably prevent tragedies like the airplane crash mentioned in Chapter 4 and disasters like the Chernobyl nuclear reactor meltdown.

But Personal Productivity Is Not the Key

The analysis in Chapter 7 showed that the main stimulus behind industrialization and the developments of the modern, bureaucratic organization in the nineteenth century was the tremendous productivity increases that could be obtained through functional specialization and the use of new tools. If a technology-induced increase in the workers' individual productivity could drive this great change, it may seem natural to ask if computer-based increases in personal productivity today could have the potential to play a similar role. In my view, the answer is no.

The reason is that the decisive innovation in an organizational perspective was specialization itself—not the tools that followed. The potential for organizational change built on specialization and an increase in individual productivity was therefore largely exhausted already by this first transition, and even the tremendous increases in productivity that has taken place since the modern factory was developed in the last half of the nineteenth century has not changed the organizational principles of the Machine Bureaucracy in any significant way. We have therefore no reason to believe that a further increase in productivity at any isolated step in a process—even if it is substantial—in itself should be enough to change the picture significantly. Output of the total organization may well increase greatly, but as long as the improvement is built on isolated achievements at single steps in the process, the organization itself is not likely to change very much.

The basic characteristics of the technologies involved are very different, moreover, and the keys to exploit them therefore quite dissimilar. In contrast to the specialized machinery of traditional industry, the computer is a general, information-processing machine that is able to adapt to an extremely wide array of tasks. The strength of information technology is therefore first and foremost its ability to support coordination and planning, and to carry automation (including automated coordination) to new levels of complexity and sophistication. Information technology should therefore be expected to affect first of all the design and coordination of work processes and the linkages between different tasks, and achieve its greatest effects through directing physical processes of far greater complexity with superior efficiency and flexibility and with much less overhead than before.

EXTENSIONS TO THE CONSTRUCTIBLE SPACE

Isolated elimination of routine jobs in itself, then, offers fairly limited extensions in the space of constructible organizations. Nevertheless, the potential increases in personal productivity should allow some changes. The most important opportunities are probably connected to de-specialization and an increased use of self-service.

Elimination of Routine Jobs

The bounded improvement in personal productivity effected through the office tools and cell automation described earlier has fairly little to offer with respect to new organizational structures. The main opportunity in that direction lies in the elimination of routine jobs. We have touched upon this already. Many of the tools in the personal support category do the kind of work that was previously provided by secretaries and various kinds of assistants.

Routine jobs may also be eliminated by more comprehensive changes, such as in the accounts payable function at Ford (Hammer 1990, Hammer and Champy 1993), which will be described in some detail in Chapter 13. However, in that case we are talking of a thorough reorganization facilitated through the use of the coordinative power of a database, not of reductions based on increases in personal productivity.

The groups hardest hit by elimination based on personal productivity tools have up to now been filing clerks, typists, draftsmen, and assistants performing various kinds of calculations. In the long run, most routine office jobs are in danger—as their functions are either automated or eliminated. The routine jobs with the best chance of survival are physical or personal services. The janitor and the cleaner will survive, for instance; we will still need some people in the canteen, and most organizations will prefer a human receptionist to greet and direct visitors.

De-specialization and Knowledge Support

Broadening the span of competence through the use of system-supported skills has somewhat more to offer, since it may allow us to decrease job specialization. Perhaps we should rather call this re-integration or even *de-specialization*—to emphasis that we are now able to alleviate some of the problems that job specialization created in the first place.

De-specialization is not a universal option. It builds on two pillars: easy retrieval of information on the one hand, and embedded knowledge and AI on the other. These tools primarily support de-specialization of jobs that require people to collect information from many sources for further processing, or for use in decision making on the basis of law, rules, or regulations—the archetypal bureaucratic kind of job after Weber's definition. The important aspect of de-specialization is that it, by reducing the number of steps in the work process, also reduces the need for information transfer, one of the most time-consuming activities in any large office, and a major source of errors and misunderstandings.

The main reason that functional specialization met with much less success in the office than in the factory can be found precisely in the much higher volume of information that has to be transferred from person to person as part of the work process there. In the factory a piece of hardware coming down the assembly line embodies most—if not all—of the information needed by the workers. The information is absorbed quite literally at a glance, and, consequently, one attracts very little penalty—if any—in the form of increased time for information transfer when one increases functional specialization.

A transaction so simple that it only needs to be registered or stamped can be processed in much the same way in a white-collar "line." As soon as it becomes a little more complex, however, requiring some kind of assessment and decision making (what might more readily be termed a *case*), it will normally be accompanied with a lot of written information—usually both the basic information collected at the outset as well as the information accumulated while it has been passed along the various steps in the work process. Often, there will also be a need to transfer informal, oral information.

Any increase in functional specialization in the office will therefore normally incur a considerable overhead in the form of information transfer. Not infrequently, absorbing all the relevant information and making sure that one understands it correctly takes longer time than doing the actual work. As noted earlier, numerous information transfers also create ample opportunities for errors, misunderstandings, and loss of information. We have probably all been victims of such mishaps in our encounters with bureaucratic structures. Indeed, many of us have been guilty of producing them as well.

Reducing the number of information transfers in an organization will therefore contribute greatly to its productivity, especially since interpersonal communication itself is so difficult to make more efficient. As our previous analyses have shown, this is the most recalcitrant of all our innate constraints when it comes to tool support. Despite all our gadgetry, it takes about the same time to transfer information from one mind to another today as it did a hundred years ago-and, if we talk about people at the same location, it takes the same time as it did *10 000 years* ago.

How far can the concept of de-specialization be developed? Can we, for instance, imagine computer-supported superprofessionals covering many disciplines, or supermanagers taking over the responsibilities of entire present-day management teams? What the distant future will bring is not possible to foretell, and history has taught us not to try. In the foreseeable future, however, such a scenario is simply impossible, because the knowledge that can be embedded in systems, even in AI-systems, is mainly of the "hard" kind: simple facts, or pretty simple if-this-then-that rules. Even advanced AI systems are extremely limited compared to a human mind.

All our "softer" knowledge; our experience; our tacit knowledge; our ability to interpret facts from a context and previous experience; our ability to discern the important from the unimportant, to judge and weigh information and decision alternatives is impossible to embed or mimic in a system. In a professional and managerial position, extensive experience and background knowledge is always needed to respond sensibly to problems or execute tasks in a satisfactory way. Even if we could build a system that would allow persons without such experience and background knowledge to respond adequately in many or even most instances (a daunting, but perhaps not impossible task in certain circumstances), they would be at a complete loss when more complex situations arose. Or, even worse, they might think—erroneously—that they had a good answer and then happily execute it, since they did not know enough about the implications to understand their own shortcomings.

The limiting factor, then, for integrating professional and managerial jobs is not so much the nature of the tasks themselves, but rather the extent of the knowledge and experience that is necessary to fully understand their implications. For some jobs (for instance, in sales) the number of personal, external contacts that must be maintained is also a limiting factor on the number of functions one person can shoulder. Everyone with experience in sales activities knows that personal contact is extremely important and that it cannot be totally supplanted by more "efficient" computer-mediated, semiautomatic communication (except for fairly inexpensive items).

Self-Service

However, the opportunities range further than this. Of particular interest is the possibility of offloading tasks onto the customer, thus removing it from the organization altogether. Supportive systems with elements of AI and/or embedded knowledge may allow for much more extensive self-service than we have been used to. Automatic teller machines have already introduced us to personal support systems that allow us to complete some kinds of bank transactions ourselves. The types of transactions that have been made available for self-service so far have been few, but there are more advanced machines (and systems) coming up, and the concept should be possible to develop to the point where the bank itself all but ceases to exist (we shall return to that particular case in the next chapter).

There are doubtlessly a large number of areas where computer-supported self-service will surface. Both airline tickets and other tickets are already sold this way, betting systems should be eminently possible, and insurance (at least some kinds, and more advanced than the travel insurance you can buy from vending machines at some airports) is a product that should also lend itself to similar self-service systems. The filing of applications for various purposes is another area open for computer-supported self-service solutions.

Although self-service is a phenomenon all by itself, it can also be seen as an aspect of de-specialization, since the logic behind both is the same. Systems guide us through; because they "know" how things are to be done, they help us get at the necessary information, prompt us for our contributions, and then perform the transactions on our behalf. The organizational effects may be profound—a lot of specialized jobs will disappear because customers take over, and large parts of existing organizations may be eliminated.

Conclusions

The various improvements in personal productivity discussed earlier have already made possible changes that have had significant impact on organizations, and more is bound to come. As personal productivity continues to improve and cell automation and self-service proliferate, organizations of all sizes will be able reduce their payrolls further—at least in the parts of the organization where the improvements are implemented. This is of course not the only source of workforce reductions—it is not even the most important one, as we shall see later. However, it will allow for significant reductions. A reduction in the number of employees will also allow organizations to reduce the number of administrative layers somewhat—in particular, de-specialization should contribute to this.

However, the changes are relatively simple: by and large, they consist in workforce reductions. Even if de-specialization may involve an integration of jobs and thereby a marked reduction in the need for information transfer, it provides no particular platform for really inventive organizational changes. There are no genuinely new principles involved—the IT-based advances in personal productivity mainly represent improvements and extensions of the development process started in the eighteenth century.

Granted, the improvements are dramatic in some respects and may foster significant local changes in many organizations, as when typing pools are dissolved, assistant draftsmen made superfluous and jobs broadened. The improvements in productivity can even be said to be of epochal proportion in quite a number of scientific and engineering disciplines. Organizationally speaking, however, they do not significantly expand the space of constructible organizations, nor do they build significant pressures for evolution in totally new directions.

GROUPS AND TEAMS

All organized activities are instances of cooperation, and, in that sense, cooperation can be thought of as more or less synonymous with organization. When talking about cooperative work in connection with the use of information technology, however, it is the team and the work group that is in focus. The discussion in this section will therefore be limited to that level; a group small enough to let each member have more or less direct contact with all the other members.

I have quite intentionally made a distinction here between the concepts "team" and "work group." Although these expressions are frequently used as synonyms, at least in everyday speech (I often do so myself), they have distinctly different connotations in a more precise theoretical context. A group or work group is a fairly loose term, designating any relatively limited number of people who work in conjunction with one another for a common purpose. A team in its more precise sense is a small and tight-knit group with a common purpose, a strong sense of commitment, and a genuinely shared responsibility for the outcome of their work (Katzenbach and Smith 1993). It is this genuine commitment and shared responsibility that serves to distinguish the true team from the work group, not a particular way of working. Since many authors are less stringent about this term, however, and everyday use is far less rigorous, I will use the word "team" fairly broadly in the following. Regardless of definitions, moreover, teams and work groups should have the same kind of needs for coordination and work support and thus reap the same benefits (and share the same problems) from using information technology.

The use of computers in group support is one of the aspects of computer use that receives most attention as we make the transition from the twentieth to the twenty-first century (together with multimedia, the Internet, networking and the concept of "electronic highways"). In my view, this attention is not warranted by its actual contribution to organizational transformation and efficiency (this goes for multimedia and the Internet as well). It is, however, easy to understand why it arouses so much interest. It talks directly to our primate, emotional side; it is all about humans being human together, rather than being machine-like parts in a machine-dominated organization. Using a term from organization theory, Cooperative Computing and the development of groupware may in many ways incarnate the human relations movement of the computer scene.

Cooperation among humans is almost synonymous with communication. The exchange of views and ideas, the transfer of information, and working out decisions and making them known involve copious amounts of communication, with meetings as the main instrument. People who continuously grumble about "all the time thrown away in meetings" only demonstrate that they do not understand the nature of human cooperation or the burden of coordination placed upon us by any organized activity. They may simply believe in commanding instead of cooperating, and thus feel no need for advice, for discussions, or for building motivation.

There are of course good and bad ways to conduct meetings, and in many, more work could be accomplished in less time. Some meetings are undoubtedly even unnecessary—but I also know about a good number of necessary meetings that were never held, to the detriment of the organization in question. The fact is that any organized activity will require meetings, and, the more dynamic the situation is, the more meetings will be required. It is no accident that the supreme military commanders in critical situations or during major offensives meet continuously during the most intensive phases to coordinate the efforts of their respective services—they are not locking themselves into their separate offices to do "real work."

It is no wonder, then, that much of the work being done in the area of cooperative computing involves either support for face-to-face meetings or tools for electronic meetings. Johansen (1988) even concludes that such efforts can best be categorized according to their support for meetings or activities related to meetings. I would like to propose another classification scheme, however: *meeting support, work support,* and *infrastructural support.*

Meeting Support

Meeting support involves both systems to support face-to-face meetings and systems designed to allow fully "electronic" meetings by way of computers. Work on such systems started quite early in the computer era—for instance, quite a lot of the original work of Douglas Engelbarth, the "father" of groupware and graphical user interfaces, involves systems for the enhancements of meetings. Work on support systems for face-to-face meetings and "electronic" meetings started at about the same time.

Meeting Support Systems

The main approaches to meeting support systems have been various forms of electronic white boards and group decision support systems. The aim has been to provide tools for better structuring of meetings, easier integration of contributions from the participants, and better documentation of the results.

The results so far have been fairly meager. It is difficult to make tools that truly contribute to real-time, human communication processes, and it is even more difficult to make them so easy and intuitive to operate that they are adopted for use outside the rather narrow circle of groupware developers and enthusiasts. I think there are potentials for improvement here, however, and I believe that the electronic white board will slowly develop into a useful tool—but that development will take many years. Perhaps the most important initial contribution will be the ability to retrieve and display information from corporate and external databases, to provide a common platform for discussion, and to quickly satisfy needs for ad hoc information that may arise during meetings.

Most of the development in this area has been devoted to meetings in administrative environments that work mainly with language (text)— that is the case with all the systems described in Johansen (1988). This can perhaps be explained by the background of the researchers, their institutional settings, and the all-too-common preoccupation with the problems of top management.

However, the analysis of where the computer contributes most to enhance our own abilities suggests that the potential for useful meeting support tools should be much greater in the professions already working with highly graphical applications, such as printing, advertising, architecture, and engineering design. Electronic white boards in those environments, in the form of large-screen, common workspaces, could serve as very important productivity instruments for design groups. And if, in the future, one succeeds in harnessing more advanced graphics and animation for the display of more administratively oriented information, the electronic white board may gain in importance even here.

Electronic Meetings

Among the tools for meeting support, those meant for supporting fully "electronic" meetings have aroused by far the most widespread interest. They may involve telephone, video, computer conferencing, and screen sharing. Screen sharing means that everybody participating in the meeting can see and access the same picture on their displays. The focus of development lies in the direction of video conferencing, preferably combined with screen sharing. With a sufficiently large screen and sufficient bandwidth on the transmission lines, it would then be possible to conduct workgroup meetings onscreen. One part of the screen could be occupied by the live pictures of the participants; the rest could be available to material for presentation and manipulation.

Simpler solutions may involve telephone conferencing with screen sharing or real-time computer conferencing (with all the participants on-line at the same time). Traditional computer conferencing, in which participants log on at different times and keep exchanges going for days and weeks, does not seem a viable tool for meetings, but for easy exchange of written statements and expositions—it is more like an electronic journal or bulletin board.

The analysis in the previous chapters indicates that such solutions will be a good tool for groups where the participants know each other, and will make it easier to maintain cooperation in spite of geographical separation. It also suggests that the improvements will be especially important for those who work with strongly graphical applications—geographical separation is more of a handicap for them than for groups working mainly with text and numbers. However, the need for colocation and face-to-face meetings cannot be totally eliminated—at least not yet.

Work Support

Meetings are certainly indispensable to coordinate and reach decisions. They also quite often function as problem-solving groups. Thus they encompass most aspects of group work. However, groups do not only work when they meet, the members also work by themselves on their part of the group assignment. Most of that work is probably accomplished with the help of various personal support systems, but, in addition, groups need tools that provide a common framework, and help integrate the various contributions. Electronic mail, conferencing systems, and group authoring programs (programs supporting the production of joint documents or other forms of joint information presentations) are such tools, along with common databases.

A typical example of computer-supported group work was quoted in Chapter 9 (from McKersie and Walton, 1991), where telephones, a conferencing system, remotely accessible databases, and word processing were used to produce a joint document with a number of remotely located managers. As we noted, that document could doubtlessly have been produced without computers, but probably with lower quality. More advanced tools such as video conferencing and screen sharing will further increase the edge that computer-based systems will give over pre-computer tools. Even here, however, I think the potential is greatest for work involving strongly numerical and graphical applications, such as engineering design (CAD). By having a common database representing the total object to be designed as basis, a true design-group-oriented CAD tool should offer both full coordination and coherence of the overall design parameters and of the interfaces between modules, while, at the same time, allowing the individual designer to work on his/her part of the assignment. When fully developed, however, such a system becomes much more than groupware—it becomes a very complex system for coordinating the work of a total organization or even many organizations. We shall return to this subject in Chapter 13.

Although workflow tools do not, strictly speaking, belong to the groupware class, all the vendors insist that they belong there. They probably do so because groupware as a concept is very much in vogue, and also because they do not have very many other products to include under the groupware heading, except for calendars and email systems. Workflow tools are meant to manage work processes and to speed work along from point to point in the process, and they also take care of some of the most routine aspects of that process (Thé 1995). As such, they build on a rather traditional approach to office work, aimed more at speeding it up than changing it. The underlying model is still that of a chain of individual caseworkers each doing an incremental part of a total task. The products provide instant transport of all electronically stored material between caseworkers and also make it much easier to monitor progress and to find out where in the process a particular case is at any particular time. Householding functions save time for caseworkers with chores such as filing and routing.

Workflow tools can undoubtedly increase productivity in most procedural environments, but in the process they tend to cement existing routines and inhibit more creative solutions built on automation and elimination of tasks.

Infrastructural Support

To function properly, groups require a certain infrastructure. By tradition, we would say that they need office space for work and meetings; they need a common "memory" in the form of files and archives; they may need support personnel of different kinds. We would also prefer groups to work at the same location and in adjacent offices, not only because of the efficiency (easy access and no travel time), but also because colocation is generally deemed necessary to build the team-spirit that is so important for successful teams. Friendship and team spirit need a certain volume of interaction to grow, preferably ample and regular informal contact. The close proximity of a common work area is required to achieve that.

Computer-based systems can improve such group infrastructures in several ways. The most obvious one is perhaps the database—when everyone have easy access and can use the same information as a basis for their work, the general coordination of a group is automatically improved. Group calendar systems can also be of help if members spend much time away from a common office and have difficulty keeping tabs on each other to arrange meetings, etc. Computer-based project management systems represent an improvement over earlier tools and can significantly increase the flexibility in larger projects when it comes to tackling unforeseen events and changes in plans and priorities.

Then there is the issue of personal communication. When analyzing the merits of electronic communications in Chapter 9, I concluded that the new channels still did not measure up to face-to-face contact. However, I also concluded that video conferencing would allow us to reduce the number of required face-to-face meetings and could function quite satisfactorily in many instances, especially for people who already knew each other well. When we now discuss the subject of group infrastructural support, it is interesting to consider the possibilities for using electronic communication to improve team building in teams that cannot, for various reasons, work in the same place.

The attempts that have been made to create electronic "spaces" for spontaneous and informal communication have not been very successful (Johansen 1988), however. The technology has been too constraining to allow for the casualness required for successful informal interaction to develop. Small screen formats, mediocre sound quality, and the high price of video communication have combined to limit the usefulness of video conference systems. Computer conferencing systems and bulletin boards have actually shown some capacity for creating and maintaining electronic "cliques," but mainly among young people or others with time to spare. The trouble is that communication is a time-consuming affair, and, no matter the quality of the channel, communication with more people subtracts more time from the time available for "real work."

With the greater availability of bandwidth that is bound to come, possibilities for "virtual groups" may improve, however. With sufficient bandwidth we can have not only videophones, but video-wall rooms (let us nickname them *vidwams*) where one or more walls consist of a high-definition video screen showing a corresponding room in another location. With sufficiently advanced sound systems, it should be possible for geographically separated groups to achieve a fair semblance of the experience of actually being together in the same room.

Such rooms should also contain or give easy access to video cubicles (let us call them *vubicles*) where single persons or small groups could sit down to have a closer chat with someone at "the other side." *Vidwams* could serve partly as relax areas, where people could come in to see if anyone was there, partly as meeting rooms or rooms for presentations—or may be even as canteens. It is likely that the effect of seeing and hearing even in such an electronically mediated way would help build stronger ties and loyalties than geographically separated groups could otherwise achieve. Let us just remember that the time constraint, mentioned earlier still apply: *vidwams* will not make it possible to work closely with significantly *more* people than before—even if successful, they will only allow about the *same number* of people to work closely together in spite of geographical separation.

EXTENSIONS TO THE CONSTRUCTIBLE SPACE

Could group support tools then give rise to new ways of group cooperation, or even new organizational schemes? Many people seem to think
so—especially, of course, proponents of groupware and what is termed
computer-supported cooperative work (CSCW). Greif, for instance, con-
tends that (1988, p. 6): "CSCW research is examining ways of designing
systems—people and computer systems—that will have profound
implications for the way we work."

It is not entirely clear what those implications will be, however. The
speculations cluster around a small number of themes. The main argument is that computer-based tools will increase group productivity and
creativity through improved coordination and communication, by allowing groups to do more work in real-time group mode than before (direct
work on the same screen, for instance), and by providing better support
and structure for the work done individually. It is also believed that
this improvement in group productivity and increased communication
capacity will result in increased emphasis on teams, more horizontal
communication and thereby flatter and more democratic organizations
(see, for instance, Drucker 1988, Johansen 1988, Greif 1988, Keen 1991,
O'Hara-Devereaux and Johansen 1994).

This is by no means clear. Johansen, whose account of groupware
products and research is very factual and realistic, makes his own reservations in the introduction to his book *Groupware* (1988). After underlining
that his conclusions "lean toward the upsides of groupware," he lists his
concerns—among them that there may be too many meetings, overdone
teams (too many participants without reduction in other responsibilities),
increased control over team members, too much structure, and a tendency
for people to only join teams that use the systems they know. Rockart
and Short (1991), on their part, question the long-term implications of a
disintegration of usual structures and reporting relationships.

It should come as no surprise that I also belong to the skeptics in this
area. I do not doubt that computer-based systems can provide valuable
tools for improved group coordination and communication and, in some
instances, increase productivity significantly. But I do not think that the
improvements will be sufficient either qualitatively or quantitatively to
transform group work or make groups and teams so much more effective
that organization structures can be radically changed.

As mentioned earlier, the gist of group work is communication—
sharing information and views, building a common understanding of
problems, and forging common decisions. These are exactly the areas
where the analysis in Chapter 9 suggests that computers can contribute
the least. To comprehend the ideas and thoughts of other people, we still

have to listen and read, and it matters little how fast information can be transferred from computer to computer when the time spent to write, read, speak, and listen does not change. We still need to reflect upon that information at our own pace to respond sensibly to it. Working in groups simply takes a lot of time and effort, and it does not seem very likely that we can escape these fundamental constraints in the foreseeable future.

I do not mean to suggest that computer-based systems will be entirely without impact on the way groups work. Neither do I think there will be no new opportunities for organizing. But I do think that the effects in this area will be much less dramatic than the CSCW enthusiasts predict. The kind of improvements in group productivity delivered by systems such as coauthoring systems, meeting assistance, electronic mail, and group calendars will not change the nature of the tasks that groups can tackle in any significant way. They will only allow groups to become somewhat more efficient, produce work of somewhat higher quality, and function more independently of physical proximity.

Moreover, an increase in the productivity of groups and teams in itself should not have too much of an impact on organization, aside from strengthening the general trend toward reduced manpower requirements. The production aspect of groups and teams really only gets exciting when we transcend the boundaries of the group itself and look toward integration within the total organization—as when engineering design groups work through systems that link their work directly not only to other design groups, but (through a common database) also to the groups working with production, sales, and distribution.

For the organization as a whole, the reduced dependence on colocation may turn out to be the most important opportunity, especially if effective means (such as vidwams) can be found to foster real team spirit and the development of a common organizational culture across geographical divides. That would make it easier to exploit other aspects of computers as well. For example, many companies with geographically dispersed manufacturing operations could benefit considerably from a close co-ordination of those operations—to the point of running them as one integrated factory based on integrated computer systems encompassing both sales, production, and warehousing/distribution. However, the spirit of independence of such plants will mean that they will often resist close coordination with sister plants under the auspices of what is perceived as a remote and faceless division management in the division headquarters. If vidwams, videophones, conference systems, and electronic mail could help to establish cross-plant work groups and a primary-group identification among key personnel from all the plants as well as the headquarters, such an organization would be much closer to succeeding with tight coordination than before. The same technique could possibly be used to build cross-company loyalties at select levels in multinational companies, supporting more direct coordination efforts built on other aspects of computer use.

To achieve this is not easy, however. Even systems such as those discussed here do not make it possible to increase the total communication volume very much. The people who participated would therefore either have to reduce their communication with the people they work with locally, thus putting some of their local relationships at risk, or significantly increase the amount of time they allocated for communication. To use expressions from network theory (Lincoln 1982), computer-based systems would not make it possible to significantly increase neither the density nor the connectivity[1] of organizational networks, although the links could possibly be others, span greater geographical distances, and thus change the structure of both inter- and intracompany networks. It is therefore doubtful whether the use of information technology will be the decisive factor that allows team-oriented organizations to achieve flatter and more democratic structures. Computers *can* help flatten the organization, but not because of groupware—it is rather the systems for personal support discussed in the preceding section and the automatic coordination coming up in the next chapters that will provide the major impetus in that direction.

It is also quite doubtful whether it was the prospects of groupware and computer support that arose the interest and faith in teams in the first place. As Johansen (1988) quite correctly notes, the increased emphasis on team-oriented organization probably has reasons other than computer technology. Johansen himself points to deregulation, the trend toward contract work, increasing geographic spread for companies, and the declaration of team-oriented companies as models for the business world.

There may even be more basic reasons for the emphasis on teams and the interest for groupware, however. Both the debates about teams and the development of groupware are products of the academic and professional communities (which include most managers), which have a well-developed propensity to prefer teams. Their educational backgrounds have accustomed them to professional discourse as an indispensable tool

---

[1] The *density* of a social network is a measure of the number of links between the nodes (nodes can be persons or groups, depending on the level of analysis). It is calculated as the ratio of actual ties to potential ties. The *connectivity* denotes the degree to which nodes are linked to other nodes either directly or indirectly (through other nodes). A maximally dense network (for instance, a group where every member has a direct link with every other member) will also have a maximum connectivity, but a fully connected network (for instance, a hierarchical organization where everyone is linked to the top manager through their bosses) can have low density (as when no one in a hierarchy has links with people other than his or her boss.)

for developing ideas and solving complex problems, and their jobs more often than not require them to work in close cooperation with colleagues in their own profession as well as people in other professions. Most of them *like* discourse-rich environments; they *want* to work in groups, and would quite naturally like to see the team concept gain ground—hence a fascination for groupware.

By this, I do not mean to say that groups and teams are not important, or that professional discourse is superfluous—on the contrary, discussions are indeed indispensable for much of the work that professionals do, such as planning, product development, business development and administration and problem-solving in general. Let us also not forget that after the family, the team is probably the oldest and most basic organizational structure we have. But the feeling that teams are all-important and an answer to most of the problems of contemporary organizations may reflect just as much the local work environment of the team champions as the functioning of large organizations in their entirety. To the extent that the team concept is growing in importance throughout the organization, as indeed seems to be the case, this growth could also be an artifact of progressing automation and elimination of routine jobs: automation largely passes by jobs of the kind that professionals use to have, and thus increases the proportion of team-oriented work in the organization even if the absolute number of people working in teams remains the same.

Consider, for instance the control room operators in the fully automated paper mill mentioned in Chapter 10. To tune the factory and squeeze maximum production and the desired quality out of it, operators can no longer work in isolation: they may have to team up with both process engineers, product specialists, and marketing people. In that sense, the workers have been changed from isolated operators responsible only for discrete steps in the production process to team members with joint responsibility for the total result. Thus, it seems to constitute another example of the transition from hierarchical, command-chain organization to a team-oriented approach in industry.

Appearances are deceptive, however. A closer analysis *also* suggests that the job as control room operator is not a continuation of the earlier manual work but, rather, an (incidental) appropriation of the work of the production manager and his immediate subordinates—a group of people that has *always* had to function more or less as a team. It is thus not a question of the transformation of jobs or job roles: the former jobs of the control room operators—when they controlled the discrete production steps in the factory—have simply been eliminated through automation, and the operators themselves have been thrust upon a totally new set of duties and responsibilities, requiring an entirely new set of job roles— resembling rather closely that of the production management team.

The sum and substance of this is that teams are important because they are superior instruments for coordination and problem solving, and, as more and more routine work is eliminated, because a larger and larger proportion of the work that is left in the organizations will be the kind of work that requires cooperation and teams. *Paradoxically, therefore, computers may enhance the importance of the work group and team not through support for them, but rather by eliminating most of the jobs that do not belong in groups or teams in the first place.* Then, of course, the technology may also facilitate group work and make groups and teams even more useful and flexible than they used to be.

12
Routines and Automation

"The machine yes the machine
never wastes anybody's time
never watches the foreman
never talks back."
Carl Sandburg, *The People, Yes*, 1936

AUTOMATION—THE CORNERSTONE OF COMPUTING

Routine Automation

Information technology has the potential to let us attack all kinds of tasks that involves handling and processing of information. In general, we may say that most work will be touched by information technology, at least as a supportive tool, and many types of tasks will be wholly or partly automated or eliminated, since the programmability of computers has given automation a strong, new boost. The more routine the task is, the easier it will be to dispose of, but computer-based automation will continue to evolve over the coming decades—much as mechanical automation and the use of energy sources such as water, coal, and oil were developed during the nineteenth and twentieth century—and it is likely to reach levels we cannot even imagine yet.

The first and most basic application of computers has been just to automate simple routine tasks. This is still the dominating way to use computer-based systems—from word processing (automating important parts of the tasks earlier associated with the production of typed or printed text) to accounting (automating the arithmetic and most of the reporting) and claims processing in the insurance business (automating a great deal of filing, writing, and control). Such automated routines are in fact the most important part of any computer-based system—even those that seem to concern quite different matters. A program for finite element analysis, for instance, helping engineers to decide on the optimal form and thickness of mechanical parts, works simply by repeating programmed routines based on mathematical formulas; a CAD system draws, redraws, fills in surfaces, and adds shadows by doing just the same. Computer-based systems will also often direct and even pace the work of their users. Typical examples of this are systems for caseworkers in large white-collar bureaucracies, such as the system for dental claims processing in a large insurance company described by Zuboff (1988), which is briefly mentioned in Chapter 10.

Computer-based systems thus generally incorporate explicit routines on two levels: the closed routines "hidden" in the application program's internal functions and the open routines that incorporate the dialogues with the users and structure their work. Quite often, in the heated discourse about the wondrous feats that information technology can pull off, and its great potential for society, organizations, and individuals, we seem to forget that in the end it all boils down to this: routines consciously designed and programmed by real humans, and dumb machines that ultimately derive their great powers from their immensely fast execution of these routines.

The creation of such *programmed routines* is obviously a development that falls within the bounds of the basic coordinating mechanism that Mintzberg (1979) calls *standardization of work*. Its immediate forerunner is the explicit routine, which was developed on the basis of writing and became the main coordinating tool of the modern organization. I have positioned programmed routines accordingly in Figure 13-1 on p. 315. However, in my view they represent an advancement in relation to explicit routines that is greater than the original development of explicit routines and the blueprint of the modern organization.

The traditional use of explicit routines requires that the workers learn all the routines belonging to their task, or at least learn those that are used most often, and remember when and how to retrieve the others. Experience shows us that only routines that are thoroughly learned (internalized) are systematically used in the daily work situation; others may be overlooked, forgotten, or fall into disuse for various other reasons. The process of renewing or changing routines is also difficult, because it requires workers to "actively forget" the old routines and thoroughly learn the new ones. Since the number of routines that can be retained as active in a work situation is fairly low, the repertory of any one organization member will be naturally limited, and the capacity for branching (alternative routines) will be low.

When routines are programmed into computer-based systems, the situation is quite different. First of all, a significant number of routines can be automated completely. Second, the routines that enter into the user dialogue can be much more numerous and diverse, since the user does not have to remember them all actively, but just how to operate the system and relate to the dialogue. This can be compared to the difference between our active and passive vocabularies—which is quite significant, as anyone who has learned a second language will know. In addition, the system can incorporate assisting features giving users a broader span of competence.

A good example is the system developed at IBM Credit (Hammer and Champy 1993). IBM Credit finances the computers, software, and services sold by IBM—it is a profitable business to IBM, and quite large: if independent, IBM Credit Corporation would rank among the Fortune 100 service companies. Prior to redesign, each application for credit went through a five-step procedure, taking on average six days to complete before a quotation letter could be delivered to the IBM field salesperson who had requested it in the first place. During these six days, the deal was still vulnerable for several reasons: the customer might obtain financing elsewhere, fall prey to another computer vendor, or even cancel the acquisition altogether. The pressure to reduce the turnaround time was therefore considerable, and it was also highly desirable to reduce the number of calls from impatient sales representatives wondering where their customer's application was sitting.

A closer look revealed that the actual work on an application averaged only 90 minutes—the rest of the time it was either sitting on a desk or was on its way between the five desks it had to visit before completion. A total redesign was then undertaken, where most of the applications were completed by a single caseworker, supported by a new computer system. How? Hammer and Champy explain (Hammer and Champy 1993 pp. 38–39):

> How could one generalist replace four specialists? The old process design was, in fact, founded on a deeply held (but deeply hidden) assumption: that every bid request was unique and difficult to process, thereby requiring the intervention of four highly trained specialists. In fact, this assumption was false; most requests were simple and straightforward. The old process had been overdesigned to handle the most difficult applications that management could imagine. When IBM Credit's senior managers closely examined the work the specialists did, they found that most of it was little more than clerical: finding a credit rating in a database, plugging numbers into a standard model, pulling boilerplate clauses from a file. These tasks fall well within the capability of a single individual when he or she is supported by an easy-to-use computer system that provides access to all the data and tools the specialist would use.
>
> IBM Credit also developed a new, sophisticated computer system to support the deal structurers. In most situations, the system provides the deal structurer with the guidance needed to proceed. In really tough situations, he or she can get help from a small pool of real specialists—experts in credit checking, pricing, and so forth. Even the handoffs have disappeared because the deal structurer and the specialists he or she calls in work together as a team.

Hammer and Champy claim that IBM Credit in this way cut the average process time to four *hours* and increased the number of deals handled *100 times* without any increase in workforce.

The IBM Credit case represents a quite innovative use of computers to redesign the work process, it is not exactly an implementation of a run-of-the-mill administrative system. However, even in more commonplace systems, which often represent little more than an "electrification" of older, manual routines, we can usually find traces of all the strong points of computer-bases systems exploited by IBM Credit: automation of simple routines, implicit structuring of work, embedding of rules, and support for decisions. As the sophistication of the user organizations as well as the system vendors and software developers grows, we can expect them to increasingly take advantage of the more advanced possibilities.

What and How Far Can We Automate?

Automation has proved to be a very powerful approach for increasing output and improving an organization's competitiveness. Especially in material production, it has been the most important determinant of organization for the last 150 years at least. Therefore, we can expect organizations in general to continue to explore the possibilities offered by automation, and to seek to increase their output per employee. In my view, the potential is still great, and just as great—if not greater—in the white-collar as in the blue-collar sector. Computers are new as human tools, and it stands to reason that we are only in the beginning of a long and exiting development. If the technology's history so far has any predictive value at all, the coming decades (and even centuries) will see continuous, rapid improvements both in the basic technologies, in available hardware products, and in application systems that will consistently dwarf earlier achievements. Both in the factory and in the office, our efforts to automate work have just started.

It is not easy to define the kind of work that will be automated into oblivion and which tasks that will survive—our present knowledge and experience provides a meager model for extrapolation and our imagination is a guide of dubious merit when we speculate about the possibilities in the longer run. However, with due caution, the possibilities seem to be greatest in three broad areas:

1. Material production (especially factory production).
2. Immaterial production and services—any product or service that mainly consists of information, information processing or information procurement.
3. Internal administration in all trades.

In spite of 150 years of improvement, there are still massive opportunities for increased automation in factory production—indeed, considering the immature nature of information technology (compared to the long history of mechanical technology), we have barely scratched the surface. Still, we tend to automate on the conceptual basis of mechanical engineering, and the most astounding innovations, in my view, await the development of production methods that are natively dependent on a copious use of processing power.

So far, we have probably come farthest in this direction in the process industries, where we have also seen some of the most spectacular improvements in productivity over the last couple of decades—whole production units such as refineries or paper mills have been totally automated. Great strides have also been made in mechanical industries, however. As early as in the late 1970s, for instance, Fujitsu built a metalworking factory not far from Mt Fuji that covered 20 000 square meters, employing 82 workers on the day shift and only one control room operator during the night. His only task was to surveil the working industrial robots and automatic machine tools from a central control room. A traditional factory of the same size would have employed almost ten times as many people, and there were still plans for reductions at that time (Hatvany et al. 1985).

If we turn away from material fabrication, the possibilities for automation are generally excellent in almost any business that deals mainly in information, especially when we include computer-supported self-service as an aspect of automation. The most extensive automation can be achieved when the information is structured, and especially when it is quantitative. Banks are prime examples of such businesses. They have been the subject of major changes over the last decades, and there is more to come. I shall elaborate somewhat on this in a moment.

For businesses such as newspapers and publishing houses, often hailed as the archetypal information-mongers, we must distinguish sharply between the editorial side and the distribution activities—of which printing has been (and still is) the central part. Writing and editorial work is highly labor-intensive and it will have to remain so (even if it can be computer supported through the use of word processing and the like). On the distribution side, printing is already highly automated, but electronic channels and media do offer the possibility of further automation. However, drastic changes here will require the customers to change their habits and to leave paper as the preferred medium. I think this will happen more slowly than many enthusiasts believe, and the reason is simply that screen technology still falls far short of the portability, comfort, and ease of reading offered by printed media—and it is likely to do so for a good number of years yet. The exception is the kind of concise factual information that up till now has been found in dictionaries, encyclopedias, directories, news clippings, and the like, and where reading comfort is not a very important issue. For this kind of information, digital media have already gained an important position, and may rapidly achieve dominance.

Leaving the subject of single lines of business, there are also significant automation possibilities in internal administration in all kinds of trades. The function where computers are most widely applied is probably accounting, where it has lead to considerable staff reductions. However, even areas such as the administration and use of customer data (as in insurance companies), sales (on-line order registration and semiautomatic fulfillment, or even self-service ordering over the Internet or through customer terminals), and logistics (automatic restocking through point-of-sale registration, etc.) have been the focus of much change.

The prospect of automation in the office has been the subject of much discussion. Arguments have centered on whether general office work can be automated at all, and many research projects have concluded that such work in its very nature is too unstructured and dependent on human judgment to allow significant automation. I shall return to this discussion later in this chapter, and will only say at this point that I think the possibilities are far greater than many people would like to think. However, the development of automation will happen in close interplay with the development both of information technology, other technologies, and methods for analysis and design, and it is not possible to predict the developments very far into the future.

It is perhaps easier to say something about where the opportunities seem to be most slender—to point out the work that depends too much on the human faculties computers cannot mimic (at least not yet), or that require physical skills and dexterity machines cannot match. There seems to be three broad classes of such work:

1. Work where judgment and creativity are central—for instance, research and development, design, policy making, journalism, artistic work, and management other than routine supervision.
2. Work where human physical dexterity and skill are paramount, as in handicrafts, the performing arts, domestic work, and chauffeuring. Some jobs are safe because we *want* humans to perform them, as in handicrafts and the performing arts; other remain safe because they are (at least for the time being) very difficult to automate, such as much domestic work, transport, and repair work.
3. Work where the emotional component of dealing with a fellow human is important, such as psychiatry, much sales and service

work (especially personal services such as hairdressing or waiting at tables), and teaching.

Many jobs have components from more than one of these classes—waiters also depend on their dexterity to do their job, and craftsmen often combine skill and creativity. Work such as nursing combines all three. When a job scores high on one or more of these properties, it means that it depends on human qualities, and the incumbents will be difficult to supplant by nonhuman agents or automatic procedures.

A word of caution is warranted, however. Even if we may think so, the human aspect of a job is not always the most important to us. We readily forgo the social pleasures of exchanging everyday niceties with a bank clerk in order to retrieve money faster and more conveniently from an automatic teller machine, and we have been swift to prefer the low prices and fast throughput of the self-service store to the old over-the-counter shop. Our culture has put increasing value on efficiency and in many ways fostered an acceptance and even glorification of neutral impersonality in business matters—conditioning us to tolerate or even prefer the self-service concept in more and more situations. Indeed, the reluctance many senior citizens show in front of self-service devices is not only grounded in their unfamiliarity with the appropriate techniques; it is just as much grounded in the fact that their cultural values have not adjusted to accept the absence of human contact in those situations. Jobs that look safe now because of their emotional component may therefore be in danger if this trend continues—such as the more routine aspects of teaching, which may become seriously threatened by "self-service" learning based on multimedia computers, with their combination of programming, video, sound, and databases.

The Potential of Evolving Automation—An Example

To illustrate some of the potentials of automation and the iterative nature of its development, I would like to elaborate on these ideas in an example. And since automation so far has progressed farthest in the factory, I think it is more interesting to use an example from the white-collar world—where the changes have scarcely begun.

Up until the computer entered the scene, automation in the realm of administrative work was sparse. Punch card equipment was probably the most advanced, and it may have been the only example of true automation. Bookkeeping machines and mechanical desk calculators more approached the nature of tools. Even punch card equipment was a modest achievement compared with the extensive automation in the production of material goods.

The computer, however, is profoundly changing this state of affairs, and the changes have proceeded further than most people realize. A large part of the work that is strictly procedural and routine in nature has already been automated to a greater or lesser extent, especially work associated with large files of administrative information—and the pace is accelerating. But the automation is often gradual and fairly unobtrusive (for everyone except those made redundant). It is not always easy to spot for an untrained eye. For a familiar example, let us take a short look at the development most banks have gone through since the early 1960s.

Traditionally, banks were mainly filing and accounting organizations. Before the computer era, they used mechanical bookkeeping machines of various kinds. For each transaction, the customer's account card was manually located in the filing cabinet, placed in the appropriate machine, and the amount deposited or withdrawn was entered manually on the keyboard. After the record was completed, the file card had to be put back into its folder in the cabinet. This work was carried out in central filing or bookkeeping departments, and the inputs for their work were the receipt forms and vouchers they received from the various branch offices and departments that had the direct customer contacts. Typically, there were separate departments for different types of accounts—one for savings accounts and another for checking accounts, for instance. To get an overview of the bank's total relationship with a particular customer would therefore involve several persons and quite a lot of work.

This was a very labor intensive setup, and was only feasible when there were few transactions. The number of transactions was low because society still mainly operated in the cash mode—wages were paid in cash; goods and services were paid in cash. Besides, it was cumbersome both to deposit and to withdraw money—you had to go to a branch office of your bank,[1] bring with you your bank book, and wait your turn at at least two different counters. I can still remember the stuffy atmosphere of the savings bank of my childhood savings account—where you first walked up to the appropriate counter, presented your errand and your bank book, and then waited until the teller called your name through a loud-speaker. The counters, moreover, were different for withdrawals and deposits, although the teller window was the same.

There were also a number of instruments to conclude transactions outside the premises of a bank, such as the check, the giro, and the credit card.

---

[1] In some countries, such as Britain, one even had to go to the particular branch that administered one's account. In Britain this system partly survived even up until quite recently—as late as 1990, a Norwegian journalist working as a correspondent in London lamented the fact that he had to have one account in a branch office in the suburbs where he lived, and another at a branch in the city center, where he worked. The downtown branch office would not allow him to draw money on his suburban account and vice versa.

As long as bookkeeping was manual, even they depended on a fairly low volume to be viable, and it was not until the introduction of computers in the 1960s that the banks were ready to promote a more active use of bank accounts, with personal checks as an important feature. It was also computers that made it possible for the credit card companies to start their rapid expansion.

At first, the computer-based systems only replaced the manual files and the bookkeeping machines. Still, the customer's interface with the bank was as it had always been, and the receipt forms, the vouchers, and the checks were still collected and registered at a central location. Some of the manual operations were eliminated even at this stage, however, such as the retrieval and replacement of account cards, work with the bookkeeping machines (being replaced by punching), and much accounting work. The punching and the automatic processing by the computers were so much faster than the old methods that the transaction volume could increase many times over without an increase in the workforce. Moreover, printouts of the account balances could be distributed to the branch offices, giving them much better information on their customers.

Then came the next step—terminals at the counter, allowing the clerks to register the transaction directly in the database, eliminating the need for a central punching department. At first, the systems generally did not operate in realtime—transactions concluded at the counter terminals did not update the production database directly but were collected for batch processing (usually during the night). Since then, the trend has been a development toward true on-line systems with real-time updating of the production database.

This change did eliminate many routine jobs in central bookkeeping departments, but the instant availability of customer information also facilitated a significant reorganization at the customer interface—the counter. Specialization was reduced, to the effect that most of the usual transactions (deposit, withdrawal, currency exchange, cashing of checks, etc.) could be completed by any one of the clerks working at the counter. A lot of paper-pushing was eliminated in the branches, and branch offices were furthermore authorized to give loans and credit to a larger degree than before.

The next step was to introduce automatic teller machines, allowing customers to wrap up some of the transactions themselves. Later development has provided EFTPOS[2] terminals in shops, allowing you to use your smart card to pay for what you buy, thereby concluding a direct and immediate transfer of money from your account to the shop's. Quite a

---

[2] Electronic Fund Transfer at Point Of Sale—the card reader and auxiliary equipment that lets you pay with your bank card in shops and elsewhere.

few banks now also allow customers (at least professional customers such as companies) to link up to the bank's systems, and complete certain types of transactions from their own computers, and an increasing number are making it possible for customers to access such services through the Internet. The net result is that a lower and lower percentage of the transactions are concluded on the bank's own premises or involve any of the bank's employees.

The development just described has been gradual, with each new step building on the preceding one. The degree of automation has increased for each step, both by direct automation of tasks and by eliminating the need for certain operations altogether. If we look at the rise in transaction volume over the last 40 years, productivity has increased enormously, and the service level for most customers (those who can handle cards, teller machines, and computerized answering devices!) has improved dramatically. But, to a surprising degree, all this has happened without the banks making any real changes to the basic definition either of what a bank account is or of what a central file is. Most banks still regard the account as their basic entity, not (as one should think) the customer—some even to the extent of sending separate account statements in separate envelopes for each account a person might have. What we consider a revolution is so far *not* a result of a radically new concept of banking; it is just a consequence of having made the mechanics of record keeping infinitely more efficient through automation. It is also another example of how change that is basically quantitative can have results that are perceived as qualitative by the user.

If you take a closer look, moreover, the banks are still plagued by a solid heritage of their original paper-based systems. Giros and checks, for instance, still require a great deal of manual handling (including punching) and represent a drain on the banks' profits, since banks are generally not able to (or do not dare to) charge their customers what it really costs to process paper-based payments.

But, the story does not end here. Banks seem ripe for much larger changes over the next thirty years than over the last thirty, and some banks may be able to operate with only a fraction of the workforce that is common today—even with the most sophisticated of current systems. We shall return to that a little later, but, at this point, we must first confront the debate on the limits to automation, especially for automation in the office.

LIMITS TO AUTOMATION—REAL OR IMAGINARY?

The Debate on Office Automation

There is significant disagreement on the future possibilities of automation in the office. Although no one would deny that a lot of jobs in accounting and filing have disappeared, and that even more such jobs will go in the future, doubts have been raised about whether less narrow jobs can be automated. Most office jobs are simply seen as being too diverse, involving too many exceptions, and requiring too much judgment to be defined in the exact algorithms needed for a computer. In one sense this is true; in another it is not.

It is certainly correct that most classical "office work" does not readily lend itself to straightforward automation. Numerous studies on this subject in the early 1980s, where the researchers monitored the activities in various kinds of offices, showed that office work was very complex, and even seemingly trivial tasks required quite a lot of knowledge, judgment, and nonroutine activity (see, for instance, Maus and Espeli 1981, Lie and Rasmussen 1983, Strassman 1985, Long 1987, Schmidt and Bannon 1992).

The general conclusion from these studies and many later discussions is that early hopes of automating the office in the same way as factory production were naive and built on an superficial and overly simplistic understanding of the nature of office work. There were simply too few repetitive activities that could be automated, tasks were too unstructured to lend themselves to automation, there were too many exceptions to the rules (insofar as there were any formalized rules at all), too much of the activity was concerned with uncovering and correcting errors, and the activities generally required the collection of information from many different sources and the execution of considerable judgment. Long, summing up his review, says (1987, p. 51):

> Overall, conclusions based on a realistic picture of the office and its occupants suggest that the scope for the outright "automation" (elimination) of jobs in the near future is quite small, except with respect to semi-professionals and some routine information-handling and coordinating roles.

The conclusion drawn by Long, Strassman, and Schmidt and Bannon, as well as many others, is that the main scope for computers in the office is to support the work of professionals and managers: "Stimulating an improved quality of performance or the provision of new and/or better services," as Long puts it (1987 p. 46). The growing number of people occupied with R&D activities concerning computer supported cooperative work, or CSCW (to whom Schmidt and Bannon belong), are especially vocal in this respect.

It is undeniable that the possibilities for directly automating more complex office jobs are limited, in the sense of having a computer system replace humans by more or less mimicking their behavior. But that does not mean that automation in a wider sense of the word is blocked.

Even in material production, directly mimicking human behavior is not the way we normally automate—we do not design machines that wield or directly mimic the use of traditional hand tools. True, there are some examples where precisely that happens, as when a paint line is robotized by letting human spray painters guide robot arms equipped with spray guns by hand until they "learn" the painting movements. But in most industrial automation, automation is in large part achieved by exploiting the intrinsic properties of machines, not by building human-like automatons. In my view, that will also be the strategy that will continue to revolutionize material production. The real potential in the future lies in matching the intrinsic properties of computer-controlled production systems with new materials and production processes that cannot be utilized without them. New advances such as chemometry—the use of sophisticated sensors and mathematical models for the control of production processes—is perhaps a harbinger of things to come (Lundberg 1991).

I believe that the situation is the same even when it comes to office work and that the studies mentioned earlier overlook the fact that even if most of the activities of office work themselves cannot be automated, the peculiar properties of computer systems—especially their processing power and the coordinating effects of their databases—can nevertheless be harnessed to *eliminate the need to carry out large sets of activities altogether.* The job cuts achieved through this can be as just as dramatic as those effected through classical automation. Consider the following example.

Task Elimination: An Example

One of the most cited examples of the elimination of a whole set of tasks is the reorganization of the accounts payable function in Ford in North America (Hammer 1990, Hammer and Champy 1993). Indeed, this project is probably one of the cornerstones behind the term "business process reengineering."

The accounts payable function consisted of typical, old-fashioned office work—the clerks in the AP departments checked invoices against purchase orders and receiving documents, and (if the three matched) then authorized payments. The work sounds simple, but of course it was more complicated than this. Quite often, the three documents did *not* match. The delivery might be different from the order, and the invoice could easily differ from both. Several kinds of information had to be collected and compared, missing papers had to be located, inconsistencies cleared up, and so on. There was need for copious amounts of communication, with people within the company as well as suppliers sending the invoices.

Looking at an accounts payable office in isolation, one might well conclude that the scope for automation is scant, and that the best solution would be to offer the people working there various support tools to make their work more effective (for instance, electronic mail).

Initially, that was probably also the project team's conclusion, since they were working to reduce the head count in its account payable departments, which totalled more than 500 employees just in North America. The project was part of a company-wide offensive to regain ground lost to the Japanese in the late 1970s and early 1980s. The initial analysis proposed a project that would use computer support to reduce the number of people to 400, which must have seemed pretty good. However, Ford had recently bought a 25% interest in Mazda, and Ford executives noted that the (admittedly smaller) Japanese company handled the comparable functions with only five people.

A deeper analysis—sparked by this, and taking the total problem domain into account—revealed that most of the work in the accounts payable departments was a consequence of the intrinsic shortcomings of paper-based administration, and that computer-based systems could simply *eliminate the need to carry out of most of the work* in the first place, by offering a superior *integration of the information* with a more far-reaching *implicit coordination* as a result.

Ford's subsequent project ended up eliminating the accounts payable departments in its traditional form altogether. Instead of using 500+ labor-years to check and compare invoices against purchase orders and receiving documents, and then authorizing payments, all purchase orders were registered in a database. When a shipment arrived at the receiving dock, it was immediately checked against that database. If matched by a purchase order, it was accepted and registered as received (if a match is not found, the delivery was returned). The system then automatically generated a payment transaction and prepared the check. As the system went into operation, Ford notified its suppliers that invoices were no longer accepted (they would go directly to the trash bin); they should just send the goods. Ford estimated that the change reduced the work needed to handle the control and payment functions (which is really the reason for an accounts payable department) by 75%. In addition, there were no longer any discrepancies between the financial and physical records to worry about, material control became simpler, and financial information more accurate.

This is a prime example of the possibility for eliminating work through deep analysis of the problem domain, of the strong effects of the inherent coordination in a unified database, *and* of the value of the integrity of the information it delivers.

Mazda's achievement was even greater and apparently also effected through the coordinative effect of the database:[3] Mazda in effect delegated the full responsibility for stocking the production line to their suppliers. The suppliers were therefore allowed access to Mazda's production planning and control system and could deliver their parts directly on the line, coordinated with the succession of cars coming down it. All Mazda needed to do, then, was to count the number produced of each model—knowing that, they also knew exactly how many parts they had received from their various suppliers. The beauty of that system was not only the total elimination of parts administration and accounting on Mazda's side, but also the automatic exclusion of faulty parts from the payments (they would be eliminated by quality control during production).

Banking: A Possible Next Step

To elaborate somewhat, let us return to banking to discuss what extended automation and new concepts for using the strong properties of information technology can allow. Until quite recently, what has been exploited is relatively straightforward automation through the exploitation of the range and speed of the database, as the accounts (the central administrative files of the bank) have become available for access not only in the main office, but also in branch offices and even in shops and the customer's own office or home.

This concept can be extended further, however. It is already technically feasible to conclude nearly *all* kinds of payments—be it the purchase of a new car or of a bus ticket—as direct transactions against bank accounts. It is just not economical for small amounts yet, due (mainly) to the cost of telecommunications and the banks' transaction systems. But, in not too many years, it will become economical for almost all purposes. Further, apart from simple payments, a much broader spectrum of transactions will be possible to complete via office terminals, automatic teller machines, or home computers. What will then happen to the banks?

Consider the following. As a private bank customer, I have fairly limited requirements—I need to keep my money in a safe place, I need to pay bills and receive money from employers and others, I need to deposit money to earn interest, and from time to time I need to borrow. I also need to receive information on my transactions and the current balance of my account(s). How can I get these services most conveniently?

---

[3] Strangely enough, I have not found any account of what Mazda actually did to achieve this result, neither in the book by Hammer and Champy nor anywhere else. The information about Mazda was related to me by the manager of a productivity program sponsored by the Royal Norwegian Research Council.

Not by venturing out on the streets to seek out a branch office (mind the opening hours) or by mailing checks!

To me, the perfect solution would be a "banking system" residing on my own PC. For safety, it could incorporate a card-and-code based identification system (there are already PC readers for traditional bank and credit cards available, and the PCMCIA standard for external peripheral devices could provide even more advanced possibilities). Off-line, I could set up my transactions, and then ask the PC to execute them. A short (and thereby cheap) automatic call to the bank's central computer would download my instructions, upload confirmations, upload notifications of other transactions concluded toward my account since my last connection, and update the balance and transaction history kept by my local database. That way, I would always have a complete history of transactions available without bothering the bank (after all, it is my money and my information), and I could play around with statistics and budget information as much as I wanted.

The upload could also contain the bank's current offers on interest rates, it could include electronic invoices from my creditors (which means that I could send my own invoices through the system as well). Perhaps I could also deposit a mortgage bond on my house in the bank, giving me a credit limit within which I could grant myself loans at the then-current terms (contained in the latest upload). Another advantage would be that I could have the same access to my "local" banking services no matter where I was in the world, as long as I had access to a public telecommunications network.

There are already services available from a number of banks incorporating parts of this concept. However, they are not yet complete and do not yet adhere to common standards. If the interface between such a local system and the bank's system was standardized, and not proprietary to the bank (or if one of the proprietary interfaces was emulated by others and thereby established as a de facto standard), I could not only use the system for my business with one particular bank, but use it to obtain competing offers and conclude business with other banks as well, not to mention insurance companies, stockbrokers, mutual funds, and others. In my view, the growth of financial services on the Internet will greatly contribute toward such standardization, and create a very different type of market for financial services than the one we are used to.

A logical conclusion to such a development could be that there would no longer need be any need for banks in the traditional sense—what I would need would first of all be a clearing central that could carry out the money transfers (also the many small transfers coming as a result of electronic payments in shops, etc.) and keep an officially authorized version of my transaction account(s). Then I would need various service providers to offer me alternatives for depositing money, for loans, for buying stocks or parts in mutual funds, and so on. The clearing central could even be organized as a public institution (a new role for the central bank, when paper money becomes almost extinct?), operating on a regional, national, or even on an international basis.

Technologically, such a development is already perfectly feasible, and there is no need for exotic new inventions. Commercially, development along these lines is highly probable, as the development in basic technologies makes the necessary equipment and communication capacity cheap enough—even if it is too early to predict the specific directions and speed of change. As hinted earlier, the new development in Internet banking will probably speed the development toward the fully electronic bank further. Of course, such banks will not take over the whole market, at least not in the foreseeable future. There will still be sizeable customer segments that prefer more old-fashioned services. But we will have a much greater segmentation of the market, and there will be more competition— also internationally, since fully electronic banks should be able to compete equally well on a global basis for many types of services. The main constraints will be legal provisions (a number of countries would perhaps not allow such banks to do business with their citizens) and the question of confidence—to put your money into an account, you have to trust the bank. Not everyone would feel attracted to even high interest rates offered by—for instance—an Internet bank located in Grozny, Chechenya.

"Digital money" in the form of reloadable smart cards are another interesting development in this connection. Such a card could be loaded with money from one's bank account, and then used for all kinds of purchases (as cash and credit cards are used today) as well as for paying bills over the telephone network. The card and the payment system would incorporate advanced cryptography to ensure maximum security and should allow payment without leaving "electronic traces" in the form of name or account information. Interestingly enough, a number of the European central banks have supported research on such systems through the European ESPRIT program. If we view this in the context laid out earlier, there could be a possibility for an international network of clearing centrals run by the central banks[4] (or by the European Central Bank), serving cash cards as well as the "personal bank" described earlier, or even a (very potent!) combination of the two.

---

[4] A Norwegian commission presently working to propose new banking laws has already suggested that the clearing function in Norway should become a responsibility of the Norwegian central bank. The basis for the proposal is the delays in money transfers consciously implemented by banks in order to hold on to their float revenues.

Whatever the direction and speed of development, one thing is for sure: The banks will have to change more during the next 25 years than in the previous 50, and the facilitator will be the mounting automation provided by information technology—automation that increasingly exploits the special properties of computer-based systems. Banks, or the corporations that replace them, may end up as largely automated organizations with very few employees, and there may also be considerably fewer of these companies left. If earlier communication revolutions in historic times teach us anything, it is that improved communications brings death to local business. When it becomes possible to reach out beyond geographically delimited markets, it also means that all will face a proportionally larger set of competitors. As some take advantage of the situation and expand aggressively, local businesses who thrived mainly because of lack of competition will find themselves in great trouble, and they will be bought up or driven out of business in large numbers.

The larger and more perfect markets emerging from this process will foster greater focus on price and performance, and the result will be—just as in conventional brand-name business—that a small number of players will grow large and destroy the others. If the Internet becomes as important for a number of trades as many people think, it spells not only opportunity for all in those trades, but also ruin for most of them. We can already see this development starting for booksellers and record shops. The only alternative to agressive growth will be to concentrate on niches where the big players cannot or do not bother to compete—but these niches are not big enough to sustain more than a fraction of the original players. The Internet, then, is no more of a boon to the small, local business than the railroad, the car, and the telephone were. Like them it is, on the contrary, an exterminator.

Circumventing the Maginot Line

If we relate these examples—one real and the other (so far) imaginary—to the debate on the scope for automation in the office, we can see that the barrier created by the inherently indeterminate nature of office work—by many regarded as a Maginot line against automation—can simply be circumvented. Quite spectacular achievements can be made without having to force the presumed barrier at all.

Consider the Ford example: With a traditionalist approach, it would indeed be very difficult, if not impossible, to develop a computer system that could automate the accounts payable function—that is, to make a system that could automatically compare purchase orders, receiving documents and invoices, check for consistency, investigate and resolve mismatches, take corrective action if necessary, and finally authorize payments. Taking those tasks for granted would therefore create problems for automation. In fact, that was in all probability what the project team at Ford first did (Hammer 1990, Hammer and Champy 1993). If their initial efforts (in line with the arguments of Long and the CSCW proponents) only aimed at providing the people in the accounts payable departments with better support tools for their jobs, they were actually quite clever to achieve a projected improvement of 20%.

When they rethought the problem in light of their discoveries at Mazda, however, the people in the project realized that most of the tasks and routines in accounts payable were nothing more than consequences of the way work was traditionally defined and organized, it was *not* intrinsically necessary for the reception and payment of shipments from Ford's suppliers. When they managed to analyze the deeper functional necessities behind the existing procedures, they could therefore specify a system where the computer's strong properties were used to completely rearrange work and eliminate a whole slate of operations.

This example becomes even more interesting when we consider the subject of groupware and computer supported cooperative work: One can easily envision a solution to Ford's problem along the lines of CSCW—with workflow tools to speed electronic or scanned documents around the caseworker circuit, with email to enhance their cooperation and their contact with the suppliers' accounts receivable people, and with conference systems and videophones to solve the most difficult cases. It is, however, difficult to see how even the most exquisite system along these lines could have approached the efficiency attained by the project finally carried out by Ford, which relied on task elimination instead.

Of course, the Ford case is not an example of pure automation; it includes both automatic routines and the coordinative effects of a common database for purchasing, inventory, and accounts payable. However, that is the nature of successful computer-based systems—they usually exploit several of the strong aspects of information technology simultaneously. This creates problems for orderly analyses and expositions such as the present one (I must wait until a later chapter to discuss the coordination part), but not for the application of the actual systems.

EXTENSIONS TO THE CONSTRUCTIBLE SPACE

Shrinking the Organization

Automation, then, allows us to abolish work both through straightforward task automation, as in a pulping plant, and by task elimination, as described in the example from Ford. The development in banking really incorporates both. Quite often, we will see that organizations are able to reduce their head count even as they manage to increase their total production—banks are good examples of this, even if they have increased the size of their organizations over the years. Many people take this as a proof that computers do not deliver the productivity they should, but looking at size alone is grossly misleading. If we look at the volume of bank transactions—any kind of transactions—the number of transactions per employee per year has increased dramatically over the last 35 years, as computers have taken over for bookkeeping machines, counter terminals for forms and vouchers, auto-giros and customer terminals for manual giros, and finally card-operated teller machines and EFTPOS-equipment for checks and cash transactions. Viewed in this light, the banks have achieved a very impressive increase in productivity.

Moreover, they have done so while drastically reducing the size of that part of the organization that performs the bookkeeping operations, the original main function of the bank. Because of the increasing use of computers, bookkeeping has actually been collapsed to a small fraction of what it was.

The reason the bank organizations have not shrunk dramatically in the same period has been an increase in other aspects of the bank's activities. Tasks such as arbitrage, sales, and advisory activities have grown considerably in volume, along with customer contact at the counter and the various functions necessary to assess risks and give loans, manage funds, and so on. The structure of the bank's organizations has thus changed quite markedly, away from an overwhelming emphasis on mass transaction processing toward a relatively high proportion of more varied work of a professional nature.

If the development in banking conforms to the scenario outlined earlier, however, the future reduction in workforce requirements will not be offset by new demands for services, and we will witness a further contraction of the banking organizations, as more and more functions are automated or eliminated. We may also see more specialization, not only in niches, as today, but as a general trend that almost no bank can escape, and where some banks will specialize in highly automated routine services (high-volume, low-value transactions), whereas others will develop into highly competent financial service organizations concentrating on nonroutine (low-volume, high-value) transactions.

Organizational Truncation

There are more dramatic examples of task elimination, however. Especially within the process industries, such as paper production and oil refining, advanced automation has led to an outright truncation of the organization. Almost all of the manual tasks in production—which means practically the whole factory organization—have been eliminated. This development has been analyzed in some detail by Zuboff (1988), who bases her book partly on the automation-based transformation of two pulp mills and one pulp-and-paper mill.

Before automation started in these factories, each step in the process was run by skilled workers who controlled locally their particular vat, boiler, or blender. They had some contact with the production steps directly ahead or after their own but were otherwise isolated from the rest of the process—except when something really went wrong, and the whole factory had to stop. This fragmented control of the production process naturally meant that a considerable number of coordinating positions were required—the total production process had to be coordinated by foremen, supervisors, and, finally, the plant manager. Mechanical automation had allowed a fair degree of centralization of control, but it was only when computer-based systems entered the scene that it was possible to thoroughly automate the production processes and eliminate next to all manual positions.

What happens, then, when a production process is fully automated and the control of the entire factory is centralized not only to a single control room, but (in principle, at least) to a single terminal?[5] As Zuboff (1988) shows, the persons in the control room are suddenly, with the support of the system's processing power and information concentration abilities (modern process control displays are highly graphical), in a position to directly control and run the entire plant, without any intervening organizational apparatus. Of course they do not run the plant in the sense that they manually control the process (which execute under the control of computer programs), but they supervise it *and* are able to improve it by tuning the program parameters as they gain experience with the equipment and the way it operates. The depth of their control has been dramatically increased—they almost literally run a joystick-controlled factory.

What has really happened here is that the systems have *eliminated the entire operating organization* at the factory floor, the entire operating core in Mintzberg's terminology, and left only the roles of the production manager and his support team relatively intact. The organization has not only been reduced in size; it has been *truncated*—one part, which was earlier the largest one, has simply disappeared, and only machines have come instead. Of course, there is still need for small teams of workers

---

[5] Normally, you will see a number of terminals in a control room. That is more an expression of the present state of the technology (requiring several screens to display all vital information) and safety precautions (the need to have more than one person available in case of emergency), than of the technology's basic characteristics.

to maintain the plant and to tackle emergencies, but the daily control of the production process can be left to one person (in principle), or (more likely in practice) a small team of persons. According to Mintzberg (1979), such an elimination of an operating core configured as a Machine Bureaucracy will mean that the total organization is going through a metamorphosis. Its character changes in a profound way, since staff and management, populated by many more team-oriented professionals, will now come to dominate its structure.

It is very interesting to note how this has generally not been understood in plants that have been automated. Almost without exception, the jobs in the control room have been defined as transformed versions of the local control jobs earlier performed by skilled workers, and it has been the workers who have been trained to fill them. Our analysis here, however, indicates that the control room jobs are not a continuation of the work on the factory floor at all; rather, they represent the key plant management responsibility: to direct the operation of the plant such that it achieves optimal performance, given the existing business objectives (product and quality mix).

Before automation, the managers and their process engineers had to pursue this goal indirectly, working through supervisors and foremen, trusting both their judgment and the judgment of a large number of skilled workers. Improving the quality or yield was very difficult, since so much of the process depended on tacit knowledge, and the control over process parameters was quite crude.

When such a factory is fully automated and the whole organization at the factory floor is eliminated, control can be exercised directly, without human intermediaries. In addition, control over the production process is dramatically improved, since it can be based on accurate measurements, parameters can be adjusted in minute increments, and systematic experiments can be made in order to improve both yield and quality. The direct control of the total process and the tuning activities are definitely not a customary part of rank-and-file factory work; they belong squarely to the traditional domain of management and engineering.

Quite naturally, this mismatch has led to conflicts between control room operators and production managers, their subordinates, and staff. Zuboff describes this in some detail (1988) and explains the reasons quite accurately. Clever control room operators will, after some time, develop a deep understanding of the total process and will increasingly be able to tune it for greater economy, increased production and/or improved quality. Managers, who do not have direct access to the control systems and the information they provide about the processes, will fall behind and will not be able to either direct or control the operators' work in a meaningful way. Frustrated over losing their positions as those who can best comprehend the total process, they will often try to reassert their authority by giving the operators directions anyway—directions that are likely to be inferior in most cases, since they are based on inadequate information and a lack of experience with the system. The operators, in their turn, will feel this both as an encroachment on their newly found responsibility and an affront to their professional competence. Both parties will suffer, together with the plant's economic performance.

Ideally, then, control room responsibilities should have been left with plant management and the engineering staff, and the systems designed accordingly. It is they who should have been trained to use the systems for controlling and optimizing production. If it is desirable, for moral or political considerations, to appoint former workers for such jobs, one should be very conscious of the implications and provide educational programs, discretionary powers, and benefits that match the real responsibilities of the job—because, in the highly automated factory, it is the people who master the systems and understand the information they provide who decide the profitability of day-to-day operations.

Hyperautomation

Already, information technology has helped us develop the extent and sophistication of automation far beyond what was possible by mechanical means alone. Looking into the future, the scope for progress is still vast, and the limits are difficult to define. Advances have already been dramatic enough to warrant a new term to distinguish this new breed of automation from mechanical automation as we have seen it develop over that last century: it could be called *hyperautomation*. Hyperautomation is the computer-dependent variant of automation, and it can be mapped under that entry in the taxonomy of coordinating mechanisms shown in Figure 7-1 on p, 165 (as I have done in Figure 13-1 on p. 315). In principle, hyperautomation is not different from automation, but, just as for computer-based information storage, the sheer power of the new tools is so great that they are nevertheless qualitatively different.

We may see great organizational changes in connection with hyper-automation, as in the examples described earlier. By shedding almost all the workforce in its operating core, a company can be transformed from a Machine Bureaucracy to something much more like an Administrative Adhocracy (Mintzberg 1979). There is also no doubt that the use of information technology will make such transitions possible for a much larger number of organizations than mechanical automation ever could.

Hyperautomation also makes it possible to integrate a much greater span of organizational activities into one coordinated process, not least because it allows the automation or elimination of significant administrative processes. We have thus already seen process-oriented automation expand along value chains (Porter 1985), even outside the boundaries of the principal organization.

Prominent examples of this can be found in the automobile industry, which has for a long time been at the forefront of automation. When building their new factory in Sunderland in northern England, for instance, Nissan invited important suppliers to establish their own factories at the perimeter of their main plant site and tie directly into Nissan's production control system. The objective was to have the suppliers deliver their parts directly on the assembly line, to save storage space and handling costs.

As soon as the basic body of a new car is put on the painting line in the Nissan main plant, a transponder is attached to it, containing the complete specifications for that particular car.[6] This is particularly important, since the broad range of colors and options offered today's customer virtually ensures that no two adjacent cars coming down the line will be identical (the company claims to offer customers 20 000 varieties of their vehicles). When the body leaves the paint line, the transponder is read by the the central production control system, which broadcasts the information to the subassembly stations and component supply points as well as to the suppliers that are tied into the direct delivery system. The manufacturer of seats, for example, receives the necessary specifications three hours before the seats are to be fitted (Christopher 1992). Only then do they start their own production, assembling the front and rear seats to match the car model, colors, and other details determinded by the model and the customer's choices. Every 15 to 20 minutes, a transport shuttle leaves their factory, taking the finished seats directly to the appropriate supply point at the assembly line, where they arrive just before the car they belong to.

What we see here is an extremely tight coupling of a number of independent organizations, a coupling that is even tighter than you will normally find between departments within a single organization. Nissan's own plant, by the way, operates according to the same principles—its press line for body panels, for instance, is carefully synchronized with assembly, to the point where the total amount of doors, hoods, and trunk lids in process amounts to less than what is required for one hour's production.

Even though these supplier organizations all have their own independent owners, administrations, and economies, for the purpose of producing Nissan automobiles, they function as one amalgamated organization with

---

[6] This information is drawn from the company information package distributed by Nissan.

a common coordination infrastructure. We shall return to this kind of organizational setup in Chapter 16, since it constitutes a new organizational configuration.

Hyperautomation is a tool that offers dramatic new opportunities for the design of organizations, and one that may also greatly affect the development of society. The possibility of organizational truncation and the establishment of strongly coupled organizations are genuinely new extensions of the constructible space. However, the new tools and even the new organizational configurations work fairly well with established organizational practices and structures. For all the work that is not eliminated by the new systems, it is eminently possible to use common structures and coordinating mechanisms. Though I am not certain, I would guess that the remaining operating cores of both Nissan/Sunderland and the suppliers are predominantly Machine Bureaucracies, and that staff and management still operate much as they used to. It would certainly be possible. This fact is perhaps also one of the main reasons why hyperautomation has developed so fast, and organizational truncation and the development of strongly coupled organizations have kept pace with this development. It is only natural that more unconventional approaches (if they are possible) will take a longer time to develop and deploy.

Consequences for Society

As we have just seen, the consequences of extensive automation are dramatic for the organizations involved. The more organizations exploit the potential computers offer in this direction, the more the consequences will also be felt on the societal level. Increasing automation will irrevocably change the labor market, and the great advances in productivity will provide a steadily increasing material prosperity, if the accompanying environmental problems can be solved.

The developments in the labor market have actually been underway for some time, apparently as a continuation of a long trend starting with industrialization and the mechanization of agriculture. First, industry overtook agriculture as the major employer, but, as industrial productivity increased through automation and increasing use of energy, it was overtaken by the service sector (including public services and administration). The further contraction of the industrial sector can easily be interpreted as a continuation of this trend, trailing the agricultural sector by a number of decades.

However, even without venturing into a discussion of the development of a service economy, information economy, or the postindustrial society, it can be stated that we are experiencing a break with this development; we face a new situation with unclear consequences. The significant difference between former developments and the present is that, up until now, the routine work eliminated in one sector has always been supplanted by routine work in another. As the available positions for farmhands dwindled, up went the number of positions for factory work; and as their number in turn declined, the great white-collar bureaucracies expanded to offer a new set of jobs.

What is happening now is that the remaining routine jobs in both industry *and* in the service sector continue to be decimated, but no new ones seem to be appearing. Almost all new jobs are less routine than those that disappear. The required level of education rises, and it becomes more and more important to be able to think abstractly and to understand and manipulate symbols instead of physical objects. This tends to be true within most occupations, even traditional ones.

A simple example of this is a subtle change in the situation of secretaries who do a lot of typing. In the days of the typewriter, their core professional skill was of the action-centered type—it was the physical skill of hitting the correct keys very fast. The typewriter was a simple and very concrete tool, and its operation and few controls were well understood by the secretaries. They were the undisputed office masters of typing and editing. Today, where most professionals and managers have their own PCs with the same word-processing software as the secretaries, the situation is significantly changed. True, the secretaries are usually still the fastest key-hitters, but they are generally no longer the masters of their tool. In most organizations and departments, there will be a number of professionals who are more proficient than the secretaries in using the advanced functions of word-processing software, and the secretaries will often have to turn to them or to support personnel for help. The case is the same for errors and system breakdowns. The secretaries do not have the general knowledge about their computers to escape from even relatively simple error situations, and they again need help from someone else. Many secretaries experience this as humiliating, and as something that undermines their former position as specialists.

We often see that even extensive training does not change this situation significantly. The task of typing and editing has become so much more abstract, and the writing tool itself so exceedingly complex and symbol oriented, that it is more easily mastered by the professionals, who generally have extensive training in handling symbols and abstract problems. On the average, professionals may also have greater natural abilities in that direction to begin with.

Are we all able to live up to these new requirements? Or will there be a sizable number of people in our societies who will never find a job they can master? Will we have to stimulate the creation of more simple service jobs, which can offer a decent and respectable living to those who do not want or do not master intellectual work? At the moment, these questions do not have clear answers; they only echo growing political concerns (at least in some countries) about the "two-thirds society," where the fortunate two-thirds of the population is employed and grows more and more prosperous, whereas the unfortunate third is unemployed and only becomes poorer. Although it is not the theme for this book, this question represents a problem that will affect every aspect of society.

Another aspect of the developments outlined here is that it is not only jobs that are becoming more complex and abstract—many everyday doings follow the same trajectory. Paying bills, for instance. Not too long ago, it was possible to live by cash alone. Today, that is becoming increasingly difficult, and you suddenly have to write giros or checks and understand bureaucratic procedures. No big deal for most of us—but to the 5–10% in most western societies who are functionally illiterate, it is. As technology, abstraction, symbol manipulation and written directions seep into more and more aspects of our lives, those who have trouble reading streets signs are having greater and greater problems, and no one seems to take their predicament seriously yet—neither in business nor in government.

13
Coordination by Default

"Harmony would lose its attractiveness if it did not have a background of discord."
Tehy Hsieh, *Chinese Epigrams Inside Out and Proverbs,* 1948

Implicit coordination achieved through the use of common archives or files was the first new coordinating mechanism made possible through the use of technology, and it has played a crucial role in the development of the modern office organization. Its elegance and efficiency stem from the fact that it allows coordination to be achieved not by actively directing people, but simply by recording information and making it available. However, as long as it was tied to paper, its potential was severely restricted—the information being accessible in only one location, and normally having only one index. Therefore, it did not come fully into its own until the advent of information technology, or specifically, the structured database, which lifts these restrictions through automatic indexing, automatic search and retrieval, and electronic communication.

The Structured Database

That Significant Record

As we have noted earlier, writing was most probably created to keep records for business and public administration (Goody 1986). The first material memory technology was thus used for storing administrative information—itemized, often quantitative information such as sums of money, numbers of cattle, amounts and kinds of goods, names of people, sizes and locations of landed property. Only later did it become a medium for discourse, for art, and for accumulation of knowledge and reference material. However, because the written discourse and the accumulation of knowledge and reference material were decisive for the development of philosophy, religion, science, and politics, and thus were more visible (and exiting), those aspects of writing easily attracted most of the attention in historical analyses.

Nevertheless, the Industrial Revolution and the evolvement of modern society depended just as much on the meticulous record keeping of merchants, master craftsmen, industrialists, engineers, civil servants and, not least, their clerks. Their tidy accounts, production plans, inventory lists, file cards, protocols with customers and suppliers, details of business transactions, land registers, and tax records became the lifeblood of an increasingly complex society.

The great importance of record keeping is evidenced by the fact that all new technologies for information storage seem to make their debuts in the realm of business and public record keeping—punch card equipment and computers included. When they first ventured beyond research and was adapted for administrative purposes, it was indeed for record keeping and tabulation: The only two private customers on Univac's order books in 1948 were Prudential Insurance Company and the market research company A. C. Nielsen.

In my view, the vast improvement and extension computers bring to implicit coordination represents one of their most revolutionary aspects— and one we find behind most of the familiar success stories that circulate in the business. Paradoxically, it is also among the least talked about. The reason is probably that it does not reside in highly visible equipment such as personal computers and scientific workstations, or in their increasingly advanced software and add-ons. It does not jump at you like a fancy multimedia presentation—you cannot walk into a computer show or an office and *see* implicit coordination, unless you take the (often considerable) time needed to study and understand the applications and databases accomplishing it.

Tools for implicit coordination are nothing new. Nor is it new, either, that they are undervalued. Today, however, computers have brought new dimensions to it—even if the database, logically speaking, is in many ways just an extension of the paper-based file. The increases it offers in speed, availability and ability to handle complex information are nevertheless so great that it becomes qualitatively different. The difference is further increased by the fact that the information in a database is available for automatic operations.

The central aspects of this new functionality are the *reach*, *capacity*, and *speed* offered by the implicit coordination achieved through the use of databases.

Reach

The coordinative reach of a database is a function of the available communication arrangements. If communication lines with sufficient capacity are available, the geographical reach can cover the whole earth (and more, if that should be required!). Thus, with a true, on-line banking system, for example, a transaction registered against your account in any one branch office is immediately reflected in an updated total for that account in the central database—and so instantly available for all the other branch offices as well. You can therefore expect a coordinated response from your bank—no matter which branch office you walk into, the amount of money they would be ready to give you should be the same.

Capacity

Another important factor for of the coordinative power of a database is the number of people that can be simultaneously coordinated. As with geographical reach, there are no definite theoretical limits here—the achievable capacity is determined by the level of the available technology and is rising rapidly all the time. To my knowledge, the largest capacity displayed by single databases in 1999 were the airline reservation systems. The three largest are SABRE, Galileo, and Amadeus. At the time of writing, Amadeus is probably the largest, with 180 000[1] terminals gener- ating (probably) more than 6000 transactions per second at peak load. When the first such system, SABRE, was introduced in 1964, it taxed the capacity of the fastest machines then available with its 1200 teletype terminals (Hopper 1990).

If the development continues at the same pace—and there are no reasons why it should not—a single physical database should be able to accommodate at least 3 million on-line transaction-processing terminals in the year 2020. My guess is that we will reach that level even earlier— maybe as early as the first decade of the twenty-first century—due to advances in parallel processing and new storage media. For less trans- action-intensive applications, the number of terminals could be considerably larger. It is not necessary to test the limits of the possible performance ranges to extract great value, however.

Speed

In theory, the reach and capacity of coordination described earlier are not dependent upon computers. Information can travel the world on paper as well as on wires and airwaves, and a paper file can thus be accessible for anyone, almost without regard for distance. There are many library services in the world demonstrating this principle daily, and the Japanese *kanban* system, the tool behind the original development

---

[1] Personal communication from a representative for Amadeus in Norway.

of just-in-time production, was originally based on cardboard cards. Indeed, many smaller Japanese companies still rely on such cards in their daily production.

But reach and capacity is not everything—it must be coupled with speed. If we look again at the examples described earlier, we will see that none of them would be feasible without the instant transfer of electronic communication. And even that is not enough—it must also be combined with the instant registration, retrieval, and transmittal offered by computer systems. It is precisely this combination of reach, capacity, *and* speed that makes the database qualitatively different from the paper-based file (and from *kanban* cards, for that matter).

As an example, we can go back to SABRE, the first airline reservation system, developed by American Airlines and IBM from 1954 to 1964. Before SABRE began operation, all flight bookings and changes were received through telephones (note that telephones provide instant or almost instant transfer) and recorded manually on blackboards and index cards (Hopper 1990). When the development of SABRE started, however, the booking department of AA had begun to look really strained; by the time SABRE was finished in 1963/64, it was probably coming apart at the seams.

The reason is not difficult to see—the number of persons needed to answer all the telephones was increasing dramatically and changes to the cards and blackboards were cumbersome to effect—and, as the number of callers and clerks steadily rose, the update problems increased even faster. In addition, there was a significant time lag between the actual confirmation of a seat and the moment this was known by the other clerks, and that time lag could easily lead to trouble.

Today's traffic volume would probably not even be theoretically possible to handle the old way—already in 1990, SABRE's database contained 45 million fares from 650 airlines, there were up to 40 million changes every month, and more than 500 000 passenger name records were created every day (Hopper 1990). At the time of writing, SABRE handled booking for more than 400 airlines, 35 000 hotels and 50 car rental companies. It had over 30 000 agency locations, more than 130 000 terminals attached, and in 1996 it processed over 5200 transactions per second and peak load (according to the company's annual report for 1996). Without the automatic and extremely fast reads and writes of the central computers, this would simply be impossible.

Multiple Databases and System-to-System Communication

Even if it is not always feasible or even desirable to coordinate a set of activities through a single database, I believe that the single-database solution will become increasingly important for intra-organizational purposes as both software and hardware improve and communication lines become cheaper. It simply provides a superior solution with regard to speed, integrity, and administrative overhead. However, there will be a considerable period where solutions with multiple databases will dominate, and, in interfirm linkages, they will probably dominate in the foreseeable future.

Linking can take several forms. A database may be split physically among several distributed machines but still be logically organized as a single database. A database may also exist in several copies, with mutual updating at preset intervals. In principle, this is also simply a single database split physically. The reason for such a setup is almost invariably that telecommunication costs makes it a cheaper solution than a centralized database.

Much more common, however, is the situation where the linked databases are quite different from each other—when they use different software, belong to different applications, and run on different kinds of machines. We can then use electronic messaging to synchronize key information between them—let the databases exchange information about their states, allowing automatic coordination to take place—let orders update production schedules, invoices be matched against purchases, and payments against records in accounts receivable. The messages can either go automatically as a result of processes internal to the application programs or be triggered directly by the users.

Messaging is going to be particularly important as long as systems remain fragmented, and even intraorganizational databases are diverse and incompatible. It will allow automation of many existing routines, increase speed, and save labor hours without requiring any fundamental logical changes in the administrative structure. In fact, standardized messaging (such as EDI) tends to conserve existing practices, because of the nature of the standardization process itself. The creation of international standards for messaging involves a large number of countries, standards organizations, and trade organizations. To be accepted, any standard will have to build on widely used documents and forms that are part of the traditional way companies of the world organize and do business. The whole EDIFACT standard is a witness to this—the catalog over standardized document formats reads like an old-fashioned textbook on accounting and business administration. Examples (taken from the catalog in Thorud 1991) are as follows:

IFTMAN   Arrival Notice Message
IFTMBC   Booking Confirmation Message
CREADV   Credit Advice Message
DEBADV   Debit Advice Message

DESADV   Dispatch Advice Message
DOCAPP   Documentary Credit Application Message
PAYEXT   Extended Payment Order Message
IFTMBF   Firm Booking Message
INVOIC   Invoice Message
PAYORD   Payment Order Message

From the outside, an organization with extensive use of EDI may thus look thoroughly reformed in the way it operates, due to improved coordination, increased speed, and reduction of errors. Below the surface, however, most of the old functions and procedures might still be intact, even to the extent that the old, isolated applications still run—now only augmented by EDI-compatible front-ends. In other words, existing procedures will just have been "mechanized." But the quantitative change (increase in speed) is so great that the consequences are often perceived as qualitative.

Bearing in mind the accounts payable function of Ford described in Chapter 12, you will see from the preceding list (where you find both a DESADV, an INVOIC, and a PAYORD message) that an uninventive solution based on the use of EDI is eminently feasible, and it could easily have been compounded by the use of email and other groupware applications. The result would have been an impressive system, yielding considerably less improvement than the much more radical solution eventually adopted by Ford.

Networks of linked systems may be very large. The largest existing one is probably the SWIFT network used by banks for international money transfers. Most large banks throughout the world are connected to this network, and billions of dollars are moved over it every hour, constantly updating account databases in banks worldwide, with an unknown total of terminals attached. A transaction entered on a terminal in Oslo may withdraw a certain amount of kroner from an account in a Norwegian bank database, and update an account, for instance, in Japan with the corresponding amount of yen.[2] In turn, this would cause a Japanese bank clerk to allow the owner of the Japanese account to withdraw money without any other notice than the implicit coordination provided by the linked databases. As we have just seen, even tighter coupling can be found in the automobile industry.

Speed need not be much lower for systems based on linked databases than for those based on a single database, but it often is—there may be batch processes involved, or delays may be deliberately introduced for

---

[2] It may take some time—a day or two—because there may be old equipment and batch-oriented systems involved, or the banks may want to sit on the money for a certain amount of time to earn some interest, but, technically, the transfer could happen immediately.

other reasons, as is often the case with money transfers—the banks want their float just as in the old days, no matter how fast the technology may allow them to operate. In my view, however, only unified databases can deliver the maximum advantage from database technology. Information should be registered when and where it is created or captured, and stored in only one place to ensure full information integrity. Single databases are also much better and more efficient than messaging for coordinating a total value chain. Distributed databases, where the same information may be stored in several physical locations, will incur a great deal of processing and communication overhead to maintain integrity. As communication costs continue to fall, the central database will therefore grow in popularity.

This discussion has been focused on administrative applications. There are also, of course, important uses of messaging and common database access in areas such as sensor information (in process control and other manufacturing systems, in air traffic control and other types of monitoring systems) and in the direct control of physical devices (as in manufacturing and military systems). But the principles are the same, and the benefits derive from the same basic mechanisms: integrity of information, implicit coordination, and fast responses.

EXTENSIONS TO THE CONSTRUCTIBLE SPACE

Computers do extend the scope of implicit coordination. They offer real-time coordination almost regardless of volume and geographical distance, even across processes. But how does this extend the space of constructible organizations? In my view, there are opportunities on three main levels: inside the single organization, on the interorganizational level, and on a level where it can be debated if we are really talking about organizations at all.

The Single Organization

Banks, Automobiles, and Airplanes

As a coordinative tool inside the single organization, implicit coordination has already proved some of its mettle. We have talked a lot about banking, and there is little doubt that the coordinative power of the database is the main force behind the flexibility of modern banking. The instant or near-instant availability of account information has made it possible to eliminate a lot of back office work and control procedures, to broaden jobs, and to extend services reliably both to self-service devices (e.g., automatic teller machines) and to external agents (e.g., shops and filling stations).

However, even if the database is vital for banking, and its effects powerful in the sense that it allows any clerk in any branch office to meet a customer's request in the same way, the coordinative aspect is nevertheless fairly narrow—the clerks are coordinated in their assessment of the customer's financial status, but, aside from that, the actions of one clerk will have little or no implications for another. That even this fairly simple and narrow application of implicit coordination has led to revolutionary changes in banking is a proof of its power, and with the addition of automation—especially in combination with "intelligent" self-service solutions such as those postulated in the Chapter 11—it will eventually effect a total transformation both of single organizations and a whole industry.

The potential is even greater than this, however. To find an example, we need go no further than to an example from the previous chapter: the revolution in Ford's accounts payable departments. It was the use of a fairly simple database that made the whole thing possible, and there is even an element of cross-process coordination to be found—the database not only effected the procurement of parts and payment of suppliers; it also saved a lot of work in financial reporting. The reports became both more up to date and more reliable, since information on parts and payments was available at all times and were always consistent.

Even more illustrative is the situation at Mazda, where the same database served as a coordination point for orders, production and supplies from subcontractors. The data integrity and implicit coordination offered by the single database provided full synchronization of the entire manufacturing process ("procurement to shipment," as Hammer and Champy [1993] prefer to call it), the sales process ("prospect to order") and the order fulfillment process ("order to payment"). The same is, in all probability, the case for the Nissan factory in Sunderland, also referred to in the previous chapter, although details are lacking in the available description. Indeed, it is this potential for cross-process coordination that is the main motive for the general movement toward registering data only once—at the point of origin—and storing it in one place only to ensure integrity.

A different example of the strong coordination that unified databases can provide can be found in the aerospace industry. The Boeing 777 was the first airplane whose full structural design was done in an integrated CAD/CAE[3] system (Stix 1991, Moeller 1994). A modern jetliner is a very

---

[3] CAD: computer aided design. CAE: computer-aided engineering.

complex piece of machinery, and with traditional, paper-based design, a major part of the job is to manage thousands of drawings; correct them when there are changes; to ascertain that adjoining parts actually fit together, and that no two parts (including piping and cables) occupy the same space. This job is so complex that it is simply impossible to complete on paper—to really find out if all the parts fit, and whether cables and piping collide, physical models and full scale mock-ups have traditionally been necessary to sort things out. It was even usual that last-minute changes had to be made during the actual manufacturing of the first airplanes, due to problems that had not been discovered during the design phase.

With the 777, all the design work was done on workstations equipped with a three-dimensional (3D) design program, which made it possible to display each part as a 3D picture, rotate it to view it from different angles, test the effect of movements, and so on. Because of the integrated database connecting all the workstations, neighboring parts could then be joined together on-screen—any engineer could call up the parts adjoining the one he or she was working on to check if they fitted together. The screen even provided the telephone number of the person working on that particular part, in case there should be need for consultation.

The parts could also be assembled on-screen to modules and to a complete model of the entire aircraft, including such vitals as cabling and piping. The fit between parts and modules could thus be tested without the need to build models and mock-ups, and the software could detect if any two parts—for example, two cables—occupied the same point in space. The design program and the database, then, took care of the co-ordination and ensured that the work done by any of the thousands of engineers matched with what the others did—without the need for human liaisons.

Besides the digital design itself, Boeing also took advantage of the coordinative powers of the system to integrate about 15 different design and engineering steps into a single overlapping process (Stix 1991). Manufacturing engineers were able to write tooling specifications as soon as design on a part had started, and could provide feedback on manufacturability early in the process. Some of the CAD data could also be fed into CAM[4] systems and used directly to manufacture parts. Likewise, the same data could drive automatic testing equipment, examining parts for mechanical accuracy (mechanical tolerances are very narrow in this business). According to a November 1991 article in the *New York Times*, Philip M. Condit, then Boeing vice president in charge

---

[4] CAM: computer aided manufacturing.

of the design project, said that the system allowed the engineers in this large project to work together just like the team of less than 100 engineers who designed the B-29 bomber during World War II.

The actual size of the 777 project team, however, is not clear—the number of workstations and people actually working on the design, has, surprisingly, been impossible to ascertain. The various articles all report different numbers, and personal communication with sources at Boeing has not helped very much to clarify things, since Boeing regards the CAD system and the way it is used as a competitive advantage important enough to be shielded from detailed reporting. It seems reasonably certain, however, that the number of people involved in the design was higher than 5000, and that at least 2–3000 of them—at more than 20 sites in USA and Japan—were equipped with workstations.

The 777 project did not save Boeing time in the period up to the first roll-out of the new plane, due to the time it took to train the large number of engineers—not only to use the new system, but to "think" in 3D and to work in cross-departmental teams. However, with that job done, and the entire structure of the plane in digital form, Boeing spokesmen were confident of spectacular savings in the development of new versions. Moeller (1994) quotes Larry Olson, director of computing systems at Boeing, as saying that custom versions could be built in eight months, compared to the previous 52—an 85% reduction in lead time! It seems reasonable to expect that the system will save Boeing considerable time when they embark on the design of their next new aircraft, and that it will be extended to cover larger parts of the total aircraft design.

Bigger, Better, and Brisker

These examples illustrate the main strength of the database as an organizational tool: the ability to provide coordination as a spin-off, as an implicit effect, of the data storage itself. Coordination that earlier required significant, even massive, efforts can now be effected without any human mediation at all, with much greater speed, and with much better precision. Computer-based implicit coordination should make it possible to build and maintain *much larger organizations* than before, to make large organizations *much more responsive*, and to *improve the quality of their output*. The condition is of course that common information lies at the base of their main activities, as they indeed do in banks and in design projects. For manufacturing operations such as the Mazda and Nissan factories, a common information base must be augmented by advanced automation to achieve the maximum advantage. Indeed, the same can be said about banking, where the combination of the database, automation, and self-service will soon make it possible to run vast transaction-processing operations, covering great geographical areas, with surprisingly slim organizations.

The increased responsiveness does not only come from the speed with which one organization member can retrieve information—for example, to answer a simple customer request. It is equally important that changes in the common information base are instantly incorporated into the basis for everyone else's work. Thus, it takes considerably less time and effort for the organization to come up with a consistent response to a request that involves more than one person or group. This will be true for relatively simple cases as well as for really complex ones, such as an airline's request for a custom version of the 777. The consistency of the information and the instant updates will allow a large organization to respond in ways that were earlier only possible for organizations small enough to have almost every relevant person working in the same building—taking advantage of the richness of face-to-face communication. The integrity of the common information will also contribute significantly to product and service quality by increasing the internal consistency and accuracy of the output.

Decentralization

The implicit coordination achieved through the use of databases eliminates a lot of administrative tasks that used to be necessary to co-ordinate work. Those tasks used to be the main responsibility of middle management. However, they were also combined with decision making—and when the coordinative tasks are eliminated and middle management is correspondingly decimated, the decision making is not necessarily eliminated with them. Someone, then, still has to take care of it, and it tends to go where the information is used—which most often means a migration toward those parts of the organization where customers' requests are met. In most instances, this will mean a decentralization of authority (vertical decentralization in Mintzberg's terminology [Mintzberg 1979]). To illustrate, let us detail the banking example a little bit.

An important effect of the introduction of modern banking systems has been the transformation of work at the counter level. Before computers, or, rather, before they got terminals, the clerks working at the counter were little more than paper pushers. Their most important decisions were whether to accept a check or an identity card. The introduction of terminals (especially on-line terminals) changed that. First of all, it eliminated a lot of registration (that is, most of the paper work), even if the transaction still had to be registered. However, with an on-line system, the clerk could now immediately check the customer's balance, transaction histories could be retrieved, and accounts could be opened and closed on the spot, to mention a few of the new possibilities. Since this also meant that important parts of a customer's total relationship with the bank were available at the counter, and additional information on creditworthiness became available in commercial databases, many banks authorized some of their clerks to grant small loans and credits to customers.

This was indeed a revolution, and it was the instant availability of information at the customer interface that invited the delegation. Earlier, information had to be collected from many sources within the bank itself, where it resided in paper-based files, and the retrieval process had to follow established archival rules and mail routines. All this took time and effort—information travels slowly when it sits on paper that has to pass through several hands. To collect this information was therefore back-office work, and managers coordinated it and reviewed the results before making the final decisions.

Under the new setup, the counters were usually divided into two zones—one where customers concluded their normal transactions (such as withdrawal, deposits, payments, and so on) in terminal-equipped teller windows, and another where they could conclude more "elevated" business (such as opening an account or applying for a small credit on a salary account). This development was usually also followed by an increase in the sizes of loans and credits that branch managers could authorize.

Used for decentralization in the manner just described, computers will undoubtedly lead to a reduction in the number of organizational levels and an increase in the authority and latitude for judgment in the bottom layers of the organization. This leads many people to argue that IT is first and foremost a technology for decentralization, and that empowerment of employees and the transfer of responsibilities down the ladder of authority are prerequisites to success when implementing computer-based systems. I disagree with this view, which I consider overly optimistic, just like the claims that computers will foster a proliferation of networked teams. I shall return to this subject in the next chapter, where I will argue that computer-based systems can also be used also as a tool for centralization. In my view, computers will not force the abolishment of hierarchy, but, on the contrary, provide a platform that extends our options—the space of constructible organizations—in both directions.

Implicit Coordination as an Expression of Mutual Adjustment

In Chapter 7, I classified paper-based implicit coordination as an expression of mutual adjustment. It should then follow that computer-based

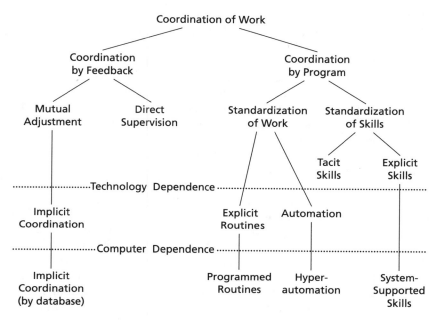

Figure 13-1: *Taxonomy of coordinating mechanisms extended by the use of information technology (preliminary)*

implicit coordination is such an expression as well (Figure 13-1). Just like its paper-based counterpart, it works by effecting an indirect, mutual adjustment between all the people who use the database for their work. In most cases, it cannot provide total coordination—designers of neighboring parts on the 777 had to talk to each other from time to time, as did people working with different aspects of the design process. But it is nevertheless sufficiently powerful to allow a radical reorganization of the entire process, and it extends some of the functionality of mutual adjustment to a potentially vast number of people.

The simple elegance of the principle of computer-based implicit coordination—where extremely detailed, complex, and time-critical coordination can be achieved without any direct coordination effort, unfettered by geographical distance—represents the second great power of information technology, on par with hyperautomation.

Coupled Organizations

In Chapter 12, we discussed the case of separate organizations tightly bound together and coordinated through common computer systems.

The focus then was on automation, but there is little doubt that the foundation for hyperautomation along value chains will always be one or more common databases, sometimes synchronized by messaging. The same will be the case with other arrangements for tight organizational cooperation. The implicit coordination provided by databases is therefore a pivotal factor when coupling independent organizations. The reason is of course the same as for single organizations: it is a very efficient co-ordinating mechanism, it requires little or no manual work, it works independently of geographical distance, and the upper limit on the number of persons or organizational entities that can be coordinated is already very large and rapidly rising.

As long as the coordination achieved through computer-based systems is sufficient, then, there will be few technical constraints on size. The main limiting factor is no longer the technology, but simply the will to cooperate and to undertake the painstaking analysis, standardization and design that is required to make such structures work. The task is already formidable for systems in single organizations, and the work required to standardize the format of information items across organizations can frighten even the most hardened project manager. Even reaching agree-ment on simple things, such as the number of digits in an order number, can be difficult enough to delay projects for considerable periods of time. This also serves to underscore the fact that such tight coupling is not easily established, and the easy way in which terms such as "network organizations" and "virtual organizations" are used today belies the effort it takes to establish them and the losses involved in opting out once the cooperative structure is working.

However, I definitely think we will see more such constructions in the future; I have already hinted that I believe they constitute a new kind of organizational configuration—but that part of the discussion must wait until Chapter 16.

On the Fringes of Organization

One of the examples I used earlier in this chapter to throw light on the way databases provide implicit coordination was airline reservation systems. The operation of all the big reservation systems is quite astonishing, if you really think about it. While you are on the telephone in the late afternoon with your travel agent in Cincinnati, mulling over if you should book that last available seat on the first flight from London to Milan on Christmas Day, I might place an early morning call to my travel agency in Oslo and snatch the ticket from under your nose—and you will know it and suffer the consequences in the same instant (give or take a few seconds, depending the current response time of the system and the alertness of your agent). You would then end up as the victim of an implicit coordination spanning half the world, taking place inside a database physically located on another continent.

What is really happening here, when tens of thousands of travel agents daily book flights for their customers on Amadeus? The coordination implicit in the common database keeps them constantly informed about everyone else's bookings; new flights; changes in pricing, departure, arrival times, and so on. Clearly, there is a strong element of organization present—if they did not have their computers and database, they would need an enormous hierarchy of coordinating managers and professionals to carry out the same work—except for the fact that the whole feat would be totally and utterly impossible to bring about without the database in the first place.

Of course, this mass of travel agents cannot be said to make up an organization in our normal understanding of the word. But no one can deny that their common database connection ensures that their behavior appears organized in certain key aspects—their actions are coordinated in the sense that *any* booking by *any* agent has the potential to modify the behavior of *any other* agent connected to the database, and that such modifications routinely occur. It is not an organization, but it is certainly organized, representing what can be considered a new kind of structure. We shall return to this discussion in Chapter 16.

14
Comprehension and Control

"Knowledge is the true organ of sight, not the eyes."
Panchatantra, c. 5th century AD

COMPREHENDING THE COMPLEX

Getting to Know

In Chapter 9, we briefly discussed how the digital computer's processing power has made it possible to handle much greater complexity than before. It is of course not only processing that is involved—as with most application areas, several of the strong points of computers are involved at the same time. In this instance both registration and storage of structured data (especially in quantitative form) and communication are essential.

This has at least two interesting aspects. First, computer-based systems make it much easier to aggregate, communicate, and display key information. Important information about sales, for instance, that used to be available only periodically (say, once each month) and lag weeks or even months behind actual sales can now be updated daily or even in real time. Second, in a growing number of instances, the computer systems will register and report information that was simply unavailable before, and thereby create new feedback chains throwing light on formerly unknown or unfathomable causal relationships. Let us explore this in some more detail.

Availability of Information

Information technology improves the availability of information in two ways. First, as Zuboff (1988) notes, the increasing use of computer-based systems means that a larger and larger part of the information used and processed in an organization is captured and registered in the organization's computers. The systems will often capture and retain information that has not been collected earlier at all, because it was too difficult or too expensive (e.g., registering every single item sold in a supermarket at the point of sale). Second, the access to this information is greatly improved both by storage in integrated databases allowing remote access and by machine-to-machine communication.

Information transfers that previously had to involve many people can now happen automatically, and with great speed. The speed itself is very important—information registered in a database is immediately available, and information communicated between computers moves very quickly. This means that you can have information continuously updated in real time, without any perceptible delay between the registration of an information item and its use hundreds or even thousands of kilometers away.

Information Concentration

However, it is of no avail to collect heaps of information if it causes our innate input channels to clog up. With increased information availability, we also need information concentration—the refinement of "raw" information into a form that is easier to comprehend. This may happen in several ways. One of the most obvious possibilities is through transformations, as when numbers are turned into graphs. It may also take place through aggregation, as when we compile statistics. Statistics can then be further concentrated by being converted to graphs. We may design compound measures—numbers that represent a weighed synthesis of several other numbers. We may let the computers select information items for us, and, for instance, only show us values that deviate from the expected.

The more of these techniques we use, the more we draw on the computer's ability to continually trace and display the relationships between a large number of variables, the more information are we able to monitor. In theory, the number is almost infinitely large, in practice there are of course limits—but the limits are only imposed by constraints on data capture and on our modeling and programming capabilities. And, even a humble spreadsheet represents a real extension of our working memory, showing us instantly the ramifications of changes in single or multiple variables, thus greatly enhancing our understanding of the total system— whether it is a budget or the layout of a logistics operation. When represented graphically, the information is even more accessible, as in modern brokerage systems, where brokers can follow (in real time) the continuous changes in exchange rates, interest rates, stock or commodity prices both as numbers (in one window) and "living" columns (in another). The columns make it very easy to note the trends; the numbers provide the precision needed for actual trading decisions. Through the constant updates they get from the screen, brokers are thus able to reflect on and manipulate more complex relationships than before.

Other examples of systems that allow us to deal with otherwise intractable complexity are modeling systems for complex physical processes, such as weather forecasting systems, and modern military fire control systems. The computerized fire control centers of modern naval units such as an aircraft carrier group can simultaneously track and engage a large number of targets—ships, aircraft, and missiles—using a diverse array of weapons (including its own aircraft). Fighter planes now have computers that allow pilots to engage several enemy aircraft simultaneously. Indeed, the military forces of the modern industrialized countries are rapidly becoming extremely computer-intensive. The Allied offensive against Iraq in January 1991 relied not only on modern weapons and a lot of firepower, but just as much on a very sophisticated communication and control infrastructure. With a high skill level in organizing and operating computerized weapons as well as communications and control systems, it is possible to achieve a planning capacity and a tactical coordination on the battlefield that is simply out of reach for less skilled and more poorly equipped forces.[1]

The ultimate goal here is of course to simplify information and crop it down to a volume small enough to absorb. This represents a new twist to an old story, but it is also strikingly different: it means simplification by *inclusion and concentration*, not by *selection and omission*. Whereas, as naked humans, we had to rely on our experience and intuition to choose the few select parameters we could manage to monitor and process, we can now build systems that allow us to monitor all or a large number of the parameters we suspect are of interest, and then have the systems select and concentrate information on the basis of programmed rules. The systems may even have heuristic properties and be able to modify themselves on the basis of accumulated measurements (artificial intelligence). I think we are just in the beginning of a very interesting development in this field.

---

[1] In addition, such coordination and control also build on the impersonal discipline, reliability and efficiency that have become part of the industrialized cultures. Precise coordination of large organizations is very difficult when one operates within a more oral culture, with its emphasis on emotions and personal relations, and where appearance may be judged more important than fact. That is probably why highly industrialized countries are so overwhelmingly efficient in large-scale battlefield warfare, much more so than their firepower alone should warrant, and why forces from less developed societies only stand a chance if they can drag the war down to the guerrilla level, where more or less isolated man-to-man or platoon-to-platoon battles dominate.

Causal Relationships

The exposure of causal relationships and the establishment of feedback loops are among the most important contributions of computer-based systems. The more the activities and information in an enterprise are committed to computer-based systems, the more the relationships between different parts of the enterprise's activities will be revealed and laid open for intervention. Because information stored in machine-readable form is so much more accessible, and the computer-based tools for analysis so much better than the old manual ones, increased use of computers will make it possible for us to uncover deeper and more complex causal relationships than before, and establish much more sophisticated feedback loops. Combined with the computers' outstanding ability to aggregate, concentrate, and present quantitative information, this will significantly expand the limits of what single persons or small groups can comprehend and direct.

If all the activities that lend themselves to digital representation are indeed represented in an integrated database, and that database is structured after a suitable model of the enterprise's business domain, it should be possible to surveil and tune the total organization's activities in a very sophisticated way—especially in manufacturing enterprises with extensive automation. The just-in-time production control systems of the automobile industry represent precisely an effort in this direction, and similar effects should be possible in other chains of enterprises making up an extended value chain (from raw materials to retailing). On a societal level, intelligent use of computer-based systems should make it possible to reveal interdependencies and establish feedback loops in public administration that could allow more efficient use of public funds.

Informating Work

To Shoshana Zuboff, it is this general contribution toward a deeper understanding and more sophisticated control of complex processes that stands out as the most important aspect of computer-based systems. We have touched upon this in Chapters 10 and 12, but I would like to introduce Zuboff's concept more directly.

In her book *In the Age of the Smart Machine* (1988), Zuboff opens with an explanation of what she calls "a fundamental duality" of information technology. While the activities of classical machines only result in concrete products, information technology in addition to this (1988, pp. 9–10) "... simultaneously generates information about the underlying productive and administrative processes through which an organization accomplishes its work. It provides a deeper level of transparency to activities that had been either partially or completely opaque." This is how information technology goes beyond traditional automation, says Zuboff, and coins the word *informate* to describe this capacity.

To Zuboff, automation and informating form a hierarchy, where informating "derives from and builds upon automation" (1988, p. 11). Automation is nearly always the goal when IT-based systems are introduced, says Zuboff, and up to now informating has come largely as an unanticipated effect, which almost no organizations have understood and very few have exploited. The informating aspect of the technology is for Zuboff the real revolutionary one, the one that will cause most of the organizational changes in the future. Although she acknowledges that IT has the potential to replace large numbers of humans through automation, in her opinion it only "perpetuates the logic of the industrial machine, that over the course of this century, has made it possible to rationalize work while decreasing the dependence on human skills" (1988, p. 10). Only informating can bring real change, as it "... alters the intrinsic character of work—the way millions of people experience daily life on the job" (1988, p. 11).

In Zuboff's view, it is only by exploiting the informating aspects, the insight it gives in core processes, that it is possible to design systems and work organization in such a way that one can reap the full benefits of information technology. In her eyes, the capacity for informating also represents an appealing aspect of the technology, because it seems to favor increased use of human intelligence, learning, and teamwork, and a concomitant decrease in hierarchy and the application of Tayloristic principles. This is simply necessary to reap the full benefits of computer-based systems.

I fully support Zuboff's view that the informating capacity of computer-based systems represents a very important and genuinely new addition to our arsenal of tools. It is absolutely central to our growing capacity for managing complex tasks and projects, and, in my view, it is one of the technology's three most important contributions—on a par with hyperautomation and the coordinative powers of the database.

However, I disagree with some points. First, I do not believe that information technology necessarily favors empowerment and a decrease in hierarchy in general. Like earlier communication technologies, it can be used both for centralization and decentralization, and it is not a given that decentralization and empowerment will be more attractive or productive in all circumstances.

Second, I do not agree that computer-based automation operates "according to a logic that hardly differs from that of the nineteenth-century machine system" (Zuboff 1988, p. 10). Even if many of the basic principles are the same as those that apply to mechanical automation, I nevertheless believe that the degree of automation we can achieve by using computers is so dramatic in comparison with mechanical automation that it represents something qualitatively new. The effects of hyperautomation and the general elimination of work that can be achieved through the use of information technology will contribute just as much as informating (or more) to the changes we will experience in our organizations and in society.

Finally, I do not agree that such automation, or the use of information technology for other purposes than informating, necessarily implies a decreasing dependence on human skills: on the contrary, it entails an *increasing* dependence on knowledge. However, the requirements for knowledge may well be unevenly distributed in the organization, and I think the narrow statement that automation decreases the dependence on human skills is based on a "local" interpretation of skill—that is, on looking only at the concrete (and presumably lost) skill of a worker who is replaced by machinery of some kind. In my view, one must look at the total set of skills required for a certain production process. To achieve a sophisticated level of automation, it is necessary to develop equally sophisticated skills in analysis, engineering, and planning to design and build the necessary machinery and computer systems and to operate the resulting production units.

This is, of course, the reason why advanced automation can only be developed and maintained by advanced industrial and scientific cultures. The skill required to automate is actually much higher than the level sufficient to carry out the work without automation—but the skill is of another kind; it is more intellective, to use Zuboff's terminology. It will also normally reside in another part of the organization, and partly even outside the organization itself—in consulting firms and the firms that make and install the necessary systems and machines. Moreover, as an increasing number of routine jobs are eliminated, the jobs left will in most instances require a higher skill level than those eliminated, which means that the average skill level in the organization will rise. However, the skills required in both the automated and the informated organization will increasingly be of the intellective kind, and the ability to work through symbols and abstract thought will become much more important.

The fact is that currently available technology already permits us to control more complex matters than we can tackle at our present level of methodological sophistication. The scale of manageable complexity is already limited not by the technology itself, but by our ability to plan and design systems, and to interact with and through them. The reason is simply that to build a system that can help us manage complex matters, we must first understand these matters thoroughly—as well as analyze and describe them very closely. Only then is it possible to design the control systems in all their painstaking detail and devise the interfaces that will allow people to use them effectively. *As we proceed along the learning curve, then, and set out to tackle more and more complex tasks, the ability to analyze and understand the problem domain, and then design the total system/organization combination becomes the crucial factor—not the technology itself.*

EXTENSIONS TO THE CONSTRUCTIBLE SPACE

By making information extremely accessible and increasing organization members' understanding of both an organization's problem domain and its internal workings, information technology adds a new contribution to its extensions of the space of constructible organizations. As recognized in the old proverb "knowledge is power," the increased knowledge should, first and foremost, make it possible for those with access to make quicker and better decisions and to supervise and direct more complex tasks and operations than before. This was, by the way, the main point made by Leavitt and Whisler in their pioneering article on the effects of computers on management (Leavitt and Whisler 1958). They predicted that top managers would be prone to use this opportunity to recentralize authority that had been delegated only because overwhelming complexity had made central decisions untenable.

What kind of opportunities will this open up? Does it primarily favor the development of more centralized, more tightly reined organizations, or of decentralized organizations, where management layers peel off and empowerment and self-organized team becomes the order of the day? The answer is not evident—just as for the telephone (Pool 1983), arguments and examples can be produced that point in both directions. In fact, the question seems to function almost like a Rorschach test: those who think central control is a good thing eagerly eye what they see as the opportunity to use automation, improved communications, faster reporting, and better information retrieval and analysis to strengthen management's grip on the organization, whereas those who would like to wrestle power away from bosses finally see their chance to decentralize operations, devolve responsibility, and empower employees.

George and King (1991) has made a thorough review of the debate on computing and centralization, drawing on 65 studies and discussions. Their material clearly shows that there are no simple relationships to be found. Numerous empirical studies can be marshaled in support of all the main hypotheses—that computer use leads to centralization, that it leads to decentralization, that they are unrelated, and that their use will only reflect the already established propensities in the organization. George and King conclude that there can indeed be a relationship, but that it is not a simple causal one (1991, p. 70): "Rather, we believe this relationship is filtered through an organization's history and context and power structure and takes form through management action in a manner best accounted for by reinforcement politics perspective." They assert that the centralization/decentralization debate in its traditional form can be declared to be over, but that research into the matter should continue in order to learn more about the intricate relationships between information technology and organizations.

For our purpose, it is still worthwhile to analyze this matter in a little more detail, taking the nature of the technology and the way it alleviates our innate constraints as the starting point.

The debate is in fact even older than Leavitt and Whisler's article, as the telephone provided some of the same advantages as computer-based systems. Pool's conclusion for the telephone was that it both facilitated some centralization of control, while at the same time allowed decentralization through a dispersal of activities (Pool 1983).

However, according to Mintzberg's definition of decentralization (Mintzberg 1979), the physical (geographical) dispersal of facilities alone does not qualify to be called decentralization in an organizational sense. True decentralization must involve a decentralization of *decision making and power*. In this perspective, the telephone appears to be mainly a tool for centralization, perhaps with the qualification that it helps to democratize the organization by making it easier to strike contacts across organizational levels and divides. (Pool cites several authors to that effect.) Pool's conclusion seems more valid for computer-based systems, however. They can indeed facilitate both centralization and decentralization. The question is what *kind* of centralization and decentralization we can achieve, and, additionally, if the potential is greater in one direction than in the other.

Possibilities for Centralization

Pool (1983) says that the telephone makes it easier to centralize control, and that, precisely because of this, it allows greater physical dispersal of operations: the *controlled* can be given a physically longer rein, since the *controller* is confident that the new means of communication will enable him to maintain the desired level of control anyway. This relationship can be seen as an aspect of a more general relationship between control, distance, and complexity. Control is inversely related both to the distance between the controller and the controlled, and to the complexity of the problem domain.

From this, it follows that any technology improving communication and/or the handling of complex information and feedback chains will improve control if distance and complexity are kept constant, and allow greater distance and/or complexity with an unchanged level of control.

There is much historical evidence to support this. Before the advent of radio and international telephone and telegraph links, for instance, masters of merchant ships had great discretion in accepting freight assignments, deciding which ports to call at, whether to do repair work, and so on. Being away from the home port for months, often years, at a time, they constantly had to (and were expected to) make important business decisions on behalf of the owner. The advent of radio, telegraph, and telephone, however, effectively reduced them to mere navigators and crew managers, since the improved means of communication allowed the owner to gradually bring the business decisions home to his own office.

Diplomacy has seen the same development—when it took months to consult one's government, the post as ambassador was really an important one in political terms. Today, it primarily covers certain administrative and ceremonial functions, in addition to public relations and local information gathering (and even intelligence activities). Pool (1983) himself vividly describe the moment when this development was brought home to American (and other) diplomats—when President Hoover took to the telephone to placate the French government after he had unilaterally declared a moratorium on all war debts on June 21, 1931 to deter the German government from defaulting on its loans from US banks. He used the telephone intensively to maintain hourly contact with the American representatives in the major European capitals, and they also conferred with each other. The calls were effective, and resulted in an agreement with the French government two weeks later. These new methods caused considerable agitation in Europe, as the instant information transfer of the telephone forced diplomats and politicians to work at much greater speed than they were used to. Pool quotes from an article in *The New York Times* (1983, p. 88):

> This breach of diplomatic precedent has startled Europe, a Belgian politician declared, relating how Europe was being hustled by new American methods. It is a new world without distances, he said, which makes diplomats feel they have outlived their usefulness when the heads of States can discuss matters almost face to face.[2]

In this example, as well as in the example of General Oyama quoted earlier, the telephone improved control because it allowed rapid collection of information at a distance. It also made order giving much more efficient

---

[2] Herbert Hoover: *The Memoirs of Herbert Hoover.* New York, Macmillan, 1952, p. 72. *The New York Times*, 28 June 1931, p.1; 29 June 1931, p.10.

and swift. It was used as a tool for centralizing both intelligence and command.

However, computer-based systems do much more than facilitate human communication—as we noted earlier in this chapter, they also make information available to anyone, and they can concentrate information and expose causal relationships not previously known or fathomed. In addition, systems with embedded knowledge, artificial intelligence, hyperautomation or clever use of implicit coordination can allow wholesale elimination of tasks. By virtue of this, information technology can facilitate centralization in at least three ways: by furnishing managers with *greatly improved information about real-time performance*, by *large-scale elimination of tasks*, and by *automated supervision*. Task elimination was discussed in detail in the previous chapter, but I will nevertheless include it here, since the perspective now is a little different.

Centralizing by Informating

As I said earlier, I do not agree with Zuboff's (1988) postulation that the full potential of computer-based systems can only be achieved through the empowerment of organizational members and a concomitant devolvement of power. I do agree that this is true in many instances, but I maintain that the informating aspect of information technology also offers a potential for very efficient centralization of power.

As we have already concluded, computers cannot move verbal information from one person to another very much faster or over a longer distance than the telephone can. But, by virtue of their processing capacity, coupled with the range and speed of database access, they can automatically collect quantitative information from a multitude of sources, aggregate it, and present it to a human in an easily accessible form. This process can happen quickly enough to present the information in real time or very near real time, and provide a central management with very accurate and adequate information about the main activities of an organization. Such automatic collection of information from a multitude of sources was what made SAGE, the first computer-based air defense system (deployed in 1958) so revolutionary. It made it possible to organize a real-time, central combat control center for the air defenses of the northern United States. This facilitation of a central command is still one of the main functions of combat control systems.

However, let us consider instead a more civil case in point, where computer-based systems allow increased centralization of control through automatic collection, aggregation, and presentation of vital business information. The much-quoted example from Benetton (Clegg 1990) provides an interesting illustration. This Italian maker of clothing (mostly sweaters and other knitwear) developed a business strategy that was based on real-time monitoring of color preferences in the marketplace by the help of a computer-based system. Their subcontractors (about 200 small family outfits in their home region in Italy) produce only undyed clothes. Small batches of clothes in assorted colors (assumed to be the most popular that particular season) are sent to the Benetton shops the world over in the beginning of each season. Every sale is registered at the cash register and transferred electronically to Benetton's central database, where it is aggregated with data from the other shops. It is thus immediately available for analysis, and Benetton's central management know straight away which colors sell and which do not in their different markets. They can then go on to dye the clothes that are produced accordingly. Changes in demand throughout the season are instantly registered and reflected in production.

The weak point in this system, by the way, is the time lag between the registration of the sales information and the delivery of the new batches of garments to the stores—the sales profile may well change in the time it takes to go through the whole cycle! Ideally, therefore, delivery to the stores should be daily; based on the sales the day before; and modified by any accumulated experience about typical variations relating to time of the year, holidays, and day of the week. The Swedish clothes chain H&M (Hennes & Mauritz) has a comparable system that lets management pinpoint slow sellers early in the season and begin selective clearance sales both to preempt their competitor's clearance sales and to draw extra crowds into their stores while the rest of the collection is still "hot."

The organizational implications of systems such as these are perhaps not visibly dramatic, but what happens is that management in the central headquarters has just as good a knowledge of the developments in the local markets as the shop managers themselves, and they get it just as fast. Indeed, because of the computer system's ability for information concentration and calculation of trends, central management probably knows *more* about the total action in the local market than the people in the individual shops. Their managerial reach then naturally extends much further down the organizational hierarchy; in fact it will extend right into the shelves in the individual stores: Because of the informating aspect of the systems, and their greatly improved overview over customer choices from day to day, management's effective *depth of control* in the organization is greatly increased—and the shop managers' freedom of action correspondingly reduced. What is left of it can often be taken care of by less experienced personnel, since it is no longer necessary to have store managers with a thorough knowledge of the local market or the trends within the industry.

One can of course argue that the information here presented to a central management could instead be fed back to the store managers, giving them a tool for ordering and organizing their sales activities. Although the feedback itself is technically unproblematic, such a procedure would not necessarily represent an improvement for the organization as a whole. Marketing and sales activities for chain stores have to be centrally initiated and coordinated to a large extent, and orders based on local modifications and expectations may just as well be less accurate than more so compared to those based on a broader material.

Anyway, the point here is not that the technology will force a develop-ment in one direction or another (we repudiated such determinism already in the introductory chapters), or that one direction will, by necessity, yield better results than another, just that *the technology extends the constructible space in both directions.* Information technology thus makes it possible to centralize command in large organizations with great geographical spread to a much larger degree than before, and it allows central management to extend its direct reach of supervision to a much greater depth in the organization. Information technology here clearly enables a significant extension of direct supervision as a coordinat-ing mechanism. The extended mechanism is qualitatively different from the previous version—much more so than the enhancements brought about by the telephone, and I believe the changes merit a separate term: *system-supported supervision* (Figure 14-1).

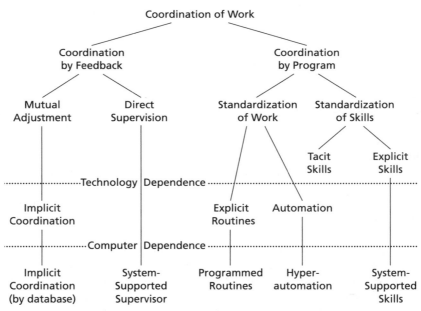

Figure 14-1:   *Taxonomy of coordinating mechanisms extended by the use of informa-tion technology (preliminary).*

System-supported supervision usually means conscious direction of work to great depth and/or great breadth in an organization, based on information gathered and presented through computer-based systems. Directions to subordinates can be given directly by personal communication (including email and voice mail), indirectly as new parameters in application programs or new routines to be followed, or they can even just follow as a consequence of deliveries of goods or other concrete actions. The core is that the results of the subordinates' work can be monitored and directed in sufficient detail through the system, in real time or with a negligible time lag.

Centralization by Hyperautomation and Elimination

Hyperautomation in Zuboff's (1988) mills led to a total centralization of control in the factory. Prior to the introduction of computer-based control systems, the physical control of the process was spread throughout the factory; afterward, control was centralized to one room. In principle, a fully automated factory such as this could be controlled from a single workstation. The qualified jobs (for skilled workers, foremen, and supervisors) outside maintenance were more or less eliminated, and the factory organization was thus effectively truncated below the level of the production manager and his support team.

One of the interesting properties of this brand of centralization is that it is often not viewed as centralization at all, and may even be mistaken for decentralization. Because the positions in such control rooms are almost invariably given to skilled workers that formerly worked on the factory floor, it is not infrequently interpreted in terms of devolvement of responsibility and decentralization of power. To me, it is obviously the opposite: a centralization of power built on the elimination of lower organizational levels. As I argued in Chapter 12, the new powers of the control room operators are not a result of devolvement, but of a de facto functional promotion. The fact that control room operators often find themselves in conflict with their superiors over how the system should be run only corroborates this—as their new responsibilities force them to assume large parts of the role of production manager, it is just natural that such a conflict will develop. Maybe it will be easier to see this if we perform a thought experiment with *Ceramico*, the enterprise of Mrs Raku—Henry Mintzberg's archetype of a growing organization (Mintzberg 1979), briefly described in the beginning of Chapter 3.

Mrs Raku started out by doing everything herself, and obviously had full control of every aspect of her business. In other words, centralization was total. As soon as she started to employ others, control began to slip, but it remained strong as long as everyone worked in the same room. As the enterprise expanded ever further, finally becoming a divisionalized corporation, Mrs Raku had to rely on a growing hierarchy of managers, and her direct control over day-to-day activities diminished sharply. She probably felt the frustration that so many entrepreneurs show when they suddenly have to work through others, and she became a "normal" top manager—far removed from the everyday details of business, and obliged to work through echelons of people with wills and views of their own.

Now, imagine if information technology made such strides that Mrs Raku could totally automate production (except for maintenance and transport), as well as most of the administrative work—having the sales-people in the field update the production system directly, the designers' CAD systems seamlessly link up with the computers controlling the production machinery, purchases and payments handled more or less automatically through EDI-type transactions, and so on. Maybe she could then get almost all the information needed to run the company directly from the computer systems, and could gather the few people who really needed to make decisions in one room—or at least along one corridor. Then much of her lost control would return, and the enterprise would become re-centralized—in the sense that routine work and the work of middle management would be eliminated, concentrating control in far fewer hands. Here, both hyperautomation and system-supported supervision would be used to its fullest potential, and to use an alluring metaphor, we could say that Ceramico would become a *joystick organiza-tion*—a company where all or almost all activities were directly controlled by one person or a very small group of persons, with the help of sophisticated, computer-based systems.

This possibility is not as far-fetched as it may sound—in fact, the hyper-automated pulp mill and the modern automobile factory (e.g., the Nissan Sunderland facility) represent long steps in this direction, and we can expect the development to continue. The great communication capacity of computer-based systems also opens the possibility to stretch the depth of control in joystick organizations over large geographical distances. The most likely early candidates for such large-scale centralization will probably be process industries with a global market as well as a global spread of their production facilities and sources of raw materials.

Centralization by Remote Control

The success of the modern organization was built (among other things) on extensive use of standardized, explicitly described work procedures. In a way, the use of such standardized procedures represents a "remote control" of organization members—their work is, to a large extent, directed by rules laid down by a combination of managers and staff personnel, saving huge management resources compared to organizations based on direct supervision. And, as noted in Chapter 12, administrative computer programs, with their embedded routines, coordination mechanisms, and directions for work, make it possible to extend and refine this control.

However, the increasing sophistication of computer programming can be exploited to increase such "remote control" even further by embedding AI-like functions and making systems active in supervising and directing workers—to let systems assist or even replace human managers.

An example of a fairly simple system of this kind is given by Zuboff (1988), in the case of the WFSS system of Metro Tel discussed earlier. All the maintenance work was registered in the WFSS, which also held a database with the necessary information about all the workers. The system automatically scheduled the workday for each worker, taking into account the location of the tasks (including which floor in the building) and their expected duration to minimize travel time and achieve a workload that had the best possible fit with the length of the working day. The workers started their day by logging into the system to receive a printout of that day's work and reported back to the system for each task that was completed. Even if there were still foremen in the organization, they now worked primarily through the system, entering tasks and monitoring workers through the statistics produced as a result of the task data—the information about completion, etc. logged by the workers. The algorithms in the system then set priorities, calculated the time for completion, and scheduled work for each individual worker.

Siemens in Norway employs a similar system for its nationwide crew of computer maintenance engineers.[3] Their system also includes an inventory database, because, to offer speedy fixes, the service personnel keep a select inventory of spare parts in their cars at all times. When the system "sees" that they need new parts, replenishments are automatically dispatched by post.

An example of a more complex system is a suite of programs used in the Mrs. Fields cookie shop chain (Walton 1989). The company tried to incorporate into the programs Debbie Fields' own expertise in running cookie shops, developed in the early days of her enterprise when she personally managed one of them. As Walton notes, cookies are perishable products, and success depends on good management. As the number of cookie shops grew from a few to dozens and then to hundreds, it became more and more difficult for Debbie Fields and her growing numbers of managers to ensure that the store managers ran the shops the way they

---

[3] Personal communication from sources in Siemens Norge.

wanted them to. Training and supervision were extremely time-consuming, since the shops were geographically dispersed, and the company relied on a young and inexperienced work force with high turnover rates.

The company attempted to solve these problems by applying a number of computer-based systems. For instance, a voice mail system allowed Debbie Fields to address all her employees (or select ones) directly whenever she wanted, and an email system allowed the employees to address her. The core system, however, was a program called the Daily Planner. In this program the company tried to embed as much as possible of Debbie Fields' own experience, selling techniques, and management principles.

Every day, the program required the store manager to enter a number of information items, such as a daily sales projection (based on sales the same day last year, adjusted for a growth factor), the day of the week, the weather, and whether it was a school day. Walton quotes one of Mrs Fields' regional managers, Tom Richman, describing how the program worked from a store manager's point of view (Walton 1989, pp. 36–37):

> Say, for example, it's Tuesday, a school day. The computer goes back to the store's hour-by-hour, product-by-product performance on school-day Tuesdays. Based on what you did then, the Daily Planner tells him, here's what you'll have to do today, hour by hour, product by product, to meet your sales projection. It tells him how many customers he'll need each hour and how much he'll have to sell them. It tells him how many batches of cookie dough he'll have to mix and when to mix them to meet the demand and to minimize leftovers.
>
> The computer revises the hourly projections and makes suggestions. The customer count is OK, it might observe, but your average check is down. Are your crew members doing enough suggestive selling? If, on the other hand, the computer indicates that the customer count is down, that may suggest the manager will want to do some sampling—chum for customers up and down the pier with a tray of free cookie pieces or try something else, whatever he likes, to lure people into the store.
>
> On the other hand, the program isn't blind to reality. It recognizes a bad day and diminishes its hourly sales projections and baking estimates accordingly.

The Daily Planner was not issuing orders that the store managers *had* to follow. It was meant as a guiding and suggestive tool. Inexperienced store managers followed its advice most closely; older hands allowed their own experience to override the system when they thought it best. They needed to keep sales up, however, because their daily results were picked up by a store performance monitoring system, revealing their results to the headquarters based "store controllers." Results lower than expected were sure to attract immediate attention. The computer systems in the shops also helped in a number of administrative tasks, such as workforce scheduling, interviewing of applicants, payroll, and maintenance of bakery equipment.

It is interesting to compare this use of computer systems with the thought experiment we just performed on the case of Henry Mintzberg's Mrs Raku. Debbie Fields readily admitted how difficult it was for her to delegate authority when the company began expanding. Like almost every entrepreneur, she was loath to relinquish her direct control of the baseline activities in her company: "Eventually," she says (Walton, p. 39), "I was forced, kicking and screaming, to delegate authority, because that was the only way the business could grow." So, she tried to hold on to that control through the use of computer systems. She tried to remote-control her shop managers, automate performance control, and establish a communication system that would let her completely bypass middle management. In my view, this represents a serious effort to build the kind of systems suite described in our discussion of Mrs Raku, to create a real-world example of a joystick organization.

If we compare this with a traditional approach to standardization of work—such as the extremely detailed handbook reportedly governing all aspects of work in McDonald's hamburger restaurants (Morgan 1986)— the distinguishing feature of systems like those used by Mrs Fields are their dynamic features. They do not only contain static rules; their algorithms adapt their output according to circumstances (such as time of the year, day of the week, weather, if it is a school day), to the actual sales volume, as well as to a constantly updated repertory of past experience (sales were related to performance on the same day in previous years). Moreover, they do not only answer queries; they "act" proactively, giving directions for corrective action when input (in the form of registered sales) deviates from what the systems' designers (and thereby top management) deem appropriate or acceptable. In addition, the systems (unlike a handbook) report sales directly to centrally placed managers, providing them with the ability to monitor performance on a daily basis, or even in real time, if they so wish. This combination of system-supported supervision, programmed routines, and a dash of artificial intelligence creates a very powerful extension of the explicit routines of the traditional Machine Bureaucracy.

When systems replace managers, as in the examples described here, we should expect problems to crop up if the systems severely reduce the amount of human interaction. After all, humans are social animals and normally crave a certain level of social contact. As we have already seen, this is exactly what happened in the case of Metro Tel's WFSS—most workers missed the old days when they worked in one building as a member of a fairly stable team, and had frequent contact with their foreman and fellow workers. The new situation turned their job into a lonely one, traveling between largely unmanned switching centers and only reporting to computer terminals.

In Siemens there are fewer complaints, probably because many of the service engineers work in small communities throughout the country and would not have had any interaction with colleagues anyway, and because they meet users all the time on their calls (often people they know from earlier visits). They have been deprived of their daily telephone contact with the central service organization, though. Finally, Walton does not report any problem of this kind from Mrs Fields, which may indicate that there were at least no major difficulties. In that case, it seems reasonable to assume that store managers fulfilled their social needs through their constant interaction with crew and customers.

Possibilities for Decentralization

It seems quite evident, then, that information technology can allow for increased control and centralization of power, just as the telephone has. But what about the promise of decentralization of authority and empowerment of employees?

According to Mintzberg's definition, Pool's example of the telephone's decentralizing effects was not an example of decentralization at all, only of dispersed activities. We might add that the reason dispersal was allowed was precisely the improved control over distance that the telephone provided. Thus, the telephone conserved or increased centralization of power and stands out first and foremost as a tool for extending the control of the centers of management—if one is not ready to accept the arguments of McLuhan, Boettinger, Cherry, and others (Pool 1983) that the telephone is functioning as a democratizing tool, allowing easy contacts across levels and departments. "On the telephone, only the authority of knowledge will work," Pool quotes McLuhan (1983, p. 61)[4]. Although I readily acknowledge that any technology that makes communication easier and less formal will have some democratizing effects, I think that the matter is considerably more complex than the quote from McLuhan indicates, and that the telephone in itself plays a fairly minor part in the democratization of the workplace we have seen especially in the latter part of the twentieth century.

When we turn to information technology in its full breadth, however, we face a different situation—computer-based systems represent more than a new communication channel and can extend the possibilities for genuine decentralization in several ways.

---

[4] The quote is from Marshall McLuhan's *Understanding Media*, New American Library, 1964, p. 238.

Decentralization by Information Availability

Perhaps the most basic contribution is the integrity and availability of information stored in databases, as many middle-management tasks can be eliminated by making updated information directly available anywhere in the organization. Not all of the decision making disappears, though, and it tends migrate toward that part of the organization where the information is utilized—often positions at the customer interface. Frequently, this will also lead to decentralization of a number of other decisions that are connected to the same complex of information and customer services. In banks, for instance, people working at the counter were authorized not only to open and close accounts, but to grant limited credits and small loans as well. The implicit coordination obtained by immediate registration of the new credit or loan in the system ensures that an enterprising customer cannot obtain an undue amount of loans by approaching different clerks in a number of subsidiaries. Before the on-line age, this problem was one of the reasons why banks had to centralize such functions.

Decentralization by De-specialization

Another opening that we have discussed already is de-specialization, where the use of embedded knowledge, artificial intelligence, and artificial memory makes it possible for single persons to cover a broader set of tasks than before. Thereby, it facilitates decentralization, especially in connection with increased availability of information. If a broader set of tasks can be gathered in one hand, it means that there will be less need to collect information at more central points in order to make informed decisions. It is not a universal option; it will mainly support jobs that require people to collect information from many sources for further processing, or for use in decision making on the basis of laws, rules, and regulations. De-specialization has its limits, since only "hard" knowledge is possible to embed in ordinary systems or AI systems—tacit knowledge, the kind of "feel" developed through experience, is extremely difficult to extract and implement.

Decentralization by Increasing the Depth of Control

This title may sound self-contradictory—especially after the discussions earlier in this chapter. However, the informating aspects of the technology should also be able to serve as a basis for decentralization in the sense of pushing decision-making powers down and outward in an organization.

The focus here is on the scale of manageable complexity in an organizational context. We have already touched upon the enormous improvements computers have provided in tackling complexity in the scientific and engineering sector. Models of the atmosphere, of waves, of crude oil reservoirs, of pollution—to mention a few of the applications that can be found on the many supercomputers and scientific workstations of the world—enable us to study and predict the behavior of physical systems that are vastly more complex than anything we could ever hoped to tackle in the past. But complexity is also a challenge in terms of organization. Summing up his book *Images of Organization*, Gareth Morgan says the following (1986, p. 339):

> I believe that some of the most fundamental problems that we face stem from the fact that the complexity and sophistication of our thinking do not match the complexity and sophistication of the realities with which we have to deal. This seems to be true in the world of organization as well as in social life more generally. The result is that our actions are often simplistic, and at times downright harmful.

Morgan here points to a central aspect of our continuous struggle to cope with the world, and, more narrowly, to keep complex organizations going and ensure that our actions have the intended outcomes. But it is not only the simplicity of our thinking that represents a problem—part of the trouble can also be found in the limits of our coordinative tools and abilities. Complex tasks require great efforts in coordination, which tends to build hierarchy: information must be gathered and related, and informed decisions can only be made by those with a position central enough to provide them with the necessary information. Information technology has the potential to revolutionize our abilities even in this respect—the new tools for personal support, the coordinative powers of the database, the greatly increased scope for automation, and the informating capacity of computer-based systems converge to improve our capabilities. This is perhaps the very essence of the computer as a tool—that it gives us an unprecedented handle on complexity in almost any area of application: It informates work, and greatly increases our depth of control by providing a more complete understanding of the problem domain as well as exposing more of the consequences of our own actions.

The introduction of CAD in the structural design of the Boeing 777 is an interesting case in point. The "living" model of the evolving airplane provided the designers with an immediate and much better understanding of how the results of their own work meshed with that of others in the project. The individual designer as well as the cross-departmental teams obtained a depth of control earlier achievable only through laborious procedures rooted in a fairly extensive project hierarchy. The new control, moreover, was much more powerful than the old one, since it was based on a tool that could adequately reflect the dynamics of the running design process and thus provide almost real-time control.

The CAD system thus meant that repercussions from an addition or change in the 777 structural design could be ascertained very quickly, both horizontally (for adjoining parts) and vertically (for the subsequent steps in the engineering process). Cross-departmental teams replaced significant parts of the traditional project hierarchies, and considerable decision making power was moved closer toward the origins of design. In this case, then, the informating aspect of a computer-based system provided an increased depth of control, which was, in contrast to the examples reviewed in the section on centralization, exploited by decentralizing power and giving new responsibilities to the lower levels in the organization—which is more in tune with Zuboff's (1988) conclusions.

There are not many examples of this brand of decentralization, however, where depth of control—not sharing of information or despecialization—is the central feature. There could be several reasons for this. First, management traditionally seeks control. Where possibilities for increased depth of control are found, one can assume that managers on various levels will be attracted to it and motivated to exploit it for centralization. Second, increased depth of control is often not planned for—the possibility only surfaces as an unintended effect and is difficult to discover and handle. The pulp mills described by Zuboff (1988) provide examples of this. Third, complexity is difficult—as noted in Chapter 8, the bottleneck for building systems to handle really complex tasks is no longer found in hardware, and not even in basic software, but mainly in our ability to understand the problem domain, analyze the tasks, and design the appropriate systems. Fourth, the decision-making power that is decentralized may not really be centralized in the first place—actually, without the benefit of computer-based systems, it may not even exist as a practical possibility! To illustrate this last proposition, which may seem puzzling, let us consider two examples—one actual and one hypothetical.

We have already discussed airline reservation systems in some detail. Looking at the numbers associated with them, it strikes one at first as fairly massive aggregations of information, but perhaps not too complex—after all, an airplane is an airplane; a seat is a seat; and, even if there are lots of them, the relationships in the database seem simple enough. In its first version, that may also have been the truth. But, as always, when new opportunities open up, humans gradually develop new ways of exploiting them, building complexity along the way.

First of all, a seat is not simply a seat—there are several classes, each with different pricing. This may even imply physically different seats, as first class always has and business class often has—especially on international flights. The number of seats of each type will vary among the particular airplanes, and this must of course be reflected in the database. Pricing is quite differentiated, as airlines try to attract passengers to seats that would otherwise be empty. Airplane seats are perishable commodities; an empty seat at takeoff is equivalent to income irretrievably lost, and the airlines will therefore try to vary prices for particular seats on particular flights to squeeze the maximum profit out of each planeload.

The art of balancing pricing for maximum profit per flight is called *yield management*, which is today viewed as one of the airlines' most important competitive instruments. Good yield management can mean the difference between loss and a handsome profit, and reservation systems allow analysts to manipulate seat pricing and the ratio of differently priced seats in a way that was previously simply impossible. To quote Hopper (1990, p. 121),

> Computers review historical booking patterns to forecast demand for flights up to a year in advance of their departure, monitor bookings at regular intervals, compare our fares with competitors' fares, and otherwise assist dozens of pricing analysts and operations researchers. During routine periods, the system loads 200 000 new industry fares a day. In a "fare war" environment, that figure is closer to 1.5 million fares per day.

The real decision-making power in this case falls to the pricing analysts and operations researchers, especially since many of the changes will be time-critical, and there will be little time for review by line management. The better the systems become, the closer they will come to real-time control, and the less room there will be for direct management involvement, other than as a source of general policy directions. In Mintzberg's terminology, this will amount to horizontal decentralization. Insofar as the decision-making opportunities are new and only made available through the (informating) quality of the systems, it is a power that emerges directly at a decentralized location in the organization.

We can also note that the implicit coordination of the database will then manifest itself—making the new fares immediately available directly at the customer interface the world over and guide travel agents' advice to customers. It is important to note that this coordination is indeed direct and without human intermediaries—the actions of the travel agents and the people in the ticket offices, and even customers who buy directly via Internet, are directly modified by the information entered in the database.

Now for a hypothetical example of an optimizing system (a kind of yield management system) for the health sector in Norway. Norway has a very comprehensive, public health care system, designed to provide (practically free of charge) every citizen with all health services needed. The administration and funding of its various parts are split among the national administrative level, the counties, and the municipal authorities, causing serious suboptimalization because vital feedback loops have been severed through the system's very design.

The system works like this: if you get sick, the national health service pays your benefits until you are well again and can resume work. Now, say you need hospital treatment—simple surgery, for instance. The hospitals are run by the counties, and it does not matter to them (economically) that you are on sick leave, because your benefits are paid out of central government budgets, not theirs. So they can safely leave you waiting for hospital admission for months—even if your operation will cost only a fraction of what you receive in benefits while waiting.

If the counties had been a little more sophisticated, they might at least have calculated their tax loss while you were sick and figured out that it would pay to operate quickly anyway, but they do not. Even if you get so sick that you need help and care at home, or admission to a nursing home, it does no economic harm to the county[5]—these services are run by the municipal authorities and are paid over their budgets. When you finally get treated, the hospital (county) will kick you out as soon as possible and leave you to the municipal services again if you need further help. This is really a classic case of suboptimalization, caused by a failure to establish the necessary feedback loops. The authority that controls the treatment is isolated from the economic consequences of a failure to treat the patient.

The reasons for the resilience of the established system are in large part political/ideological (treatment shall be given to everyone without considerations of economic character, employed should not have advantages over unemployed), but also that very few people have actually realized the problems caused by the lack of feedback and the costs associated with it, even if there have been some very convincing small-scale trials. On top of this comes the problem of solving the problems by administration—the complexity of a coordination effort involving all levels and elements of the national health care system seems truly overwhelming.

Technologically, however, it should be quite straightforward (even if it would require substantial investments and a lot of work) to create a suite of computer systems that would allow a health administration officer to calculate the projected cost of your treatment; match it against the cost of your benefits; check the costs and waiting times of the nearest hospitals

---

[5] Lest anyone who is not familiar with the health care system in Norway is led by this to believe that you are not admitted to a hospital in an emergency, I hasten to add that you are indeed; the delays apply to conditions that can await treatment (even if there are bound to be borderline cases). I should also point out that hospitalization is free—and, as we know from economic theory, when a service or a commodity is free there tends to be an escalation in demand and a need to regulate it by queues. Of course, the severity of the cases in the queues is a function of the total resources used on health services, and that is where the political discussion focuses.

and at hospitals farther off; check the prices and available capacity of certified private hospitals in Norway and other countries, and then make a decision representing a sensible tradeoff between your comfort and well-being and the cost to the health care service. Such a system would also allow the health administration to determine the total performance of the entire national service and tune the capacities of its various parts to achieve the best possible result in view of the given priorities. Because it would lay bare economic causal relations that have hitherto been obscured by the very complexity of the system, it would also give politicians a much better instrument for their decisions.

In short, a quite conventional (albeit large and complex) suite of systems could provide a degree of control over a very complex part of the public services that would be almost unthinkable with traditional tools, and much of the control would end up in the hands of officials at the "customer" interface.

The national health service is perhaps an extreme example, but there are bound to be innumerable large and small spheres of activity where suboptimalization exists because of obscured causal relations and severed feedback loops. Computer-based systems could be used to close those loops and reveal the causal relations, and thus give people in responsible positions much better instruments to manage the complexities of their domains of responsibility—and even to extend their responsibilities considerably. The most serious obstacle for such developments is not technical, but, rather, a question of that old primal part of ourselves: closing feedback loops, revealing causal relations, and extending responsibilities for someone inevitably means that others will lose their large and small empires, have their budgets suddenly linked with someone else's, and so forth. Such changes are bound to be painful and to feed organizational and political infighting, and they will be difficult to effect—no matter how rational they seem when viewed from the outside.

The Migration of Power

All the examples in this chapter—of both centralization and decentralization—have one thing in common. The systems build directly on the most central properties of computer systems: their ability to store very large amounts of information cheaply and indefinitely; to retrieve that information rapidly, reliably, and independently of physical location; and to present it in an accessible form, possibly also with a few analyses performed automatically before presentation. By eliminating paper-bound information flows and by automating information processing and presentation, the systems make it possible to bypass traditional paper-processing administrative hierarchies and deliver the necessary information directly where it is needed. And, as noted earlier, when the middle layers of the organization are bypassed (and partly eliminated), decision-making power tends to follow the information upon which it is based. It migrates toward the "hot spots" in the organization, the places where the needs for decisions arise.

Here, we see the interesting split that is illustrated in the examples presented in this chapter. Customer-related decisions are pushed toward the customer interface, supported by systems used to retrieve information relevant for single transactions, for specific customer-related tasks, or for critical operations in a production process—whereas coordinating and controlling power relating to the whole organization is drawn toward the top, exploiting automation and/or automatic gathering and presentation of information on an aggregate level. In those cases, as we saw in Boeing, where the total result is dependent on a very complex process where no single point in the organization can decide, power migrates toward the process seniors (senior professionals—those who head the project teams).

The location of such "hot spots" may vary from organization to organization, but will most commonly be found at the top (the *strategic apex* in Mintzberg's terminology), the customer interface, and the critical stages in the production process. In service industries, such as banking and insurance, the customer interface will often also represent one of the most critical stages in production. Power and authority should therefore tend to migrate toward those critical decision points, moving aggregate information upward and task-specific information downward. This can happen to a large extent without disrupting the general structure of the organization—a Machine Bureaucracy can survive this process with flying colors and come out strengthened and rejuvenated. As Thompson says, commenting on what he considers the postmodern theorists' premature burial of bureaucracy (Thompson 1993, p. 190, italics in original),

> Organizations *are* frequently becoming leaner and more decentralized, but these trends can be interpreted very differently than the fundamental break with centralized bureaucracy present in postmodern imagery. Essentially what we are seeing is a duality in which the decentralization of the labour process and production decisions (through mechanisms as diverse as profit centres, subcontracting and quality circles); is combined with increased centralization of power and control over the spatially dispersed, but interdependent units.

However, not everything is preserved. The middle layers of any organization easily become big losers in this process, because much of their raison d'être is just aggregation and processing of information for superiors, and channeling of information among subordinates. As power migrates toward the strategic and operational levels, therefore, the middle layers in the organization should shrink significantly. Moreover, to exploit the potential benefits of computer-based systems, it is necessary not only to let this migration of authority and responsibility happen, but to promote it actively. It is also necessary to empower the people working in the nonmanagerial "hot spots." Even if the framework becomes more tightly controlled (such as strengthened financial controls), the discretionary powers of the people in the hot spots should nevertheless be increased, if the benefits the new tools can provide are to be fully exploited.

It is also extremely important to understand that these jobs will change radically in the process—they will incorporate parts of the roles formerly filled by managers and professionals on higher levels, and demand more advanced skills, a more pronounced talent for abstract thinking, and a greater feeling of responsibility for the organization as a whole. Not everyone will be ready or able to make this transition.

It turns out, then, that Pool's proposition for the telephone holds up well for computer-based systems—the same technology that allows centralization can also support decentralization. But, as George and King argue, the movements in those two directions are neither similar nor mutually excluding—the relationships between computer-based systems and organizations are intricate and dependent on many factors, both social and technological. However, computer-based systems will facilitate the movement of aggregate information for business guidance toward the strategic apex, and information relevant for actual transactions or production processes toward the customer interfaces and factory floors—information that formerly had to be painstakingly collected, processed, and moved in paper-based information flows, involving many people and organizational levels, and even information so complex in origins or processing that it had not been available with traditional tools at all. Leavitt and Whisler's (1958) prediction that middle management would fall upon hard times is valid indeed.

Control: The More Sinister Aspects

So far, we have only discussed new opportunities for centralization and decentralization in a normal, democratic setting, where due respect for human rights and the right to privacy is taken for granted. Unfortunately, that is not always a valid assumption. It makes one shudder to think what Hitler or Stalin could have achieved with information technology—and even more at the thought that they were probably not the last of their kind to appear on the world scene.

Information technology gives people bent on control and surveillance a dangerous new set of tools. For example, in many countries today, you can have a small chip implanted in your dog (usually in the neck), carrying a unique identification number (Hesselholt et. al. 1992). If the dog becomes lost, an appropriately equipped police or veterinarian can read out the number by placing a reader at the appropriate spot over the chip. A national register will then inform them of the owner's name and address. The system is also useful for breeding purposes, and it is now routinely used to identify dogs in important sled races. Such systems are even applied to identify fish in fish farms for research purposes. The possibilities of this technology are daunting indeed.

A similar technology has been implemented for the collection of toll fees for automobiles—around several Norwegian cities, for example, one can find electronic toll stations. As a subscriber, you will have a chip glued to the windshield of your car, and each time you pass through the toll station, a computer system picks up the car's identity, checking it against the central database for the city to see if you have paid. If your subscription is valid for a number of passages rather than for a period of time, the system will deduct one passage from the number you have left. It performs this operation in the few tenths of a second it takes you to pass the antenna and reach the pole with the warning light and the camera. If you have five passages or less left, a white signal will flash at you, and if you have none left or do not have a chip at all, a red light will flash and your car and license plate will be photographed. A few days later, you will receive the appropriate bill in the mail. You are not supposed to pass at speeds higher than 70 kilometers per hour, but taxi drivers have assured me that the system seems to work well past 100. I have not had the nerve to test that for myself.

One can well imagine that Hitler would have been very pleased with the ability to implant such a chip into every Jew and put up detectors in their homes and in relevant public places—and that Stalin would have taken the opportunity to do the same with suspected "enemies of the state." Judging by the enormous surveillance machinery revealed when the former East Germany collapsed, one might even ask if some leaders would perhaps be prepared to equip *all* their citizens with such a convenient identification tag, and have the muscle to actually do it. Still more chilling, it is probably only a matter of a decade or two before computers can recognize faces quite reliably, making surveillance even easier and harder to detect.

Used in this way, information technology would become the first realistic tool for achieving a measure of control at the level of or even beyond that described by Orwell in *1984*, since much of the surveillance could be automated. Access to any area could be automatically controlled, every citizen could be assigned individual restrictions on movement, and the patterns of movement of persons and even groups could be continuously monitored and analyzed by computer systems, alerting the attention of human surveillants only when anything suspicious turned up.

Hopefully, this is somewhat beyond what we would expect in democratic societies and the organizations in which we work. Indeed, to forestall unwanted surveillance, governments increasingly impose new laws and regulations restricting both their own and private corporations' leeway in collecting and using information on private citizens. For instance, Norwegian authorities have instructed the company collecting the toll fees in Oslo that they are not allowed to store information in their database about when and where a particular car has passed. Only the balance of the car's subscription account may be retained.

In spite of this, there is already talk about equipment that can be installed in every car—recording not only the amount of use, but when, where, and with what speed. The idea is that it will allow the authorities to price the use of roads directly, not only through excise duties and toll fees, and to price it differently according to date and time of day. No doubt, well-meaning people will also advocate the use of such gadgets for catching speeders and generally controlling the behavior of drivers in order to increase safety.

Related to this is the ability to monitor performance. Some of you may recall the controversy raised in the early 1980s when Wang introduced word-processing systems that allowed supervisors to monitor the performance of secretaries (the number of characters typed). Similar controls can easily be devised in many work situations involving computers. Not only can one monitor the amount of work, but often also speed, quality, the number and length of breaks, and general work patterns. We have certainly entered an age where vigilance against unwarranted surveillance and control—private as well as public—is more important than ever before. Have you, for instance, ever thought about the record of your travels that some airline reservation systems keep accumulating? Or the spending patterns revealed by your credit card accounts? The history of telephone calls registered by your telephone company? Remember that with the new digital switches now in operation in most modern countries, the destination and duration of every single telephone call can be recorded and stored.

To complete this chapter, I will relate a story brought to my attention by Professor Jon Bing of the Norwegian Research Center for Computers and Law. This story shows that even the activity pattern reflected in the database of your local electricity board may have amazing potentials.

In the late 1970s Rudolf Clemens Wagner, one of the central terrorists in the notorious German *Rote Arme Fraktion* was surprised by the police and arrested in his flat in Hamburg. How had the police tracked him down? They suspected that he lived in Hamburg, but they had no idea about where. They knew, however, of some occasions when he was demonstrably elsewhere in Germany, participating in RAF activities. By matching his suspected travel pattern with the database over electricity consumption kept by the Hamburg Electricity Service and analyzing the resulting data closely for other clues, they were left with a very small number of flats—and in one of them, the suspect was found.[6]

However chilling these examples may seem, let us not make the mistake of labeling information technology an "evil" technology. The general qualities of computer systems that allow such monitoring are the abilities to record information automatically; to store very large amounts of information cheaply and indefinitely; to aggregate, transform, and analyze it automatically; and to present the results in an easily accessible form. They are the same abilities that make Benetton's extended production system possible, and the examples presented here just show us that IT can, like any other technology, be used for both good and bad. It is up to us and our own vigilance to ensure that the technology is not used for oppressive purposes.

---

[6] The example is reported in more detail in the third annual report of the German Federal Data Protection Commissioner, 1981, p. 50.

V
The New Organizations

In the four chapters in Part IV, we analyzed the way computer-based enhancements to our preconditions for organizing extended the space of constructible organizations. The main extensions can be summed up thus:

- Increases in personal productivity eliminate routine jobs. This tends to increase the ratio of team-oriented jobs in organizations.
- Computer-based systems allow improved group cooperation over distance and can improve social cohesion in teams and groups who cannot otherwise meet. The prospects of dispersed organizations ("virtual organizations") are improved, but social and emotional constraints limit their attractiveness.
- Automation and hyperautomation allow large-scale elimination of work, even of work that cannot be automated directly. Organizations may be truncated, thereby totally changing character and even structural configuration—generally in adhocratic direction.
- The implicit coordination achieved through databases also allows for extensive elimination of work. The potential is great for both simpler (banks) and more complex work (engineering design). This will allow for much larger organizations than before; it can make large organizations more responsive and improve the quality and diversity of their output.
- Computer-based systems also make it easier to couple separate organizations closer together. The coordination may be very strong, as in extended value chains that are wholly or partly automated under common control programs.
- Implicit coordination can support large entities that are organized, but still not constitute organizations in the classic sense.
- Computer-based systems allow extensive centralization of power through informating. Management can surveil performance in real-time, both aggregate and in detail, and supervision of subordinates can be automated ("remote control"). Work elimination also contributes to centralization.

- Computer-based systems may allow increased decentralization through improved information availability, de-specialization and by increasing the depth of control. Decentralization mainly takes the form of a migration of customer-oriented decisions toward the organization's periphery (the customer interface).

In a way, we have now fulfilled the original purpose of our investigation. We have analyzed information technology's strong and weak points, we have established how it allows us to alter the set of organizational preconditions, and we have analyzed how these improved preconditions in their turn allow for new extensions to the space of constructible organizations.

However, we have still not fully analyzed the consequences of the combined effects of these extensions. The discussion has verged on combining two or more of the extensions at several points in the last four chapters; however, to do so would have anticipated later discussions and caused a break in the narrative. I have therefore waited until the last three chapters to bring the whole picture together. Moreover, since Mintzberg's structural configurations were so centrally positioned in the discussion of the organizational platform in Chapter 3, I cannot end this book without discussing if and how the extensions to the space of constructible organizations combine to modify the configurations and perhaps create altogether new ones.

This discussion will come in Chapter 16, "The New Configurations." Before that, however, I must discuss two other topics that are central for understanding how intimate the connection between organizations and computer-based systems are becoming: that is, what will it *really* mean to build organizations with information technology? In Chapter 15, "Toward the Model-Driven Organization," I will therefore first discuss the status of computer programs as building blocks of organizations, when organizations are viewed as patterns of action in line with the discussion in Chapter 2. As such programs become ever more prominent parts of the organizational fabric, action theory will have to confront this problem. Next, I will return to the conceptual model, which was first discussed in Chapter 7. We noted there that this model was at the heart of the emergence of the modern organization, which was built within the literate paradigm. At first, organization designers were probably not aware that they were actually constructing models and using them for organizational improvements. Later, however, and especially after computers and computer programming were introduced, the concept of the model and modeling activity became very explicit. Models will be extremely important for the organizations of the future—indeed, we seem to be heading toward a situation where active models will make up the central elements in most organizations.

15
Toward the Model-Driven Organization

"From the moment of birth we are immersed in action, and can only fitfully guide it by taking thought."
Alfred North Whitehead, *Science and the Modern World*, 1925

ORGANIZATIONS: PATTERNS OF ACTION, PATTERNS OF LOGIC

Before going on with the analysis, I would like to address the question of the status of computer programs—the logic governing the computers—as compared to human actions in organizations. This is especially important, since I have supported a combination of an action and a systems approach to organization theory.

I have argued that the modern organization was a product of the literate society and the literate mind. Its defining feature, and indeed its foundation, was the explicit, conscious design of the recurring patterns of action that constitute organizations. Whereas the patterns of action that constitute organizations just *emerged* within the traditional oral paradigm, they were to a much larger degree *consciously constructed* within the modern literate paradigm. I also held that automation represented the utmost in such design, but deferred to Silverman (1970) and others in reserving the term "action" for human actions, talking instead about "machine movements." I could also have used the term "behavior," which, according to Silverman, only designates observable, outward conduct, and can thus also be used for the operations of inanimate matter. In Silverman's sense, "action" is more than behavior, it implies the meanings the actor attribute to the actions, and meaning is something that cannot exist outside a sentient mind.

Even if they embodied a modest amount of logic, in the form of "canned actions," automatic mechanical machines could still be seen as belonging to the old world of tools used to augment human work. As such, they could fairly easily be contained within the original perspective of the action theorists, reflected in Silverman's definitions of "action" and "behavior." When we enter the computer age, however, the distinctions begin to blur, because the computer, as it now appears, is not first and foremost a machine in the old sense of the word. The ability to store and execute programs has made the computer a new kind of universal machine, and modern microelectronics has increased the amount of logic per gram of matter by so many orders of magnitude compared to mechanical automation as to create an altogether new class of machines. Even the average PC must chiefly be looked upon as an exceedingly complex system of logic, a logic that represents (in executable terms) an extremely large repertory of "canned actions" designed and implemented by systems analysts, designers, and programmers.

Thus, even if the computers and programs themselves are inanimate and cannot attach meaning to their behavior any more than a pebble on the beach, the programs are the result of a painstakingly detailed analysis and design, full of both meaning and intent on the side of their creators—a process Yates and Benjamin (1991, p. 77) call the "capturing of procedural knowledge in computer programs." This meaning and intent is to a considerable degree preserved in the structure and functioning of the programs. Of course, even computers running sophisticated programs cannot be viewed as actors on par with humans (for instance, no program has yet passed the Turing test[1]), but they preserve and display too much of their creator's intents and interpretations to be brushed off as inanimate in the old sense of the word. When using a program in the course of their work, people will to a large extent be compelled to view a designated part of the world (the problem domain that the program addresses) through the eyes of the program's creators. Most users will also have an acute feeling of engaging in a kind of *interaction* when they work with their computers—not only of wielding a tool, as when one uses a hammer to drive in nails. This interaction will of course be partly self-referential, since

---

[1] The Turing test is an experimental setup where a person is put in a room with a terminal and a keyboard, connected to a computer in another room that is either controlled by a program or by a person. The person in the first room is then asked to determine if there is a machine or a person in the other end by typing questions on the screen and watching the answers. No program has (to my knowledge) been able to consistently pass as human in such tests. A particularly elegant way of deciding the nature of the respondent that has been used is not to pose any questions at all. A computer will wait patiently for ever (if its programmer has not anticipated such a situation), whereas a human, after a fairly short while, will start asking if there is anybody out there, or if something is wrong.

the computer's response will regularly include feedback on the user's own actions, but it also constitutes, in large part, an interaction with the logical structure created by the program's designers.

This is, by the way, why it is so extremely important that systems analysts and designers have a keen understanding of the meanings prospective users will attach to the system's responses—and not just concentrate on the organization's objectives, the designated problem domain and the tasks the system should support/supplant/eliminate. That is what cognitive ergonomics is all about. (A good discussion of many of the details in this process can be found in Eason 1988).

When we use computers in an organizational context, therefore, the result will not only be a system of recurring patterns of live human action—which we now should call *living patterns of action*—but a system where such patterns of action are intertwined with patterns of logic residing in computer systems, logic that represents carefully designed *programmed patterns of action*. In fact, the combined patterns of action of people and computers may be so tightly integrated and intertwined that it is difficult to conceive of them as separate systems—which, indeed, I believe to be wrong anyway.

To me, it is therefore impossible to escape the conclusion that this logic, these patterns of programmed action, must be regarded as an important part of the total system of actions that constitute an organization. Likewise, the process of program development must also be included, since it is there that the patterns of programmed action are determined and translated into executable logic. To underline the importance of this process and its vital role in the construction of both present and (especially) future organizations, we may even rename the program development process *program construction.*

The introduction of computer-based systems therefore creates a new level of sophistication and complexity in organizations. It also creates a new level of abstraction, since actions will be tied to symbols to a much higher degree than before and the formalization inherent in the programmed patterns of action will permeate much of the dialogues. The structure and functioning of the organization will no longer be determined only by living patterns, created and carried out in real time by the organization members and the members of relevant parts of the environment. Programmed patterns, consciously designed, will increasingly influence the structure and functioning of the organization. They will influence them directly, because important parts of the organization's structure and functioning will be implemented in computer-based systems, and they will influence them indirectly as well—because the nature of these programs will exert strong influence even on the live actions of their users.

THE ASCENDANCE OF THE ACTIVE MODEL

When explicit, conscious design was put to use as a tool for the construction of organizations, the conceptual model became its alter ego. The deliberate analysis and the conscious planning and design processes opened the organization and the work procedures to innovation and systematic improvement, starting it on a trajectory that differentiated it more and more from the familial-social-commercial continuum of organization that characterized preindustrial society.

At first, the introduction of computer-based systems seemed only to be a matter of continuing this process, especially since it all started with discrete applications for narrow sets of tasks, such as accounting and filing, exploiting the most basic properties of computer-based systems. When applications expanded beyond the single task, and we learned to link them, we entered the next level of computer use—where focus was shifted toward larger groups of tasks or even complete processes, and where the new, computer-based coordinating mechanisms emerged as important tools. It is this second level that has produced most of the examples presented in the preceding chapters; and it is on that level most of the development efforts today are concentrated, at least in larger organizations. There is still much to do there—we are far yet from exhausting the primary properties of computer-based systems and the basic, computer-dependent mechanisms for coordinating and directing work.

However, as the use of information technology is both broadened and deepened and our theoretical sophistication grows, I believe we will see a development away from the (relatively) simple application of the basic coordinating mechanisms toward a third level, which will be characterized by a potentially dramatic ascendance of the conceptual model to a dynamic and much more commanding position in the daily life of organizations. This is when the difference between computer-based and previous tools will really start to show.

From Passive to Active Models

The foundation of this development is the programmability of computers and their rapidly increasing power, which provide the basis for the increasingly rich repertory of software we have at our disposal. These programs are the result of an analysis and design process much more detailed and deep-probing than any earlier, with the possible exception of the design of fully automatic mechanical machines—which also presupposes a detailed, complete, and unequivocal description of the tasks to be executed. But mechanical automation is necessarily so much more limited in scope that it really cannot be compared to computer-based systems.

In the construction of computer programs, the modeling process itself has become a conscious activity to a much larger degree than before. Although the Machine Bureaucracies of the literate paradigm were certainly consciously constructed, the designers were probably not aware that they were actually first working out a (however rudimentary) conceptual model to use as a blueprint. Today, we have taken a significant step forward, as detailed, conscious modeling has become a normal part of systems design—which means that it is also increasingly a prerequisite for organizational design, even though organization people have not yet looked seriously at the methods of systems design as a tool also for purely organizational development (which I think they should). There are now several well-developed methodologies available, and the three leading factions have even joined forces and created a common modeling language called UML (Universal Modeling Language), which seems set to play an important role in the future (for an introduction to UML, see Fowler 1997).

There is also a good number of computer-based tools for modeling available, and there is a clear development toward a closer and closer integration between analytical tools, modeling tools, and program development tools. Ideally, the model should be the main focus of program construction and maintenance, and the actual computer program code should be generated more or less automatically by a combination of modeling tools and program development tools. Considerable resources are today dedicated to this end, in both the commercial and academic worlds.

Computer-based systems are therefore increasingly not only systems; they are also much more clear-cut representations of conceptual models than previous organization structures. We may in fact say that a computer-based system incorporates its own model while also representing that model's expression—or at least a part of the expression, since there will usually be human actors involved in a system-oriented dialogue (the exception is, of course, purely technical systems without organizational references). Even that dialogue will, however, be strongly constrained by the system's inherent model, which can only allow actions (accept input) that are defined within it. In addition to being descriptive, therefore, the model inherent in a computer-based system is not only a passive blueprint for design, it is also *active*, in the sense that it becomes a part of the ongoing patterns of actions constituting the organization. Its role in this web of actions is moreover not only receptive, but even directive, in that its reservoir of programmed actions can generate responses that guide or direct the actions of its human operators. Even the most humble computer-based system, therefore, involves the modeling of a part of the organization's problem domain.

Take, for instance, Ford's accounts payable system described earlier. This system implicitly represents a model of the relationships between the functions of buying, receiving, and paying for goods; and it stores the information pertaining to those functions. In the model there are unequivocal definitions of what an order is, what a delivery confirmation is, what a payment is, and how they are related. When a shipment is received, information about it is no longer communicated to another clerk for processing—when keyed in on the terminal as a confirmation of a match with an outstanding order, the information is instead communicated to the system (and thereby to the model). According to the definitions built into the model, the system then automatically updates the inventory record and generates a payment transaction. In addition, everyone with access to the system can immediately see the status of that delivery if they need to and act accordingly.

As long as the systems are few and they only address narrow, isolated parts of the problem domain, the potential advantages of the single, computer-extended coordinating mechanisms we have discussed in the previous chapters will dominate. When systems multiply, their fields of operation will increasingly meet or even overlap, resulting in both a need and a wish to integrate their operations in order to reap the full benefits of systems use. In turn, this will necessitate a more comprehensive and unified conceptual model of a growing part of the organization's problem domain, a model that will be incorporated into the web of integrated systems. If this web of systems becomes sufficiently comprehensive, we will reach a situation where the major part of the operative actions constituting the organization (the interactions that are directly relevant for the organization's purposes) will be directed toward and through the computer-based systems, and not directly toward other humans.

Somewhere around that point, we will cross a threshold. The main constituting part of the organization will be the integrated computer-based systems, their programmed patterns of action, and, implicitly, the conceptual model they are based on. The coordination of the organization members will then be mediated mainly by the systems and thereby (logically) by the model, not by direct human communication. Such an organization will not only be model based; it will be *model driven*, and the model, integrating several of the computer-dependent coordinating mechanisms, will constitute a supermechanism for coordinating organizations.

In my view, this development harbours a second paradigm shift in human organization. Paradigm shifts are often proclaimed these days; there is hardly a more misused word in computerdom, where even quite modest product innovations are trumpeted as paradigm breakers. So, it is with some reluctance I bring it up. However, the transition from a passive, descriptive model and the three original technology-dependent coordinating mechanisms to an active model and the five computer-dependent ones constitutes a deep shift in the structure and inner workings of organizations, a shift that in my view is at least comparable in scope to the shift from the oral to the literate paradigm. I propose to call this emerging paradigm the *computerate paradigm*.

I believe that most large organizations will reach a stage where they are model-driven, and that the computerate paradigm will thus supersede the literate. However, it will not completely replace it, since the literate paradigm will still live on as the preferred frame of reference for organizations where it proves too difficult to implement active models. We should also bear in mind that the oral paradigm still dominates in the realm of small organizations, and is likely to do so in the foreseeable future. Kuhn's natural science paradigms replace each other totally; if the term is to be used in organization science, we will have to accept the notion of layered paradigms.

Early Examples

Can we find examples already? I believe we can. There are indeed organizations that have already approached the computerate paradigm, at least for part of their operations. Let us review a couple of the organizations discussed earlier with this new perspective as a guideline. Perhaps the most instructive example is the Boeing 777 case discussed in Chapter 13, since it involves the kind of model we are most familiar with: a model of a physical object.

The really interesting part of the Boeing example—and what makes it a prototype of model-driven organization—is that the CAD system the engineers worked with did not contain unrelated data or data sets, but a carefully defined conceptual model of the organization's main problem domain, the airplane. On the workstation screen, each engineer at all times—and at his or her own discretion—had access to the visualized, fully updated (in real time) model of not only his or her own design, but of all the adjoining designs and indeed the model of the total construction (if so authorized). The evolving model also allowed project managers at all levels to follow the progress of work in real time.

If we believe the reports, the system had two main advantages: it eliminated large parts of the traditional project bureaucracy needed to handle drawings and coordinate the efforts of the many designers and design groups, and it allowed for the integration of previously discrete steps in the design and engineering process. There is little doubt that this advance in coordination did not come from an improvement in direct interpersonal communication, but was rooted in the way the project members now communicated *indirectly but collectively* through their individual interactions with the evolving model of the aircraft. By changing the part of the model within his or her area of responsibility, the designer would *automatically* communicate that change to all the other designers, who could, in turn, respond directly to the change if it had consequences for their own work. And, when project groups had to meet (which they still had to) to decide upon design parameters or questions related to physical production, they had the advantage of having a common, unequivocal, and updated conceptual model as a basis for their discussions.

Now, the nature and advantages of models are fairly easy to understand as long as we stick to the design of physical objects such as airplanes. Can we imagine administrative models of this kind?

Let us return to the airline booking system: we can now reinterpret it as a quite interesting model. Seemingly, it represents just a collection of aircraft models—much simpler than the Boeing 777 model, of course, but still aircraft models. In this problem domain, which concerns the sale and administration of airplane passenger capacity, only a few of the airplane's properties are of any interest—mainly the number of seats, seating arrangements, speed, and range.

However, the booking system does not exist to model individual, physical airplanes, but to model flights—that is, particular airplanes flying particular runs at particular times. The same physical airplane will therefore appear a large number of times in the database, each time associated with a different set of departure and destination points and departure and arrival times (maybe also with different seating arrangements, if they are modified between flights—which they sometimes are). Because locations and points in time are represented in the model, the system is even capable of modeling something much more complex—namely, the full web of all the flights present in the database, with all the possibilities they offer for interconnections and transfers to cover routes not served by direct flights. This is the part of the model that the travel agent and the passenger see and care about. To the airlines, there are other aspects of it as well—for instance requirements for crews, catering, and fuel.

For the purpose of seat reservation, then, and even for a number of the airlines' administrative tasks, the chief instrument for coordination is the system and thereby its inherent model of that particular problem domain. For seat reservation, the system is in fact the *only* coordination instrument. We can therefore say that seat reservation is an example of an activity that is 100% model driven. True, the users of this system do not constitute a traditional organization, but there seems to be no fundamental reason why "proper organizations" should not be able to base the full weight of their coordination needs on active models in the same way. It will perhaps not be possible for all organizations, due to the nature of their problem domains, but in many instances I believe it will mainly be a question of learning how to model and handle really complex domains.

Another interesting example, which we have already discussed at some length in Chapter 14, is the cookie shop operation of Mrs Fields. The system called the Daily Planner was meant to incorporate as much of Debbie Fields' own experience, selling techniques, and management principles as possible, in order to enable the inexperienced shop manager to run a shop like a professional (and to keep him or her within the style of operations that Debbie Fields preferred). The system would generate directions to the shop manager based on a number of parameters and an internal repository of rules.

We can now easily see that the people who made the system did in fact create a fairly complete model of the cookie shop's problem domain, and constructed a program that expressed that model quite effectively. For the shop managers, it must have been almost as if Debbie Fields were standing right next to them throughout the day. To the Mrs Fields organization as a whole, it meant that supervision was by and large effected through this system and the model it represented, and to implement changes in policy or in product mix would first and foremost be a matter of changing the system (and thereby the model).

I do not have information about the flexibility of the system—if it was able to adapt to local patterns of demand, for instance—but such flexibility is certainly possible in principle. A general model can be built to adapt itself through accumulation of local data (e.g., sales patterns), and thus adjust to some extent to different local mixes of contingency factors. However, the adaptation can never exceed the limits set by the definitions in the original model. If, for example, the ethnic mix of the neighborhood is not defined as a parameter in the model, it cannot be used for local adaptation, unless the local operators are authorized to modify the model itself.

A Typology of Models

If we look at these examples, the models show clear differences in both design and operation. The differences arise from their differences in purpose and are manifested through how they use and combine basic system properties. Can we discern some main types? The answer is a cautious "yes"—there are indeed clearly distinguishable types of models, but we encounter the same problem here as we do with Mintzberg's (1979) coordinating mechanisms and their corresponding organization types: organizations in real life seldom represent pure forms. However, if we reconcile ourselves with the fact that our concepts, theories, and models can never represent or explain the full richness of real social phenomena, we can nevertheless appreciate how apt archetypes can help us see and understand important, often decisive, aspects of reality. Even if their explanatory power is limited, they can nevertheless be of great help and make it possible for us to analyze problems more accurately and to design more functional organizations.

I propose three basic kinds of models, then, each based on a combination of computer-dependent coordinating mechanisms, and each representing a main direction in the computer-based enlargement of the space of constructible organizations. They are the *regulating model*, the *mediating model* and the *assisting model*. For an informal characterization, we may nickname them respectively the "boss model," the "peer model" and the "sage model."

The Regulating Model

As its name implies, the purpose of the regulating model is to direct and control the activities in an organization. Regulating models often incorporate extensive automation, and the organizations that have come closest to being driven by regulating models today are probably the most advanced manufacturing organizations, for example, a number of process industries and automobile manufacturers. Perhaps the properties of regulating models are most visible in operations such as the Nissan factory in Sunderland, briefly described in Chapter 12. The production control system there manages virtually all aspects of the assembly process, including the timing of deliveries from the key suppliers located around the perimeter of the factory premises. Actually, we may well view the combined production control systems of both the Nissan factory and its suppliers as one supersystem, based on a master model, driving the operations of the combined organizations.

The model behind the Daily Planner of Mrs Fields is also an example of a regulating model—it both directs the work of the personnel in every shop *and* controls their performance—but it is different from the Nissan model in one key aspect: it does not include the lock-step coordination of a production process with numerous interdependent steps. In the Mrs Fields organization the shops are independent from each other, and have no need to coordinate their actions the way the different stations on an assembly line must. The coordination here is first and foremost a matter of regimentation—of securing a scrupulous and uniform execution of company directives. We may therefore say that there are two kinds of regulating models: a *linked* model, driving organizations where tasks are *inter*dependent, and an *atomistic* model, driving organizations where they are *in*dependent.

The regulating model depends mainly on system-supported supervision, programmed routines, and hyperautomation, but it also often incorporates implicit coordination. If we look at the completed taxonomy of coordinating mechanisms in Figure 15-1 this should indicate that regulating models imply a combination of Mintzberg's direct supervision and standardization of work—in other words, a merger of real-time and programmed coordination. This is exactly what I believe the development of sophisticated and comprehensive regulating models will tend to effect. The richness, interactivity, and computational capacity of computer-based systems will allow us to blend the two modes in a way not previously possible, and thus allow us to construct organizations that are large, extremely efficient, agile, and flexible. In the extreme case, regulating models may allow what we have termed a *joystick organization*: an organization where large parts of the activities are either automated or directed

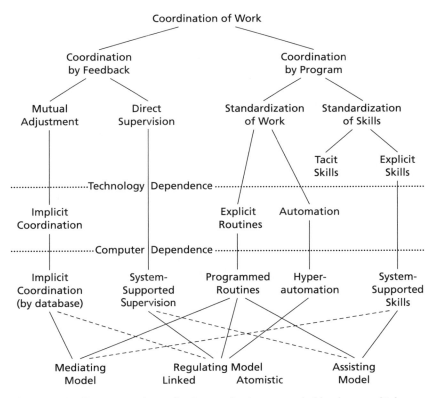

Figure 15-1: *Taxonomy of coordinating mechanisms extended by the use of information technology (complete).*

by the systems, but where key parameters and activities are controlled and carried out in real time by the management.

The flexibility of an organization driven by a regulating model cannot, of course, transcend the limits of the model, since all allowable actions and action alternatives must be predefined and incorporated in it. Regulating models are only possible to use when tasks, their execution, and their interrelations can be defined in necessary detail beforehand. This is a tough demand, but not impossible—it has also been a prerequisite for mechanical automation, for much factory work, and for large parts of the work carried out in earlier white collar bureaucracies such as banks and insurance companies. And, since computer-based systems can accommodate much richer models and provide much better work support than was previously possible, the prospects for building strongly regulated organizations are now greatly improved and will continue to improve in the future.

The Mediating Model

There is, however, work that is too complex and with circumstances too dynamic for tasks and outcomes to be defined beforehand—or even work that involves designing new products or processes, essentially creative work where the process steps can be known, but not their content. This is the kind of work where organizations are drawn toward the configuration Mintzberg calls an Adhocracy, and where coordination must rely on mutual adjustment or an adaptation of it. When efficiency cannot be sought primarily through pre-planning and programming, the goal must be to achieve the best possible exchange of information and ideas, to speed the process of mutual adjustment, and to ensure that conflicts are resolved and agreements reached with a minimum of effort.

This may sound like a cry for groupware and "networking"—but it is not. That does not mean that the kind of systems gathered under the banner "groupware" do not have a mission, or will not be part of systems built on a mediating model—it only means that direct human-to-human communication is very time-consuming, often inexact, and very often directed toward a set of people that includes many who do not need the information and omit a few who actually do. We will be much better helped if we can let the systems do as much work as possible on their own, as well as help us make our own communication more precise and directed toward *only* those who need it and only *when* they need it.

An organization driven by a mediating model, then, is much more than an organization consisting of teams communicating via computer networks, accessing common information bases, and coauthoring electronic documents. If we say that an organization is model driven, the model and the suite of systems built on it must incorporate so much of the organization's functionality and dynamics that the organization members will work and communicate mainly with the *system* and thus the model itself, and *not* with particular people. This only pertains to task-related communication, of course, not social exchanges.

The situation can be pictured as a group of people playing a board game. They may chat and joke, but their effective contributions toward their common goal (to have fun by finishing the game) and their effective, game-relevant communication with each other is made solely through their separate, individual interaction with the board and the game's rules (which are reflections of the game model). The consequences they suffer are partly a result of the vagaries of the rules, and partly of the other players' moves (their contributions). Any player's options at any point in time are a result of the rules (the model) and the accumulated results of all the players' previous moves; all players have a full view of the situation at any time; and the information available is always current.

The CAD model that was the centerpiece of the Boeing 777 design project is precisely an example of such a model. The CAD system was the main tool both for the people working at the design and for those doing the preparations for manufacturing. The resulting structural model of the aircraft, which resided in the system's database, then functioned as the project's prime communication medium. The way it functioned is instructive. Changes were primarily *not* communicated directly to those concerned and those who might possibly be concerned; they were simply entered into the system (model). Those who *were* concerned could then extract that part of the information they needed when they needed it. Just as importantly, the information was not entered into the system in separate, dedicated operations, it was in fact *created* there as a part of the normal work process, as the designers and others used the system as a tool for their day-to-day work. Creation and communication were thus merged into one process, ensuring that the database always contained the latest version of everybody's contribution. When meetings were necessary to decide on design parameters or other problems, all the participants could therefore draw their basic information from the same coherent source. Moreover, the CAD system itself could eliminate a lot of work by automatically finding and exposing problems such as spatial conflicts, as well as helping to quickly resolve questions where the system contained the pertinent information. The system thus provided the main tools for work, structured the communication by acting as medium, made the communication a lot more precise because of its criteria for information entry and information creation, and made the communication process much more selective by eliminating most of the communication that takes place "just to be on the safe side."

The models behind the organization-like features of travel agent behaviour when coordinated by reservation systems are also mediating models. They may seem to be regulating, in the sense that the systems only allow certain actions and also contain inviolable rules on how transactions are to be effected, but the essence of systems such as trading systems and reservation systems is not to direct and control the actions of the users, as it is in production control systems such as Nissan's or Mrs Fields'. Their purpose is to ensure that all the users have access to the same status information at any time, and that this status information *always* (in real time) reflects the accumulated sum of all the users' system-relevant actions. In this way the users' actions can be perfectly coordinated by mutual adjustment without a single direct user-to-user message. The users only have to access the information that is *immediately* relevant for their own purposes and can safely ignore the rest.

The mediating model depends mainly on implicit coordination and programmed routines, but it may also contain aspects of system-supported skills to support professional work. The model's revolutionary aspect is that it makes *true mutual adjustment* a real alternative in much larger organizational settings than before. With earlier technology, mutual adjustment in organizations of more than a handful of people was only possible through representative and consultative schemes, which often generated a lot of overhead—as in the project bureaucracies of large design projects, with their innumerable drawings and time-consuming modification procedures. Comprehensive mediating models will effectively remove the theoretical upper limit for true mutual adjustment. The model requirements will be no less stringent than for regulating models, however, the problem domain must be accurately and sufficiently described, and all relevant relations between the significant items in the domain must be mapped. This is a very demanding task, but I believe we will gradually develop the necessary skill, methods, and tools to tackle it in an increasing number of instances.

The Assisting Model

There are tasks and organizations that do not belong to either of the two kinds described thus far—organizations where the "product" is professional judgment, and where there is little interdependence between tasks other than a need to conform to professional quality standards. Those standards will moreover typically be products of independent professional communities, rather than intra-organizational authorities. Examples of such organizations are universities, courts of justice, investment analysts, law firms, and consulting firms with mainly senior personnel (consulting firms where a lot of juniors do most of the work according to centrally produced methodologies are more akin to the Mrs Fields operation[2]). Even organizations processing mainly nonstandard cases—such as government departments and other political and nonpolitical staff organizations—may belong to this class.

Such organizations have limited needs for coordination in the sense that there is little interdependence between tasks. Their main goal is most often to secure high professional standards and efficiency in work. Often, an important aspect will be to produce outcomes that are as correct as possible according to professional standards and as uniform as possible for comparable cases. The model (and the systems) will therefore mainly aim at a best possible support for the professional staff and their work, giving them easy access to both task-specific and general information, professional standards as well as precedents.

The assisting model may seem to resemble the atomistic regulating model in the sense that both aim to produce consistent outcomes. The crucial difference is that the regulating model incorporates a "correct" behavior and a number of "correct" action alternatives drawn up by the organization's technostructure and sanctioned by management. Its aim is to lead (and goad) often inexperienced employees toward the "correct" organization behavior. The assisting model, on the other hand, aims at supplying experienced professional employees with a tool that allows them to exercise their professional judgment in the best possible way.

If the model is limited to this, however, it is debatable whether it is able to drive an organization at all in the way the other two models can. To be complete, it must include the relatively modest coordination and control functions even such knowledge organizations have. An assisting model will therefore depend on both system-supported skills as well as programmed routines. Sometimes, there will also be a small dose of system-supported supervision—since one of the main concerns of management in such organizations often is to ensure that cases are processed in due time and that inquiries and requests receive prompt answers.

The assisting model does not, in my view, offer the potential for change and increase in productivity that the two other models do, since there are

---

[2] This is not intended as a derogatory remark. Everyone with some experience in this business knows that there are, by necessity, two kinds of consulting: the nonstandardized, "every case is unique" type, which requires experienced consultants who can craft a suitable approach in each case, and the standardized, volume type, where fairly rigid methods are necessary to produce consistent results with less experienced personnel.

definite limits to how far this kind of work can be automated, eliminated, or radically changed. As noted earlier, "soft" knowledge is generally not possible to incorporate into systems, and wherever individual human judgment and experience are central, computer-based systems will have limited impact.

SOME REQUIREMENTS FOR MODEL-DRIVEN ORGANIZATIONS

Model Precision

The decisive factor for the feasibility of a model-driven organization is of course that the model and the systems that build on it represent the organization's problem domain in a sufficiently detailed and correct way. This includes the requirement that the model is unambiguous and that the information contained in the systems has the necessary precision. The need for such a high degree of formalization may seem to be contradicted by the use of computers to achieve goals such as flexible automation (allowing a large number of variants to be produced without retooling) or free-text searches in large text bases, but this is a deceptive and superficial impression. Behind the apparently effortless flexibility of advanced systems one will find extremely detailed and time-consuming analysis and design processes, where all the options and functions have been defined and described with utter precision. Actually, the development effort needed for really large and complex systems is often counted not in man-years, but in man-centuries.

The higher the precision is, then, both in data and in the definition of their relationships, the better the prospects for eliminating or automating both work and coordination. When the precision degrades, so does the usefulness of the model. There is, for instance, a definite threshold of precision below which the model of the Boeing 777 would be largely useless, because measurements would not be within the necessary tolerances.

The same can be said about booking systems. If departure and arrival times could only be specified to the nearest half hour, or if there was an error margin of plus or minus 10% on the number of seats, its value as a coordinative tool would be destroyed. This effect can be observed from time to time in the real world, when delays due to bad weather, industrial actions, or heavy traffic force reality out of synch with the plan-based model. The results are missed connections, empty seats and lines of angry passengers.

We can also easily see that Ford's accounts payable system would be less than perfect if deliveries were not registered, incomplete deliveries were recorded as complete, or vice versa—or if the system did not specify the exact amount of money to be paid when goods were received and accepted.

Clearly, then, building such models is easiest when the relevant information is quantitative or possible to assign to clear categories (which do not overlap)—that is, when the information can be put into structured databases, and where unambiguous relationships can be defined between data elements. However, especially for models exploiting system-supported skills, considerable effects can also be achieved with information in less structured forms, such as text and pictures. For these purposes, the concept of hypertext may prove very valuable and allow more extensive use of unstructured data than existing tools do.

Skill and Effort

I argued earlier that Zuboff's contention that automation implies a decreasing dependence on human skills is only correct in the "local" sense—in that it has tended to reduce the skill level needed at the factory floor (with the notable exception of some advanced machine tools and other instances of machinery that demanded fairly sophisticated knowledge on the part of the operators). However, both automation and industrialization have sharply increased the need for skills in analysis, planning, and engineering. Sophisticated automation, therefore, presupposes much more advanced skills than craft production both at the company level and in the society as a whole.

This is even more true in the era of information technology. First, the technology itself is extremely complex and continues to balance on the leading edge of engineering knowledge. Indirectly, it is even heavily dependent on advanced basic research in physics, materials, and mathematics. Second, the use of information technology in an organization presupposes extensive knowledge not only of the technology itself and of the target processes or tasks, but of how to analyze and model those tasks. To develop more comprehensive systems and successfully implement them in the organization, organization theory and work psychology become important as well.

When we approach the model-driven organization, the demands grow further. As work is increasingly informated, and more and more routine tasks are either automated or eliminated, the remaining work will to a large degree be conducted onscreen. It will require a fairly advanced ability to think abstractly, understand symbols, and work through symbol manipulation. We will need an advance in skills—at least in total skills, but often at all or most levels in the organization as well. The new skills are indeed different from the old, and almost always of a more abstract nature (more intellective), but they are not less demanding. They often necessitate quite sophisticated theoretical knowledge.

The parallel with industrialization also extends to the increasing need for a professional technostructure. As noted earlier, computer-based systems always require a higher degree of formalization and standardization than manual procedures. This presupposes a detailed analysis of the relevant tasks and an understanding of how they relate to each other—an undertaking that can be very demanding in itself. Then the new combination of system and tasks must be designed, preferably in such a way that the most powerful aspects of the technology are exploited. This is no mean task, either (as they learned at Ford). To build models and system suites for the model-driven organization only raises the demands further. And, just as before, any subsequent change in the organization or the way it works means changing the model as well as the systems, requiring planning and analysis on the same level as the original effort—making the need for a competent technostructure a permanent one in every organization of some size that uses computer-based systems for more than simple tool substitution.

In fact, since the use of computer-based systems requires significantly more work on analysis, planning, and system construction than previous technologies, and the use of such systems automate or eliminate large numbers of jobs, the size and importance of the technostructure must increase in both relative and absolute terms as computer use expands. However, just as during industrialization, the increased efforts and resources that go into analysis, planning, and systems construction will pay off handsomely—if the process is soundly managed. In computer-intensive industries, therefore, competitiveness will increasingly hinge on the competence of the technostructure and on its ability to combine systems competence with knowledge about organizational structuring and development. Top managers for this new combination (the title, if drawn from a constructivist vocabulary, should probably be *pattern manager*, but I suspect that something like *organization design manager* will sound more attractive) should find themselves as sought after as top CEOs, and top professionals in the field should become the brightest stars in the professional firmament in the first half of the twenty-first century. Correspondingly, CEOs without understanding of computer-based systems and the way they interact with the organization will find themselves on an increasingly overgrown sidetrack.

16
The New Configurations

"Life is a petty thing unless it is moved by the indomitable urge to extend its boundaries. Only in proportion as we are desirous of living more do we really live.'
José Ortega y Gasset, *The Dehumanization of Art*, 1925

The analysis in Chapter 3 concluded that coordination is the linchpin of organization. In most of my subsequent discussions and analyses, I have therefore concentrated on the evolvement of coordinating mechanisms, especially on how technological innovations affect existing mechanisms and allow new ones to emerge. These changes are the main enablers behind the appearance of new types of organizations, whether they are genuinely new types or just represent variations or extensions of old ones. Therefore, they also serve as the main avenues for extending the space of constructible organizations.

Part IV outlined what I see as the significant computer-dependent co-ordinating mechanisms, based on the previous analyses of how computer-based systems enhance our capabilities for work, communication and information storage and retrieval. I discussed their potential for extending the space of constructible organizations, using both actual and imagined examples. Although I hinted at possible new organizational configura-tions, the discussions were focused on the separate coordinating mechan-isms and their individual potentials.

In Chapter 15, I also evoked a more integrative perspective by arguing that the implementation of models in computer-based systems for the first time makes it possible to work with *active* models rather than passive, turning models into a kind of supermechanism for coordination. Models are no longer paper-bound descriptions used as passive blueprints for design; they are embodied by computer-based patterns of programmed actions, and thereby become part of the total sum of the patterns of actions that define the structure and functioning of an organization. When an organization model becomes sufficiently comprehensive and sophisticated and is implemented through a sufficiently integrated system suite covering the essential parts of an organization's problem domain, the active model will begin to govern and drive the organization's most significant patterns of actions. What I have termed a *model-driven organization* will then emerge—a new and revolutionary phenomenon in the organizational world, which will become increasingly dominant in the realm of medium-to-large organizations in the coming decades.

However, the picture painted so far is still somewhat fragmented, and it would be advantageous to arrive at a more consolidated view, as Mintzberg (1979) does with his structural configurations: "natural clusters" (1979, p. 302) of the elements of his study (the coordinating mechanisms, the design parameters, and the contingency factors) that seem to capture the salient features of most organizations into five broad classes. *We may ask, can Mintzberg's configurations be modified in any way in the computer age, and can we see altogether new configurations on the horizon?*

An interesting aspect of this analysis is Mintzberg's (1979) proposition that we will find in each configuration a dominant pull on the organization, indicating the direction in which the organizational structure will develop if it is not checked by environmental factors or control problems. If the concept of pulls is correct and the pulls are correctly described, we may learn a lot by looking at if and how computer-based systems will change the barriers for how far an organization may be pulled in the desired direction.

In this chapter, I shall discuss the impact of information technology on each of Mintzberg's original configurations, assess their potential for modification, suggest their possible evolutionary paths, and try to determine if they have the potential of transforming themselves into new, computer-based variants. I will then propose two altogether new configurations, the *Meta-Organization* and the *Organized Cloud*.

EMPOWERING THE SIMPLE STRUCTURE

I suggested in Chapter 5 that we could regard the Simple Structure and the Adhocracy as the two fundamental organizational configurations, since they represent the two basic ways of coordinating work. The Simple Structure is perhaps the simplest of all the configurations, at least when we talk about organizations larger than the handful of people who are able to communicate freely all to all. To use Mintzberg's own words (1979, p. 306, bold type in original),

The Simple Structure is characterized, above all, by what it is not—elaborated. Typically, it has little or no technostructure, few support staffers, a loose

division of labor, minimal differentiation among its units, and a small manage-
rial hierarchy. Little of its behavior is formalized, and it makes minimal use of
planning, training and the liaison devices. It is, above all, organic. In a sense,
Simple Structure is nonstructure: it avoids using all the formal devices of
structure, and it minimizes its dependence on staff specialists. The latter
are typically hired on contract when needed, rather than encompassed permanently within the organization.

Coordination in the Simple Structure is effected largely by direct supervision.
Specifically, power over all important decisions tends to be centralized in the
hands of the chief executive officer. Thus, the strategic apex emerges as the key
part of the structure; indeed, the structure often consists of little more than a
one-man strategic apex and an organic operating core.

The typical Simple Structure is the start-up, the small entrepreneurial
firm owned and managed by the founder, but even larger organizations
can be dominated by strong and charismatic leaders. This is even more
common in less developed countries, still greatly influenced or even dominated by the traditions of oral culture, and where the literate forms of
organization have correspondingly less appeal. In the European/
American sphere, it probably had its heyday with the great American
trusts in the late nineteenth century (Mintzberg 1979). Sometimes, organizations with other configurations will temporarily take on some of the
characteristics of the Simple Structure if a serious crisis renders their
more elaborate decision-making schemes inadequate. However, both in
the latter case and in the case of the great American trusts, we may question the purity of the configurations—if an organization is very large, it
will be impossible even for an extreme autocrat to have that kind of
direct, personal control over day-to-day operations that is the hallmark
of the Simple Structure. Such an organization will therefore have strong
bureaucratic features, but people will tend to look more toward the
top manager's apparent preferences than to written rules, and the top
manager will feel completely free to intervene in any matter or decision
anywhere in the organization.

Extending Direct Control

In the classic Simple Structure the defining feature is an extremely centralized control over day-to-day affairs, most often concentrated in the
hands of one person. The predominant force pulling on such an organization is the *pull of the strategic apex to centralize* (Mintzberg 1979)—to use
direct supervision as far as possible, and without any delegation. We find
this very poignantly expressed by Debbie Fields (Mrs Fields cookie shops)
in the statement quoted on p. 335, where she concedes being "forced,
kicking and screaming, to delegate authority, because it was the only
way the business could grow." This statement, by the way, also serves

to substantiate an assumption that underlies Mintzberg's arguments though it is not made explicit, namely, that growth is always a paramount objective—for entrepreneurs and administrators alike—and that the desire for growth in most cases is even stronger than the desire for control.

In the conflict between their wishes for control and growth, the entrepreneurial managers of growing firms typically agonize over the delegation of power to a layer of middle management. The reason is not only that they dislike the fact that they will be separated from the direct contact with the people in the operating core. As they see it, the problem is that the associated growth most often also means an increased reliance on the more efficient standardization of work as a coordinating mechanism. In turn, this means that more power is relinquished, in this case to the professionals in the technostructure who design and maintain the standardized work rules.

To Simple Structure managers, the most appealing aspects of the technology will therefore be those that improve control and eliminate work, so that the size of the organization can be kept down and direct control can be retained. I believe they will be pleasantly surprised by the potential if they can rise above their natural distrust of professional experts—because, if they really want to exploit the new possibilities offered by information technology, they will also have to accept the need for a competent technostructure to build and maintain the new systems.

In order to increase control, the manager of the Simple Structure will of course want to exploit system-supported supervision, which is the computer-dependent version of direct supervision. This alone should make it possible to extend the size of a genuine Simple Structure considerably. Further, the use of programmed routines with a strongly regulating content will make it possible to direct the actions of employees to a much larger extent and to a much greater detail than before. Insofar as the top manager can supervise the content of these routines directly, the use of this coordinating mechanism may give greater sense of control than traditional written routines. This will especially be the case if the systems allow fairly easy adjustments of rules and/or parameters. Such systems may therefore also allow Simple Structures to grow larger without becoming fully-fledged Machine Bureaucracies. However, there is a threshold here where control will cease to come directly from the hands of the top manager and pass into a process of rule standardization where the decisive influence is wielded by a larger set of people. The organization structure will then topple over and become a variant of the computer-supported Machine Bureaucracy discussed in the next section.

Finally, extensive hyperautomation and elimination of work can allow extensive reductions in the number of employees in an organization, while keeping up or even increasing its economic size. This may allow Simple Structures to expand further into the territory of mass-producing Machine Bureaucracies than before. However, since the Simple Structure cannot easily accommodate really large organizations, such an expansion would probably at some point lead to either stagnation or a transition to a computer-supported bureaucratic form.

It is of course also possible that the increased flexibility offered by computer-based automation can be harnessed to lower the production costs of small batches or even semi-tailor-made products to a level where they can compete directly with the products of traditional mass-producing Machine Bureaucracies. In such a case, a multitude of small Simple Structures may develop and effectively replace formerly dominant mass-producers. This would be in line with the ideas of flexible specialization on the basis of craft traditions put forward by Piore and Sabel (1984). As they point out, such developments have taken place before, although on a different basis. In particular, they point to the developments in the textile industry in Italy's Prato area in the 1930s and 1950s.

To exploit computer-based systems to extend operations without relinquishing control, managers of Simple Structures will have to learn quite a lot about the technology and the systems in use in the organization, since they will have to use the systems themselves in order to achieve the control they want. They will also have to learn to work closely with the computer professionals in their new technostructure. In fact, a significant part of their control efforts will have to be channeled into the supervision of systems construction and maintenance.

In short, I believe that computer-based systems have enlarged the space of constructible organizations considerably in the direction of allowing increased size and economic clout for organizations configured as Simple Structures. Technology-conscious entrepreneurs and autocrats should therefore have the opportunity to invigorate this configuration and perhaps even increase its importance relative to other configurations. In organizations that have grown too large for the pure configuration, it should be possible—at least in a number of instances—to revert back to a more clean-cut situation through significant workforce reductions coupled with computer-supported supervision.

Does this mean that the configuration itself is modified, or is it only a matter of an electronic invigoration of the traditional Simple Structure? I think there is a continuum building here that will eventually pass the threshold to a qualitatively new configuration.

Even moderate use of computer-based systems will allow a Simple Structure to outgrow the limits of its pre-computer forebears without changing very much in principle. However, as system use develops and covers larger and larger parts of the operations, things begin to change.

Control is increasingly effected through the systems, and a growing part of the top manager's time is devoted not to supervision in the form of face-to-face contact, but to systems design, parameter setting, and system-supported supervision. With maximum exploitation of the technology, the result should approach the organization described in the thought experiment with Ceramico at the end of Chapter 14.

Emergence of the Joystick Organization

At this point, I think the threshold has definitely been crossed, and a new, computer-based configuration has emerged. I think this new breed needs a name of its own. I propose to keep the name suggested in the discussion of the hypothetical Ceramico example, and will thus call this computer-dependent version of the Simple Structure the *Joystick Organization*.

It will definitely be model driven and rely on a regulating model with a clear emphasis on information aggregation (system-supported supervision) and easy manipulation of key parameters in the controlling systems (programmed routines). There will often be extensive automation in the operating core, even to the point of organizational truncation. The top manager will run the organization mainly through interaction with the systems, not with people—other than a few close assistants. The Joystick Organization will continue to cherish the centralization of the Simple Structure and will keep its forebear's organic structure and low degree of specialization and formalization. It will thrive in the same environments (simple and dynamic), but it may grow larger than the Simple Structure, at least in economic size. Contrary to the Simple Structure, however, the new configuration will have a significant technostructure, since it will need a sophisticated IS department to take care of (and often develop) the extensive systems needed for its daily operations. The head of this department will be one of the top manager's closest collaborators.

Some readers may protest that such a revival of a modernized Simple Structure flies in the face of the common prophecy that information technology will first and foremost promote flatter organizations and a greater reliance on teams, cooperation, and devolvement of power. My answer to this is that the technology in itself does not promote any particular arrangement; it is an enabler that opens up possibilities in a number of directions—just like earlier technology. Within the constructible space available to them (the local space, which is the constructible space restricted by local contingency factors), individual actors will exploit the technology in the direction they prefer. People who favor cooperation and devolvement will seek out features supporting teamwork and decentralized decision making; people who want control will move in the opposite direction.

As an illustration, we may note that all the while Marshall McLuhan was writing about the democratizing effects of the telephone in the corporation ("On the telephone only the authority of knowledge will work."[1]), Harold Geneen was using the telephone as one of his prime instruments of control at ITT (some would even say instrument of terror!). To keep his subordinates on their toes, he would telephone them at any time, day or night, demanding rapid answers to questions about their operations (Schoenberg 1985).

PERFECTING THE MACHINE BUREAUCRACY

The Machine Bureaucracy is the epitome of the modern organization—indeed, many organization theorists just call this structural configuration the Modern Organization. Its defining feature is its use of standardization of work processes as its main coordinating mechanism. It achieves its efficiency through mass-production of goods or services in a highly rationalized operating core. The degree of formalization in the organization is high, and most tasks are highly specialized. Since the operating core of the Machine Bureaucracy can only achieve its impressive productivity through continuous production at a high rate of facility utilization, and since changes in the production setup are costly and time-consuming, it craves a high degree of stability in its environment. Often, it tries to influence its environment both directly and indirectly to increase stability.

To manage the normally quite complex organization and maintain its operating core, the Machine Bureaucracy has both an elaborate administrative structure and a well-developed technostructure. In fact, Mintzberg (1979) points to the technostructure as the key part of the organization, even if the formal power resides in the line managers (Mintzberg 1979, pp. 316–17, bold type and italics in original):

> **Because the Machine Bureaucracy depends primarily on the standardization of its operating work processes for coordination, the technostructure—which houses the analysts who do the standardizing—emerges as the key part of the structure.** This is so despite the fact that the Machine Bureaucracy sharply distinguishes between line and staff. To the line managers is delegated the formal authority for the operating units; the technocratic staff—officially at least—merely advises. But without standardizers—the cadre of work study analysts, job description designers, schedulers, quality control engineers, planners, budgeters, MIS designers, accountants, operations researchers, and many, many more—the structure simply could not function. Hence, despite the lack of formal authority, considerable informal power rests

---

[1] Marshall McLuhan, *Understanding Media*, New American Library, New York, 1964. Quoted in Pool 1983.

with the analysts of the technostructure—those who standardize *everyone else's* work.

Typical Machine Bureaucracies are well-established, large organizations such as banks, insurance companies, automobile companies, airlines, and government services (e.g., the Customs Service or Social Security). Even the police and the armed forces are usually configured as Machine Bureaucracies. Because it is first and foremost a configuration for mass production, the Machine Bureaucracy is optimized for efficiency within a quite narrow domain, and it cannot easily adapt itself to another. It is definitely not able to live with very dynamic or very complex environments. However, its efficiency in producing standardized goods and services is so superior that it has become the dominant structural configuration for larger organizations in all modern societies. The overwhelming majority of us seem, in most instances, to prefer these standardized, cheap products to the more tailor-made (but also more expensive) products we could have had from enterprises with other configurations.

According to Mintzberg (1979), the main pull on a Machine Bureaucracy is the pull of the technostructure to standardize—that is, to increase and refine the use of standardization of work processes as the organization's coordinating mechanism. This reflects the inclination and training of the technostructure and also serves to strengthen its power in the organization.

An elaboration of the standardization of work is indeed one of the main avenues that information technology opens up, and unchecked technostructures thus have ample opportunities to engage in their favorite pursuit. However, dependent on the nature of the organization's operating core and the skills and vision of its technostructure, several scenarios are possible. The most important are *staying within tradition, truncation through automation or self-service*, and *flexibilization*.

Staying within Tradition

The dominant approach today is to stay within tradition, using information technology mainly in a reinforcing way—that is, to make existing procedures more efficient. Programmed routines are gradually substituted for explicit routines, there is incremental automation of routine tasks, and management uses information available in the systems to improve its control over the organization and its operations. Even what are regarded as state-of-the-art improvements do not necessarily bring a Machine Bureaucracy out of the traditional mold—groupware, workflow tools and even business process reengineering (BPR) can well be applied within the traditional structure. For example, the reengineering of Ford's accounts payable function did not change Ford into an nonbureaucratic organization. It is even doubtful whether the accounts payable function itself became less bureaucratic through its reengineering. It can be argued that by shifting the handling of payments over to a set of programmed routines, the task rather became *more* strictly standardized than before, and the company's relationship with its suppliers *less* flexible. Instead of receiving the shipments as they came and sorting out any problems afterward, all deviations from the agreed delivery schedules were now immediately detected and triggered the same, standardized response: a rejection of the whole shipment and a demand for a corrected one. However, the change also entailed that the internal coordination in Ford improved dramatically and that the company's relationship with its suppliers became far better coordinated and much more closely controlled, since the new system allowed the control to take place in real time, and not after the fact. This is how the benefits traditionally have accrued within the Machine Bureaucracy: through increased and improved design, control and regulation.

Truncation

Of course, if the process of automation and elimination is carried far enough, most or even all of the operating core may become automated, effectively truncating the organization as in the process industries described by Zuboff (1988) and discussed in Chapter 12. According to Mintzberg, the configuration then changes to a variant of the Adhocracy (Mintzberg 1979, p. 458, italics in original):

> The problem of motivating uninterested operators disappears, and with it goes the control mentality that permeates the Machine Bureaucracy; the distinction between line and staff blurs (machines being indifferent as to who turns their knobs), which leads to another important reduction in conflict; the technostructure loses its influence, since control is built into the machinery by its designers rather than imposed on workers by the rules and standards of the analysts. Overall, the administrative structure becomes more decentralized and organic, emerging as the type we call the *automated adhocracy*.

However, there is an important difference between the traditional automation Mintzberg refers to and the computer-based hyperautomation that is our subject. Design and control are not laid down once and for all before installation of the machinery. The reason is simply that computer-based systems are so much more complex than mechanical systems—they allow much more sophisticated and flexible automation. They may also allow a truncation by a combination of hyperautomation and increased self-service, which is what we will see at least in large sections of the market for banking services and payment transactions.

In any case, the result is that an organization with a hyperautomated operating core will need a sizable and competent technostructure not only to look after it, tune it, and continuously improve it, but also to prepare the extensive parameter controls that such systems allow and assist the line organization in their use of these controls. The more sophisticated the organization becomes in using information technology and the more it (hyper-) automates, the more the technostructure will grow and the more important it will become.

An organizational truncation based on information technology should therefore result instead in an *Administrative Adhocracy*—the configuration Mintzberg designates for organizations with very complex technical systems. Just like its sibling, the Operating Adhocracy, an Administrative Adhocracy is mainly project oriented. However, in contrast with the Operating Adhocracy, its projects are not organized to fulfill customer needs, but to take care of the Administrative Adhocracy's own internal needs: the upkeep and development of a mass-producing operating core.

If the organization is not too large, automation extensive, and the top manager of the appropriate kind, such an organization may even revert to a Simple Structure or become a Joystick Organization. Even if it keeps a team-based management style, it may approach the Joystick Organization, since the top management team in such an organization may develop a very dominating position.

The Rise of Flexible Bureaucracy

The most exiting development, however, goes along the flexibility dimension and can provide us with a revitalized version of the Machine Bureaucracy, supplying the mass commodities and services of the twenty-first century. The key here is the transition from *inflexible* to *flexible* standardization.

The Achilles Heel of Machine Bureaucracy

The Machine Bureaucracy was developed as an organization for cheap, reliable mass production of standardized products and services. In order to maximize productivity and minimize the need for training, it depended on a high degree of job specialization, detailed prescriptions and rules for the execution of work, along with fairly rigorous standards of quality and generous amounts of control. This produced a type of organization with unsurpassed efficiency within its very narrow problem domain, but this efficiency was bought at the price of an almost total inability to tackle problems that was outside its underlying conceptual model and thereby not defined in the implemented routines. In short, the Machine Bureaucracy is extremely inflexible compared to other organizations, especially the Simple Structure and the Adhocracy. In manufacturing, the costs of retooling for a new product are considerable; in white-collar bureaucracies, it is both time-consuming and expensive to change operating procedures and to train people to solve new classes of problems.

This is why a Machine Bureaucracy is not suited for dynamic environments or for products that cannot be standardized, and why Piore and Sabel (1984) and Pine (1993) believe it needs to be relieved as the dominant configuration for producing goods and services in advanced economies. Piore and Sabel, in particular, argue that the main reason behind the apparent sluggishness of the world economy the last couple of decades is precisely the mismatch between the increasingly saturated and more rapidly changing world markets on one hand, and the Machine Bureaucracies' inflexibility and dependence on long, uninterrupted production runs at full capacity on the other. The uncertainty about market developments deters new investments, and the great costs of renewing products—not to mention changing lines of business—impede the ability of the economy as a whole to shift resources quickly enough between changing demands.

Will the Answer Be Small and Nimble or Big and Flexible?

The remedy proposed by Piore and Sabel is to stimulate the growth of technology-based flexible specialization, based on the pattern of craft production. The companies they envisage will typically be fairly small (most of them would probably be Simple Structures) and flexible enough to be able to shift their production quickly between a fairly wide range of products and do so with moderate costs.

Pine, in his turn, describes how old style mass production is giving way to mass customization, where flexible production lines can deliver products with great variation, where product development cycles have been shortened, and lead times reduced to a point where even cars can be delivered to customer specifications within a few days. Pine lists three forms of companies that make up what he terms the "New Competition": Japan, Inc. (the typical Japanese manufacturing company), the Flexible Specialization firms described by Piore and Sabel, and the Dynamic Extended Enterprise, exemplified by the renewed American corporation. Pine says that although the three forms are clearly different, they are all variations of the model offered by Piore and Sabel, bringing back much of the flexibility of the craft-based firms of the American System of Manufactures (described briefly in Chapter 7).

However, as Pine's own examples show, it is not only the craft-based, small-scale company that can achieve flexibility. Computer-based systems may also allow the development of a more flexible Machine Bureaucracy, which may answer at least parts of the challenge of more dynamic markets, and become formidable competitors both for craft-based production and traditionalists among their own kind. The basis for this is of course the extreme (and increasing) richness and flexibility of computer-based systems, so dramatically different from traditional machinery and media for automation and implementation of routines. By relying on information technology and appropriate reorganization, bureaucracies in both manufacturing and service industries can become much more agile and achieve much greater flexibility in their production.

Flexibility can be increased in three ways: by having a richer set of pre-defined (and routinized) problem definitions and responses, by increasing discretion at the organization perimeter—something that will improve the organization's capability to deal with problems within its problem domain but inadequately provided for in established routines—and by making it cheaper and easier to change the routines themselves. All of these will also help to improve an organization's agility. Agility will likewise be enhanced by more efficient and rapid internal coordination and by the availability (especially to top management) of more comprehensive and timely information about various key aspects of the organization's performance. The discussions in the previous chapters have established that computer-based systems can make significant contributions in all these areas.

First of all, computer-based automation can produce more complex products and accommodate much larger variations in product types. I believe we have only seen the beginning here, since we have only started to exploit the vast potential of computer control in our development of production methods and materials. Even now, car manufacturers are able to produce not only cars with different colors and a wide selection of options on a single assembly line, but even different models—and still operate according to the rather extreme just-in-time principles reported from Nissan's Sunderland operation. This means that the mix of models can be changed dynamically not only from day to day, but, in principle, from hour to hour. This is a considerable improvement over the situation not too many years ago, wherein one assembly line could only produce one model with a fairly limited number of options. Of course, not even these factories can suddenly change their production to boats or airplanes, but this increase in flexibility—which is still primarily built on traditional materials and production methods—is nevertheless a harbinger of a future development where even greater flexibility will be available. We may, for instance, imagine materials and production machinery that do not depend on molds, but, rather, can produce any shape designed in a CAD program on the fly. Actually, we already have a beginning in stereolithography, where a resin is hardened by an ultraviolet laser beam "drawing" on its surface, layer by layer forming a three-dimensional object on a platform that is successively lowered into the resin bath. This process is still very slow, cumbersome, and expensive, but already it is efficient enough to replace a lot of traditional wood, plaster, and plastic modeling in the making of prototypes.

The same principles apply to clerical work, only to a greater degree, since offices have much less mechanical equipment (which is the least flexible part). Both automated and programmed routines can be very complex, and allow for a large number of predefined actions. Of course, it is also possible to prepare a great number of alternatives in a manual environment, where routines are documented in writing. However, the limits of human memory and the cumbersome nature of written documentation will combine to restrict the variation that can be sustained in practice. Well-designed computer-based systems can easily extend the practical number of routines considerably and assist in choosing the right one for each occasion. System-supported de-specialization may increase flexibility further by increasing the range of tasks that one person can execute, thus making it possible to accommodate greater variations in task mix than before. This has been evident for a long time in banks, where the introduction of counter terminals led to a significant de-specialization.

We may also return to an earlier example. The changes at IBM Credit involved automation of the larger part of the work and extensive computer support for most of what was left. The caseworkers thus achieved a much broader span of competence. In addition to the documented leap in productivity, we should expect the new setup to provide greater flexibility in setting up nonstandard deals, although Hammer and Champy do not comment on it. They do, however, include IBM Credit among their examples of organizations that have increased employee empowerment—something that normally entails greater ability to tailor responses to customer requests. We have also concluded earlier that the migration of power toward the decision-making hot spots in the organization should lead to greater flexibility and agility for bureaucratic organizations.

Just as important as an increased repertory of predefined routines is the ability to change routines or establish new ones quickly and cheaply. In a manual environment, changes are theoretically straightforward to implement, since all it takes is to describe the change and circulate it to all concerned. However, as all who have lived in and with such organizations know, it can be extremely difficult to make changes take hold, and override established patterns of action. The required effort can be quite considerable even for small changes.

One of the great advantages of computer-based systems in this respect is the way they can be equipped with options and parameters for adjustments in their functioning. We saw, for instance, how the people responsible for yield management in American Airlines could use the reservation system to implement instant changes in the prices and options available on flights throughout the world—changes that would probably have taken weeks to effect by manual means. And, despite the fact that many view bank systems as both archaic and hard to change, there is absolutely no doubt that banks today have more room to maneuver than they did 40 years ago when it comes to rapid changes in their products—whether it is to meet attacks from competitors or to accommodate general changes in their customers' preferences. It has, for instance, become much easier to vary interest rates, to let interest rates depend on the dynamic size of deposits, to differentiate payment options, and to combine accounts in various ways.

Looking at existing systems, one will of course find great differences in how pliable they are, but rigid systems are more a result of poor analyses, poor modeling, and poor design than of technological constraints. Naturally, there are limits to the flexibility that can be achieved without renewing or replacing the systems (which involves great cost and effort), but I believe we have a long way to go before the potential is exhausted.

Big Will Still Be Better

Like Paul Thompson (1993), I therefore disagree with the postmodernist contention that information technology is paving the way for a decisive break with Machine Bureaucracy as the dominating structural configuration of larger organizations in the advanced economies. *On the contrary, I believe that information technology is already supporting the development of a leaner, much more flexible and much more agile type of bureaucratic organization than the classic Machine Bureaucracy.*

This new type of organization will depend mainly on hyperautomation and programmed routines but will also draw on the other computer-dependent coordinating mechanisms represented in Figure 15-1 (p. 361). When sufficiently advanced, it will be model driven, relying on a regulating model with an emphasis on programmed routines, hyperautomation, and (depending on the type of production) implicit coordination. The middle layers in the organization will be severely decimated, some of their power migrating upward and some downward. Through the use of improved information access and increased spans of competence, discretionary powers in matters related to specific tasks or customers will be decentralized to the operating core. Top management, however, will have much better control of the operations overall, both through their access to much better and more timely information and through the much improved process control they achieve through their command over the systems used by the operating core.

This kind of organization will be much better equipped than its predecessor to tackle variation in its environment, because it reacts much faster to changes, has a wider repertory of standardized responses, and has a greater ability to vary its product mix. To phrase it in the language of Ashby's Law of Requisite Variety (1956), it will contain within itself a greater variety than the classic Machine Bureaucracy, and it will therefore be able to live with more variation in its environment. Because such an organization will be much more change oriented in general, it will also have a greater ability to accomplish those major changes that must come when the demands from the environment finally outstrip its normal range of responses. I propose the name *Flexible Bureaucracy* for this configuration, to denote both its strong points and its origin.

The Flexible Bureaucracy will retain most of the design parameters of the Machine Bureaucracy, such as behavior formalization, vertical and horizontal job specialization, large operating unit size, vertical and limited horizontal decentralization and action planning. However, whereas the Machine Bureaucracy usually relies on functional grouping, the Flexible Bureaucracy will use its computer-based systems to maintain market-oriented grouping or even matrix-like structures. The Flexible Bureaucracy will be able to thrive in more complex and dynamic environments than the Machine Bureaucracy. It will retain strong technocratic control, since the computer professionals required to design and run its comprehensive systems will find a natural home in the technostructure.

I believe that this computer-based version of the bureaucratic configuration will prove a far more vigorous successor to the Modern Organization (Machine Bureaucracy) than the craft-oriented alternative proposed by Piore and Sabel, and, accordingly, that *flexible standardization* is a more likely solution to the problems of the classic Machine Bureaucracy than flexible specialization. Far from promoting the small organization, information technology (which is in its essence an automating and coordinating technology) will invigorate the larger organizations and make them still more formidable competitors. Indeed, of the three forms of New Competition that Pine (1993) defines within the field of mass customization, two of them (Japan, Inc., and the Dynamic Extended Enterprise) correspond much more closely to the Flexible Bureaucracy than to the craft-based type of firms envisioned by Piore and Sabel.

As a part of their metamorposis, Machine Bureaucracies are now experiencing a period of contraction while they hyperautomate an increasing part of their operating cores and shed organizational layers by gradually shifting their coordination toward the computer-dependent coordinating mechanisms. This is, by the way, a process that has really been underway for quite some time—as early as around 1970, the employment figures of large manufacturing companies such as General Motors, Philips, and Unilever started to drop, whereas sales and capital expeditures continued to grow (Huppes 1987). After they have made this transition, they may well start to grow again—even in employees—although their most decisive growth will still be in economic size.

The adaptability of the Flexible Bureaucracy is not limitless, however. If it is confronted with problems not defined in its underlying model or requests outside the available range of responses defined in its systems, even as they are supplemented by empowered employees, it will come up against the same need for fundamental changes as a Machine Bureaucracy. Indeed, so will all organizations with a heavy reliance on computer-based systems. Even the IT-based Simple Structures will find that they cannot "turn on a dime" as easily as their noncomputerized brethren. Because of the enormous amount of analysis, planning, and design needed to create comprehensive systems and the conceptual models they must be based on, the required effort for major change can indeed be large. There are numerous examples of such changes that have turned into catastrophes when major new systems have been severely delayed, have suffered massive cost overruns, or have even stranded altogether. However, there are also numerous examples of successful projects of this kind, and as our knowledge improves, our experience accumulates, and the software tools become better, the successes will probably slowly increase their share of the total. The Flexible Bureaucracy will, as other computer-dependent configurations, have another advantage: the people working in them will be more used to, and thereby probably more receptive to, change.

THE ENDURING PROFESSIONAL BUREAUCRACY

The Professional Bureaucracy is similar to the Machine Bureaucracy in the sense that it is meant to produce standardized goods or services in an efficient way. It differs from the Machine Bureaucracy in that its production process (Mintzberg: "operating work") is too complex to rely on low-skilled operators working according to explicit routines. As Mintzberg says (1979, pp. 348–49, italics in original),

> We have seen evidence at various points in this book that organizations can be bureaucratic without being centralized. Their operating work is stable,

leading to "predetermined or predictable, in effect, standardized"[2] behavior, but it is also complex, and so must be controlled directly by the operators who do it. Hence, the organization turns to the one coordinating mechanism that allows for standardization and decentralization at the same time, namely the standardization of skills. This gives rise to a structural configuration sometimes called *Professional Bureaucracy*, common in universities, general hospitals, school systems, public accounting firms, social work agencies, and craft production firms. All rely on the skill and knowledge of their operating professionals to function; all produce standard products or services.

For their operating cores, the Professional Bureaucracies rely on professionals—people who have received their main training in independent educational institutions. (The exceptions are of course these educational institutions themselves; they tend to count many of their own graduates among their employees.) This education not only provides them with the basic knowledge they need to carry out their work, it also teaches them what to expect from their professional coworkers and how it is customary to coordinate activities with them. The education normally also serves to indoctrinate the professionals with norms about ethical standards and proper conduct both toward fellow professionals and customers/clients. Even in those instances where systematic education continues after hiring (as in hospitals that educate specialists), the content and process are fully controlled by standards set by the larger professional community. There is little room for organization-specific programs. In their work the professionals work relatively independent of their colleagues but usually maintain a close relationship with the customers or clients they serve. Their decisions and the way they carry out their work are determined not so much by in-house rules as by their own judgment, built on the standards of their own profession.

Whereas Machine Bureaucracies generate their own standards and rely on formal authority, then, Professional Bureaucracies apply standards set by self-governing professional associations and rely on the authority of recognized expertise. The main pull in such an organization (Mintzberg 1979) is to professionalize—to extend the supremacy of professional expertise throughout the organization. This pull has three main expressions. Occupational groups not yet recognized as separate professions will strive toward such recognition, the recognized professional groups will fight for the inclusion of more prestigious tasks into their domains and if possible secure statutory monopoly on their jobs, and all the professionals will vigorously defend their own autonomy and join in the effort to

---

[2] Mintzberg here quotes himself from his definition of bureaucracy in an earlier chapter, which he refers to in a parenthesis I have left out here.

keep control of the organization and relegate the administrative apparatus (including the managing director) to a subordinate, staff-like position.

This tendency is easy to observe, not least in hospitals (at least in Norwegian hospitals). Almost every occupational group in hospitals has worked systematically to establish a separate profession, complete with its own separate education and statutory provisions for a monopoly on certain positions. The doctors were first, followed by nurses, and later we have seen the same development for most of the other groups, such as physiotherapists, physical chemists, occupational therapists, and nursing assistants. The establishment of new professions has often taken place in conflict with existing ones, since it usually has involved staking out claims to tasks that already belonged to one or more of the established groups. The archetypal conflict here has been (and still is) the conflict between doctors and nurses, as nurses over the last 100 years have fought fiercely and with great perseverance to improve their standing and their education, and to take over a significant part of the work that was earlier the domain of medical doctors.

Hospitals are also characterized by a single-minded concentration on formal qualifications when evaluating people for new positions, even within the professions. To cross the border between two professions is impossible altogether—regardless of actual knowledge and experience—without going through the full educational program of the new profession. If the certificate is missing, the door is totally blocked. And, as hinted earlier, the educational programs of the different professions are totally separate, with no common tracks or courses.

The occupational turf in a hospital is by now largely cut up and occupied by the various professional groups, and the fight for larger domains or more prestigious tasks increasingly amounts to a zero-sum game. The hospital organization is therefore very rigid and extremely difficult to change. In such organizations one would expect game theory to apply in many instances, and it is interesting to see that alliances and conflict lines among the professions indeed seem to comply. There is, for instance, a conflict between nurses and nursing assistants, since the latter dislike to be supervised by nurses and moreover want to move up toward nursing status and take over some of the nurses' responsibilities (and positions). The nurses, on their hand, have been nibbling away at the doctors' domain for a century, and these two groups still have their skirmishes—not least in the area of administrative duties and responsibilities in the hospital wards. What is more natural, then, than mutual sympathy and goodwill between doctors and nursing assistants? Neither group threatens the other, and the nursing assistants have no trouble accepting the professional authority of the doctors. In fact, many doctors will claim that they really do not need the (now) university-educated nurses, that they would prefer to recruit only nursing assistants (who receive more limited education) and then teach them what more they need to know themselves. So far, however, the nurses have had the most success.

This main pull of the Professional Bureaucracy—the pull to professionalize—will receive no particular support from information technology. Actually, the Professional Bureaucracy is probably the configuration where information technology provides the most limited platform for change. The reason is simply that the gist of the work in such organizations consists of professional judgment, which typically requires the kind of "thick" or "soft" knowledge that is (at least currently) impossible to impart to computer-based systems. A number of expert systems that aid in tasks such as fault finding and medical diagnosing have indeed been developed, but they cannot—and are not intended to—replace the professionals. Rather, they are meant to function as tools for the professionals, speeding up assessment and improving the quality of their work.

Some Ruffled Feathers

There are of course exceptions to this general pattern. First, a growth in self-service may become a threat to some professional groups. For instance, an increasing number of brokerages now offer customers direct access to their stock-trading systems, enabling customers to conclude deals directly from their own PCs. Although the brokerages still perform the back-office functions, this development may reduce the need for stockbrokers quite significantly and diminish their position compared to the more routine-processing back-office staff.

Second, not all Professional Bureaucracies are in the service sector (even if the largest and most visible ones are). The configuration can also be found in manufacturing in the form of craft enterprises (Mintzberg 1979), which is the configuration favored by Piore and Sabel. They will be vulnerable to the development of hyperautomation and flexible production and the pressure for change implied by this development.

Traditionally, the craft enterprise depends on craftsmen who use relatively simple tools to produce standardized goods. Because their tools are simple and often general, it is relatively easy for them to shift their output to new products if the markets change. This flexibility makes up for some of their lack of productivity compared to the Machine Bureaucracies. However, in their competition both with Machine Bureaucracies and with other craft enterprises, they increasingly have to invest in more powerful tools and even computerized equipment. This tendency is described by Piore and Sabel in the case of the textile industry in Italy's Prato district and the Japanese metalworking industry.

To Piore and Sabel, this is a proof of the vitality and adaptability of the craft enterprise. To me, it is instead a development that will serve to reduce the importance of the independent craft enterprise in manufacturing, since the increasing use of computer-based equipment will tend to level out the field between the different configurations. The necessary investments per employee in the craft enterprise will approach those of the competing Machine Bureaucracies (gradually becoming Flexible Bureaucracies), and the flexibility of the Machine Bureaucracies' production machinery will approach that of the craft enterprise's.

This convergence in technologies will also result in a convergence of the required skills. Even if both the craft enterprise and the Machine Bureaucracy have traditionally relied on action-centered skills (Zuboff 1988), they have been very different in kind. The craft enterprise has employed highly skilled craftsmen who perform a broad range of qualified work; the Machine Bureaucracy has employed largely low-skilled personnel who have received the limited, specialized training they need in-house or even on the job. However, as the use of computer-based equipment increases, both types of organizations increasingly need operators with the sophisticated, *intellective* skills required to master the new equipment. Simultaneously, the degree of automation will tend to rise, and computer-based systems will be employed to automate the coordination of larger and larger parts of the production process, even spanning organization borders, as in the Nissan Sunderland example. Craft enterprises, in my opinion, will therefore experience a strong pull toward the Flexible Bureaucracy configuration, or toward the Administrative Adhocracy if they are able to automate their production completely. In some instances, information technology even renders whole crafts superfluous, for instance, traditional typography (as printing once eliminated the need for scribes).

We can expect such trends to continue, and Professional Bureaucracies whose professional work can largely be automated, eliminated, or routinized will also develop toward other configurations, such as a Machine Bureaucracy, a Flexible Bureaucracy, or an Administrative Adhocracy— depending on the nature of the changes they go through.

In the majority of the Professional Bureaucracies, however, the dominating tasks fall into one or more of the three categories least susceptible to automation (listed on p. 282): work where qualities such as creativity, judgment, artistic skill, and emotional content are central. The professions are therefore likely to continue their dominance in these organizations, and there is little reason to believe that they will change configuration or that the configuration itself will be significantly modified. As Mintzberg says (1979, p. 367),

The professional operators of this structural configuration require considerable discretion in their work. It is they who serve the clients, usually directly and personally. So the technical system cannot be highly regulating, certainly not highly automated.

The professionals will therefore prefer systems that assist them in their work and enhance their professional capacities. However, for the same reasons, they will also take a favorable view of systems that automate or eliminate the most routine aspects of their work, and especially systems that reduce the need for an administrative staff. The potential of information technology in the case of the typical Professional Bureaucracies is therefore a development toward somewhat slimmer organizations, with a higher proportion of professionals than before, and with sophisticated support systems both for professional and administrative needs. There will be no dramatic changes justifying the proclamation of new configurations, not even for the model-driven version of the Professional Bureaucracy, which will depend mainly on the assisting model.

A New Line of Conflict

The technology does, however, hold a potential for increasing the antagonism between professionals and administrative staff. The latter, which is usually configured and run as a Machine Bureaucracy, tends to hold the view that professionals are a bit on the whimsical side, and that a more "structured" approach to work and better cooperation would improve both their productivity and the quality of their work. They (and even the organization's owners) may easily see information technology as a means to improvement through injecting more control and standardization into the professional sphere, and maybe even automate or eliminate some of their tasks. In such a process the administrative staff would also improve their own position in the organization. This is of course anathema to the professionals, as Mintzberg points out in the continuation of the preceding quote:

> As Heydbrand and Noell (1973)[3] point out, the professional resist the rationalization of his skills—their division into simply executed steps—because that makes them programmable by the technostructure, destroys his basis of autonomy, and drives the structure to the machine bureaucratic form.

I believe this will be an important source of conflict in Professional Bureaucracies in the years to come. The conflict will of course become

---

[3] Heydbrand, W. V. and Noell, J. J., "Task Structure and Innovation in Professional Organizations," in W. V. Heydbrand (ed.), *Comparative Organizations*, Prentice-Hall, 1973, pp. 294–322.

most severe in organizations where significant parts of the professional work *can* be automated or eliminated, and where the organization may even be posed for a change of configuration along the lines indicated earlier. Many Professional Bureaucracies also have strong "manufacturing" aspects, for instance, hospitals—where the flow of patients through the wards and the throughput in terms of the number of patients treated can be likened to the flow of materials and output of finished goods in a factory. Such resemblances—real or apparent—can provide platforms for attacking the traditional autonomy of the professions, and the availability of sophisticated, regulating computer-based systems for a variety of administrative and production-oriented purposes can only strengthen those platforms.

The position of the computer professionals themselves will also be interesting. Will they establish themselves as the kernel of a new techno-structure, allied with the administrative staff, or will they seek acceptance as a new professional group? So far, the first alternative has been most common, something that can be explained both by history (computers were usually first brought in by the accountants in the administrative staff) and by the computer professionals' aptitude for logic as well as systems and efficiency engineering. Because their work always tends to encroach on the autonomy of the other professionals, it is also quite likely that they will have problems being accepted as a bona fide professional group separate from the administrative staff.

REINTEGRATING THE DIVISIONALIZED FORM

The Divisionalized Form is not a configuration in the same sense as the others; it is in a way a second-order form, a structure for the coordination of relatively independent organizations—organizations that have their own structural configurations and that could well exist as independent entities. As Mintzberg says (1979, p. 381),

> The Divisionalized Form differs from the other four structural configurations in one important respect. It is not a complete structure from the strategic apex to the operating core, but rather a structure superimposed on others. That is, each division has its own structure. As we shall see, however, divisionalization has an effect on that choice—the divisions are drawn toward the Machine Bureaucracy configuration. But the Divisionalized Form configuration itself focuses on the structural relationship between the headquarters and the divisions, in effect, between the strategic apex and the top of the middle line.

As noted in Chapter 7, the Divisionalized Form of the modern era was pioneered by Edgar J. Thomson of the Pennsylvania Railroad and Pierre du Pont and Alfred Sloan, Jr. of GM. It is primarily a configuration for organizations that are too large or too diverse to be managed as centralized structures organized in single tiers of functional departments. Most often, it is an answer to market diversification either through growth or through takeovers (conglomeration). There are a number of intermediate forms between the Machine Bureaucracy and the Divisionalized Form, however; Mintzberg (1979) counts four subtypes.

The *Integrated Form* is characterized by purely functional divisions, each performing a step in the corporation's total value chain, and it is only a small step away from the departmentalized, monolithic organization. The divisions are locked into a common planning system and generally lack the freedom to buy from or sell to other than their sister divisions. If such an organization starts to seek wider markets by diversifying production in its divisions and allowing them to sell some of their output directly to outside customers, it changes to the *By-product Form*. Central planning is still pervasive and the needs of the sister divisions dominate, but some more freedom is introduced. If diversification and growth in the by-product sector continue, the open market may at some point in time become more important to the divisions than the corporation's internal market, and the organization moves on to the *Related Product Form*. At that point, the demands from customers in the open market become more important to the divisions than their internal, corporate commitments, and they require a much more substantive independence. The end of the line is the *Conglomerate Form*—the pure version of the Divisionalized Form—where the divisions are fully independent and often totally unrelated.

In this pure form the corporate headquarters will be small—Mintzberg mentions the case of Textron, where a staff of 30 executives and administrators oversaw 30 divisions with combined sales of more than $1.5 billion (of late 1960s denomination). Corporate management will concentrate on monitoring the divisions' financial performance and on issuing policy for long-range planning. Typically, there will also be a small legal department, and in many instances an industrial relations office.

The process can also run in the other direction—from a conglomeration of unrelated companies to a tight-knit, divisionalized corporation. When du Pont took over control of GM from William C. Durant, even the monitoring and planning functions were not established, and it was at the very most a holding company—Durant managed it with the help of two to three assistants and their secretaries (Chandler 1977). Du Pont and Sloan quickly established stringent reporting and planning procedures and allocated the divisions to separate market brackets. Over the years, control was gradually tightened, and more and more common functions were instituted. Mintzberg (1979, p. 405) cites Wrigley[4] to the effect that in the mature GM, "The central office controls labor relations, market forecasting, research, engineering, quality control, styling, pricing, production scheduling, inventory levels, product range, and dealer relations; it decides what plants are to be built, and what cars; it styles them, and it tests them on the corporate Proving Ground." There is also extensive use of standardized parts across divisions. Mintzberg concludes that the modern GM has moved almost all the way toward a Machine Bureaucracy, and is best characterized as exhibiting the Integrated Form variant of the Divisionalized Form.

Differentiated Centralization

This illustrates the two pulls acting on the Divisionalized Form—one decentralizing and one centralizing. The pull underlined by Mintzberg in his total model of the main five configurations is the pull of the middle line (division management) to balkanize—to decentralize, increase the divisions' freedom of action, escape too detailed central planning, and reduce their dependence on the sister divisions. On the other side, the Divisionalized Form is a configuration created not for the love of decentralization as such, but as a remedy for the mounting control problems experienced as organizations (especially Machine Bureaucracies) become very large. The strategic apex in a Divisionalized Form, then, delegating authority only by necessity, will almost always be on the lookout for ways to achieve stronger central control.

Corporate management's objectives will differ, however, according to the nature of the enterprise. The main distinction here is between companies with totally unrelated divisions (true conglomerates) and companies where the divisions have related products or markets, and where synergies or increased economies of scale are conceivable (which was the case in GM). In true conglomerates the strategic apex will concentrate on monitoring results and on managing corporate finance; in companies with possible synergies, its ambitions will also cover cross-divisional planning and coordination.

Information technology will also offer new possibilities for Divisionalized Forms, and not only on the corporate level. The divisional level—the changes possible within the divisions themselves—is also very important. However, they are more or less equal to the possibilities for individual organizations discussed under the other headings in this chapter and therefore do not need separate treatment here.

---

[4] Wrigley, L.: *Diversification and Divisional Autonomy*, D.B.A. thesis, Harvard Business School, 1970.

Consequently, we can concentrate on the corporate level, where the main dimension for change is the centralization/decentralization dimension outlined earlier, and where the main differences in attitudes are dictated by the level of affinity between divisions.

In true conglomerates, companies where there are no potential synergies between divisions, the incentive for cross-divisional, central planning is of course limited. However, corporate headquarters may well partake in the planning process in the separate divisions, or at least use their plans to monitor their progress and trigger corrective action at an early stage in the case of underperformance. The supervision may be purely financial or may cover a broader range of indicators. System-supported supervision offers ample opportunity for strengthening and refining such monitoring of financial and other quantitative information. With the proper systems in place for conducting day-to-day business in the divisions, monitoring may even take place in real time or almost real time, as in the reporting systems of Benetton and Hennes & Mauritz. This will provide corporate headquarters with several options for development: closer control and participation in the daily affairs of the divisions, management of more divisions with the same staffing, and a reduction of headquarters staff while maintaining or even improving control.

In addition to improved monitoring, computer-based systems will also make it possible to elaborate the financial integration of a Divisionalized Form considerably, regardless of subtype. With sophisticated systems, corporations may run what amounts to internal banking systems, where internal transactions are netted (also across borders), liquid reserves are pooled, and internal loans and deposits are made. Many large companies, such as the Norwegian conglomerate Norsk Hydro, have had such systems for years already. At Hydro, which is regarded as one of the world leaders in this field, all transactions by divisions and their sub-sidiaries are made toward central, internal accounts managed by corporate finance—no division or subsidiary ever sends money directly to another or to major suppliers, not even across borders. If a subsidiary in Norway needs to pay a supplier in the United States, payment is made in Norwegian kroner to corporate finance in Norway, who will then pay the supplier in dollars from its accounts in the United States—accounts that in turn receive payments from Hydro's American operations for goods and services purchased elsewhere in the world. All external loans, deposits, and currency transactions are made by corporate finance. In this way the number and size of external currency transactions and ordinary bank transactions are minimized.

Hydro even operates a bank for its employees in Norway—complete with automatic teller machines installed in its offices and subsidiaries around the country, where employees can withdraw money with their

Hydro cards. The bank accepts deposits and gives loans to employees, always at better terms than those offered by ordinary Norwegian banks.

The advantages discussed so far also apply to the other subforms of the Divisionalized Form—those where there are more or less clear synergies or economies of scale to be realized by coordination across divisions. However, in such organizations, the strong coordinating powers of computer-based systems can also be brought to bear. In addition to system-supported supervision, both implicit coordination, programmed routines, and hyperautomation can be applied to overcome the information and control overload that earlier prohibited unified coordination of the divisions. I believe that this will allow reintegration of operations in a large number of instances, reducing the number of divisions or even transforming Divisionalized Forms to clean-cut Machine Bureaucracies or Flexible Bureaucracies. In so doing, they may also cross the threshold to become model-driven organizations, depending mainly on the regulating model.

We have seen some developments lately that point in this direction—a growing number of companies have taken advantage of computer-based just-in-time systems to eliminate regional warehouses and coordinate distribution nationally or even internationally. HÅG, for instance, a Norwegian producer of desk chairs, delivers made-to-order chairs from its manufacturing plant in the mountain town of Røros directly to customers over most of Europe within five days of receiving the order.[5] This feat is made possible by a sophisticated just-in-time production management system and cooperation with a forwarding agent who runs operations with the help of a computer-based distribution system. The condition is of course that the order stays within the range of upholstery in stock. Dell, the American PC maker, runs a similar operation from its plant in Ireland.

Multinational companies are increasingly lumping national markets together in larger geographical regions and have restructured both manufacturing and distribution along the new boundaries, supporting them with sophisticated logistics systems. In Scandinavia we have seen quite a number of such moves now, as companies have organized their Scandinavian operations under one umbrella, establishing a joint headquarters in one of the capitals, often supplying the whole region directly from a single facility.

As our experience grows and systems mature, it should be possible to achieve a much higher integration than we experience today. The result could be larger, faster, and more nimble multinationals, which means increased competition for businesses who believe they are local and

---

[5] Personal communication with the project manager for the JIT implementation.

have advantages because of their small size. Still, it does not seem that the extensions of the space of constructible organizations will contain variants of the Divisionalized Form that amount to new configurations, neither for the conglomerate variant nor for the more tightly knit firm—at least as long as we maintain the condition that all the elements of the organization shall have the same owners or at least answer to the same corporate management. When it comes to the coordination of totally separate companies, however, we approach something new: the Meta-Organization, which will be discussed later in this chapter.

TRANSFORMING ADHOCRACY

Mintzberg views the Adhocracy as the youngest of his five basic configurations. As a configuration for larger, formal organizations, this is probably correct, even if it also represents one of the two primal coordination mechanisms. However, I suspect that closer study would find that variations of it have been in use for centuries and even millennia, especially in teams of craftsmen constructing buildings, ships, or other large objects.

The Adhocracy comes into its own when the environment is so dynamic that it is difficult to standardize products and perpetual innovation is necessary; and the innovative work is so complex that it requires the efforts of many experts or expert groups. Adhocracies must therefore bridge specialization in a much more dramatic way than Professional Bureaucracies, where experts cooperate by enacting their establish professional roles and adhering to their own group's particular standards. In Adhocracies the experts have to give and take, to pioneer new approaches that may break with established procedures, and to arrive at joint solutions incorporating elements from them all. Because experts are so central to the innovations that Adhocracies live by, they must also hold wide power—at least in in practice if not in formal designation. Describing the design parameters of the Adhocracy, Mintzberg says (1979, pp. 432–3, bold type in original):

> **In Adhocracy, we have a fifth distinct structural configuration: highly organic structure, with little formalization of behavior; high horizontal job specialization based on formal training; a tendency to group the specialists in functional units for housekeeping purposes but to deploy them in small market-based project teams to do their work; a reliance on the liaison devices to encourage mutual adjustment—the key coordinating mechanism—within and between these teams; and selective decentralization to and within these teams, which are located at various places in the organization and involve various mixtures of line managers and staff operating experts.**
>
> **To innovate means to break away from established patterns. So the**

innovative organization cannot rely on any form of standardization for coordination. In other words, it must avoid all the trappings of bureaucratic structure, notably sharp divisions of labor, extensive unit differentiation, highly formalized behaviors, and an emphasis on planning and control systems."

Adhocracy comes in many varieties, since organizations may border on other configurations or have to meet special conditions. Mintzberg mentions at least seven variants, with the Operating Adhocracy and the Administrative Adhocracy as the most important ones. (He does not say it explicitly, but they seem to represent two main classes, whereas the other five are subtypes). The Operating Adhocracy is the classic form, where the teamwork is undertaken to serve the customers' needs directly, and where the operating core and the administrative staff constantly mix and merge in project teams. In the Administrative Adhocracy, however, the operating core is cut off from the administrative part of the organization because it needs another kind of structure since it is automated (most often it will be a Machine Bureaucracy) or even done away with completely and contracted out to other organizations. The rest of the organization, structuring itself as an Adhocracy, can then concentrate on the innovative part of the work, leaving the isolated operating core to crank out the products. Typical Administrative Adhocracies include newspapers, where the editorial staff faces the awesome task of creating a new paper every day (different down to the last letter), while the printing plant and the distributing organization—always physically separated from the editorial offices, often even organized as separate companies—can concentrate on stream- lining their repetitive duty of providing the subscribers with (from their point of view) the same wad of printed paper every day. As we have already concluded, information technology (especially by enabling much more extensive automation) will make it possible to structure more organizations as Administrative Adhocracies in the future.

The other subforms defined by Mintzberg, such as the Entrepreneurial Adhocracy (a hybrid of Adhocracy and Simple Structure) and the Divisionalized Adhocracy (a cross with the Divisionalized Form) will differ significantly in the extent to which they benefit from computer- based systems. The Entrepreneurial Adhocracy, which is really an Operative Adhocracy (usually a high-tech start-up) with an owner/ manager who is also an outstanding professional (and recognized as such), will not benefit any more than small Operative Adhocracies in general. The Divisionalized Adhocracy, however, stands to gain more. As Mintzberg defines it, it is essentially a Divisionalized Form with an environment so complex that simple divisionalization does not suffice—it has to implement a matrix structure. A true matrix organization does away with the unity of command that is the hallmark of Machine

Bureaucracies and conventional Divisionalized Forms, and requires close, team-oriented cooperation between the two (or even three) dimensions found in the matrix.

It is indeed conceivable that the strong coordinating powers of computer-based systems—which can allow a Divisionalized Form to change into a Machine Bureaucracy or a Flexible Bureaucracy—can help a Divisionalized Adhocracy to collapse one of its dimensions. For instance, in a product/market matrix (the most common one), the coordination of production and shipment of goods may be streamlined to such an extent that the organization may be able to collapse its matrix to essentially a market-based Divisionalized Form served by a common product division. As noted earlier, we have indeed seen tendencies in this direction lately, as a number of multinational companies have considerably enlarged the geographical regions served by one organizational unit.

The Communication Bottleneck

Regardless of which subtype of Adhocracy we study, however, the central problem is the copious communication needed to coordinate through mutual adjustment, the coordinating mechanism required for the kind of tasks that Adhocracies are designed to tackle. To quote Mintzberg once more (1979, p. 463),

> People talk a lot in these structures; that is how they combine their knowledge to develop new ideas. But that takes time, a great deal. Faced with the needs to make a decision in the Machine Bureaucracy, someone up above gives an order and that is that. Not so in the Adhocracy. Everyone gets into the act. First are all the managers who must be consulted—functional managers, project managers, liaison managers. Then are all the specialists who believe their point of view should be represented in the decision. A meeting is called, probably to schedule another meeting, eventually to decide who should participate in the decision. Then those people settle down to the decision process. The problem is defined and redefined, ideas for its solution are generated and debated, alliances build and fall around different solutions, and eventually everyone settles down to a hard bargaining about the favored one. Finally, a decision emerges—that in itself is an accomplishment—although it is typically late and will probably be modified later. All of this is the cost of having to find a creative solution to a complex, ill-structured problem.

Although this is all necessary to solve one-of-a-kind problems, it is devastating for any attempt to compete in the field of routinized work. Adhocracies are ill equipped to handle ordinary, routine tasks, and, if they want to move in such a direction, they must transform their structures— for instance, to Professional Bureaucracies (for consulting based on standard methods and a repertoire of tested solutions) or Machine Bureaucracies (for volume production of goods). Such transformations are, by the way, seldom made without conflict and the defection of a number of experts. Those who prefer innovative work and adhocratic organization will fight fiercely against the changes, and, if they lose, a number of them will probably jump ship to join other companies more in tune with their preferences. They may even choose to set up a company of their own. This is in accord with the main pull on an Adhocracy, which, according to Mintzberg (1979), is the pull of the support staff to collaborate—which translates into the experts' insistence on organizing work in projects and participating in decision making on all levels.

How, then, if at all, can information technology help to ease the exceptionally heavy burden of communication that is the core problem of the Adhocracy? Saturated as they are with communication, and with a consistent pull toward cooperation, we should expect these organizations first of all to benefit from systems supporting communication and teamwork—that is, they should benefit more than other configurations from the use of groupware tools of all denominations. I do indeed believe they will be able to use such tools profitably, but success will not be ensured—they will need fairly firm coaching in order to use such tools for increased productivity rather than simply for increasing their volume of communication and probing their (always interesting) subject matters to even greater depths.

However, as concluded earlier, groupware (e.g., coauthoring systems, systems for meeting assistance, electronic mail and group calendars) is not going to revolutionize any type of organization—not even Adhocracies. The reason is that these types of systems really only support and facilitate the various kinds of interpersonal communication that constitute the traditional means for mutual adjustment. They do very little to reduce the required communication volume; on the contrary, by offering improved channels they tend to *increase* the total amount of communication instead.

Groupware will therefore only allow Adhocracies to become a bit more efficient (provided the necessary coaching), to produce work of somewhat higher quality, and to function more independently of physical proximity. Groupware products will not have the power needed to allow structures very different from today's Adhocracies, since they simply do not tap into the most powerful aspects of computers.

Ascendance of the Interactive Adhocracy

The strong points of information technology, however, offer other possibilities—perhaps not so obvious, but much more interesting. The attack point is, even here, the volume of communication needed for coordination. However, the thrust is not in the direction of better tools for this communication, but toward reducing the need for such interpersonal communication in the first place.

How can that be accomplished? The answer lies in the mediating model and the power of implicit coordination. If an Adhocracy can model its problem domain to sufficient depth and with sufficient rigorousness, it can also build systems that will shift the larger part of the coordination burden from explicit interpersonal communication (which has to be carried out in addition to the actual work itself) to a much more terse and efficient kind of communication, directed *toward the system* (or complex of systems) and *effected as an implicit part of the actual work.*

An early example is, as we noted, the CAD system used for the structural design of Boeing 777. Before the introduction of the new system, all coordination in the project organization had to rely on direct interpersonal communication, meetings, and circulation of drawings—all burdensome efforts that came on top of the actual design work. With the CAD system in place, the need for much of that communication was simply eliminated, since the required information could be presented through the system to anyone at any time. Additionally, the information itself was created and fed into the system as an integral part of the work process and required little or no separate effort.

Unlike the implementation of groupware, then, the introduction of comprehensive systems based on a mediating model will allow quite dramatic changes—even large organizations may achieve real-time or close-to-real-time mutual adjustment, in some aspects comparable to the kind of coordination achieved in small groups. Adhocracies based on mediating models should therefore become much more efficient, since they will spend far less time and effort on coordination than they used to. They should also be able to react and adapt significantly faster to changes in their problem domains. This variant of the Adhocracy is definitely different enough from its traditional forebear to justify a new name: it could be called the *Interactive Adhocracy*, to connote the way it depends on pervasive, real-time, interactive systems to sustain the dynamic mutual adjustment that is the defining feature of adhocracies.

The Interactive Adhocracy will retain almost all the main design parameters of the Adhocracy, such as organic structure, selective decentralization, horizontal job specialization, high percentage of professionals/experts, and a concurrent use of functional and market groupings. The liaison devices of the Adhocracy will, however, be largely supplanted by the mediating model.

While keeping and even strengthening the superior problem-solving capability of the traditional Adhocracy, the Interactive Adhocracy should be able to come substantially closer to the other configurations in efficiency, and it should therefore emerge as a viable alternative in a much larger number of cases. To bring the creative power of this kind of organization to bear on problem domains that have, as yet, not been able to sustain the costs of an Adhocracy should be a very exciting prospect in a world where most markets experience increasingly rapid changes and a mounting pressure for innovation.

There are two important limiting factors for the construction of Interactive Adhocracies. One is the extent to which the problem domain can be modeled with sufficient rigorousness to be implemented in a suite of computer-based systems. As we travel along the learning curve, however, and our tools and methods improve, we will be able to do so for an increasing number of organizations. The other major factor is the need for synchronization of goals and objectives. The "anarchistic" nature of Adhocracies means that their members must internalize their organization's goals and objectives to a larger degree than necessary in more hierarchic configurations. As Khandwalla[6] says about the Adhocracy (quoted in Mintzberg 1979, p. 435),

> The job of coordination is not left to a few charged with responsibility, but assumed by most individuals in the organization, much in the way members of a well-knit hockey or cricket team all work spontaneously to keep its activities focused to the goal of winning.

This will be even more true in an Interactive Adhocracy, where the volume of interpersonal communication will be significantly lower than in a conventional Adhocracy. If model-mediated mutual adjustment is to be used on a large scale, sustained attention to the maintenance of a comprehensive team spirit and loyalty toward common goals will be required. Without a common understanding of the organization's goals and objectives and of their own role in the total picture, the members of the organization may end up pulling in opposite directions, compromising the viability of the model.

NEW: THE META-ORGANIZATION

So far, we have only looked at the evolution of Mintzberg's original five configurations. However, information technology may also permit the construction of totally new configurations. The discussions in Chapters 12 through 14 have hinted at two: one emerging from the strong coupling of independent organizations, the other emerging from the very fringes of organization. I will call them, respectively, the *Meta-Organization* and the

---

[6] Khandwalla, P. N.: "Organizational Design for Change," *Learning Systems, Conceptual Reading*, 5 (New Delhi, India, 1976).

Organized Cloud. Table 16-1 (p. 402/3), lists the main characteristics of these two and the three modified configurations discussed earlier.

As we concluded in Chapters 12 and 14, the strong, detailed, and extensive coordination that can be achieved through the use of unified computer-based systems makes it possible to achieve a new kind of integration between separate organizations. Organizations such as those comprising the manufacturing system centered on the Nissan factory in Sunderland are indeed coordinated more closely than sister departments within most single organizations. Whether or not the organizations involved have separate owners, their operations are so intertwined and they depend so critically on each other for their daily operations that it seems very reasonable to view them as a single organizational entity. However, the fact that they have separate owners, separate economies, and separate chains of command and are joined only in a contractual arrangement makes it difficult to classify such clusters as Machine Bureaucracies or Divisionalized Forms—even if they resemble these configurations in many ways. There is also a continuum of such arrangements—from the very long-term, inclusive, and tight arrangement of the Nissan's Sunderland operations, to more temporary hookups such as the ones that may be established in the construction business to bid on a specific contract.

There are various terms in use for such arrangements, most often *network organization, networked organizations*, or *virtual organizations*. As they are used today, they are given quite varied interpretations, ranging from the one we are discussing here (a close cooperation between separate organizations) to single organizations where a large part of the members rely on information technology to work away from the organization's premises. The last phenomenon does not necessarily involve any new organizational developments at all. As Mintzberg points out (1979), physical distribution of services (or people) does not necessarily involve any decentralization of power, especially not when the dispersal is facilitated by much improved communication equipment—which is precisely what makes it possible to keep the normal chains of command regardless of distance. Instead, I will apply the term *Meta-Organization* to entities consisting of two or more closely coupled organizations. This term serves both to indicate the layered nature of such organizational constructs and to avoid the misleading connotations that can be attached to the other terms.

Particularly, I find the term "virtual organization" superficial and misleading—if we extend to it the connotation of "virtual" in other computer-related terms, such as "virtual memory," "virtual disks," or even "virtual reality," (a perfectly postmodern oxymoron), a virtual organization should be a simulated organization—the kind you play with in

Configuration	Main Coordinating Mechanism	Main Design Parameters	Main Contingency Factors
Joystick Organization *Early examples: Possibly some centralized franchising operations.*	Regulating model, emphasizing system-supported supervision and programmed routines.	Centralization and organic structure. Little specialization, except sophisticated technostructure; little formalization.	Small to medium size, nonsophisticated technical system *or* hyperautomated operating core, simple, dynamic environment (possibly hostile), or strong power needs of top manager.
Flexible Bureaucracy *Early examples: Possibly some advanced JIT producers.*	Regulating model, emphasizing hyperautomation, programmed routines, and (depending on the problem domain) implicit coordination.	Behavior formalization, vertical and horizontal job specialization, usually market grouping or matrix structure, large operating unit size, vertical centralization and limited horizontal decentralization, action planning.	Medium to large, regulating, hyperautomated technical system, environment that is simple to moderately complex and stable to moderately dynamic, technocratic control.
Interactive Adhocracy *Early examples: Possibly some design projects using advanced CAD systems.*	Mediating model, emphasizing implicit coordination. Project oriented. Experts have much informal power.	Organic structure, selective decentralization, horizontal job specialization, training (large percentage professionals/experts). Functional and market grouping concurrently.	Often fairly small, but can become large if problem domain is well suited for modeling. Complex and dynamic environment, sophisticated and often automated technical system.

Meta-Organization *Early examples:* *Possibly supplier clusters such as the most advanced ones in the automobile industry.*	Regulating model, emphasizing hyperautomation, programmed routines and (depending on the problem domain) implicit coordination.	Strongly formalized cooperation between a number of independent organizations. Vertical product specialization and functional specialization among organizations, vertical centralization and limited horizontal decentralization, action planning.	Medium to large, regulating, hyperautomated technical system, environment that is simple to moderately complex and stable to moderately dynamic, technocratic control.
Organized Cloud *Early examples:* *Reservation systems, trading systems.*	Mediating model, emphasizing implicit coordination.	Nonmanaged, self-regulating, except for operation of providing system. Sophisticated technostructure.	Small to very large, simple but extremely dynamic environment, sophisticated and fully automated technical system.

Table 16-1:   *Main characteristics of the three modified and two new structural configurations. Format adapted from Mintzberg 1979.*

computer-based management games, an imaginary organization that does not affect reality at all. Only *real* organizations can act in the *real* world.

I also prefer to avoid the term "network," which has a distinctly egalitarian connotation that does not fit many of the actual examples. Whatever the relations are between the participants in the Nissan setup, for instance, they are surely not equal. Also, the term "network" seem to imply that one can fairly easily connect and disconnect to the structure; if there is one thing that is true about setups such as the one in Sunderland, it is that it takes copious amounts of work and long-time commitments to establish it, and, once established, it is very expensive to change both setup and participants.

A Meta-Organization may of course also consist of equal partners, with no single partner occupying a dominating role. The present terms are used with a considerable degree of looseness, however—even fairly simple cooperation endeavors such as common marketing efforts, a number of common projects, or the use of email for coordination seem to arouse the enthusiasm of the IT community and earn the participants a pioneer status, even if it is not at all different from what was earlier achieved by traditional means. In contrast, to call a construct a Meta-Organization, the activities of the different participants should be directly and unequivocally coordinated through a common systems infrastructure, preferably with a high level of automation.

Constructs resembling Nissan's in Sunderland may also exist within the boundaries of a single organization, as when a company with a number of manufacturing sites unites the coordination of their operations with a unified production control and delivery system, providing the sales force with something that looks and behaves like a single source. However, when such arrangements are set up within a single organization, it will fall into other categories that have already been discussed earlier in this chapter—notably in the sections on the Machine Bureaucracy and the Divisionalized Form.

In a Meta-Organization the participating organizations are closely bound together by comprehensive systems and are usually member of only one or two Meta-Organizations—at the very most a handful. In the case of multiple memberships, the organization will frequently have a corresponding number of different sites, with each physical site serving only one particular Meta-Organization. The common systems will typically coordinate a large part or even the total set of activities in the members' organization. The process of setting up the Meta-Organization requires considerable efforts over extended periods of time and is replete with planning and design in painstaking detail. Once set up, is not easily dissolved, since the process of replacing a member is almost as costly as setting the whole thing up in the first place. Members are usually specialized in relation to each other and totally dependent on each other for the combination to succeed. Because of the efforts involved, the number of members in a Meta-Organization will typically be single-digit or double-digit, but increasing standardization may facilitate larger Meta-Organizations in the future.

The main purpose behind Meta-Organizations is to automate coordination of processes across the member organizations. They will therefore depend on regulating models, emphasizing hyperautomation and programmed routines. Depending on the problem domain, they may also use implicit coordination. The main design parameters will resemble the Flexible Bureaucracy's: a strong formalization of cooperation, vertical product specialization among members, vertical centralization both inside the member organizations and in the cooperative effort itself, and a preponderance of action planning. The Meta-Organization's technical system and preferred environment will be the same as the Flexible Bureaucracy's—indeed, the Meta-Organization's goal will, to a large degree, be to function (for production purposes) just like a Flexible Bureaucracy.

In spite of the considerable efforts needed to establish them, I believe we will see a growth in the number of Meta-Organizations in the future, and I believe the most prominent form (at least for a long period of time) will be clusters of suppliers built around dominating buyers, even though there will also be a growth in cooperative efforts between more or less equal partners.

However, I am generally skeptical toward the very optimistic attitude many commentators take on the prospects for imminent success of more temporary arrangements of this kind (for example, in the construction business, which is often subject of such discussions). This optimism, in my view, vastly underestimates the difficulties and efforts involved in going beyond the email stage and setting up really close cooperation based on the use of common (or communicating) systems in areas such as design and production control. Not only is the level of systems standardization still far away from what is needed for easy hookups; the organizations involved are almost guaranteed to use different data formats and, even more important, to have different understandings of important terms and categories. For instance, when Elkem[7] wanted to compare the performance of the different furnaces at its Norwegian and American smelters, it turned out that the terms and parameters used to measure performance were so different between the sites that it was simply impossible to make a comparison. To obtain meaningful data, it would be

---

[7] The Norwegian metals company that is among the sponsors of the research behind this book.

necessary to carry out a full revision and standardization of the terms and parameters used at the different sites—an effort so overwhelming, and sure to meet with so much local resistance, that the project was shelved for an indefinite period.

Supplier Clusters

The supplier cluster alternative, such as the Nissan example, is most easily established—not because it is technically easier or requires less work, but because a powerful buyer can demand cooperation from its subcontractors and more or less guarantee their benefits. Such a configuration will also tend to be more stable, since the leadership position will never be questioned. It is interesting, however, to speculate on whether or not there will be any impetus toward takeovers. Will the dominant buyer prefer to acquire the suppliers when they are already functionally almost as a part of its own organization?

Early in the automobile era, there was a strong movement toward such vertical integration, with Ford's legendary River Rouge plant as the pinnacle (Beniger 1986). Ford's ultimate ambition was to start with iron ore in one end of the factory and roll out finished automobiles in the other, keeping up an uninterrupted production flow throughout the complex. The task proved too difficult, however, and the River Rouge plant was not competitive compared to plants where materials, parts, and subassemblies were purchased from specialist companies.

It may be argued that information technology now has made it more realistic to tackle such complex coordination problems, as setups such as the Nissan plant indeed indicates. However, a number of the old arguments are still valid. Specialist companies will generally be more competent in their fields, since they serve several customers and accumulate superior experience, and since they can devote their full energy to a limited set of problems. The fact that they are not a formal part of the buyer's organization also means a reduced financial risk in case of a reduced demand for cars. I therefore believe that the Meta-Organization solution will be very stable in these circumstances, since (from the point of view of the dominant buyer) it combines the advantages of competitive know-how and reduced financial risks with a level of coordination fully comparable to what could be achieved through ownership.

The Meta-Organization will also tend to be quite stable in terms of membership, since a change of supplier can be very expensive for the suppliers involved as well as the buyer, due to the high costs of systems development and adaptation. In the Nissan Sunderland example there is the added stabilizing requirement that the most important suppliers are physically located on the ring road around Nissan's main plant.

Equal Partners

Cooperation among equal partners seems to be more difficult to establish and maintain, which should not come as a surprise. The costs involved in setting up a Meta-Organization are high, and the benefits of cooperation can be difficult to ascertain before hand. Moreover, a considerable level of mutual trust must be present from the outset, since the implementation of common systems and common procedures implies that the participating organizations will have to reveal many of their internal functions, problems, and even company secrets to each other. Such close cooperation will also easily put constraints on the activities of the member organizations—it may, for instance, be considered disloyal to do certain kinds of business with companies that are competing with a partner.

A successful Meta-Organization consisting of equal partners will tend to be somewhat unstable, since the partners will be fairly likely to develop different ambitions for the evolution of the partnership. One or some of the companies may well try to build a leading position at the expense of others; some companies may want to proceed toward a merger; some will play brakemen; and some may leave altogether for what they see as more exciting opportunities elsewhere. In the event that the cooperation is successful and free of conflicts, merger may well be a frequent outcome in the longer term.

NEW: THE ORGANIZED CLOUD

At the end of Chapter 13, I discussed briefly the organizing effects of reservation systems. Even though we do not consider this far-flung mass of people an organization (as it was defined in Chapter 3), the fact remains that all these tens of thousands of travel agents and others—using, for instance, SABRE or Amadeus—are perfectly coordinated in those aspects of their work that pertain to reservations for the flights, hotels, and car rentals that are listed there. In those aspects, they are even more strongly and efficiently coordinated than most members of conventional organizations. As I remarked at the end of the discussion, even if this arrangement is not an organization, it is certainly organized—and I think it is unsatisfactory to dismiss this phenomenon as not belonging to the realm of organizations just because it does not fit the traditional definitions. I propose to call it an *Organized Cloud*. The cloud metaphor here is derived more from astronomy than meteorology—picture the travel agents as a cloud of stars, held together by the gravity of the their common database.

Organized Clouds are by and large products of the computer age, as they are totally dependent on the powerful implicit coordination of the database to exist—they represent perhaps the most completely model-driven organizations we know today. Their databases represent complete mediating models of their problem domains, and all interaction between the members takes place via these models.

However, we may say that they have a humble ancestor in the traditional marketplace, and somewhat more discernible progenitors in the stockmarkets and commodity markets that developed after 1700 (the world's first real stock exchange was established in London in 1698)—especially since the late nineteenth century, when traders started to use telegraphs and telephones. However, it is the reach, capacity, speed, and the interactive nature of the database that has made possible the formation of really significant Organized Clouds, and it is the almost instant information dissemination and feedback provided by the systems that breathes life into the clouds and turns them into such powerful attractors.

Perhaps the most interesting clouds at the moment are the trading systems for stocks, currency, and commodities, which have substantially changed the behavior of the financial markets. Because of the almost instant conclusion of deals and broadcast of pricing, the pace of the markets have increased dramatically over the last decades, and in the course of the 1990s the development of program trade (trade initiated by computers programmed to react to certain price levels) increased the speed further. There is also a discernible trend toward growth in the biggest clouds (the trading systems based in London, New York, and Tokyo, the top three financial centers of the world), and trading is increasingly done on a global basis—especially for currency. As Yates and Benjamin (1991) point out, it will certainly be technically feasible to organize global markets. I think we can expect to see the development of a hierarchy of clouds on global, regional, and national bases, with the main focus on global and regional clouds. Currencies and commodities in particular are increasingly moving toward global integration, stocks probably toward a regional emphasis with a number of premium stocks traded globally, whereas small companies and local start-ups will continue to be traded mainly on a national basis. We may also see a development of some sector clouds on a global basis, with a single trading center (and thereby a single database) contracting most of the business in one industry—for example, shipping or gold mining.

The definition of an Organized Cloud is by no means clear. Clouds exhibit some of the properties of proper organizations (as defined in Chapter 3). If we start out with the two previous examples, it is fairly evident that cloud members do not have a common goal in the sense that members of a normal organization have (or should have!). Although cloud members are very interested in the availability of clouds suitable to their purposes, and will willingly pay fees to have access to them, they do not have a common purpose relating to any *specific* cloud—they do not look toward the interests of a cloud in the way any loyal organization member would look toward the interests of his or her organization. However, cloud members do have *similar* purposes. The travel agents all want to book airplane seats and hotel rooms; the traders all want to trade. It is precisely these similar interests that bring them into the cloud in the first place. In their transactions as cloud members, however, they look only toward their own or their clients' narrow interests, and most of them will even be member of several clouds simultaneously: travel agents will use several reservation systems, stockbrokers may have access to several trading systems. They will quite expediently use the one that offers them the best services and the most favorable terms, just as when they shop for other products and services in the marketplace.

It would also be a little meaningless to say that clouds have a division of labor—admittedly, the members all fend for themselves, but their activities are not part of an overall effort to achieve a common purpose. Essentially, clouds are non-managed: there is no central authority that can issue orders to the members, aside from determining some basic rules. Clouds do, however, have accepted mechanisms for reaching decisions (deals), and there is a rudimentary power structure concentrated around the framework of rules for actions within the cloud's sphere of interest: There are supervisory bodies, rules about membership, and mechanisms for expulsion or punishment in case of misconduct. There is also a common memory, represented by the central database, and there is definitely a communication structure. Finally, the activities of the members are co-ordinated in the sense that the actions of one member have impact on the actions of other members—within an accepted problem domain and within an accepted set of rules.

In contrast with the Meta-Organization, the Organized Cloud typically coordinates only one or a few of the members' activities, and members are typically members of several clouds. Membership is defined in terms of subscription to a service or something similar (both organizations and single individuals can be members), and access is usually simple, by means of a defined (even standardized) interface. A new member can typically be up and running in a matter of days or even hours. The Cloud is built on narrow, standardized interaction; members all act alike in their transactions as Cloud members; there is no specialization and no interdependence except for the logged results of the (atomized) actions.

The Organized Cloud always depends totally on a mediating model, emphasizing above all implicit coordination. Its main design parameters are that it is essentially nonmanaged and self-regulating, except for the provision of the system itself. It has a sophisticated technostructure run by the providing organization—which is probably structured as a Machine Bureaucracy or Flexible Bureaucracy. It can be small or very, very large—membership in large clouds today number in the tens of thousands, some even hundreds of thousands, and in the future clouds may consist of millions of members. Typically, clouds exist in a simple but extremely dynamic environment. The technical system is of course fully automated.

If we accept markets and exchanges as Organized Clouds, the configuration has been around from time immemorial and has served very important purposes. It may even be argued that a market-based economy as a whole can be viewed as an Organized Cloud, although, on a societal level, it is inseparable from other powerful organizational structures, both political and nonpolitical. Indeed, clouds seem to be particularly well suited for market-like purposes where the objective is to match buyers and sellers, takers and suppliers, within a framework of open information about crucial parameters such as prices, volume, and bookings. However, the much improved communication infrastructures provided by information technology, coupled with the unsurpassed coordinating powers of the database, provide an altogether new and vastly more powerful basis for this kind of organization. As the prices for systems and communication continue to fall, as more and more businesses and private homes are equipped with computers and data communication links, and as the Internet (or its eventual successor) provides standardized access and payments, the formation of clouds will become viable for purposes with much lower yields than airline reservations and transactions in the stock and currency markets. The Organized Cloud—in its modern guise an organization fully driven by a mediating model—could well emerge as one of the defining features of future societies.

RELATING MODELS AND CONFIGURATIONS

In Mintzberg's theory, each of the five coordinating mechanism gives rise to a particular structural configuration. Even if all large organizations will have sub-units and or pockets of deviating structures depending on different coordinating mechanisms, there will normally be a dominating mechanism that will permeate the organization and determine its overall structure.

In contrast with this one-to-one relationship between coordinating mechanism and structural configuration, the analysis in this chapter has shown that two of the three coordinating models proposed in Chapter 15—the mediating model and the regulating model—can support more than one configuration. However, models belonging to any of these two classes can vary considerably in scope—that is, in how comprehensive repetoirs of organizational actions they cover. When we include this dimension the seeming indefiniteness is resolved, in that the comprehensive and restricted versions give rise to different configurations. The relations between the different kinds of active models and the new structural configurations are summed up in Figure 16-1.

The *Mediating Model* is the basis for both the Interactive Adhocracy and the Organized Cloud. Models supporting Interactive Adhocracies will tend to be comprehensive, covering a broad set of activities, since they must support all or the major part of the activities in a complete organization. Models supporting Organizational Clouds, on the other hand, will tend to be quite restricted, supporting only the narrow activity that is the business of the cloud.

The *Regulating Model* will probably be the most widely used, at least for some time to come. It can support Joystick Organizations, Flexible Bureaucracies, and Meta-Organizations, as well as aspects of Divisionalized Forms. The Joystick Organization will tend to be simple and on the smaller side, but the model will be comprehensive in the sense that it supports a large part of the organization's total activities. The Meta-Organization will tend to be large and complex, but the model, although often quite complex in itself, will be restricted to those parts of

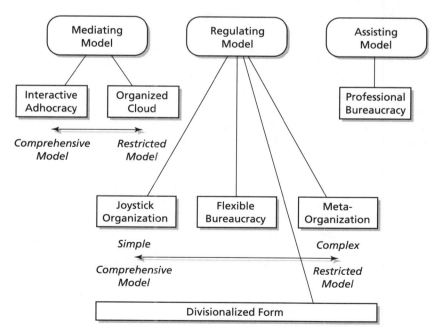

Figure 16-1: *Main model dependencies of the various configurations.*

the activities that are involved in the relationship between the partners in the Meta-Organization. The Flexible Bureaucracy will fall between these two—it will usually be more complex than the Joystick Organization, but less so than the Meta-Organization, and will usually employ models that are less comprehensive than the Joystick Organization and more so than the Meta-Organization. However, there will be great variation here—we may well see large Flexible Bureaucracies that are more complex than most or all Meta-Organizations, and there may also be Flexible Bureaucracies developing models as comprehensive as any Joystick Organization's.

Whereas the Meta-Organization is a configuration where certain aspects of separate, independent organizations are very strongly coordinated, the Divisionalized Form represents an arrangement to coordinate and control a number of organizations that are either part of or owned by the same corporation, and that are too complex taken together to be managed as one intergrated organization. The kind and degree of model support here will vary widely across the span of the different subforms of the Divisionalized Form. As noted under the discussion earlier in this chapter, highly integrated Divisionalized Forms may be able to use comprehensive models to reintegrate into Machine Bureaucracies or Flexible Bureaucracies, whereas true conglomerates may apply model support to achieve superior performance control and streamlined, common financing.

The third model, the *Assisting Model*, supports only one main configuration, one that is not among the IT-based configurations: the Professional Bureaucracy. The reason is that it is only assisting—helping professionals to perform their tasks better and/or more efficiently. Although it can be very advantageous (securing much greater consistency and quality in an organization's products and services) and also facilitate considerable reorganization of work in particular organizations, it cannot in my view support genuinely new structural configurations. Even a model-driven Professional Bureaucracy will remain a Professional Bureaucracy. Although an increased span of competence and programmed routines make it possible to reshape work processes to a certain degree, the structure of the organization as such will not change much as long as the professional judgment of experts, as well as the norms of the professional groups and of the greater professional community, lies at the heart of the organization and decides the main features of the work process.

17
Concluding Considerations

"He who bears in his heart a cathedral to be built is already victorious. He who seeks to become sexton of a finished cathedral is already defeated."
Saint-Exupéry, *Flight to Arras*, 1942

LONG ON CONSTRAINTS, SHORT ON POSSIBILITIES?

Some readers may perhaps at this stage feel a sting of disappointment—missing more spectacular technical predictions, more thrillingly novel organizational configurations, and more splendidly liberating organization structures. They may also feel that I have given too little attention to the more fashionable contemporary visions and ideas debated in the industry today. For instance, where is that virtual, networked knowledge organization based on multidisciplinary teams, assembled on the go for a particular challenge, meeting and working over the Internet and delivering its products in digital form directly to the prosumer? If you have not seen it here, it may simply be because you did not look hard enough—or because you mistook the physical topology of a technical device such as the Internet for an organizational structure. I shall elaborate a little on this.

Let us take a closer look at the virtual networked organization outlined above. It would probably be a project organization put together to solve a particular task or deliver a particular product or set of products. To do so, the task at hand would have to be broken down into subtasks, which would be distributed among the members of the organization. These members would then have to coordinate their work and monitor it so that they would be able to produce the desired result at the agreed time, with the agreed quality, and within the agreed budget.

This coordination could be effected in several ways. First of all, one of the project members could act as a main contractor, determine everything, hire in the others, plan their work, and monitor and direct them as they progressed. What kind of organization would we then have? I leave it to the reader to decide. Then, of course, the task could be very unstructured and pioneering, demanding a highly creative effort and involved cooperation between a multitude of experts, all with a stake in the result. What kind of organization would we then have? Again, I leave the answer to the reader. If in doubt, consult Mintzberg's short descriptions of the main properties of his structural configurations quoted under the appropriate subheadings in Chapter 16.

My point here is simply that an organization coordinated over the Internet is not necessarily a particular kind of organization any more than an organization coordinated over the telephone is—or an organization coordinated via telegraph or by smoke signals or messages speeded back and forth by horse riders. Here, we should especially remember the crucial difference between *dispersing* an organization physically and *decentralizing* its decision making. The nature of the communication channels has no necessary bearing on either, although better means of communication tend to make it easier to disperse people.

In my view, the metaphorical thinking that dominates much of the debate about information technology and organizations today—which base organizational concepts more or less directly on products or technological solutions—is not so much a result of profound insight as it is a sign of a rather limited understanding of the deeper relationships between technological capabilities and organizational opportunities. Organization structure and functioning are more dependent on the nature of an organization's main coordinating mechanisms and decision making arrangements than on the nature of its physical communication channels.

Does this contradict the postulation of five new IT-enabled configurations earlier in this chapter? I believe not—since those configurations are primarily based *not* on new communication arrangements, but on *new methods for coordination.* New communication equipment may constitute a part of the technological basis for these new coordination methods, but its application does not necessarily create new organizational forms all by itself.

Practical Theory

The main reason for the apparent lack of really exotic new organizational forms in my analysis is that my goal has been first and foremost to obtain results that have practical value. It is of course possible to make bolder predictions and envision more breathtaking organizational structures. There is, indeed, no lack of such prophecies. Being a consultant as well as a researcher, however, my goal was not only to achieve an understanding of the basic relationship between information technology and organization, but also to produce practicable models and theories—close enough to real life to enable me to offer better advice about how my clients' organizations can really come to grips with this new and exciting technology. I have therefore, throughout my analyses, striven to temper the purely technological possibilities with the basic human constraints and preferences that will continue to limit and shape our use of any new technology. This has implied a definitive departure from the technological stream-of-consciousness literature represented by, for instance, *Being Digital* by Nicholas Negroponte and *Microcosm* by George Gilder, and a concentration on the kind of technology use that is possible and probable in a normal human and social setting.

To use a simple illustration from another technological domain: the fact that we can easily build cars that go faster than 250 kilometers per hour, and that most commercially available cars can go faster than 150, does not by itself make it practical to use such speeds routinely in densely populated areas. In fact, most countries do not deem it practical (and, hence, legal) to use such speeds under *any* circumstances (except for competitions on specially designated tracks).

Likewise, the fact that information technology makes it possible for people who live in the most remote corners of the globe to work on common documents, pass email to each other, and even (in a number of years) confer via high-quality videophones does not by itself mean that organizations consisting of only such scattered individuals will be desirable or even viable other than for very special (and marginal) purposes. This is what the idea of the *space of constructible organizations* is all about—to delineate the realistically available alternatives for organizing work within a given culture and with a certain technological level.

Can theory be at all helpful in practical matters? One may perhaps think that answers to practical problems are best sought by accumulating experience, but, in this case, I soon concluded that we most of all lacked an adequate body of theory that could help us analyze experience and advance our understanding of the deeper relationships between information technology and organization. The link here is really quite straightforward. Without adequate theory, practical questions about how to take advantage of information technology—like the ones I mentioned in the introduction, that came from the audience when I lectured in the late 1980s—simply cannot be credibly answered. Without theory to help us interpret our experiences, we will not be able to understand much about what is going on and why, let alone chart a viable course into the future and sense potentials unrealized so far.

In order to provide the kind of practical, effective advice I wanted to be able to give my clients, then, factual knowledge and experience is not enough. To obtain a sound understanding of a particular field, experience, factual knowledge and theory are *all* mandatory. Sometimes an unconscious, everyday theory-in-use (Argyris 1980) may suffice, but for the large, complex organizations of our age, explicit scientific theories are necessary as well.

As JoAnne Yates says, summing up her very interesting work on the development of methods and technology for management control and communication in American industry between 1850 and 1920 (Yates 1989, pp. 274–275, my italics):

> Perhaps the most obvious implications concern communication and information technology. James R. Beniger has recently argued that the "Control Revolution" that began in the late nineteenth century contained the seeds of today's information society. Certainly, there are some parallels between the revolution in office technology of the 1880–1920 period and the revolution of the last twenty-five years. Recent innovations in computers and telecommunications have been so spectacular that contemporary commentators tend to focus solely on the technology, seeing it as the driving force causing changes in other parts of the organization. The case studies in this book, however, illustrate some of the problems with simple technological determinism. Technologies were adopted, not necessarily when they were invented, but often when *a shift or advance in managerial theory* led managers to see an application for them. Moreover, technologies were often adopted simply to facilitate existing managerial methods; potentially more powerful applications, such as the use of the telegraph for railroad dispatching, were ignored for long periods. *The technology alone was not enough—the vision to use it in new ways was needed as well.*
>
> A related implication for contemporary issues concerns both communication technology and geographical dispersion. Just as the telegraph once opened up possibilities for wider domestic markets and more scattered production facilities to companies such as Scovill and Du Pont, worldwide telecommunications systems are now doing the same for international markets. The historical cases suggest, however, that the real potential of these networks cannot be realized through a simple extension of existing patterns of communication. *Real gains await innovative thinking about underlying managerial issues.*

Therefore, when we encounter a new and uncharted territory like the interplay between computers and organizations, "nothing will be so practical as the development of a good new theory," as Daft and Lewin (1993) note (with due reference to Kurt Lewin[1]). As Yates attests, the future can seldom be forecasted by extrapolation, and to envisage potential new arrangements, it does not suffice to make empirical investigations of the current best practice. Without theory, we cannot distinguish between the significant and the insignificant, we cannot easily perceive causal relationships, and we cannot predict likely outcomes in new situations. Even

---

[1] Another, older Lewin. Daft and Lewin here refer to the article "The Research Center for Group Dynamics at Massachusetts Institute of Technology" by Kurt Lewin, appearing in *Sociometry*, 1945 (vol. 8), pp. 126–135.

today we are in the infancy of computer use, and no one would seriously propose that our results so far fathom the technology's potential or contain the complete blueprint for any future best practice.

So, first of all, we need a good theoretical foundation for the interplay of information technology and organization. Equally important, this foundation should not be built in isolation, but should relate directly to the established body of organization theory. It is very unlikely that the introduction of a new technology alone (albeit a powerful one) should alter the basic principles of human interaction beyond recognition, and by segregating the study of computers and organization from the rich body of organization research, we are bound to forgo major insights and take on a crippling burden of parallel research. In a field where there are many different and partly competing theoretical approaches, it is also of significant scientific interest to test established theory by systematically applying it to new problems. To me, this is also a matter of practical concern; a large part of today's managers know a lot about organization theory and feel quite at home with the main lines of argument. Linking a theory of information technology and organization to one of these traditions will make it much easier for them to relate to it, to understand it, and to use it for their own purposes. This was also one of my reasons for anchoring my analysis in Mintzberg's configurations. They have proved to be very useful tools for my analyses, and I also feel they have passed their introduction into the computer age with flying colors, showing their strength through their adaptability.

SOME SUGGESTIONS FOR THE PRACTICAL USE OF THIS BOOK

It is possible to work for improvement in an organization on several levels, from the discharge of a single task to the structuring of the total organization. However, single tasks are normally not very interesting targets—and tasks are, in themselves, not tenable analytical units if you want to take full advantage of the new possibilities offered by information technology, since any task is likely to be a construction shaped by reigning conventions and traditional tools. Tasks are, moreover, loci of functions, and function-oriented analysis becomes all too easily bogged down in detailed descriptions of existing routines, obstructing our comprehension of what the organization is really doing and restricting our creativity in the design of new solutions.

To obtain a satisfactory level of insight and understanding, it will usually be necessary to analyze the problem domain quite carefully in order to secure both a tenable technological solution and a good implementation of it, even in quite small and simple projects. If the goal is (as it should be) to go beyond traditional arrangements and make full use of the new technology, it is very important that the initial analysis aims at getting behind existing work arrangements to capture the gist of the work at hand—or, rather, its objectives, since the work (the present tasks) itself may be superfluous within a new framework.

This is not a trivial requirement. A good example is the accounts payable function in Ford. The key to the radical improvement achieved there was *not* a system that made the work of the accounts payable department more efficient; it was, on the contrary, the realization that the invoice itself—and hence most of the traditional accounts payable function— could be *eliminated* through the creative use of information technology. Such breakthroughs are the dramatic goal of most reengineering projects, but they are notoriously difficult to achieve—there are no surefire methods available, since in the end all radically new solutions hinge on the inspired creativity of the project team members. The best we can do in the way of methodology is to devise a number of coaxing exercises—as Davenport suggests in his very thorough study (Davenport 1993)—and hope that creativity will manifest itself. Of course, such a process is not entirely serendipitous; good coaxing strategies will produce much better results than bad ones.

To avoid being trapped by existing procedures, it is necessary to employ a top-down approach in the initial analysis, starting with the primary objectives at the highest organizational level relevant to the project: What is, quite simply, the nature of the products and services we aim to provide? The goal should be to describe the desired implementation of these objectives at the level of products, services, customers, or clients, and to chart the way they are related. I would propose an object-oriented approach for this, since it will force us to focus precisely on the central objects and help us avoid function analysis with its penchant for detailed descriptions of existing tasks and routines. Consequently, I would use object-oriented concepts and charting notations as tools in this work and for documentation—for instance those provided in Jacobson, Ericsson, and Jacobson (1994). There are also several comparable approaches available, although many would say that Jacobson et al. have presented the best one so far. One of the Jacobsons, Ivar, is also one of the *Three Amigos* behind the new, unified modeling language, UML (together with Grady Booch and James Rumbaugh).

The analysis should then proceed on one to three main levels, depending on what is appropriate for the project in question: product-related possibilities, process-related possibilities, and structure-related possibilities. These levels correspond to the three levels of IT utilization discussed in this book, as shown in Table 17-1. The boundaries between these three levels are of course blurred, but, by and large, there is a correspondence that is useful for both analysis and design.

Products and Services

Information technology has become one of the main enablers both for improvements in products and services and the development of totally new kinds of products and services. Very often, such advances hinge on one particular aspect of the technology. For instance, the development of services as diverse as today's flexible and efficient airline reservation systems, automatic teller machines, and electronic toll fee stations has been totally dependent on the existence of powerful databases with remote access.

When we have a reasonably clear picture of the objectives of the organization unit we are working with, its customers, their requirements, and the kinds of products and services we would like to provide, our design work can therefore be helped by a careful look at the discussions in Chapter 9 ("The IT-Based Preconditions"), which is about the strong and weak points of information technology and where it offers possibilities beyond earlier technology. Some of the central aspects of this discussion are further elaborated in Chapter 11 ("The Individual

Level of Analysis	Level of IT Support
Products and Services	**Direct utilization of information technology properties**
Changes in products and services or the development of totally new ones made possible by the use of information technology.	Discussions mainly in Chapter 9, some in Chapter 11, emotional defenses in Chapter 10.
Processes	**Computer-dependent coordination methods**
Cross-organization coordination and integration of tasks involved in the production and delivery of particular products and services or classes of products and services.	Discussions mainly in Chapters 12 through 14, some in Chapter 11, emotional defenses in Chapter 10.
Structure	**Active models**
Integration and information technology-based coordination on the level of the total organization.	Discussions in Chapters 15 and 16.

Table 17-1:   *The relationships between levels of analysis and levels of IT support.*

and the Group"), which also brings up the subject of self-service—a very important factor in several business areas in the future, not least financial products and services. To avoid being unduly constrained by the contemporary technological level, and to plan more realistically for some years into the future, Chapter 8 ("Information Technology Characteristics") should also prove useful. Finally, to temper the techno-optimism and avoid the emergence of an unbridled "chip-chip-hurrah" mentality, I would recommend Chapter 10 ("Emotional Barriers and Defenses").

Processes

Even though processes and services usually rest mainly on one aspect of information technology and thus depend directly on specific hardware and software products, their provision often involves more complex organizational processes spanning several organization units. Or, to view it from the opposite perspective, practically all medium-to-large organizations will have a number of processes that are central to their operations, some of which will produce and deliver products and services to outside customers/clients, and some of which will serve vital administrative needs. The key to these processes is coordination—of the efforts of those who are part of the process and of the customers, suppliers, and other parties inside and outside the organization.

To fathom the new possibilities for coordination provided by information technology, it should be useful to look at the chapters in Part IV. Chapter 11 ("The Individual and the Group") is perhaps the least interesting here, but it offers some ideas on the usefulness and limitations of information technology in the coordination of workgroups and teams. Chapter 12 ("Routines and Automation") should offer inspiration in the field of automation and task elimination, and Chapter 13 ("Coordination by Default") provides important signposts for forays into the exiting realm of implicit coordination—a coordinating mechanism with huge potential. Chapter 14 ("Comprehension and Control") outlines the possibilities arising from the greatly improved availability of information provided by information technology, especially the possibilities for centralization and decentralization and the concomitant migration of power within the organization. Finally, Chapter 10 ("Emotional Barriers and Defenses") is useful for avoiding the worst pitfalls of too technocratic approaches.

Structure

Today, most of the focus in the literature on information technology and organization is on the process level. Compared to the situation a couple of decades ago, when systems were still viewed mainly as specific tools for rather narrow functions in the organization, this represents a significant step forward. It is also a step up onto a higher level of complexity, perhaps the highest level we can presently handle with some confidence. However, as we gradually integrate our processes, even they will become candidates for closer integration and coordination. We then reach a level where the whole organization—and often a part of its environment as well—must be described in the same model and served by a set of intergrated systems. This involves rising to yet a higher level of complexity—today barely within reach and only for organizations with a well defined and fairly narrow problem domain. Tackling integration at the organization level will require thorough understanding of the relationship between work, technology, and organization, and we will need advanced methods for analysis, description, and modeling. At this level, organization structure becomes one of the paramount issues.

Organization structure is a subject of considerable interest already at the process level, as key processes can involve large numbers of people and many organization units. To achieve the best possible results, it is always important to choose structures that match our objectives and the nature of the required processes and systems central to those processes. Sometimes, we have a choice between process designs calling for different structures, and it is important to know the strengths and weaknesses of those structures if the desired results are to be achieved. However, structure first becomes a paramount concern when we do not simply approach a single process, but try to go one step further and integrate processes, support functions, systems, and system use across the total organization.

When we work at this level, the matters discussed in Part IV are still important, but the most significant contributions should come from the two first chapters in Part V. Chapter 15 ("Toward the Model-Driven Organization") should serve to increase our understanding of the potential of conceptual modeling, and point the way to how such models can form the basis for really comprehensive computer-based systems—and thus allow organizations to achieve new levels of integration and coordination. Chapter 16 ("The New Configurations") discuss in greater detail what the potential is for different types of organizations. This should help make us more aware of the potentials of our own organization and the ways in which it could (and could not!) be transformed, maybe even into a totally different configuration.

LIMITS TO FLEXIBILITY—BUT NOT TO COSTS?

Throughout this book I have tried to maintain a prudent attitude to the potential of information technology, especially to the possibilities we have for actually reaping its promised benefits through practical implementations. It is a very complex technology, difficult to master even in itself, and when it is inserted into such complex social constructs as our modern organizations, it is indeed a challenge to understand and manage the compounded ramifications.

I would therefore like to temper the fairly upbeat tone of the last two chapters with a few words of caution here at the end, with reference to my own discussions and to those taking place within the field of information technology and organizations. I will consider two issues in particular: flexibility and cost. They are, in fact, intimately related.

First of all, I believe that the case for flexibility has been overstated in the general debate on these matters. I do agree that information technology will allow us to build more flexible organizations that can respond more quickly and more accurately to changes in their environment and challenges from their competitors. Hyperautomation can accommodate much more variation than traditional automation, and increased spans of competence will have similar effects. I have detailed my views on this subject in Chapter 16, particularly in the section on the Flexible Bureaucracy. However, as indicated in that section, this flexibility is highly circumscribed—if the organization comes up against a problem that requires responses outside the functional scope of its systems, it will often prove much *less* flexible than an organization without any systems at all. The reason is simply that in order to respond it will have to modify its systems, which is necessarily a thorough and costly process for any significant change.

In theory, a computer-based organization can of course resort to ad hoc manual solutions just as easily as a non-computerized organization could, but that will hardly be true in practice. The technology-dependent organization will neither have the workforce nor the culture to revert effortlessly to such traditional means of doing business, and it will often experience great trouble in the process. Not that it would necessarily help if it did revert—the reason for its predicament would probably be that one or more of its competitors had developed the more comprehensive systems capable of meeting exactly that kind of challenges. If so, even an adequate manual solution would be of little use, since it would be too expensive to maintain over an extended period of time compared to the more efficient systems deployed by competitors.

If the new demands are such that they can be met by small adjustments or additions to the existing systems, these problems are manageable—a solution can be in place in a matter of days, weeks, or a few months (depending on the scope of the changes, the technical nature of the system, the quality of the underlying models, and the competence of the IS staff). However, from time to time, organizations that depend heavily on information technology will face a situation where the underlying structure of their systems and/or the basic technological solutions they employ cannot accommodate the necessary changes. They will then have to renew one or more of their systems completely, or face a situation where they may have to leave the field in question altogether, ceding it to the competition.

Total renewal of principal systems is a major operation involving considerable risk, high cost, and a significant period of time. The thorough analysis, the modeling, the creative efforts involved in designing new solutions that will have to last for quite a number of years, the painstaking labor to work out the design in sufficient detail, then the challenging process of rendering the design into executable program code, of testing the code, and finally the implementation of the new system in the organization, all this combine to make such projects major undertakings. Often, the great cost and considerable time required to do a thorough job on analysis and design tempt people to take shortcuts, frequently with catastrophic results. The systems either end up without critical functionality or the development process gets bogged down in endless and ill-structured modifications.

When talking about such major changes, it is also important to realize that after the introduction of new systems and routines, the people working in the organization will need considerable time to bring their performance up to par with the new tools and within their new work environment. No system can deliver peak performance without able and experienced operators, and all the important new adjoining routines must also be mastered. This is a fact often overlooked by the champions of perpetual change. Because the very fabric of any organization consists of well-established patterns of action, it stands to reason that one cannot rearrange those patterns too extensively too often and at the same time maintain an efficient organization. I started my career in the personnel department of a shipyard, and I still remember my experienced superior telling me that it would normally take a newly hired hand without previous experience a full year to reach the expected normal performance for an unskilled laborer there. It would be strange if it should take very much less time to develop the proficiency needed to make full use of advanced new computer-based systems in a new organizational setting with significantly redesigned tasks.

My message here is not that the problems are insurmountable, nor that they are so severe that they will pose a permanent threat to the IT-based organization. I merely want to underscore the fact that the increased productivity and flexibility provided by information technology come at a cost, as do all other improvements, and that the use of this technology increases the height of the steps in the stairs leading upward—in terms of cost, efforts, *and* rewards—just as the transition from craft production to the modern organization did. Figure 17-1 illustrates the relative merits of these three generations of organizations when it comes to flexibility, productivity, and cost of change.

It is of course possible to prepare the organization for the system renewals that has to come at certain intervals. Apart from maintaining adequate financial capabilities and an organization-wide realization that change is necessary (which are general measures important for any type of change), minor changes as well as major new development efforts can be speeded up and achieve much higher quality levels if the organization and its functional requirements are analyzed and modeled on a continuous basis—not just when a specific need arises. As I mentioned at the end of Chapter 15, any enterprise with aspirations to become a model-driven organization should have a pattern manager, and one of the duties of this office would be to continuously maintain and update the conceptual model of the organization and its problem domain. All changes to existing systems, as well as all new systems, should have this model as their foundation.

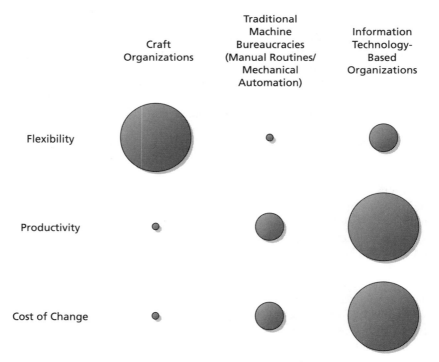

Figure 17-1: *The relative merits of three generations of organizations. The areas of the circles do not correspond to exact values; they are only meant to illustrate the relative levels of performance and resource requirements of the different generations.*

If such a model is sound, it will ensure that the systems that are implemented will be better prepared for later changes; the changes will be consistent in their basic features, and new systems will be much easier to integrate with older ones. In a large organization the maintenance of such a model may require the full-time work of several persons, but the cost involved will be recouped many times over through reductions in development costs and increases in systems quality.

THE KNOWLEDGE FACTOR

Throughout the pages of this book, I have repeatedly stressed the complexity of large computer-based systems and their intricate interplay with the organizations that use them. I have also touched upon the considerable skills in analysis, planning, organization, and engineering that is necessary to create, implement, maintain and use these systems and design the organizations that can make the most of them. This is a fact that cannot be stressed too strongly. I do not think there is any other widespread technology where relative differences in knowledge and skills are so decisive for the success of an investment. Two similar firms can therefore invest the same amount of money in the same systems and experience radically different results.

In a business world hunting for competitive advantage, this is an often neglected fact—even though it is widely acknowledged in IS circles that the best programmers work several times faster than the average, and produce far better programs with fewer errors to boot. Some of the same is true for systems analysts, and even on the purely technical side, the difference between a good engineer and a mediocre one can translate into hours and days of system downtime. In a future where organizations are becoming increasingly model-driven, superior organization designers and Organization Design Managers ("pattern managers") will also become very important—even crucial—for the competitiveness of large organizations.

The firm with superior knowledge and skills both in the systems and the organization area, and with these skills combined in a cross-disciplinary professional organization with a management team that can also think business, will therefore have a *significant* competitive advantage, which will be more important the more IT-intensive a business is. Today, both hardware, quite sophisticated standard software and software tools are freely available to all, and news about radical new and profitable ways of exploiting IT get around quickly. Experience has also shown us that the barriers to entry that are erected by early adopters of innovative systems tend to erode over time even if they are initially successfull, as customers and competitors gradually find ways of circumventing the defenses and break the lock-in.

However, teams with superior knowledge and skills take time to build, are fairly inconspicuous, and very hard to replicate. Experience across diverse organizations, from football clubs to universities, shows that such superior teams exhibit a significant tendency toward self-reinforcement, and that established superiority in skills and knowledge is possible to maintain over long periods of time. For those of us who look for an unobtrusive competitive edge, this should be a very interesting option, and for those of us who really love computers and their intricate interplay with organized humans, it is indeed a heartening conclusion to this book.

References

Agor, Weston H. (ed.) (1989): *Intuition in Organizations: Leading and Managing Productively*, Newbury Park, CA, Sage Publications.

Anderson, John R. (1990): *Cognitive Psychology and its Implications*, Third Edition, New York, W. H. Freeman.

Argyris, Chris (1980): *Inner Contradictions of Rigorous Research*, New York, Academic Press.

Ashby, W. Ross (1956): "Variety, Constraint and the Law of Requisite Variety," in Ashby, W. Ross: *An Introduction to Cybernetics*, London, Chapman and Hall. Reprinted in Buckley, Walter: *Modern Systems Research for the Behavioral Scientist*, Chicago, IL, Aldine, 1968.

Ashby, W. Ross (1962): "Principles of the Self-Organizing System," in Foerster, Hans von and Zopf, Georg W. (eds): *Principles of Self-Organization*, New York, Pergamon Press. Reprinted in Buckley, Walter: *Modern Systems Research for the Behavioral Scientist,* Chicago, IK, Aldine, 1968.

Asimov, Isaac (1975): *Asimov's Guide to Science, Vol. 2, The Biological Sciences*, London, Pelican Books.

Augarten, Stan (1984): *Bit by Bit: An Illustrated History of Computers*, New York, Ticknor & Fields.

Baran, Nick (1991): "Breakthrough in Holographics Memory Could Transform Data Access," Microbytes column, *Byte*, January 1991.

Barber, Paul (1988): *Applied Cognitive Psychology: An Information-processing Framework*, London, Routledge.

Bartlett, Christopher A., and Ghoshal, Sumantra (1989): *Managing Across Borders*, Boston, MA, Harvard Business School Press.

Beals, Carleton (1970): *Stories Told by the Aztecs Before the Spaniards Came*, London, Abelard-Schumann.

Beniger, James R. (1986): *The Control Revolution: Technological and Economic Origins of the Information Society*, Cambridge, MA, Harvard University Press.

Berger, Peter and Luckmann, Thomas (1967): *The Social Construction of Reality*, London, Penguin Press.

Bertalanffy, Ludwig von (1973): *General Systems Theory*, Harmondsworth, UK, Penguin Books.

Bijker, Wiebe E., and Law, John (1992): *Shaping Technology/Building Society. Studies in Sociotechnical Change*, Cambridge, MA, The MIT Press.

Bing, Jon, and Harvold, Trygve (1977): *Legal Decisions and Information Systems*, Oslo, Universitetsforlaget (University Press of Norway).

Booch, Grady (1991): *Object Oriented Design*, Redwood City, Benjamin/ Cummings.

Boulding, Kenneth E. (1956): "General Systems Theory—The Skeleton of Science," *Management Science*, 2, pp. 197–208. Reprinted in Buckley, Walter: *Modern Systems Research for the Behavioral Scientist*, Chicago, IL, Aldine, 1968.

Boyd, Robert, and Richardson, Peter J. (1985): *Culture and the Evolutionary Process*, Chicago, IL, University of Chicago Press.

Braverman, Harry (1974): *Labor and Monopoly Capital: The Degradation of Work in the Twentieth Century*, New York, Monthly Review Press.

Bright, James R. (1985): "Evolution of Automation: Electric Lamps," in Rhodes, Ed, and Wield, David: *Implementing New Technologies: Choice, Decision and Change in Manufacturing*, Oxford, Basil Blackwell, 1985.

Buckley, Walter (1967): *Sociology and Modern Systems Theory*, Englewood Cliffs, NJ, Prentice Hall.

Buckley, Walter (1968): *Modern Systems Research for the Behavioral Scientist*, Chicago, IL, Aldine.

Buckmann, Peter (producer) (1991): "Hansatid," a series of 3 television programs about the Hanseatic League produced by the Norwegian National Television and broadcast in January 1991.

Bush, Vannevar (1945): "As We May Think," *Atlantic Monthly* 176 (1), June 1945. Reprinted in: Greif, Irene (ed.) (1988): *Computer Supported Cooperative Work: A Book of Readings*, San Mateo, CA, Morgan Kaufmann.

Campbell-Kelly, Martin (1997): *A History of the Information Machine*, New York, Harper Collins.

Ceruzzi, Paul E. (1998): *A History of Modern Computing: 1945–1995*, Cambridge, MA, MIT Press.

Chandler, A. D. Jr. (1977): *The Visible Hand: The Managerial Revolution in American Business*, Cambridge, MA: Harvard University Press.

Chinnock, Chris (1997): "Digital Ink Gives New Meaning to Paper Recycling", *Byte*, August 1997.

Christopher, Martin (1992): *Logistics and Supply Chain Management—Strategies for Reducing Costs and Improving Services*, London, Pitman Publishing.

Clarkson, Mark A. (1991): "An Easier Interface," *Byte*, February 1991.

Clegg, Stewart R. (1990): *Modern Organizations: Organization Studies in the Postmodern World*. London, Sage.

Coad, Peter, and Yourdon, Edward (1991): *Object Oriented Analysis*, Second Edition, Englewood Cliffs, NJ, Prentice Hall.

Cohen, John (1980): *The Lineaments of Mind—In Historical Perspective*, Oxford, W.H. Freeman.

Crozier, Michel (1964): *The Bureaucratic Phenomenon*, Chicago, IL, University of Chicago Press.

Daft, Richard L., and Lewin, Arie Y. (1993): "Where Are the Theories for the 'New' Organizational Forms? An Editorial Essay," *Organization Science*, 4 November 1993.

Dahl, Helmer (1984): *Teknikk, kultur, samfunn: Om egenarten i Europas vekst*, Oslo, Ingeniørforlaget.

Davenport, Thomas H. (1993): *Process Innovation: Reenginering Work through Information Technology*, Boston, Harvard Business School Press.

Drucker, Peter (1988): "The Coming of the New Organization," *Harvard Business Review*, 1988 (1).

Eason, Ken (1988): *Information Technology and Organizational Change*, London, Taylor and Francis.

Ellis, Henry C., and Hunt, R. Reed (1989): *Fundamentals of Human Memory and Cognition*, Fourth Edition, Dubuque, IA, Wm. C. Brown.

Eriksen, Trond Berg (1987): *Budbringerens overtak*, Oslo, Universitetsforlaget (University Press of Norway).

Fineman, Stephen (ed.) (1993): *Emotion in Organizations*, London, Sage.

Flam, Helena (1993): "Fear, Loyalty and Greedy Organizations," in Fineman, Stephen (ed.) (1993): *Emotion in Organizations*, London, Sage.

Fowler, Martin (1997): *UML Distilled. Applying the Standard Object Modeling Language*, Reading, MA, Addison-Wesley Longman.

Galbraith, Jay R. (1977): *Organization Design*, Reading, MA, Addison-Wesley.

George, Joey F., and King, John L. (1991): "Examining the Computing and Centralization Debate," *Communications of the ACM*, July 1991.

Geschwind, Norman (1979): "Specializations of the Human Brain," *Scientific American*, September 1979.

Gleick, James (1988): *Chaos—Making a New Science*, London, Sphere Books.

Goffman, Erving (1959): *The Presentation of Self in Everyday Life*, New York, Doubleday.

Goffman, Erving (1970): *Strategic Interaction*, Oxford, Basil Blackwell.

Goffman, Erving (1974): *Frame Analysis*, Cambridge, MA, Harvard University Press.

Goldberg, Philip (1989): "The Many Faces of Intuition," in Agor, Weston H. (ed.) (1989): *Intuition in Organizations: Leading and Managing Productively*, Sage.

Goody, Jack (1986): *The Logic of Writing and the Organization of Society*, Cambridge, Cambridge University Press.

Granovetter, Mark (1985): "Economic Action and Social Structure: The Problem of Embeddedness," *American Journal of Sociology*, 91 (3).

Graves, Robert (1960): *The Greek Myths: 1*, Revised Edition (first published 1955), Harmondsworth, UK, Penguin Books.

Greif, Irene (ed.) (1988): *Computer Supported Cooperative Work: A Book of Readings*, San Mateo, CA, Morgan Kaufmann Publishers.

Hamilton, Gary G., and Biggart, Nicole Woolsey (1988): "Market, Culture, and Authority: A Comparative Analysis of Management and Organization in the Far East," in Winship, C., and Rosen, S. (eds): "Organizations and Institutions: Sociological Approaches to the Analysis of Social Structure," supplement to *American Journal of Sociology*, 94.

Hammer, Michael (1990): "Reengineering Work: Don't Automate, Obliterate," *Harvard Business Review*, 1990 (4).

Hammer, Michael and Champy, James (1993): *Reengineering the Corporation—A Manifesto for Business Revolution*, London, Nicholas Brearley.

Hannan, Michael T. and Freeman, John (1977): "The Population Ecology of Organizations," *American Journal of Sociology*, 82 (5).

Hannan, Michael T. and Freeman, John (1984): "Structural Inertia and Organizational Change," *American Sociological Review*, 49 (April).

Harvey, David A. (1990): "State of the Media," *Byte*, November 1990.

Hassard, John, and Parker, Martin (1993): *Postmodernism and Organizations*, London, Sage.

Hatvany, J. et al. (1985): "Advanced Manufacturing Systems in Modern Society," in Rhodes, E., and Wield, David: *Implementing New Technologies: Choice, Decision and Change in Manufacturing*, Oxford, Basil Blackwell, 1985.

Havelock, Eric (1986): *The Muse Learns to Write—Reflections on Orality and Literacy from Antiquity to the Present*, New Haven, CT, Yale University Press.

Heller, Martin (1991): "AI in Practice," *Byte*, January 1991.

Hesselholt, N., Ockens, E., Christensen, E., Elling, F. and Mikkelsen, M. (1992): "Identifikation af hunde med microchips," *Dansk Veterinærtidsskrift*, 75 (14). English summary.

Hochschild, Arlie R. (1983): *The Managed Hearth*, Berkeley, University of California Press.

Hochschild, Arlie R. (1993): "Preface," in Fineman, Stephen (ed.) (1993): *Emotion in Organizations*, London, Sage.

Hofer, Myron A. (1981): *The Roots of Human Behavior. An Introduction to the Psychobiology of Early Development*, San Francisco, W.H. Freeman.

Hollway, Wendy (1991): *Work Psychology and Organizational Behaviour—Managing the Individual at Work*, London, Sage.

Hopper, Max D. (1990): "Rattling SABRE—New Ways to Compete on Information," *Harvard Business Review*, 1990 (3) p. 121.

Huppes, Tjerk (1987): *The Western Edge—Work and Management in the Information Age*, Dordrecht, Netherlands, Kluwer Academic.

Jacobson, Ivar, Ericsson, Maria, and Jacobson, Agneta (1994): *The Object Advantage: Business Process Reengineering with Object Technology*, ACM Press Books/Addison Wesley.

James, Peter, and Thorpe, Nick (1994): *Ancient Inventions*, New York, Ballantine Books.

Johansen, Robert (1988): *Groupware: Computer Support for Business Teams*, New York, The Free Press.

Kahneman, Daniel, Slovic, Paul, and Tversky, Amos (eds) (1982): *Judgment under Uncertainty: Heuristics and Biases*, Cambridge, Cambridge University Press.

Katzenbach, Jon R., and Smith, Douglas K. (1993): *The Wisdom of Teams—Creating the High-Performance Organization*, Boston, MA, Harvard Business School Press.

Keen, Peter G. W. (1991): *Shaping the Future: Business Design through Information Technology*, Boston, MA, Harvard Business School Press.

Kepner, Charles H., and Tregoe, Benjamin B. (1965): *The Rational Manager—A Systematic Approach to Problem Solving and Decision Making*, New York, McGraw-Hill.

Kitto, H. D. F. (1951): *The Greeks*, Harmondsworth, UK, Penguin Books. I have used the Norwegian translation *Grekerne*, published in 1971 by Gyldendal Norsk Forlag, Oslo.

Koolhaas, Jan (1982): *Organization Dissonance and Change*, Chichester, UK, John Wiley & Sons.

Kuhn, Thomas S. (1970): *The Structure of Scientific Revolutions*, Chicago, IL, University of Chicago Press.

Leach, E. R. (1970): *Political Systems of Highland Burma*, London, Athlone Press—University of London. First edition published in 1954 by G. Bell & Son.

Leavitt, Harold J. and Whisler, Thomas L. (1958): "Management in the 1980's," *Harvard Business Review*, 1958 (6).

Lie, Merete, and Rasmussen, Bente (1983): *Kan "kontordamene" automatiseres*, Research report no. STF82 A83004, IFIM/SINTEF, Trondheim.

Lincoln, James R. (1982): "Intra- (and Inter-) Organizational Networks," *Research in the Sociology of Organizations,* Vol. 1.

Lloyd, Peter C. (1965): "The Political Structure of African Kingdoms," in Banton, Michael (ed.): *Political Systems and the Distribution of Power*, London, Tavistock.

Long, Richard J. (1987): *New Office Information Technology: Human and Managerial Implications*, Beckenham, Croom Helm.

Lundberg, Nils H. (1991): "Kjemometri i kjømda," *Teknisk Ukeblad* (Technology Weekly, Oslo), 1991 (36).

Lysgaard, Sverre (1961): *Arbeiderkollektivet*, Oslo, Universitetsforlaget (University Press of Norway).

March, James G., and Simon, Herbert A (1958): *Organizations*, New York, John Wiley & Sons.

Maus, Arne, and Espeli, Tron (1981): *EDB i kontoret—produktivitet og sysselsetting*, research report no. 699, Norwegian Computing Center, Oslo.

McKersie, Robert B., and Walton, Richard E. (1991): "Organizational Change," chapter 9 in Scott Morton, Michael S. (ed.) (1991): *The Corporation of the 1990s: Information Technology and Organizational Transformation*, New York, Oxford University Press.

Meyer, John W., and Rowan, Brian (1977): "Institutionalized Organizations: Formal Structure as Myth and Ceremony," *American Journal of Sociology*, 83 (2).

Meyer, Marshall W., and Zucker, Lynne G. (1989): *Permanently Failing Organizations*, Newbury Park, CA, Sage.

Mintzberg, Henry (1973): *The Nature of Managerial Work*, New York, Harper & Row.

Mintzberg, Henry (1979): *The Structuring of Organizations*, Englewood Cliffs, Prentice Hall.

Mintzberg, Henry (1983): *Structure in Fives: Designing Effective Organizations*, Englewood Cliffs, Prentice Hall.

Mintzberg, Henry (1989): *Mintzberg on Management: Inside Our Strange World of Organizations*, New York, The Free Press.

Mishkin, Mortimer, and Appenzeller, Tim (1987): "The Anatomy of Memory," *Scientific American*, June 1987.

Moeller, Mike (1994): "Boeing Goes On-Line with 777 Design," *Computer-Aided Engineering*, 13 (8).

Morgan, Gareth (1986): *Images of Organization*, Beverly Hills, CA, Sage.

Morris, Desmond (1967): *The Naked Ape*, London, Jonathan Cape.

Murra, John W. (1986): "The expansion of the Inka state: armies, war, and rebellions," in Murra, John W., Watchel, Nathan and Revel, Jaques: *Anthropological History of Andean Politics*, Cambridge, Cambridge University Press, 1986.

Nadler, David, and Tushman, Michael (1988), *Strategic Organization Design*, Glenview, IL, Scott, Foresman.

Nash, Manning (1966): *Primitive and Peasant Economic Systems*, Scranton, PA, Chandler.

Negroponte, Nicholas (1995): *Being Digital*, New York, Alfred A. Knopf.

Nelson, Theodor H. (1988): "Managing Immense Storage," *Byte*, January 1988.

Noyce, Robert N. (1977): "Microelectronics," *Scientific American*, September 1977.

O'Hara-Deveraux, Mary and Johansen, Robert (1994): *Globalwork: Bridging Distance, Culture and Time*, San Francisco, Jossey-Bass.

Ong, Walter J. (1982): *Orality and Literacy*, London, Methuen.

Palme, Jacob (1995): *Electronic Mail*, Boston, MA, Artech House.

Parish, Tom (1990): "Crystal Clear Storage," *Byte*, November 1990.

Pehrson, Robert N. (1964): *The Bilateral Network of Social Relations in Könkämä Lapp District*, Oslo, Norwegian University Press.

Pine, Joseph B. II (1993): *Mass Customization—The New Frontier in Business Competition*, Boston, MA, Harvard Business School Press.

Piore, Michael J., and Sabel, Charles F. (1984): *The Second Industrial Divide: Possibilities for Prosperity*, New York, Basic Books.

Polanyi, Michael (1967): *The Tacit Dimension*, London, Routledge & Kegan Paul.

Pool, Ithiel de Sola (1983): *Forecasting the Telephone—A Retrospective Technology Assessment of the Telephone*, Norwood, Ablex.

Porter, Michael (1985): *The Competitive Advantage: Creating and Sustaining Superior Performance*, New York, The Free Press.

Psaltis, Demetri, and Mok, Fai (1995): "Holographic Memories," *Scientific American*, November 1995.

Putnam, Linda L., and Mumby, Dennis K. (1993): "Organizations, Emotion and the Myth of Rationality," in Fineman, Stephen (ed.) (1993): *Emotion in Organizations*, London, Sage.

Quick, J. C., Murphy, L. R., Hurrel, J. J., and Orman, D. (1992): "The Value of Work, the Risk of Distress, and the Power of Prevention," in Quick, J. C., Murphy, L. R., Hurrel, J.J. (eds): *Stress & Well-Being at Work*, Washington, DC, American Psychological Association.

Rachlin, Howard (1989): *Judgment, Decision and Choice—a Cognitive/Behavioral Synthesis*, New York, W.H. Freeman.

Rasmus, Daniel W. (1991): "Putting the Experts to Work," *Byte*, January 1991.

Rhodes, E. and Wield, David (1985): *Implementing New Technologies: Choice, Decision and Change in Manufacturing*, Oxford, Basil Blackwell.

Robinson, Mike (1991): "Through a Lens Smartly," *Byte*, May 1991.

Rockart, John F. and Short, James E. (1991): "The Networked Organization and the Management of Interdependence," in Scott Morton, Michael S. (ed.) (1991): *The Corporation of the 1990s. Information Technology and Organizational Transformation*, New York, Oxford University Press.

Ross, Randall R., and Altmaier, Elizabeth M. (1994): *Intervention in Occupational Stress*, London, Sage.

Rowan, Roy (1989): "What it is," in Agor, Weston H. (ed.) (1989): *Intuition in Organizations: Leading and Managing Productively*, Newbury Park, CA, Sage.

Scientific American, special issue on microelectronics, September 1977.

Sandars, N. K. (1964): *The Epic of Gilgamesh, Harmondsworth, UK, Penguin Books*.

Schmidt, Kjeld and Bannon, Liam (1992): "Taking CSCW Seriously," *Computer Supported Cooperative Work*, 1 (1–2).

Schoenberg, Robert J. (1985): *Geneen*, New York, W. W. Norton.

Scott Morton, Michael S. (ed.) (1991): *The Corporation of the 1990s: Information Technology and Organizational Transformation*, New York, Oxford University Press.

Scott, Richard W. (1987): *Organizations: Rational, Natural and Open Systems*, Englewood Cliffs, NJ, Prentice Hall.

Sharp, Lauriston (1952): "Steel Axes for Stone Age Australians," in Edward H. Spicer (ed.): *Human Problems in Technological Change*, New York, Russel Sage Foundation.

Shotwell, James T. (1961): *The Story of Ancient History*, New York, Columbia University Press. Reprint of *The History of History, Volume I*, originally published in 1939 (same publisher).

Silverman, David (1970): *The Theory of Organisations*, London, Heinemann Educational.

Simon, Herbert A. (1976): *Administrative Behavior*, Third Edition, New York, The Free Press (first published in 1945).

Simon, Herbert A. (1977): *The New Science of Management Decision*, Englewood Cliffs, NJ, Prentice Hall.

Simon, Herbert A. (1981): *The Sciences of the Artificial*, Second Edition, Cambridge, MA, MIT Press.

Simon, Herbert A. (1989): "Making Management Decisions: The Role of Intuition and Emotion," in Agor, Weston H. (ed.) (1989): *Intuition in Organizations: Leading and Managing Productively*, Newbury Park, CA, Sage Publications.

Sobel, Alan (1998): "Television's Bright New Technology," *Scientific American*, May 1998.

Stein, Richard Marlon (1991): "Browsing Through Terabytes," *Byte*, May 1991.

Stinchcombe, Arthur L. (1965): "Social Structure and Organizations," in James G. March (ed.): *Handbook of Organizations*, Chicago, Rand McNally.

Stix, Gary (1991): "Plane Geometry: Boeing Uses CAD to Design 130,000 Parts for its New 777," *Scientific American*, March 1991.

Strassmann, Paul A. (1985): *Information Payoff: The Transformation of Work in the Electronic Age*, New York, The Free Press.

Sundstrom, Eric (1986): *Work Places: The psychology of the physical environment in offices and factories*, Cambridge, Cambridge University Press.

Thé, Lee (1995): "Workflow Tackles the Productivity Paradox," *Datamation*, 41 (15).

Thompson, James D. (1967): *Organizations in Action*, New York, McGraw-Hill.

Thompson, Paul (1993): "Postmodernism: Fatal Distraction," in Hassard, John, and Parker, Martin: *Postmodernism and Organizations*, London, Sage.

Thompson, Tom (1996): "What's Next?" *Byte*, April 1996.

Thorud, Geir I. (project mgr.) (1991): *Norsk veiledning i bruk av EDIFACT Versjon 1.0*, Sekretariatet for Norsk TEDIS.

Walton, Richard E. (1989): *Up and Running: Integrating Information Technology and the Organization*, Boston, Harvard Business School Press.

Weber, Max (1968): *Economy and Society*, New York, Bedminster Press. Originally published in Tubingen by J. C. B. Mohr (Paul Siebeck) in 1922 under the title *Wirtschaft und Gesellschaft*. There are numerous translations. I have also used a Norwegian translation of some passages, printed in Egil Fivelsdal (ed.): *Max Weber: Makt og byråkrati*, Oslo, Gyldendal Norsk Forlag, 1971.

Weick, Karl E. (1979): *The Social Psychology of Organizing*, Reading, MA, Addison-Wesley.

Wiss, Joseph (1990): "Unconscious Mental Functioning," *Scientific American*, March 1990.

Wiener, Norbert (1954): *The Human Use of Human Beings: Cybernetics and Society*, New York, Doubleday Anchor.

Williamson, Oliver E. (1975): *Markets and Hierarchies: Analysis and Antitrust Implications*, New York, The Free Press.

Williamson, Oliver E. (1985): *The Economic Institutions of Capitalism*, New York, The Free Press.

Wilson, Peter J. (1988): *The Domestication of the Human Species*, New Haven, CT, Yale University Press.

Winograd, Terry (1988): "A Language/Action Perspective on the Design of Cooperative Work," *Human Computer Interaction*, 3 (1). Reprinted in: Greif,

Irene (ed) (1988): *Computer Supported Cooperative Work: A Book of Readings*, San Mateo, CA, Morgan Kaufmann.

Yates, Francis A. (1966): *The Art of Memory, London*, Routledge and Kegan Paul.

Yates, JoAnne (1989): *Control through Communication—The Rise of System in American Management, Baltimore*, MD, Johns Hopkins University Press.

Yates, JoAnne, and Benjamin, Robert I. (1991): "The Past and Present as a Window on the Future," in Scott Morton, Michael S. (ed.) (1991): *The Corporation of the 1990s: Information Technology and Organizational Transformation*, New York, Oxford University Press.

Zuboff, Shoshana (1988): *In the Age of the Smart Machine: The Future of Work and Power*, New York, Basic Books.

Author Index

Subject Index